LAST MAN STANDING

THE ASCENT OF JAMIE DIMON AND JPMORGAN CHASE

DUFF MCDONALD

SIMON & SCHUSTER
New York   London   Toronto   Sydney

Simon & Schuster
1230 Avenue of the Americas
New York, NY 10020

First Simon & Schuster hardcover edition October 2009

SIMON & SCHUSTER and colophon are registered trademarks of
Simon & Schuster, Inc.

For information about special discounts for bulk purchases,
please contact Simon & Schuster Special Sales at
1-866-506-1949 or business@simonandschuster.com.

The Simon & Schuster Speakers Bureau can bring authors to your live event.
For more information or to book an event contact the Simon & Schuster Speakers
Bureau at 1-866-248-3049 or visit our website at www.simonspeakers.com.

Designed by Julie Schroeder

Manufactured in the United States of America

10 9 8 7 6 5 4 3 2 1

Library of Congress Cataloging-in-Publication Data

McDonald, Duff.
    Last man standing : the ascent of Jamie Dimon and JPMorgan Chase /
Duff McDonald.
        p.   cm.
    Includes bibliographical references and index.
    1. Dimon, Jamie.   2. Capitalists and financiers—United States—Biography.
3. J.P. Morgan Chase & Co.   I. Title.
    HG172.D495M33 2009
    332.1'22092—dc22
    [B]   2009024144

ISBN 978-1-4165-9953-1
ISBN 978-1-4391-0971-7 (ebook)

For the two who just missed each other

Dr. Donald John McDonald
(10/23/37–09/09/08)

&

Marguerite Scott McDonald
(11/13/08–)

CONTENTS

PROLOGUE

On the morning of September 18, 2008, the phone rang in Jamie Dimon's office. It was Hank Paulson, the secretary of the treasury. For the second time in six months, Paulson had a pressing question for the chairman and CEO of JPMorgan Chase. Would Dimon be interested in acquiring the floundering investment bank Morgan Stanley—at no cost whatsoever?

During one of the most tumultuous months in the history of the stock market—stocks fell 27 percent between August 29 and October 10, 2008—the storied investment bank Lehman Brothers had already failed, the brokerage giant Merrill Lynch had been sold to Bank of America, and the insurance heavyweight AIG had received an emergency loan of $85 billion from the federal government. One of the only remaining questions was whether it would be Morgan Stanley or Goldman Sachs that fell next. The government was desperately seeking to stave off what could have been a wipeout of Wall Street. And here was Paulson, offering Dimon Morgan Stanley for the bargain basement price of $0 per share.

At the government's urging, Dimon had agreed to take over Bear Stearns for $2 a share in March 2008, in a whirlwind 48-hour deal. (The price was ultimately raised to $10.) The transaction had catapulted JPMorgan Chase to the forefront of the financial industry and established Dimon as the government's banker of last resort. "Some are coming to Washington *for* help," Sheila Bair, chairman of the Federal

Deposit Insurance Corporation, later said. "Others are coming to Washington *to* help."

Considered in a historical light, a takeover of Morgan Stanley would have been much more profound than that of Bear Stearns. Dimon was already being compared to John Pierpont Morgan, the legendary banker who was his company's founder, and this deal would have meant a reassembling of the empire that had been forcibly dismantled during the Great Depression, when banks were barred from the securities trade. Dimon, in other words, would have been sitting atop the very same empire his firm's namesake had lorded over nearly a century before.

But it was not to be. Dimon reportedly said he'd discuss it with his board, but his initial view was that his bank shouldn't do it—it would involve a bloodbath for employees on both sides, a doubling of risk, and years of distraction for the company. What's more, the ultimate cost of a deal would have been quite substantial, whether in terms of layoffs, writedowns, or a de-risking of Morgan Stanley's balance sheet. (Dimon has always said it doesn't make sense for two major investment banks to merge.) Moreover, his team was already busy preparing a bid to take over the deposits and loans of the Seattle-based bank Washington Mutual, also on the verge of failure.

The amazing thing: Paulson really didn't have anyone else to turn to. Dimon was quite literally the only chief of a major bank to have properly prepared for the hundred-year storm that had hit Wall Street with such vengeance. Everyone had known that the capital base of the financial sector had been in desperate need of shoring up, but Jamie Dimon was alone among his peers in having actually done something instead of just talking about it. As a result, of all the actions taken by the government in the fifteen months since the crisis had started, the only thing that had really worked was *giving it to Jamie*. Which is exactly why a desperate Paulson was trying to do it again. But he proved unable to persuade Dimon to pull off a third major deal in 2008. Morgan Stanley eventually pulled through. But even without this deal, Dimon's reputation continued to ascend to new heights. In the midst of the most serious and far-reaching financial crisis since the 1930s—much of it caused by plain old avarice and bad judgment—Dimon and JPMorgan Chase stood apart. Much of the melodramatic coverage of Wall Street postcrisis has focused on its flaws—the hubris and the greed. Jamie Dimon's story contains the opposites—the values of clarity, consistency, integrity, and courage. By sticking to them, Dimon has unquestionably become the dominant banking executive of his era. "Banking is a very good business if you don't do anything dumb," says Warren Buffett. "Morris Shapiro said long ago that there are more banks than bankers, and that's fundamentally the problem. But Jamie is a banker from head to toe."

1. BANKING IN THE BLOOD

Jamie Dimon is a banker by blood. His paternal grandfather, Panos Papademetriou, was a Greek from Smyrna who worked in banking before leaving Greece during its war with Turkey. He arrived in New York in 1921, by way of France and Canada, settling in Manhattan and promptly shortening his last name to Dimon. The mischievous immigrant later offered his son two stories about the changing of his name. In the first, he sought work as a busboy but found that no one would hire Greeks. "Dimon" sounded French—and Papademetriou was fluent in French—so he changed it to get a job. In the second version, he fell in love with a French girl and chose the name for amorous purposes. Either way, he clearly felt he would do better with an American-sounding French name than with a Greek one.

Panos didn't last long as a busboy— family lore has it that he was fired, and he subsequently found work at the recently opened branch of the Bank of Athens, a subsidiary of the National Bank of Greece. After working his way up to vice president in charge of loans, he left the bank in 1949 to become a stockbroker at Shearson Hammill.

Panos's son Theodore became a stockbroker, too, joining his father at Shearson Hammill in 1953, a year after his marriage to Themis Annastasia Kalos, also the child of Greek immigrants. The brokerage, founded at the turn of the twentieth century, had a national presence as well as a reputable investment banking operation. Shortly thereafter, Theodore and his wife moved to East Williston, Long Island. Just 25 miles from New York City, the village was enjoying a burst in population growth as Americans embraced the postwar suburban ideal.

Their first son, Peter, was born in 1954. Fraternal twins soon followed—Jamie and Ted Jr.—on March 13, 1956. Ted Sr., who commuted to Shearson Hammill's offices on 44th Street and Fifth Avenue in his gray Convertible Dodge, soon grew tired of the commute, and persuaded his wife to move back to New York. The family of five settled in a rental apartment in Jackson Heights, Queens, where young Jamie attended PS 69 from kindergarten through the fifth grade.

Jamie was a precocious child. His mother remembers him looking at her "as if he was an adult" as early as the age of two. He also felt a need to keep up appearances. Even as a youngster, he refused to come out of his bedroom in his pajamas if his parents had guests. He was also extremely active, prone to leaping across the room rather than walking. Fluent with numbers from a young age—he remembered phone numbers as a small child—Dimon launched his first business at the age of six, attempting to sell greeting cards. The effort failed, but there was no doubt about his enterprising nature.

In this, he took after his grandfather, Panos. An elegant and intellectual man, Panos spoke several languages, and he dabbled in psychoanalysis while dissecting balance sheets. Young Jamie's father was also an early influence, particularly in his choice of profession. Dimon later said that he learned a great deal about the brokerage industry "across the kitchen table."

For a child from a comfortable background, Jamie exhibited an unusually early desire to be financially successful. At the age of nine, he announced to his father that he was going to make a fortune when he grew up. Whether his parents took him seriously or not, Dimon never wavered from that goal. The family photo collection includes a picture of him at the age of 21 studying J. Paul Getty's *How to Be Rich*, a collection of columns he'd written for *Playboy* on the subject.

He was, in most other ways, a typical boy, getting into the occasional scrape. Dimon and his twin brother Teddy were in a kids' "gang" they called Lightning Squad, and they battled older boys (including their own brother) in the courtyard of their apartment building.

(Dimon's relationship with his parents has always been close. When he threatened to run away from home at the age of five, his mother replied by asking him where he would go. "To the woods," he said. She asked him what he would eat: "Wild berries and flowers." What would he drink? "Water from a lake." Where would he sleep? "I'll make a bed from twigs and leaves." Finally, she asked, where would he go for love? After thinking for a minute, he said, "I'll come home." In the end, Dimon decided not to run away.)

In 1967, when the twins were 11 years old, their parents gave the suburbs another shot, moving to a modest two-story house in the village of Larchmont, just north of New York City. Dimon's mother remembers asking him at bedtime a few nights after moving how he liked his new bedroom. "I don't know the shadows in the room yet," he replied. "But it'll be OK."

Dimon spent sixth grade at Larchmont's Murray Avenue School before his parents moved the family back into the city, this time to a fourbedroom co-op at 1050 Park Avenue. (Although he has accomplished much, Dimon's is not a Horatio Alger tale. He has spent the majority of his life within the same five blocks on Park Avenue, home of New York's upper class.) Ted Dimon, who eschewed borrowing money his whole life, paid cash for the apartment.

•   •   •

Themis Dimon wanted her sons to continue in school together—she was the kind of mother who dressed all the boys in the same outfits— and in April 1968, she applied for them to attend Browning, a private all-boys' school with 189 students in a pair of converted town houses on East 62nd Street that had been founded by John Browning, a close friend of John D. Rockefeller. (Rockefeller's son, John D. Jr., attended from 1889 to 1893.)

The Dimon boys were accepted, and they all completed their high school years at Browning. Dimon was in the school choir for a time, but quit in favor of sports. He played varsity soccer, basketball, and baseball. Browning was a small school, and its basketball court was also its auditorium; Dimon once broke his front teeth on the stage while lunging for a ball. (One nickname in high school was Mad Dog.) The starting center fielder on the school's baseball team, he hit over .500 during his junior year, though he never loved the sport. "My arm was always hurting and I found it kind of boring," he recalls. He also preferred to see his girlfriend after school rather than go to baseball practice.

Two years into their time at Browning, Dimon and his brother Ted Jr. met a friend to whom they have remained close ever since. Jeremy Paul had moved into Manhattan from Connecticut. Often a dinner guest at the Dimon house, Paul remembers Ted Dimon Sr. coming across more as an intellectual than a stockbroker. A student of philosophy and a writer of poetry, the elder Dimon was also a trained violinist, and played in a string quartet in the family living room during social events. Themis, too, had an intellectual bent. The year the twins went off to college, she took classes at the New School, and ultimately got her master's degree in psychology from Columbia. "Dinner at their house was really fun," Paul recalls. "It wasn't just, 'Pass the potatoes.' Whatever the topic was that day, it was taken very seriously."

In a family of outspoken individuals, Teddy had even more of a mouth than his brothers. He wasn't afraid to provoke other teenagers, either, in part because he could always count on Jamie to come to his aid. Perhaps as a result, Jamie can be fiercely protective of those close to him. Throughout his career, he has been characterized as having an aggressive personality, and he will not deny that. But he is no bully. He hates bullies.

The Dimons, who lived at 86th and Park, walked down Park Avenue to school each day, picking up Paul on 77th Street. Already punctual to a fault as a teenager, Jamie Dimon insisted that the only time Paul was late was when it was raining, just to force the Dimons to wait in the rain.

Dimon had an almost idyllic childhood. Summers were spent mountain climbing in Colorado or taking French immersion at the Université de Poitiers in La Rochelle. Confident, good-looking, and athletic, Jamie was also something of a heartthrob. "In senior year, he majored in his girlfriend," recalls one friend. When he graduated, her photo graced his personal pages in his yearbook, along with those of his parents, his brothers, and his beloved sheltie, Chippy. When it came to relationships, Jamie Dimon was *that* guy—the one to whom women were attracted, but who always seemed to have a girlfriend.

Though not the best student, Dimon never ranked below sixth in his class at Browning. History tended to be his favorite subject, but his best marks were in math, where he demonstrated an intuitive grasp of the subject. In Dimon's final year at Browning, his calculus teacher suffered a heart attack. Her replacement didn't know calculus, and the six boys taking advanced placement calculus were told that if they wanted to continue, they would have to teach the subject to themselves. Three of the students decided to throw in the towel, but Dimon and the remaining two—one of whom was Jeremy Paul—spent a challenging year of self-instruction. "As far as working experiences go, that was pretty intense," recalls Paul. "Each day we'd go into the classroom and there was no teacher, just us. And we'd sit there, trying to work our way through the problems."

Dimon also demonstrated an early capacity for ethical leadership, exemplified by an episode in an American history course. One day, the only African-American student in the class had been acting out and was told by the teacher to leave the room. Once the door closed behind him, the teacher turned toward the class and muttered, "Six hundred thousand died to free the slaves, and this is the gratitude we get." Dimon stood up, grabbed his things, and walked out the door. "He blasted me for not going with him," recalls Paul. "And he was right."

He was never afraid to challenge authority. Michael Ingrisani, Dimon's high school English teacher, continually came up against Dimon's assertiveness, which was usually punctuated by a demand to Ingrisani: "Prove it." Browning had a policy, for example, that if a student scored above 90 percent during the term, he was not required to take the final exam. In Dimon's senior year, he had earned 89 percent in English, but he tried on numerous occasions to concoct an argument for why he, too, should be exempt from the final.

"Wow," Ingrisani thought, after one of Dimon's pleading sessions. "He's negotiating. He's practicing. And he knows he has nothing to lose by trying."

. . .

Despite having been a smart, popular student, Dimon has mixed recollections of his high school years. He was a little too rambunctious, and his outspokenness grated on some teachers; he had a vague sense that a number of the more traditional among them didn't really like him. As a result, he was later told, his college recommendation letter conveyed reservations to admissions officers. That was indeed the case. After praising Dimon's "keen, analytical mind" and "self-motivation and seriousness of purpose" in the letter, Clair Smith, the assistant headmaster at Browning, added a loaded compliment: "His lack of manners, due to habits of making quick judgments and contradicting others, has been greatly improved." Reversing course once more, Smith finished on an up note: "He will be successful."

Despite graduating fourth in his class, Dimon was not accepted by the college of his choice: Brown University. He went to his second choice, Tufts, where he majored in psychology and economics. The latter proved to be his passion. After writing a paper on Milton Friedman's *Capitalism and Freedom*, he was encouraged by his professor to send the paper to Friedman himself. The economist responded with an eight-page letter, critiquing Dimon's critique. "He said something along the lines of, 'Son, I really appreciate you sending this to me. While I agree with some of your points, you're wrong about a, b, c, and d, and there's some faulty logic here and there,' " recalls Dimon. "I was blown away by it. Partly as a result of that, I always try to reply when someone sends something to me. I can't write an eight-page critique, but I try."

It was another economics paper, though, that set the trajectory of the young man's life. During his sophomore year, he wrote an analysis of the 1974 merger of Hayden Stone and Shearson Hammill in which he explored the savings one could achieve by combining an efficient company (Hayden Stone) with an inefficient one (Shearson Hammill). He knew of the transaction through his family, as his father was still working for Shearson Hammill at the time of the deal. Hayden Stone was the acquisition vehicle of one Sandy Weill, in the midst of what was the first of his two empire-building campaigns.

By this time, Jamie Dimon had actually met Sandy Weill; his parents had become close to the garrulous financier and his wife, Joan. Ted Dimon Sr., as impetuous as his son, had written Weill a memo at the time of the merger, laying out his demands if he were to stick around under the Weill regime. When the elder Dimon called Weill to ask what he thought of the memo, Weill said that he had no thoughts at all, that he'd thrown it out. He proposed that the two men get together for a drink at the private, exclusive Harmonie Club—a Jewish preserve—instead. When they met, Weill asked Dimon to repeat his "demands." "I want this . . . ," began Dimon. "Yes," replied Weill. "And I want that . . . ," continued Dimon. "No," replied Weill. And so on.

Overall, Dimon Sr. liked what he heard. This was a man who offered no bullshit, who genuinely seemed to understand the broker's concerns. He said he would allow Weill to "continue to process his trades." Translation: there might be a company name on his business card, but Ted Dimon Sr. reported to no one. He ran his own business. (Later in his career, when Jamie had become his father's superior, the son would confirm that Dimon Sr. still considered himself a free agent, that "he would never say I was his boss.")

Before long, the Weills and Dimons were spending significant amounts of time together. They spent a few weekends together in East Hampton, and the Dimons joined the Weills at one or two seder dinners. The glue of the relationship was the wives, who had lunch between classes at the New School—Joan Weill was also taking courses in 1975—and through their friendship, Dimon and his siblings came to know Weill's children, Marc and Jessica. (Friends in their teens, the three crossed paths again while working for Weill in the 1990s.)

Excited that her son had chosen a thesis topic that touched on both her family and her friends, Themis asked him if she could show the paper to Weill. "I have never seen the merger from this point of view," Weill told her after reading it. He sent Dimon a note that read, "Terrific paper. Can I show it to people here?" The forthright student seized his opportunity. "Absolutely," he replied. "Can I have a summer job?" Weill hired Jamie Dimon to work with the budgeting team in the company's consumer business that summer.

Joining his parents at the Weill house on weekends, the young Dimon peppered Weill with questions about why the company was doing one thing or another. When Weill once bragged to the younger man that all its branches were profitable, Dimon told him he was wrong. "No, they're not," Dimon said. "Four of them are losing money." Though somewhat taken aback by the young man's cockiness, Weill liked him a lot and encouraged him to keep asking questions. He figured Dimon's aggressive temperament would soften with age.

Dimon didn't much enjoy Tufts, at first. In addition, too many students didn't take school seriously enough for him. He considered it "camp without counselors." During his freshman year, he applied to transfer to Princeton, but was turned down. Eventually, he made close friends at Tufts, and grew to love the place. His classmate Laurie Maglathlin (née Chabot) recalls that Dimon didn't seem to have to study much—he was one of those irritating people who do really well without trying too hard.

Dimon excelled academically and graduated summa cum laude in 1978. A class photo shows a confident man, blithely unaware how silly he might look years later with his shaggy 1970s hairdo. Dimon applied to Harvard Business School and was admitted, but then he delayed entering, deciding he'd rather work for a bit first. Applying to about 15 companies—including consulting giants like McKinsey and the Boston Consulting Group—he received just a single job offer, from a small outfit in Boston called Management Advisory and Consulting that had been found by professors from Harvard Business School. He spent the next two years there.

He remained as headstrong as he'd been all his life. When one partner demanded he work all weekend and deliver a finished project by 9:00 A.M. Monday, Dimon dutifully did as he was asked. Come Monday morning, however, the partner didn't even show up to see the results. Dimon's first instinct was to quit. Instead, he confronted the partner, who said he'd just wanted to make sure that the project was finished promptly. "But you ruined my weekend," Dimon replied. "And because of that, I will never work on another project for you again." When colleagues told him that he wasn't allowed to make such unilateral decisions, Dimon was defiant. "Yes, I can," he said. "And they can fire me if they want to." (They didn't.) In another instance, he refused to work on a project for a cigarette maker.

"I saw some things while I was there that were just astounding," Dimon recalls. "I remember one client's CFO being just downright dishonest. I also thought the bureaucracy of many places was over-the-top. The BS that happens at so many companies—I was blown away by it. I didn't want to be a consultant, but I learned a lot there, including the idea of fundamental research. I had no idea that if you were working for a fishing rod company, you could go to the library and look at 24 fishing magazines. And that there were fishing mailing lists and that kind of thing. It opened my eyes to all of that."

. . .

Among his brothers, Jamie was alone in pursuing business. Freed by their upper-middle-class upbringing to do exactly as they pleased, both Ted and Peter chose intellectual pursuits. Peter got a PhD in physics from the University of Chicago, and Ted Jr. became an educator and an expert in a mind-body discipline known as the Alexander technique. But Jamie never lost sight of his original goal: "success."

The year that Jamie entered Harvard Business School (HBS), 1980, Wall Street was a wreck, and corporate America was stumbling after the cursed late-1970s period of stagflation. "Not many people were going into finance at the time," recalls the HBS professor Jay O. Light. "In that sense, it was a special class, people who were *truly* interested in finance, and not just following the crowd."

Dimon stood apart even among that group—which included the future hedge fund managers Seth Klarman and Steven Mandel; the future chairman and CEO of G.E., Jeffrey Immelt; and the future president of Comcast, Stephen Burke. Within weeks of arriving at school, Dimon showed his fearlessness. Discussing a case study about the financial operations of a cranberry co-op, he challenged a professor. Case studies, the bread and butter of education at HBS, involved a group approach to solving issues in highly complex business situations—usually taken from real life—for companies and their managers. "Imagine 80 or

90 people, most of them feeling insecure, that they were an admissions mistake of some sort," recalls Burke. "And Jamie raises his hand and says, 'You've made a mistake.' Everyone froze. We all thought he was committing suicide. But Jamie walked up to the board and changed a few things, and the next thing you know, the teacher said, 'Oh my God, you're right.' It was a confidence with no fear."

Jay Light noticed the same thing that Mike Ingrisani had at Browning—Dimon had a powerful independent streak, and often a different grasp of what a manager's priorities should be in case studies. He bore down on fundamental issues such as expense strategy and risk management. One day, in a class discussion of various fixed income investments, Light challenged Dimon on the concept of investing in a long-term zero coupon bond that nevertheless had a 15 percent yield-to-maturity. (In other words, although the bond offered no annual interest payments, it was selling at a price that would offer a 15 percent annualized return at maturity.) Dimon launched a bomb into the middle of class: "If you don't see the merits of investing in a 15 percent zero coupon bond, Professor Light, then you probably shouldn't be teaching this class."

James "Longo" Long, who had come to Harvard after a stint at Hewlett-Packard in California, was dismayed by what he considered the lack of concrete "business" experience of many classmates who had worked in investment banking and consulting. "These people don't know much, but they do know how to talk all the time," he thought. He'd been told that half of the education at HBS was what one learned from other students, and this didn't look as though it was going to be much. But Long took a liking to Dimon, who didn't seem preoccupied with merely impressing others, and ended up in a study group with his new friend by the end of the year. "He was a straight shooter," recalls Long. "It was fun to be friends with him, even though he could be a pretty serious guy."

(Dimon did like to unwind. He, Burke, Long, and their classmate Peter Maglathlin formed what they called the Thursday Night Club, and usually went out and drank from 90-ounce "scorpion bowls"—a lethal concoction of fruit juice and rum. The club congregated at the

Hong Kong on Harvard Square—affectionately referred to as "the Kong"—and hashed through the events of the previous week.)

At business school, Dimon was obsessed with self-improvement. On midterm exams in the first year, he performed extremely well in all but one class, the study of organizational behavior, in which he was only slightly better than average. Burke, though, had aced the midterm in organizational behavior. "It drove him crazy that he didn't do well and I did," recalls Burke. But Dimon then surprised him. He asked if he could read Burke's "blue book"—the universal medium of college exams—so that he might understand why Burke had done better. No one had ever asked Burke *why* or *how* he had done well on an exam, but he nevertheless allowed Dimon to try to do just that. Come finals, Dimon was near the top of the class. "Part of his psyche is having a strong enough ego to be willing to say, 'I want to know why you did better than me,' " says Burke. "To put himself out there like that."

He also stood out for another reason. Business schools, by their nature, tend to be chock-full of Republicans. But Dimon was a Democrat, and an outspoken one at that. He was also prone to conversational tangents on the importance of ethics and the imperative of "doing the right thing," topics that had yet to enter the lexicon of most of his business school peers.

(The independent Dimon even cultivated an outsider persona in nonacademic ways. He didn't live in university housing, instead staying in an apartment a one-minute walk from campus. He also eschewed the traditional uniform of the B-school student—khakis and button-down shirts—and wore jeans and often a blue leather jacket. His classmates actually remember that of the 75 students in their year, Dimon was the absolute worst dresser.)

Every year, new students are told that half of their grade in each course with be based on class participation. The result: a room full of overanxious overachievers trying to interrupt one another, for fear of not being noticed by the professor. On the *second* day of class in his first year of business school, Dimon was speaking when another student began wildly waving a hand. Dimon turned toward the student and said, "Put your fucking hand down while I'm talking." The student slumped down into his seat, and Dimon moved right on with what he was saying.

• • •

At the start of his second year, Dimon was vice president of the school's finance club—an indication, if nothing else, of a man who read company financials in his spare time. Judy Kent, an exceedingly attractive and feisty HBS student from Bethesda, Maryland, who had graduated from Tulane and then worked at the management-consulting firm Booz Allen Hamilton in Washington, was one of four roommates of the club's president. Early in the year, another of Kent's roommates, Sue Zadek, had met Dimon at the wedding of his friends the Maglathlins and suggested that Kent check out the young man, as he was cute and charismatic. (It was a small world back then. Zadek attended the wedding with Steve Mandel, whom she later married. Also in attendance was Jeffrey Immelt.)

A driven young woman, in her own right, Kent had earned a master's degree from Catholic University while working for Booz Allen, but she'd decided to attend Harvard for another leg up. The daughter of a real estate entrepreneur, she was the first in her family to go to college. (She claims to have been one of the classmates who watched Jeff Immelt at HBS and predicted that he would run General Electric one day.) After hearing of Dimon from Zadek, Kent grilled Laurie Maglathlin about the brash young student. Although Maglathlin was protective of her friend, she did give him a ringing endorsement.

Walking through campus one afternoon, Kent and Zadek passed by the Pub, a snack bar for students. Zadek pointed Dimon out to her, and Kent was intrigued. "In the midst of pastel shirts, here was this guy wearing all black, and sunglasses," she recalls. More interesting, though, was the fact that while he was participating in the conversation at his table, he seemed to be completely aware of everything else around him without being consumed by it. "He's sphinxlike," Kent thought to herself. Not long afterward, when Dimon called Kent's apartment to speak to the president of the finance club, she shouted out that she'd like to speak to him after the club's business had been concluded.

Handed the phone, Judy Kent asked Dimon if he played tennis. "Sure," he replied. "Fine," she said, "I'll meet you tomorrow." She remembers that although she played as hard as she could she failed to present Dimon with much of a challenge. He asked her afterward if she'd like to get a "malted." She thought the terminology charming, and said yes, and the two went to the Pub for a drink. (He didn't have any money, so Kent paid.) She walked him home, kissed him on the cheek, and resolved to see him again. "I was just so drawn to him," she recalls. "It was instinctual." A short time later, he asked her out for dinner (he paid this time), and the two were soon inseparable. He even dared to ride with her in her dented, rusty gold 1977 Cutlass. "She drove like a bat out of hell," recalls their friend Peter Maglathlin.

(There is another, more straightforward version of the story of the meeting of Jamie and Judy, told by their classmate, future G.E. chairman Jeffrey Immelt. When one executive at JPMorgan Chase asked Immelt about the dynamics in their long-ago Harvard section—specifically, how Jamie and Judy got together—he responded simply, "Judy was by far the best-looking, sexiest, and smartest girl in the class, and Jamie got to her first. That's about it.")

Judy was able to break through the young man's uncompromising exterior and connect with someone who had surprisingly vast reserves of sentimentality. Dimon, for example, worshipped the family dog, Chippy, whom he'd brought to Boston with him. When Chippy later died, the twins (Ted Jr. lived in Boston at the time) decided to bury him at night on a hill he'd enjoyed running on. Taking Judy's car, Dimon dressed his dog in a favorite rugby shirt and headed off into the night with his brother.

He remembers the experience to this day, in part because he caught a bad case of poison sumac that night, which broke out in sores during finals week. To help him write his exams without oozing all over the blue books, Judy Kent wrapped paper toweling around both of Dimon's arms, securing it with masking tape. This was true love.

Near the end of their second year, on a weekend at his parents' country place, Dimon proposed and she accepted. Shortly afterward, on a trip to New York, Dimon surprised his father by asking if he would play a piece for him and Judy on his violin. "What did you say?" asked Ted Sr., unaccustomed to such requests from the least musically inclined of his three children. "I said, 'Would you play a piece for us?' " Dimon replied. Ted Sr. did so, and when he put the violin down, Jamie Dimon told his parents that he and Judy were engaged.

Dimon and Kent graduated from HBS in 1982. Dimon was named a Baker Scholar, a distinction bestowed on the top 5 percent of each graduating class. The couple packed their bags and headed for New York City.

2. THE MENTOR

Fresh from Harvard Business School, Dimon could write his own ticket on Wall Street. In the spring of 1982, he had three job offers—from the investment banks Goldman Sachs, Lehman Brothers, and Morgan Stanley. He called Sandy Weill, then the chairman of the executive committee of American Express, to ask for advice, and Weill invited Dimon to his office for a chat. Dimon had worked at Goldman Sachs between his first and second years at business school, and that firm was ready to give him an opportunity very few people have ever refused: the chance to work at Wall Street's most prestigious (and lucrative) partnership. As Stephen Burke puts it, 95 out of 100 of Dimon's classmates would have taken the offer from Goldman. Dimon told Weill that he was close to a decision to do that very thing.

"What's more important to you?" Weill asked Dimon. "Making the most money or continuing on the fastest learning curve?" At the time, Weill was in charge of all the treasury and financial functions at American Express, and contending with his own learning curve. He floated a fourth option to Dimon. "How would you like to come be my assistant and we can learn this thing together? We can learn a heck of a lot about how corporate America works and how a diversified financial services company works. You probably won't make half of what you'd be making at Goldman, but that's a far more concentrated and high-pressure job, and I don't know what you'd be *building*."

Dimon was intrigued. The potential riches aside, one major drawback of the investment banking business is psychological. At their core, investment bankers don't actually build anything; they move other people's money from hither to yon and grab a piece of it as it's passing by. And here was Weill, offering an entrée at the very top of American Express. Dimon accepted the offer—for two-thirds of what Goldman was offering.

"My goal in life was not to be an investment banker," Dimon recalls. "I loved the concept of helping build a company . . . the whole painting. Something that was yours over a long period of time that you could be really proud of. And Sandy had done it before with Shearson. I also thought I could always change my mind if it didn't work out. It was a little risky, because Sandy was just chairman of the executive committee at American Express—whatever that meant—but he was honest with me. He said, 'I'm not sure it's going to work out here, but I think you're a smart kid and we'll see how it develops.' "

By choosing Weill over Goldman, Dimon once again set himself apart from the crowd. Although the investment banking industry had not yet reached its mid-1980s apotheosis—as caricatured by a suspender-wearing Michael Douglas in the 1987 film *Wall Street*—the 1980s bull market was already up and running, and investment bankers were feeling giddy and powerful. Most Harvard graduates would have killed for the job at Goldman that Dimon turned down. So began one of the greatest mentor-protégé relationships in the history of American business.

Sandy Weill saw Jamie Dimon for what he was: an ambitious young man with an enormous capacity for hard work. "You can't bluff your way into being a Baker Scholar," he thought. And Jamie Dimon saw Sandy Weill for what *he* was: a minor legend on Wall Street who was offering the young man a ride in an express elevator to the executive suite. And American Express was itself a prestigious institution, so it wasn't as if Dimon were forsaking Goldman Sachs for a bucket shop.

(In the meantime, Jamie Dimon and Judy Kent endured one of New York City's more painful initiation rites—the apartment hunt. The couple eventually signed a lease at 300 East 56th Street, in a 33-story building known as the Bristol in New York's Sutton Place neighborhood, and began their adult life as New Yorkers.)

. . .

Just like the Dimon family, the Weills were part of a wave of European immigrants that descended on New York in the early twentieth century. The son of Polish Jews, Sandy Weill grew up in a modest home in Brooklyn. After graduating from Cornell in 1955, he married the former Joan Mosher, then returned to New York for a $35-a-week job as a runner at Bear Stearns.

They lived in a $120-a-month apartment in East Rockaway, where their neighbors were another young Jewish couple, Arthur and Linda Carter. In 1960, Weill and Carter opened their own firm with two other friends, Roger Berlind and Peter Potoma. The firm was called Carter, Berlind, Potoma & Weill (CBPW), and soon carved out a niche as a small "research boutique," alongside another emerging outfit, Donaldson, Lufkin & Jenrette (DLJ). (As Roger Lowenstein pointed out in a profile in 2000 in the *New York Times Magazine*, ethnic divisions on Wall Street were still strong and resulted in the firm's nickname: "the Jewish DLJ.") Along with research, CBPW offered both brokerage and investment banking services.

The firm scratched and clawed for business from the conglomerate builders of the 1960s, including Charlie Bludhorn of Gulf + Western and Saul Steinberg. A couple of fortuitous hires and palace intrigues later, Arthur Carter and Peter Potoma were forced out of the firm, and Arthur Levitt—who later went on to be chairman of the Securities and Exchange Commission—and Marshall Cogan were in. The firm, now Cogan, Berlind, Weill & Levitt (CBWL; nickname: Corned Beef with Lettuce) set up shop in the new General Motors Building on Fifth Avenue, right off Central Park.

Business boomed for CBWL in the late 1960s—the firm brought in $18 million in 1969—so much so that the partners received a call one day that their clearing partner, Burnham & Co., could no longer handle the volume of trading activity they generated. Known on Wall Street as a "back office" function, clearing was vital to a brokerage firm's existence. A brokerage couldn't buy or sell stock for clients without someone to take care of the legal and logistical paperwork for it. The partners decided to build their own clearing operation, and hired Frank Zarb, another Brooklyn-born up-and-comer, to build out a back office. "The idea was simple. We had to conquer the back end of the business as well as the front end," recalls Zarb. "If we didn't, we really couldn't be a leader."

The company ran a lean operation, but nevertheless poured scarce resources into the expansion. Its timing couldn't have been worse, as the stock market soon went into a tailspin. But as Monica Langley points out in *Tearing Down the Walls*, her biography of Weill, he had an insight that would shape the rest of his career. "You can't control income," he told his worried partners. "It varies based on conditions outside of our control. But you can control expenses." Taking charge, he slashed executives' salaries by 25 percent and those of the rank and file by 10 percent. This would be the start of Weill's reputation as a ruthless cost-cutter, a skill he would pass on to Dimon.

By maniacally focusing on costs, CBWL positioned itself to buy distressed assets from competitors sagging under their own bloated operations. In March 1970, Weill and his partners made their first such move, taking a Beverly Hills brokerage office off the hands of a struggling McDonnell & Co. Next up: Hayden Stone, a nationwide brokerage with 62 branches that was facing its own financial challenges. After a dramatic series of negotiations, CBWL swallowed its much larger rival in September 1970, and changed its own name to CBWL-Hayden Stone.

Over the next decade, Weill and his partners went through the same motions again and again, buying H. Hentz & Co., Shearson Hammill (the deal that brought Ted Dimon Sr. into the fold), and Loeb Rhoades. "We had this machine," Weill told the *New York Times Magazine*. The firm changed its name with similar frequency. In 1974, it was Shearson Hayden Stone; in 1979, Shearson Loeb Rhoades.

Weill's growing reputation was rife with contradictions. Somewhat inarticulate and unpolished, he nevertheless had "the vision thing" and had the ability to see several steps ahead and sniff out opportunities for deals. Despite his growing stature, he continued to think of himself as an outsider. His religion was a part of that perspective. Sandy Weill was Jewish, and although he and his partners had built the second-largest securities firm in the country after Merrill Lynch by 1980, and there were plenty of successful Jewish firms on the Street (Goldman Sachs, Bear Stearns, and Lehman Brothers, to name three), anti-Semitism still loomed large in other quarters.

A broker from the start, Weill never lost the habits of the profession. "The joke about Sandy was that you could stand on his desk and take all your clothes off and he wouldn't take his eyes off the tape," recalls Mary McDermott, who started working for Weill right out of college and went on to work with him for the better part of the next 30 years.

For much of the 1970s, too, Sandy Weill had a young protégé named Peter Cohen, who had originally been an assitant of one of Weill's partners, Marshall Cogan. When Cogan left the firm, Cohen essentially became Weill's shadow. A tough and analytic study, he was a precursor to Dimon, a man who pledged his early career in allegiance to Weill. He was both Weill's numbers man and his hatchet man, and had the tough-guy looks to go with his role.

After several years as Weill's go to guy, Cohen surprised his boss by announcing in 1978 that he was leaving the firm to run Republic National Bank for the billionaire Edward Safra. Weill soon enticed Cohen back, but the mentorship was over. Cohen was now a player in his own right at Shearson.

As the 1980s started, Weill was still in deal-making mode. In early 1981, he began talking to American Express's chairman and CEO, Jim Robinson, about a possible union. Both men saw the consolidation trends in financial services, and they agreed that the idea of the large brokerage firm partnering with the iconic credit card company made sense.

In March 1981, Prudential Insurance announced its purchase of Bache Halsey Stuart Shields, a brokerage firm. Suddenly Weill was up against a firm with far more financial resources than his own, and he realized that he needed to make a deal. Within a month, Weill and Robinson announced a transaction. American Express bought Shearson for a cool $1 billion. Shearson Loeb Rhoades became Shearson American Express. Sandy Weill remained CEO of the brokerage business and became chairman of the American Express executive committee. Soon afterward, he ran into Ted Dimon Sr. "Now they can't get to me anymore," Weill said, revealing, not for the first or the last time, the deep-seated insecurity that drove him to succeed.

. . .

When Dimon first hooked up with Weill at American Express in 1982, Weill still believed he had made the right decision in selling his company to Robinson. Enjoying the social whirl of New York's corporate elite, he had a car and driver and the prestige he had long craved. "Sandy nearly forgot how to drive while he was at American Express," recalls Weill's longtime PR chief, Mary McDermott. He also got down to business, quickly negotiating the purchase of two regional brokerage firms to bolster Shearson: Foster & Marshall in Seattle and Robinson Humphrey in Atlanta.

Dimon felt he'd made the right decision as well. Most MBAs toil in obscurity for years before they get their shot at the big time. Dimon was immediately exposed to deal making at its highest levels. Weill later concluded that perhaps he gave the young man too much responsibility too soon, inflating an ego that would cause Dimon problems in getting along with others. At the time, however, having such an ambitious and intelligent aide more than outweighed the frustration of putting up with his impatience.

Dimon and Weill's first major project together was not a Sandy Weill special. Instead of snapping up a cheap competitor that was on the ropes, in 1982 he and Dimon found a way to help American Express dump a poor investment without having to swallow the associated losses. At the time, the economy was reeling because the Federal Reserve chairman Paul Volcker had raised the federal funds rate to 20 percent in 1981—this was the tough medicine he thought necessary to cure the stagflation of the 1970s. The result was the worst recession since the Great Depression, with unemployment levels not seen since the 1930s. The rate increase also caused the fixed-income market to crater, leaving American Express with long-term municipal bonds that were now significantly underwater.

Coincidentally, American Express had been planning to lease space in the World Financial Center (WFC), then being built by Olympia & York—the investment vehicle of Canada's Reichman brothers—just above Battery Park. Throwing Dimon headlong into his first deal, complete with late-night negotiations at a suite in the Waldorf-Astoria hotel, Weill came up with something akin to a three-way trade in baseball. Instead of leasing space, he argued, they should buy a new building in the WFC. In exchange for buying a building in what was an extremely tough real estate climate, the Reichmans would then buy American Express's old corporate headquarters. The company could then use the gain from that sale to offset the losses from selling the municipal bonds, thereby avoiding a situation in which it would have to report a significant earnings decline. In the process, Amex traded out of municipal bonds that yielded just 1.375 percent, for treasury securities yielding 11.5 percent. "Jamie was an important part of building a fact base so we could make our points to other people in the company or on the board," recalls Weill. "He was a very quick student."

That success notwithstanding, it wasn't long before Weill began to feel stifled by the formal, bureaucratic American Express. It was nothing like Shearson. He realized that his role as chairman of the executive committee was a hollow one that gave him no authority whatsoever. And in January 1983, when Alva Way, the president of American Express, resigned, Weill made a serious miscalculation. At Robinson's request, he ceded the role of CEO of Shearson to Peter Cohen in exchange for a "promotion" to president of the overall company. What he'd done was relinquish control of an operating business, and he became, as Monica Langley put it, "a president without portfolio." After buying his company, Robinson had taken less than two years to effectively castrate Weill. (Cohen played his part, too. He later told the reporter Jon Friedman that he had pushed Weill "up and out.")

Despite seeing Weill treated this way, Dimon remembers Robinson fondly. He saw Robinson as a smart man who worked hard and was well connected, although also as one who ran an unnecessarily bureaucratic shop. "They protected that Amex brand like you wouldn't believe," Dimon recalls. "The customer service was fabulous."

Shorn of operating responsibilities, Weill decided that he needed another deal to keep himself relevant. His first target: Investors Diversified Services (IDS), a Minneapolis-based provider of financial services. With his trusty B-school tool in hand—the Hewlett-Packard HP-12C calculator—Dimon played a central role in the negotiations, shuttling between New York and Minneapolis, where he met with IDS's financial team in a hotel. In a shock to Weill, Peter Cohen effectively blocked the deal when it first came up for a vote. Weill's onetime protégé had stabbed him in the back. And although the deal eventually got done, Weill still felt marginalized by Cohen, and in need of yet another deal.

Around this time, Dimon reported to Tufts that he was vice president and assistant to the president of American Express. He described his job as "exhilarating, demanding, and a lot of fun." There was no doubt it was demanding, especially considering that there'd been no training program or guidebook to help him navigate his entrée into the world of high-stakes deal making. Even Sandy Weill would admit that he has never been much of a teacher, and that if Dimon wanted to learn the ins and outs of the business, it was largely up to him to be a self-starter. Luckily for Dimon, he was exactly that.

· · ·

Jamie Dimon has always been a man in a hurry, and in matters of the heart, he was no different. He'd proposed to Judy Kent while they were still at Harvard. When it came time to actually get married, however, there was one issue that the couple needed to navigate. Kent was Jewish. Her parents, after briefly entertaining the notion that Dimon might convert to Judaism, realized the folly of the idea when Kent explained to them that while Dimon respected other peoples' faith, he did not want to be confined by organized religion and "that there was no point in raising the conversion issue whatsoever."

Dimon, referring to himself as "the great compromiser," agreed to meet the rabbi who was to marry them. "I wasn't even speaking to him at that point, as I was so mad," Judy Dimon recalls. "Things were getting pretty tense." The two men had a brief conversation in which the rabbi tried to convince Dimon that he need not *change* to become Jewish. But Dimon wouldn't budge. "I am what I am," he said, and the issue was closed. When he and Judy next spoke, Dimon informed her in no uncertain terms that although he would allow the rabbi to marry them, he would give the man just ten minutes. She could write her vows, and he would write his own. The ceremony, on May 21, 1983, in Washington, D.C., went off without a hitch.

Judy was working at Shearson at this point, as an assistant to Joseph Plumeri, the colorful Italian-American director of marketing and sales at the firm. Plumeri remembers Kent as whip-smart but always a little frazzled. She always had runs in her stockings, so he once gave her 25 pairs for Christmas.

Judy Dimon worked at Shearson for three years as a vice president in marketing before quitting her job two months after the arrival of Julia, the couple's first child, on May 25, 1985. Almost immediately, though, she dove into a second career in the nonprofit sector, taking a job as executive director of the Spunk Fund, a foundation focused on improving the lives of impoverished young people. She later became involved in the Children's Aid Society in New York, helping support inner-city schools. Her sacrifice was rewarded by Dimon's own commitment to family, however constraining his career demands might be.

The conventional wisdom about Dimon is that he has few interests outside the office, a simplification that irritates him. "I love music and I read a lot and I exercise and play tennis and I ski," he says. "So I don't play golf. So what? I think it would be fair to say that when the kids were born, they became my outside hobby. I cut way back on the other stuff and devoted as much time as I could for the family. I still do. Until they were about 15 we never took a vacation without them. The kids and their friends would say I was around a lot, even though I thought I wasn't. But they probably felt that way because when I was there, I would *be* there."

· · ·

In late 1983, Weill had a new mission. The American Express subsidiary Fireman's Fund, a property and casualty insurer, had run into operational and accounting problems and was dragging its parent down with it. Playing fast and loose in a highly competitive insurance environment, the unit's management had boosted premium growth without a coincident increase in reserves, and a sudden spike in insurance claims was causing massive losses. Worse, it appeared that executives had tried to cover up their miscalculations. In late 1983, a $230 million increase in the Fireman Fund's reserves caused American Express to report its first earnings decline in 36 years.

Robinson asked Weill to head to San Francisco and resolve the problems. Weill was reluctant to do so—it wasn't hard to see that he was being exiled—but he also realized he really had no choice and acquiesced. He took Dimon along with him, as well as Bill McCormick, a senior American Express executive. The three spent several weeks together before launching an audacious turnaround in early 1984, in which Weill fired 15 percent of the unit's employees and raised premiums. This stanched the losses, but the division remained a drag on American Express's balance sheet—the unit needed another $200 million in fresh capital in November—and Robinson soon decided he wanted to unload it. Weill saw an opportunity.

Knowing that Robinson wouldn't be too sorry to see him go, Weill proposed to his boss that he buy Fireman's Fund from the company. Though concerned about giving the impression that Weill had gotten the better of him, Robinson nevertheless allowed him to explore the possibility of a deal. At this point, Dimon suggested that Weill approach Warren Buffett. The two men met with Buffett briefly in New York and then flew to his Omaha headquarters to pitch the legend on the idea of funding a buyout.

Buffett was interested in their proposal—he offered to buy 20 percent or more of the unit if it was sold—and the pair left Omaha thinking an opportunity was at hand. In May 1985, Weill made his proposal to the board: American Express would keep 40 percent of the business, Warren Buffett would own 40 percent, and Weill would own 20 percent, pursuant to a number of conditions and guarantees. Weill had hired Morgan Stanley to represent him in the deal.

For reasons of its own—including a desire not to be embarrassed if Sandy Weill managed to take profit that could be theirs alone—the board rejected the idea. "It was a weird situation," Dimon recalls.

"Someone said at the time that American Express couldn't do a deal if Sandy, Morgan Stanley, and Warren Buffett were on the other side. That's part of the reason Sandy had offered to let them keep 40 percent, so if they thought it was a little cheap, they'd make it back on the back end. But I really hope that wasn't the reason they didn't do it, because that would be pretty stupid."

The prospect of partnering with Warren Buffett was dead. Weill sensed that Robinson had outmaneuvered him. He'd given up his operational responsibilities, and was now being treated as an adversary by the board of the very company he worked for. He decided he had to resign, and he did on Monday, June 25, 1985. "Sandy never fit in there anyway," recalls Alison Falls McElvery, one of his assistants at the time. "On the one hand, you had all these upstanding, pressed, and beautiful people like Jim Robinson who just reeked of money. And then you had Sandy who would yell down the hallway to ask someone how their weekend had been." (This despite the fact that Weill had a greater net worth than Robinson.)

The question for the 29-year-old Dimon: should he go with Weill? Jim Robinson offered to keep Dimon on as a vice president in another role, and by that point he could have worked anywhere else he wanted, maybe even at Goldman. "It was a complex decision," Dimon recalls. Many friends, including Stephen Burke and Andrall Pearson, president and chief operating officer of Pepsi, told Dimon this was *his* chance to cut bait, to admit that his gamble on Weill had not panned out. After all, he now had a wife, and a child just a few weeks old, to care for, and Weill wasn't getting any younger. Dimon discussed the future with his Harvard buddy Peter Maglathlin that summer on vacation at the Kents' summer house in Delaware's Bethany Beach. "Is this guy washed up?" Maglathlin asked. "Does he even have another act?" "I have faith in Sandy," Dimon replied. "Something's going to happen."

It was surely a mix of factors—loyalty, an appetite for adventure, a conviction that Sandy Weill had another run left in him—that led Dimon to ignore his friends' advice and resign from American Express along with his boss. Weill offered to pay Dimon $100,000 a year to stay on as his assistant, although American Express covered the cost temporarily. McElvery decided to join Weill as well. Dimon remembers being reluctant to take money from Weill, despite the fact that Weill was by that point a very rich man. "I didn't like it," Dimon recalls. "We weren't earning anything. I figured I could take money on the come for a while, and if we figured anything out, I could get paid then. I wasn't particularly fond of the idea."

. . .

New York City is chock-full of former Wall Street highfliers who have offices paid for by the companies they used to run but no actual job to speak of. They're called elephants' graveyards. At the time, American Express was large enough to have graveyards in several locations including offices in the Seagram Building at 52nd and Park. Weill chose that location, in no small part because The Four Seasons restaurant— home of the original "power lunch"—was on the building's ground floor.

In his earlier heyday, Weill had promised John Loeb Sr. of Loeb Rhoades an office for life when Shearson bought Loeb Rhoades, an obligation American Express had taken on when it had subsequently purchased Shearson. It was Weill's turn to go to the graveyard now, though, and in an ironic twist he found that American Express had put him in a suite with Loeb.

After settling into their offices in July 1985, Weill, Dimon, and McElvery expected new job opportunities to come pouring in. Letters of support did arrive, but there were no jobs to speak of. The two men often had lunch together at The Four Seasons—they called it the "company cafeteria"—and Weill's taste for martinis led to afternoon naps on the couch in his office. He ate in The Four Seasons' exclusive Grill Room so often that the restaurant assigned him a "negative reservation"—his table would be waiting for him unless he called to tell them he was *not* coming to lunch that day. Weill wore a suit to work every day, just in case a chance meeting might pop up. Dimon also took his non-job very seriously. "Jamie would sit on the floor and open up annual reports to see what we could do next," McElvery recalls. "Once, we'd created our own merchant bank model, and Sandy hit some button on the WaNG computer and erased it before I had a chance to save it. Jamie nearly killed him."

James Calvano, who'd been vice chairman of American Express Travel Related Services—he'd run Avis Rent-A-Car previously—lasted just six months more than Weill at the company, and was now in the same boat, looking for his next gig. While playing golf with Calvano one day, Weill asked him, "What do you want to do?" Calvano replied that he wanted to run a company. "Well, come with us," Weill responded, "We'll go find one." Calvano was intrigued. "Who have you got?" he asked. "Me and Jamie," was Weill's unembarrassed response.

By that, Weill meant he would have meetings with people, then return to the office and offload any research about a prospective opportunity on Dimon, whose desk was littered with prospectuses and financial statements. Buried in the numbers for 12 to 14 hours a day, Dimon grew especially fond of Warren Buffett's missives out of his Omaha-based Berkshire Hathaway. "He was smitten whenever anything came out from Berkshire Hathaway," recalls McElvery. "He would say, 'You have to read this! It's the greatest annual report I've ever read! He's brilliant!'"

One meeting that stuck in Dimon's mind was with Ivan Boesky, then the reigning practitioner of "risk arbitrage" on Wall Street. His specialty was betting on whether proposed mergers would come to fruition or failure, and he was one of Wall Street's flashiest players. "I remember thinking he was a little paranoid," recalls Dimon. "Because in his office he had this phone bank from which he could listen into any one of his employees' phone calls. It looked like a cockpit. And he had cameras in every room. It was totally bizarre."

The first exciting possibility for Weill and Dimon came in late fall 1985, when Warren Hellman, the former president of Lehman Brothers who had moved to San Francisco, alerted Weill to a possible opportunity. BankAmerica, one of the country's most prestigious commercial banking franchises, was bedeviled by a rash of underperforming loans, its stock was in free fall, and the company's management team was under fire. It was possible, Hellman told him, that the board might consider wholesale change at the top.

After meeting with Hellman in San Francisco, Weill and Dimon crunched the numbers and determined that if Weill could arrange a $1 billion capital infusion—plus $10 million of his own money—he could reasonably propose to BankAmerica's board that they install him as CEO. Weill even swallowed his pride and asked Jim Robinson and Peter Cohen if they wanted in on the deal by providing a commitment letter for the $1 billion. (Cohen was by this point a true Wall Street *macher*. He'd bought Lehman Brothers Kuhn Loeb the previous year for $380 million. It didn't bother him, as Bryan Burrough and John Helyar pointed out in *Barbarians at the Gate*, that one critic of the deal— Lehman's in-house chef—mused, "Shearson taking over Lehman is like McDonald's taking over 21." He had emerged from Sandy's shadow once and for all.)

Around this same time, Mike Holland, the former CEO of both Salomon Asset Management and First Boston Asset Management, who was now running money for himself and some friends out of his own office in the Seagram Building, read an article in which Weill complained that no one called him for lunch anymore. And so Holland picked up the phone and invited him to lunch.

The two men agreed to meet—at The Four Seasons, naturally— and upon sitting down, Weill began talking about his plans for a potential takeover of BankAmerica. Holland was friendly with Bill Wyant, a leading analyst of commercial banks at the time, and he proposed to bring the two men together in Weill's office. When Holland and Wyant walked into Weill's office, they found that they were to be questioned by both Weill and Dimon.

"Who's this young pup?" Holland thought to himself. Wyant tried to convince Weill that the deal didn't make sense, that the bank's balance sheet didn't provide the solidity to do with it what Weill was hoping. Dimon countered that the banking analyst didn't know what he was talking about. "Sandy let that little whelp go on as if he were some sort of senior statesman, didn't he?" Holland said to Wyant when the two men departed.

BankAmerica's board rejected Weill's entreaties not once but twice. It was back to the drawing board. Adding insult to injury, it turned out that Joan Weill's psychiatrist had engaged in insider trading of Bank America's stock after she told him about her husband's attempted power grab at the firm.

In May 1986, while he and Dimon were still casting about for something that they could sink their teeth into, *Fortune*'s Carol Loomis wrote an article with a tongue-in-cheek headline in the form of a classified ad: "Sanford Weill, 53, Exp'd Mgr, Gd Refs." It was praise and critique rolled into one, because despite his "Gd Refs," Weill still lacked meaningful employment. His second career had taken on a distinct whiff of failure by this point, and Jamie Dimon couldn't help wondering what life might have been like had he taken that job offer at Goldman. "I was looking into the abyss a little bit, pretty much a kid who was not getting experience nor making money in the meantime," recalls Dimon. "Of course I thought I might have made a mistake."

Having stuck by Weill through his trials at American Express and in the empty days that followed, Dimon certainly knew that his position at Sandy's side would be inviolate if a big deal ever did come to pass. But that was starting to seem like one big "if."

3. THE SUBPRIME OF HIS LIFE

When he graduated from Harvard Business School, Jamie Dimon could never have imagined that within four years, he'd be working for a bottom-of-the-barrel lending operation in a financial backwater—and that he'd be thrilled to have the chance. But that's how it played out.

Sandy Weill and Jamie Dimon found their next gig at a decidedly unglamorous operation called Commercial Credit, a Baltimore-based lender to a huge but overlooked sector of the population: the 45 million people who shopped at Wal-Mart, with household income between $15,000 and $45,000. These were people that financial services companies generally tried *not* to do business with. (In the popular lexicon of 2008–2009, one would call Commercial Credit a subprime lender. It was a business to be shunned in the 1980s, but the pell-mell pursuit of these very customers some 20 years later would be one of the proximate causes of the financial crisis.)

It wasn't only Commercial Credit's customer base that made its business markedly different from that of most banks. Whereas typical banks borrowed money over short periods and lent it over long ones—making them extremely vulnerable to rising interest rates—Commercial Credit lent over short periods while borrowing at long. The advantage of this model was that the company didn't have to worry about a credit crunch. Its disadvantage was that if rates fell and Commercial Credit was already locked into long-term borrowings, it was vulnerable to being unable to reinvest those borrowings at their long-term cost of capital. In any event, it was a markedly different beast from a neighborhood branch banking business.

Not long after the issue of *Fortune* with Loomis's article in it hit the newsstands, Weill received a call from Bob Volland, the treasurer at Commercial Credit. Control Data, a disk drive maker, had bought Volland's company in 1968 ostensibly as a way to finance computer sales. By the 1980s, however, Control Data was ailing, and that caused complications for Commercial Credit. As a subsidiary of a failing parent, it found itself unable to tap the commercial paper market for its overnight borrowing, and had to rely on more expensive bank loans.

Ownership by Control Data, in other words, was putting Commercial Credit at a distinct competitive disadvantage. When the parent also began borrowing heavily from its subsidiary, Volland feared the worst — that his company might be dismantled to save Control Data from extinction. Worse, the company's bank lines were due to expire that September, and it seemed unlikely that they would be renewed. The model was supposed to be immune to short-term credit issues, but the model didn't account for ownership by a floundering parent company. A cash crunch was on its way.

"I didn't know Jamie Dimon from a hole-in-the-wall," recalls Volland. "But I called them up after I read that article and told them that while I wouldn't give them any inside information, I had an opportunity for them." Weill invited Volland up to New York. When Volland and Paul Burner, the company's assistant treasurer, walked into Weill's office in the Seagram Building, they were greeted by Weill, Dimon, and Greg Fitz-Gerald, the former treasurer of American Express and chief financial officer of Merrill Lynch who'd been kicking around ideas with the pair. Volland briefed the men on the opportunity he saw for someone who could pry Commercial Credit loose from Control Data.

Weill's first response shocked Volland. Weill said that he had looked at the company while he was at American Express—Control Data had hired Goldman Sachs to shop the unit in 1985—and concluded that it was "a piece of crap." Volland didn't believe that Weill had a full grasp of the issues, and continued to press his case, identifying underperforming assets that could be sold, including one unit that even leased cars to ex-convicts ("Cars for Cons"). His persistence paid off. After two hours of discussion, Weill and Dimon wanted to take the next step. Over the next few weeks, Volland and Dimon spoke several times, as Dimon burrowed through the Control Data's financials, trying to get a sense of Commercial Credit's stand-alone opportunity.

Helping Dimon with this due diligence, Weill's assistant McElvery remarked that the company was effectively a loan-sharking operation—customers paid exceedingly high rates to borrow money. Weill and Dimon were indignant, and told her that they considered the business one of helping the little guy. Her own mother chastised her for looking down on the enterprise. "Don't knock these people," she told McElvery. "They lent me the money to buy my first refrigerator."

As Monica Langley points out in *Tearing Down the Walls*, it was Dimon's legwork that made them decide to make a move. His most important finding was that although Commercial Credit had just a 4 percent return on equity—versus 15 percent for comparable finance companies—there were enough assets they could sell and costs that could be slashed to consider the 4 percent mark an attraction rather than a deterrent. The stock market likes nothing more than improved operations and balance sheets, and Commercial Credit offered plenty of room for improvement. It could be their launching pad to greater things.

The next step was to approach Control Data itself. Weill called a friend, the hotshot Morgan Stanley investment banker Bob Greenhill, and asked him to contact Bob Price, chairman of Control Data, to see if Price was amenable to a conversation. He was, and Weill, Dimon, and Greenhill flew out to Minneapolis to meet him. (Weill had enormous respect for Greenhill's judgment, his performance in a crunch, and his ability to keep his eye on the negotiating ball. Morgan Stanley also had a reputation for doing more than expected, delivering much higher-quality analysis than other investment banks.)

Although Price and Weill realized they might be able to help each other out, the discussions proceeded slowly at first. Control Data explored every alternative, including raising money in the bond market to buy some time. By September, however, they were back to the negotiating table.

Weill and Dimon considered an outright purchase. The problem was that it would require a leveraged buyout, leaving the company under an unmanageably heavy debt load. They next talked of a spin-off of the unit by means of an initial public offering. But that idea posed its own complications as well. The investment bank First Boston had roped Control Data into a unique kind of bond offering that stipulated the company would be required to make a tender offer for outstanding bonds if it sold stock in Commercial Credit. Most spin-offs sold about 20 percent of a subsidiary's stock to the public. But such a portion wouldn't raise enough money for Control Data to tender for the high-yield bonds.

All these problems led to an audacious idea. Perhaps, the deal makers wondered, the combination of Sandy Weill's reputation and pedigreed Morgan Stanley running the transaction might enable them to spin off *80 percent* of the company. It would be a blockbuster, and it proved to be the only feasible option. Bob Price and Sandy Weill agreed to give it a shot.

Weill once again tried to enlist Buffett as a coinvestor in the Commercial Credit deal. But Dimon knew better. "Sandy, Warren's not going to like this deal," he told his boss. "Why not?" Weill barked in response. "Because Warren doesn't do turnarounds," said Dimon. "This company is a hodgepodge of crap. He doesn't care that you're running it. He won't care that you're investing in it. He's just not going to do it." The two men had breakfast with Buffett in the Oak Room of New York's Plaza Hotel, and within three minutes Buffett said, "I'm not going to do it. Let's invest in the rest of breakfast."

On September 12, 1986, Control Data announced that Sandy Weill was being appointed as chairman and CEO of Commercial Credit and that the company hoped to sell a majority of the unit to investors as soon as possible. Weill accepted a $500,000 salary, with the proviso that his management team would own 10 percent of the new company through a combination of outright stock purchases and options grants.

In some ways, it was a remarkably counterintuitive move on Weill's part. As McElvery had pointed out, he was aiming for the bottom of the financial ladder, the people with the *least* money. Bankers tend to prefer the opposite. What's more, he and Dimon were effectively putting their eggs in the consumer finance basket when their peers were all trying to grab a piece of the increasingly frenetic action in stocks and bonds on Wall Street. But this focus on the unfashionable was also classic Weill. Commercial Credit was a distressed asset in an otherwise healthy industry, with bloated costs and a messy balance sheet—just the kind of company he could sink his teeth into.

And what of Bob Volland, the man who brought them the opportunity of a lifetime? Weill and Dimon had jokingly referred to him as "Deep Throat" during their initial investigations, but they cut him out the loop soon thereafter. "Bob Volland was a rogue employee regardless of the goodness of his intentions," Weill wrote in his 2006 autobiography, *The Real Deal: My Life in Business and Philanthropy*. Weill's public relations chief, Mary McDermott, thinks the issue for Sandy was a simple one: "Why would you trust someone who brought you stolen goods?"

Volland was of the opinion that the men were applying a ridiculous double standard. Realizing that Dimon didn't trust him, he decided to have it out with the younger man. Dimon told him that he thought Volland had violated a managerial code by making his original call to Weill. "There wasn't one bit of private information discussed on that call," Volland responded. "I could have had the same conversation with you." Dimon's response: "You never should have done it anyway." To which Volland could only reply, "Well, if that's the case, then *you* never should have done what you did. But you sure wanted the rewards, didn't you?"

• • •

Weill and Dimon descended on Baltimore to pretty up the company before the initial public offering, which they hoped would be just a few weeks away. Weill also launched into hiring fresh troops. He'd already spoken to his American Express pal Jim Calvano in late summer, cryptically suggesting that Calvano "meet me in Baltimore." "What's in Baltimore?" asked Calvano. "I can't tell you," Weill responded. "But what are we going to do?" Calvano queried. "We'll have lunch. I've found a place with great crab cakes," Weill said. Calvano eventually signed on as senior vice president of consumer financial services.

The former Merrill Lynch chief financial officer Greg Fitz-Gerald also joined the team, as an executive vice president and the senior financial staffer at the company. Dimon was given the titles of senior vice president and chief financial officer, which meant he was technically subordinate to Fitz-Gerald. Regardless, it was a big step up from the title of "assistant" at American Express, and given Fitz-Gerald's experience, it was an arrangement that made sense. But Dimon began to chafe against it almost immediately.

While planning the road show in anticipation of the initial public offering in October—a show in which the team visited 18 cities—Dimon sulked when Fitz-Gerald made the presentation to possible investors. Weill, noticing this, gave Dimon a share of the presentations himself. In doing so, however, he may have inadvertently fed Dimon's growing sense of his own importance. He also set a clear precedent: when it came to his protégé, the normal rules did not apply. "Jamie was in a hurry to run right through Greg, but he ended up having to be a little patient," Weill recalls. Instead of stopping Dimon, however, Weill stepped back and watched him do just that.

Weill negotiated a discounted share price of $18 for his executive team to buy stakes in Commercial Credit. Dimon put up $425,000—borrowing some from his parents—and when the shares debuted on October 29 at $20.50 apiece, he was already profiting from a job he had yet to really start. At the time, it ranked as the third-largest initial public offering ever, raising $850 million and valuing the entire company just shy of $1 billion. Dimon also received the second-largest number of stock options in the company, after Weill, a reward for having stuck by Weill through a difficult time.

The day after the company went public, Weill, Dimon, and Fitz-Gerald held their first meeting with Commercial Credit's managers in Baltimore. The first announcement was that Chuck Prince, Commercial Credit's general counsel, would be made a senior vice president. The second was that the company was going to lay off 10 percent of its staff, or 125 people, the next day, a move that would save Commercial Credit $5 million annually. Weill explained that he wanted the list done by the morning, and those laid off were to leave the building upon being informed of their fate.

Bob Volland realized he'd made a terrible mistake and pleaded with Weill not to institute such harsh measures. Commercial Credit wasn't some Wall Street firm with trade secrets the fired employees might steal; it was unnecessary to throw anybody out the door. Weill was unmoved. Volland tried another tack. Many employees commuted to Baltimore by bus in the morning, he said, and they'd be stranded with nowhere to go until the rush hour buses went in the other direction. Weill told him to hire cabs.

The Sandy Weill era at Commercial Credit had begun.

• • •

Weill's next hire shocked the staid banking world of New York. Bob Lipp, one of three presidents of Chemical Bank—he'd worked there since the 1940s—agreed to become the executive vice president in charge of consumer financial services at Commercial Credit. It wasn't just a major step down in prestige. He took a 50 percent pay cut as well. Weill considered Lipp his proof to the markets that he was serious about transforming Commercial Credit.

Lipp had realized that his upward rise at Chemical was over—the company's chairman, Walter V. Shipley, was only two years older than he—and he also knew a potential gravy train when he saw one. After a career in the bureaucratic confines of one of the country's largest banks, he was seduced by Weill's salesmanship and decided to throw his lot in with the entrepreneur. It wasn't their first dalliance, either; Lipp had been ready to join Weill if the BankAmerica deal had gone through. "The thing that actually put me over the edge was Sandy's attention to the personal stuff," recalls Lipp. "I really liked the guy."

Lipp brought his lieutenants at Chemical, Bob Willumstad and Marge Magner, with him to Commercial Credit. "Sandy had a reputation of being a great entrepreneur, of creating a lot of wealth," recalls Willumstad. "And he offered the opportunity for people to get really engaged in something. Although I must admit, I wondered for months whether I'd made the right decision." So, too, did most of the new recruits at one point or another, especially when they found out that the company would be covered by the Philadelphia bureau of the *Wall Street Journal* instead of out of New York.

Dimon and Lipp took to each other out of the gate. The intense working experience in Baltimore laid the foundations for a relationship that has endured for more than two decades. "Bob was—and is—the velvet fist," says Dimon. "He's also so smart, but he didn't wear it on his chest. And he taught me one of the most important things in my career, which is not to rest on your laurels. He would emphasize the negatives. But only when it came to the business. He always made it fun. He'd say things like, 'Hey, let's go to Kentucky and go to that place where we had those fabulous pies!' I've learned a tremendous amount from him."

Another hire who worked closely with Jamie Dimon was John Fowler, a former executive vice president at Warner Amex Cable Communications. Fowler also took a 50 percent pay cut. One of Fowler's memories is of Dimon pointing him toward the annual report of Warren Buffett's Berkshire Hathaway and suggesting that he read how Buffett ran a property and casualty insurance company in order to maximize investable assets at the lowest possible cost of money.

Fowler remembers one particular lunch meeting with Weill and Dimon at The Four Seasons. Dimon, who smoked at the time, had a cigarette brought to him at the end of lunch in lieu of dessert. A few years later, having quit smoking, Dimon chastised Fowler for keeping up the habit. He said that if Fowler quit for five years, he would donate $5,000 to a charity of Fowler's choice. Fowler took him up on the offer, and five years later Dimon paid up.

The majority of Weill's hires were refugees from big companies, people looking for less formality and more upside. "His mantra was, 'Down with the bureaucracy!' " remembers Calvano. "It was, 'This is gonna be just us guys and girls, and we'll get it done the right way.' It was very appealing, especially for those who came from American Express, which was almost Byzantine in its political nature. If you were ambitious yourself, and you wanted to do something, why not do it with Sandy?"

(Early on, Dimon suggested a board candidate to Weill: Andrall Pearson, whom he'd met through Pearson's daughter, a classmate of Dimon's at Harvard. Pearson, who was later the founding chairman of Pepsi's spin-off Yum! Brands—owner of KFC, Pizza Hut, and Taco Bell—would be another mentor to Dimon over the next 20 years. Like Dimon, Pearson was a twin. But he one-upped Dimon on that front— he and his identical twin brother, Richard, actually married another set of identical twins.)

The New Yorkers flew to Baltimore every Monday on the 7:10 A.M. flight on Piedmont Airlines out of La Guardia—a 35-minute flight— and stayed in Baltimore until Friday, when they returned home. Weill and Dimon took up residence in the luxury Harbor Court hotel, with Dimon occupying the room across the hallway from Weill's suite. Fowler took a room next door, and the three men walked to work together each day. Dimon's mornings usually began when he smelled Weill's cigar smoke seeping underneath his door, and his days ended when he watched Weill smoke a final cigar after dinner.

Although a number of other executives stayed in an apartment close to Commercial Credit's 18-story glass-and-aluminum edifice at 300 St. Paul Place, there was an unwritten rule that if you were in town and did not have some other business engagement, you ate dinner at 7:30 P.M. with Weill in a private room in the Harbor Court's restaurant. "Sandy has that kind of food fetish where he likes to order the appetizers," recalls Calvano. "He'll order your meal for you if you're not careful—so it became good practice to have something to do at night. Otherwise, you'd have to go eat those damn crab cakes every day of the week." On other nights, the "dirty dozen" as they called themselves, convened at the fancy Italian restaurant Marconi's. On seeing Weill walk in, the staff would plunk a bottle of Tanqueray gin on the table. Weill liked his Gibson before dinner.

They worked long hours, sometimes 12 to 14 hours a day. Bob Willumstad, who was helping transform the company's branch network with Lipp and Calvano, thinks they got done in six months what might have taken a year—and although it was exhausting, it was also exhilarating. "It was great fun," recalls Bob Lipp. "I often look back at those few years, the likes of which I've never experienced again. It was like going to war without getting shot at."

They made quick work of Commercial Credit's balance sheet; Dimon took the lead when it came to making the numbers work. In early 1987, they sold the company's car leasing business for $77 million plus assumption of $250 million in liabilities. They stopped making loans to kibbutzim in Israel—no one was ever sure why the company had made these loans in the first place—and curtailed all business loans. Slowly but surely, Weill and his team refocused the company on its core business of consumer finance. And the results showed. For the full year, the company earned $100 million and had an impressive 18 percent return on equity. The credit agencies had upgraded the company's debt rating from BB+ at the time of the takeover to A- a year later, and Commercial Credit was able to tap the debt markets to the tune of $100 million. In 1988, they kept going. They sold American Credit Indemnity, which insured accounts receivable for corporate clients, to Dun & Bradstreet for $140 million.

Weill did away with perks for most of the company's management ranks. He canceled all newspaper subscriptions, sending out the message that if employees wanted to read the *Wall Street Journal*, they could pay for it themselves. He ordered all company cars to be returned or bought by those using them. And he canceled a contract with a plant service, telling employees to water their own plants.

The core lending business, too, needed an overhaul. Once Bob Lipp got proper reporting systems in place, Weill saw that the cost and incentive structures at the company's lending branches were hampering profit growth. He announced that the poorest-performing 10 percent of the company's branches would receive no bonus whatsoever, whereas the top-performing 10 percent might receive 100 percent of their salary as a bonus. Believing it the best way to motivate employees, both Weill and Dimon continued to utilize this carrot-or-stick method over the years.

After a while, the executives realized that with not a single one of them living in Baltimore, they were not connected to the company. Weill started a drumbeat of, "One of us has to move," which the team properly understood as, "One of you has to move." After some discussion, all eyes focused on Dimon, who as the youngest member of the team had the fewest roots to pull up.

Because Judy was then pregnant with the couple's second child, it actually made sense for Dimon to bring his wife and daughter to Maryland with him—he didn't like being away from them. So he was the "volunteer," the only member of the executive team to do time as a Baltimorean. Judy, like many people who have lived in New York, was used to walking pretty much everywhere she needed to go, so the couple moved to Cross Keys, Baltimore's first "planned" community. "It was really hard for me to picture myself living in a suburban environment," she recalls. "So we found this ground floor apartment where Jules and I could walk wherever we needed to go. The only issue was that everybody else was twice my age." Jamie Dimon wasn't in Baltimore to make friends, though. He was there to whip Commercial Credit into shape. He didn't much care where he lived.

• • •

Working with this group of veteran executives, Dimon soon earned the nickname "the kid." But he was a notable kid, exceptional in his spongelike capacity to understand the intricacies of financial, accounting, and tax issues, while equally adept at analyzing the trade-offs between risks and returns in the company's various businesses. Bob Lipp was impressed at Dimon's ability to apply ethical standards in the gray areas of accounting rules. Dimon also managed to revive the company's commercial paper funding program, which had faltered under Control Data, bringing costs down in the process.

He also seemed perennially a step ahead. (Fowler considered him as "quick as a hiccup.") Dimon knew the company's books better than anyone else. "Not long after you started talking, he'd interrupt you, saying, 'I know, I know, I know,' " recalls his longtime colleague Marge Magner. "And he usually did." His colleagues tolerated such impatience because of his obvious focus.

It was also at Commercial Credit that Dimon cemented his reputation as hothead, engaging in frequent screaming matches with Weill. The vitriol was not reserved just for his boss. Indeed, he challenged other executives as well. One executive remembers a senior committee meeting in which the 30-year-old Dimon stabbed his ballpoint pen in the air toward Bob Lipp and said, "Bob, you're wrong on this!" All present were dumbstruck. Here was a kid just a couple of years out of business school lecturing a former president of Chemical Bank. Weill said nothing, and just chewed away on his cigar. "From that point, we could tell how tough he was," recalls the executive. "And how nobody but nobody stood up to him." (Lipp doesn't recall the specific incident, but says he had no problem with a young Jamie Dimon challenging him on anything.)

Part of what made Dimon's temper tolerable, however, was that he treated everyone exactly the same way. "He was abrasive and could make you crazy," recalls Magner. "But there was always something endearing about him." Dimon, for example, had no compunction about voicing his Democratic political views in a boardroom full of Republicans—which included former President Gerald Ford. Compulsively chewing the ends of ballpoint pens, Dimon was a most unusual hybrid, the accounting nerd who had expansive views on public policy.

He was also capable of the occasional outright power play. Sandy Weill had sensed during the IPO road show that Dimon considered Greg Fitz-Gerald an obstacle, and it was not long before the obstacle was removed. In the earliest days of forming the company, the team had a white board in a conference room showing the company's lines of reporting. One day, as a number of executives sat around the table, Dimon walked into the room, wiped out all the names under Fitz-Gerald, rewrote them all underneath his own name, and walked out. "Nobody dared change it, of course," says one executive. "It was the kind of move I never would have believed if I hadn't seen it with my own eyes." Shortly thereafter, Fitz-Gerald left the company.

Young as he was, Dimon built his own coterie of disciples at Commercial Credit. One was Charlie Scharf, a graduate of Johns Hopkins with a cocky streak akin to Dimon's. Scharf's father had been a broker at Shearson under Weill, and sent his son articles about Weill's continuing adventures in Baltimore. Scharf initially replied that he hated Baltimore, and that his father should get it out of his head that his son might actually work there after graduating; but he later asked if his father could line up an interview.

The two men hit it off. While still in college, Scharf began working for Dimon part-time, and by the end of the year he was Dimon's assistant. Life with Dimon was anything but boring. After just a few weeks on the job, Scharf was in Dimon's office when Sandy Weill walked in. Scharf stopped speaking—Weill made most employees a little nervous—but Weill insisted that Scharf continue. Before long, the young man was stammering, so Dimon took over answering Weill's questions. Before long, he and Weill were at each other's throat. Scharf was petrified. "Is Jamie going to get fired?" he thought to himself. "What the hell is going on here?" And then as quickly as it had started, the argument came to a close. Dimon had made one final point, to which Weill merely said, "Oh, OK, I get it," and turned and left the office.

Dimon's combustible relationship with Weill set the tone for how he dealt with colleagues in the early part of his career. Because he could be that way with Weill, he was that way with everyone. And this had both positive and negative effects. On the positive side, Dimon never felt the need to dance around an issue; he got straight to the point. On the negative side, he failed to hone his interpersonal office skills—because he didn't have to.

(That's not to say Dimon was unfair. In fact, to this day it is his obsession with fairness that is largely responsible for the loyalty he elicits from most people who work for him. He can and will fire people who don't measure up, but it is rare for senior executives working for him to quit of their own accord.)

"Sandy and Jamie were in a constant state of battle over their intellectual capacities," remembers Bob Lipp. "They also bet on little things. Sometimes we took the train to Baltimore, and they'd be standing on the platform, betting who would be closer to the door when the train stopped. They'd bet about anything." Once, when Weill claimed that the sun rose 30 minutes later in Baltimore than it did in New York, Dimon countered that there was only a 10-minute difference. They bet on it, and in this case, Dimon won. Their hypercompetitiveness seemed to draw them together rather than push them apart, at least for a while. A decade later, the one-upsmanship became more hard-edged—especially from Dimon's end—but in their early years together, the two men fed off each other's alpha-male energy. The dynamic paid dividends, as both worked harder as a result.

Dimon's confidence could be contagious. When John Fowler complained one day that he was making a mere $190,000 a year and was fielding a job offer for $600,000, Dimon persuaded him not to jump ship. "Wow, that's awfully attractive," he told Fowler. "But stick around, stay with this. You'll be making a million dollars a year in five years." Fowler took the advice, and got his payday. Everyone who had chosen to take a bet on Sandy Weill would be handsomely rewarded.

4. BUILDING THE PERFECT
DEAL MACHINE

Once the "platform" had been established in Baltimore, Weill wanted to prove that the Commercial Credit deal was more than a lucky break by making a splashy acquisition or two. It turned out to be much more than that. He and Dimon were about to embark on a decade of almost constant deal making. This suited Dimon just fine. "Jamie approached everything with total fury," recalls Weill's assistant Alison Falls McElvery. "Nothing was an idea that merely lingered. It was always ninety miles an hour. When I first met him, I used to call him 'the lawn mower.' He'd cut it all off before realizing that he might have made it a little short. Then he'd say, 'It'll grow back. Let's move on.'"

The template was a simple one: run the business conservatively, building fortress balance sheets that gave the wherewithal to make acquisitions during downturns, when assets were cheap. A fortress balance sheet was just what it sounded like: it consisted of ample "high-quality" capital paired with a strong liquidity position that would protect the firm from the assault of an economic downturn while also providing the ability to launch an attack on weakened competitors. To be an acquirer during boom times was to be foolish, to commit the cardinal sin of overpaying. But to pick off distressed assets in a lousy economic climate—that was the stuff of the empire builder. It was also Weill's playbook when he built Shearson from the ground up over two-plus decades beginning in 1960.

Weill hadn't invented this idea. It has been practiced and refined over the course of centuries. As the Jewish-American financier Bernard Baruch once said, "Buy straw hats in winter."

Another precept of Weill's was to add little bells and whistles to his firm's offerings, to make them more competitive. Since most financial products are commodities, the trick was to appeal to customers with something as simple as a more comprehensive account statement. If there was no way to offer a unique product, then having the lowest-cost delivery system was the only way to compete.

And a third and final one: don't go chasing the flavor of the month unless you actually know its ingredients. Just because other people are making money in something, don't be tempted to follow suit unless you understand the complexities involved and how they profit from it.

The stock market crash of October 1987 cut the price of Commercial Credit stock in half. Weill was initially shocked, along with most everybody else, but he quickly regained his nerve and exhorted his team not only to buy even more Commercial Credit stock on the cheap, but also to scour the financial landscape for an acquisition target. The crash of 1987 had not ushered in a serious recession; it had merely dealt the markets a psychological blow, so this was the perfect time to pick up a distressed asset.

It had also caused Weill to rethink his old modus operandi of consolidation within a single industry. When he took over Commercial Credit, he wrote in *The Real Deal*, he'd assumed that he'd merely buy more consumer finance companies in a drive toward consolidation. But the crash had decimated the valuations of whole swaths of financial services companies. "Wall Street firms were particularly slow to recover given that investor confidence remained shaken," he wrote, "and before I knew it, I began to see chances for a return to the securities business." The financial services conglomerate—or megabank concept—in other words, was not Weill's goal from the get-go. It was merely the result of the man's relentless opportunism. The company that would eventually become Citigroup was not a philosophical construction designed in a vacuum. It was an evolving organism that began to take shape in the midst of a crisis.

The first target was the brokerage EF Hutton. During his exile,

Weill had walked away from a deal for that firm after news of his interest had sent its stock soaring. Hutton was weakened by the crash, and Weill found its directors keen to discuss a merger. But he was to be denied again. Once word got out that Sandy Weill was on the scene, a bidding war ensued. Weill had offered $21 a share. But Peter Cohen at Shearson carried the day with a $29 bid.

It wouldn't take Weill and Dimon too long to identify another target. Their tactical approach was one they replicated again and again. The negotiating team was small, usually made up of Weill, Dimon, their lawyer Kenneth Bialkin, and Arthur Zankel, a board member who was one of Weill's oldest friends. Weill set the target, and then Dimon went after it and brought it in, identifying areas of promising growth as well as assets that could be sold off to shore up the company's capital base after a deal.

One executive who worked at Commercial Credit recalls originally considering the reputations of the two—Weill as the maestro, Dimon as detail man—simplistic. He reconsidered that position, however, when on more than one occasion Weill asked in a meeting, "Jamie, where do we put the decimal point here?" Most colleagues marveled at how smoothly the two-man tag team seemed to work. When it came time to sell units or divisions, Dimon often delegated to John Fowler and Chuck Prince, but in making a buy, it was Dimon from beginning to end.

One inherent risk of being a serial acquirer was recognizing the threshold when the conglomerate becomes too complicated to manage properly. The objective was not just to sell stock to Wall Street. These companies sold real products to real customers, and if they failed to do that well, the whole thing would come apart at the seams. This is something Weill and Dimon eventually had to face, though not for quite some time.

· · ·

The Commercial Credit crew worked harder over the next decade than most of its members ever had. For Dimon, that would hardly be a difficult mark to set, as it was his first real job. But for many of the others—Bob Lipp, Bob Willumstad, Marge Magner, Mary McDermott, and the like—this was quite literally their second or third career, and they were pulling all-nighters as they hadn't done since they were youngsters.

Weill motivated them with equity. But he demanded a commitment in return. Usually, 25 percent of any executive's compensation was in stock that vested over a three-year period. In what insiders referred to as the "blood oath," it was understood that no one was to sell those shares even after they'd vested. No one did so until the end of that decade. They were all in it together.

Dimon later said that despite the drama of all the mergers and acquisitions, it was Weill, not he, who was the deal junkie. "Sandy was always out hunting deals," he recalls. "But I don't love them. There's the systems, the people, the balance sheets, the clashes . . . they're very hard." It's not surprising that Dimon feels this way, given his inability to let the small stuff slide. Whereas Sandy Weill could easily switch his focus to the next part of his grand vision, Dimon always sweated the details. In that way, his job was much harder than Weill's.

Still, Dimon stood out for his drive. "We all worked hard, but nobody worked as hard as Jamie," recalls McDermott, Weill's longtime communications chief. Not that he was without a slower gear. In Commercial Credit's New York office on 55th Street between Park and Madison Avenues, when Weill packed his briefcase and headed home for the day, only a few minutes passed before the invariable, "Jamie says drinks at 5:00 P.M." Those on hand, secretaries included, piled into the library and had a drink.

• • •

In the 1960s, Shanghai-born Gerry Tsai was one of the most dynamic and powerful people on Wall Street, helping build the Fidelity Fund into a powerhouse. One of the common, if coarse, refrains among traders of that era was, "What's the Chink buying?" Some 20 years later, the point was inverted, and it provided Weill and Dimon with their first big strike outside Baltimore. Tsai was a buyer no more, but a seller.

In the late 1980s, Tsai, like Weill, was on his second career. He had spent the previous several years assembling a motley collection of companies into the shell of the old American Can Company. After selling the can business, he moved into retail (purchasing the likes of Fingerhut's mail-order business and Musicland/Sam Goody record stores) as well as finance (A.L. Williams insurance and the brokerage house Smith Barney, Harris Upham & Co.). He'd lately renamed the whole operation Primerica, and had been considering trying to do what Weill had set his sights on: assembling a financial services conglomerate.

Tsai's timing could not have been worse. He'd bought Smith Barney at the top of the market, in May 1987, for $750 million, and had leveraged Primerica to the hilt in the process. With the sharp drop-off in Wall Street business, the brokerage's capital-intensive business was threatening to take all of Primerica down with it.

It was the kind of deal Weill couldn't resist. Just like Hayden Stone, Smith Barney was a venerable Wall Street name that had stumbled, providing him with an opportunity to pick up a top brand at a discount. Another Chinese-American, John Hsu, Commercial Credit's chief investment officer, made the first inroads with Tsai. Hsu made it clear that not only was Weill interested in Smith Barney; he might even be prepared to take on all of Primerica. Tsai initially demurred. But Primerica continued to struggle, and he hired Lazard Frères to explore ways to raise money, including the possible sale of the company itself.

Shortly thereafter, a package titled "Greenwich" arrived on Weill's desk from the bankers at Lazard. Named for the Connecticut town where Primerica was based, it included the company's complete financials. Weill forwarded a copy to Dimon in Baltimore and told him to read it on the train to New York. Sandy Weill was in the hunt again, and Jamie Dimon was right there beside him.

Over the next seven months, Dimon dug into Primerica's businesses and financials until he was certain he understood every aspect of the exceedingly complex company. "Numbers leaped off the page and told Jamie whole stories," recalls Mary McDermott. And there were a lot of stories to tell. Although Dimon remained chief financial officer of Commercial Credit, he largely ceded the running of that company to Lipp and Willumstad while he digested Primerica's books.

The deal nearly came apart when Dimon discovered some $60 million in severance agreements for Primerica's executives in the event of a sale. Further due diligence revealed that amount to be $90 million. After raging about the excessiveness of it all, Weill engaged in a startling display of hypocrisy by agreeing to the majority of the payouts when Tsai threw in a $20 million private jet, a Gulfstream G4, as part of the sale.

Dimon eventually decided that a fair price was one share of Commercial Credit stock and $7 in cash for each share of Primerica, giving the deal a value of $1.7 billion. After a flurry of further negotiations and board presentations, the sale was announced on August 29, 1988.

Every single person involved on the Commercial Credit side would go on to give the 32-year-old Dimon primary credit for structuring the transaction. Although he eventually passed certain tasks on to others, he handled all the gory details, from determining write-downs and purchase accounting adjustments to formulating the financial projections to convincing investors and rating agencies that the newly merged Primerica would be a strong going concern.

Joe Califano, who sat on Primerica's board at the time and who stayed on after the deal, met Dimon for the first time when Dimon made a presentation about the finances and projections of the merged company. Afterward, Califano, who had worked as secretary of Health, Education, and Welfare under President Carter, walked over to Dimon. "That's the most perceptive and sophisticated and clear presentation I have ever seen," he said.

Later, when the Primerica team talked to Shearson Lehman about selling Fingerhut to that company's merchant bank, Dimon faced a man named Jay Fishman across the negotiating table. "He and I went at it several times," Dimon recalls. "A week after the deal broke down I called him up and said, 'I know we fought a lot, but I really came to admire and trust you during the process. Want to talk about coming over here?' He told me I'd got him at exactly the right time. So we hired him."

As all this was going on—the negotiations were secret—Dimon's grandfather Panos died. Dimon had managed to visit him on his deathbed beforehand and make Panos an "insider" in the first big transition of his career. He said that they were taking over Primerica, and that he was being made CFO as part of the bargain. Panos teared up in response. But even in his weakened state, Panos remained a broker to his core. During one hospital visit, he insisted that the young man needed to buy Exxon stock, immediately. "He never stopped, right up to the very end," recalls Dimon.

• • •

Weill quickly made a series of executive changes at the top of Primerica. The president of Smith Barney, George Vonder Linden, had survived its purchase by Primerica in 1987 and might have thought he could do it again. But Weill found Vonder Linden's excessive concern about maintaining Smith Barney partners' high compensation irritating.

When Vonder Linden asked Weill to stay away from a President's Council meeting of top-performing brokers in October at The Inn at Spanish Bay in Pebble Beach until the second day, Weill ignored the request and showed up on day one. He then became enraged when he learned he was not on the agenda as a speaker. Vonder Linden was soon out the door, and Weill's old friend Frank Zarb was brought in to run Smith Barney. Zarb, who'd been on the board at Commercial Credit, was a banker at Lazard at that point, but Weill persuaded him to jump ship and join Primerica.

Weill also hired the former cohead of Lehman Brothers, Lewis Glucksman, as vice chairman to run the company's capital markets business under Zarb. Dimon continued his jack-of-all-trades approach at Primerica, keeping his role at the parent company while also immersing himself in operational issues—tracking expenses; improving technology processes—at Smith Barney. Zarb tasked Dimon with overhauling the company's financial management and control functions, a job he took to with relish. In the end, Dimon got his hands in pretty much every part of Smith Barney's business, from capital calculations to performance elements to the trimming of expenses.

As a result of this change in responsibility, Dimon and his wife and two children—a second daughter, Laura, had been born on June 16, 1987—moved back to New York at the end of 1988, settling in an apartment at 211 East 70th Street. As New York addresses go, this was *not* one that mattered. There was still a long way to go. Dimon took an office in Smith Barney's longtime building at 1345 Avenue of the Americas. (In later years, the couple's children attended Spence, New York's exclusive all-girls' school.)

It was during this time that Dimon met Steve Black, who was shortly named Glucksman's deputy in the capital markets group. "Blackie" had been at Smith Barney since 1974—long before Gerry Tsai had shown up in 1987—and unlike his old boss, Vonder Linden, he had managed to stick around through the latest transition. Considered a loose cannon, Black found a friend in Dimon, another loose one himself.

To the outside world, Sandy Weill was a banking tycoon and Jamie Dimon was . . . who? When the *New York Time*'s reporter Robert Cole met with Weill and Tsai on August 29 to discuss the merger, Dimon sat in on the discussions. At one point, when Dimon tried to jump into the conversation, Cole cut the young man off. "I'm sure you're smart," he said. "But I already have two geniuses here to answer my questions. I don't need to hear from the junior genius as well."

• • •

The following year was one of wrenching change in the financial markets. Michael Milken, the junk bond king at Drexel Burnham Lambert, was engulfed in an insider trading scandal, and would soon be indicted on racketeering charges. It was a stunning reversal of fortune for the firm, which in 1986 had been the most profitable investment bank on Wall Street. An era of swashbuckling buyouts and takeovers was coming to a shattering close.

Drexel's chief, Fred Joseph, forecast a loss in the company's retail brokerage division of $40 million to $60 million in 1989 and decided by April that selling the business was better than watching it disintegrate. In different times, and with a different seller, the business might have fetched an eight-figure price. But Weill, smelling desperation, offered a paltry $4 million for 16 branch offices and about 500 brokers. On April 8, 1989, Joseph accepted the bid. While Zarb and Weill wined and dined Drexel's top producers in the hope of keeping them on board, the task of closing the deal once again fell to Dimon.

Drexel's collapse was, in and of itself, a big deal, especially considering the power the firm had wielded just months before. But there was also a growing sense that Drexel had helped much of Wall Street lose its way. Sure, the innovative use of junk bonds helped scrappy entrepreneurs like Ted Turner get their start. And although the much-chronicled junk-fueled takeover of RJR Nabisco by the private equity firm Kohlberg Kravis & Roberts provided high drama in the 1980s—trenchantly recounted in Bryan Burrough and John Helyar's book *Barbarians at the Gate*—it seemed to many observers that such profligate use of debt forced proud companies to their knees and turned the august world of corporate finance into nothing more than a debased money grab. In 1970, there had been only 10 takeovers valued at more than $1 million. In 1986, there were 346. By late 1987, nonfinancial corporate debt stood at a record $1.8 trillion, and companies spent 50 cents of every dollar of earnings to pay off creditors. The economy, in other words, was leveraged to the hilt.

"As in the Jazz Age," writes Ron Chernow in *The House of Morgan*, "much of the era's financial prestidigitation seemed premised on an unspoken assumption of perpetual prosperity, an end to cyclical economic fluctuations, and a curious faith in the Federal Reserve Board's ability to avert disaster." (The cycles continue, with the great credit bubble of the new century being premised on the exact same notions. Dimon, a student of history, is constantly in disbelief at everyone else's failure to learn from experience.)

The RJR deal, feasted on by nearly every major financier in New York, ultimately came to be seen, according to Chernow, as "the era's crowning folly." In October, the collapse of a $6.79 billion buyout of United Airlines sent the markets into a tailspin as investors concluded that without the junk bond market to fuel ever-greater buyouts, stock prices had lost a crucial leg of support. By the end of the year, the economy was headed into recession.

Britain's Barclays Bank PLC started to feel the pinch earlier than many others, and in November decided to put its U.S.-based consumer loan division up for sale. After rapid-fire due diligence at Barclays' offices in Charlotte, North Carolina, Primerica offered $1.35 billion in cash for BarclaysAmerican/Financial. The deal not only broadened Primerica's national distribution but also expanded its loan portfolio by 40 percent, to more than $5 billion.

Drexel finally filed for bankruptcy in February 1990. The capital markets were closed to it, and without access to credit—the lifeblood of a Wall Street firm—there was nothing left to do but shut the doors and clean out the desks. Fred Joseph's last-ditch move—calling Gerald Corrigan, head of the Federal Reserve Bank in New York, to plead for emergency credit, which the Fed had historically made available only to commercial banks—was met with a definitive refusal. (Eighteen years later, when Jamie Dimon insisted that the Fed actually get some skin in the game if he was to save Bear Stearns from bankruptcy, New York Fed chief Tim Geithner was more accommodating.)

Corrigan's decision wasn't exactly surprising. Drexel had alienated almost every major firm on Wall Street with its arrogance during the junk bond boom, and had then exhausted the resources of regulators and the Securities and Exchange Commission in choosing to defend Milken for well over a year before finally caving.

The combination of Dimon's shrewd number crunching and Weill's vision and salesmanship kept Primerica stock strong even as the broader markets were getting pounded. The stock was up from $21 to $28. And a December 4 issue of *Business Week* proclaimed "The Return of Sandy Weill." Weill was back. And this time, he'd brought a guy named Jamie Dimon along for the ride.

• • •

The new decade saw Dimon's achievements continue to multiply. In March 1990, Weill made him an executive vice president (EVP) at Primerica. (This was in addition to his operating role at Smith Barney.) It was all coming together. With the arrival of his third and final daughter Kara Leigh on June 20, 1989, Dimon, now 34 years old, was not only taking on greater responsibility but making a lot more money. In 1989, he had earned $660,000, up from $594,348 in 1988. This was still well below Weill's $1.54 million take, but Dimon was just slightly behind Bob Lipp—a man 17 years his senior—who had earned $810,000.

He was also closer personally to Sandy Weill than he'd ever been before. If a visitor dropped by Weill's house in Greenwich on a Sunday morning, Dimon's Volvo wagon was invariably parked in the driveway, the two men already hard at work by 7:00 A.M. Three months after becoming EVP at Primerica, Dimon added the titles of executive vice president and chief administrative officer of Smith Barney.

Weill and Dimon weren't all business. They were capable of pulling the occasional prank on each other. When Alison Falls McElvery was married in October 1990, she showed up at the church to find Dimon in a tuxedo. "Why are you wearing that?" she asked. "It's not a black tie wedding." "Sandy convinced me it was black tie yesterday, and Judy's all done up in a fancy dress," Dimon fumed.

Dimon took on an increasingly prominent role at presentations to investors and analysts. In one of the company's first meetings with analysts and investors since taking over Primerica, Brian Posner, a portfolio manager at Fidelity, thought Dimon was talking too much and too aggressively. Fidelity had been making major purchases of Primerica's stock, and Posner grew worried about whether this brash young executive had the knowledge to back up his big mouth. Posner thought he'd test the confident young CFO and said he'd like a brief on the company's insurance subsidiary, A.L. Williams. "Let's see if this guy actually knows anything about this," Posner told a colleague. Twenty minutes later, Posner turned to the same colleague and said, "Wow, he wasn't faking it."

In 1990, while the economy shrank by 1.5 percent, Primerica's stock continued to reach new heights, hitting an all-time high of $37. Primerica even briefly surpassed Citicorp in market value. Dimon jokingly mentioned to Weill the idea of going after that venerable institution. The two men laughed off the notion, but Dimon was inspired enough to muse out loud, "Wouldn't that be the mother of all deals?"

Instead, Dimon did the only thing he could do: aim low. Rather than make a run at the entire company, he merely bought shares. When Citicorp hit $8.50 a share, he picked up $50 million worth for the Primerica investment portfolio. Dimon convinced everyone at the company that the stock would have $5 a share in dividends within five years, and several Primerica executives loaded up on Citicorp for their own accounts—including Dimon, who bought some for each of his three daughters.

Around this same time, Fidelity's Posner would occasionally join either Dimon or Bob Lipp after work for drinks at Lipp's favorite hangout, the Drake hotel. The men had just one ground rule. They wouldn't talk about each other's companies. But Citicorp was always a topic of conversation. One evening, when Dimon and Posner were out along with another Fidelity portfolio manager, Citi's stock hovered around $10 a share. Dimon was distraught. "God, I wish we could buy it! I wish we could buy it!" he said. "Now is the time to buy Citi!"

Weill soon got nervous about Dimon's $50 million purchase, even as Citicorp stock was rising, and pestered Dimon to unload the position. After fighting his boss for months, he relented, selling the stake for a $30 million profit.

(Weill had more pressing concerns, however, when it was revealed that the founder of A.L. Williams, Art Williams, was being investigated about a "dirty tricks" campaign to drive a competitor out of business. Weill decided to throw Williams out of the company, causing tens of thousands of agents to quit in response. Investors drove Primerica stock down to $16.88, less than half its high of $37 that year.)

• • •

By September 1991, Weill decided to officially recognize what much of Wall Street had finally come to appreciate, that Jamie Dimon was a driving force at Primerica. Weill named Dimon, just 35 years old, president of the company, relinquishing the title to his protégé. Weill also named Bob Lipp and Frank Zarb vice chairmen.

"When Sandy told me, I almost fell off my chair," Dimon told a reporter at the time. In a lengthy handwritten letter, Judy Dimon assured Weill that her husband would make him proud.

Although he was making Dimon one of the youngest presidents of any Fortune 500 company, as well as one of the most powerful men on Wall Street, Weill was also adamant that this was not succession planning. "When somebody does something very, very well, they're going to be rewarded," he said. "[But] I don't feel very old, either." Analysts understood the point, even if they didn't entirely believe it. Fifteen years later, Weill gave it a different spin. 'Whatever gossipmongers might have said," he wrote in his autobiography *The Real Deal*, "I assumed at the time that Jamie stood first in line to succeed me eventually."

Weill had a peculiar style of mentoring. He regularly rewarded Dimon, but at the same time he often found subtle ways to impede the young man's progress by forcing power-sharing arrangements on Dimon at every turn. After making Dimon chief administrative officer (CAO) of Smith Barney in April 1991, for example, Weill then hired Bob Druskin away from Shearson Lehman, where he had been CFO, to be co-CAO with Dimon. The contradictory signals would eventually drive Dimon out of his mind, but in the early part of the decade, he still held his boss on a pedestal, and took what he was given without much complaint.

Not long afterward, both Dimon and Lipp were named directors of Primerica, another step up the ladder for Dimon. Weill later claimed that he elevated Dimon against the advice of a number of board directors who thought he was advancing the younger man too quickly. Several of Dimon's colleagues would agree. "The man was extremely sharp," recalls one. "He could do five sets of computations in his head. But given his mandate from the get-go, he had few interpersonal skills. He never had to learn them. Most of us have to go through the ranks and learn some humility, but he never had to. He was dictating to everybody from day one."

Still, Dimon was widely regarded as the man who made things happen when they needed to happen. If there were costs that had to be cut, Dimon was the man for the job. The company needed higher credit ratings? Dimon figured out how to get them. What he brought to the table was the basic ability to understand the underlying drivers of any business—the two or three things that *really* mattered—far more quickly than his peers. And through an admittedly aggressive and unyielding Socratic process, he got information out of the people that he needed to in order to make decisions about those drivers.

He was also Weill's enforcer. Widely known to be a bit of a coward on sensitive personnel issues, Weill gladly left the tough stuff to Dimon. "Sandy would yell and scream but at the end of the day it was Jamie who pulled the trigger," says a longtime colleague. Dimon didn't take perverse pleasure in firing people himself, but he certainly wasn't afraid of it, particularly if he was convinced that it was for the good of the company. If there's one thing he could not stand, it was weak links, and he never had a problem severing them.

Deals were happening all over the financial industry during this time, including the $2 billion purchase of Manufacturers Hanover by Chemical Bank. Weill explored buying Kidder Peabody from General Electric but shied away from Jack Welch's $1 billion price tag after Dimon saw the firm's fixed income operations and advised against a deal. He concluded that the traders at Kidder had too much power and were twisting the arms of their operations colleagues to take excessive risks. When a scandal involving Kidder's government bond trader Joseph Jett erupted in 1994, forcing the firm to reverse $340 million in phantom profits Jett had booked, Welch sold Kidder to PaineWebber for just $670 million. "Sandy forgot to thank me for that," Dimon laughs.

. . .

It's a well-known maxim that one of the hardest things about running a business is to maintain the ability to say no and thereby save limited resources for the best opportunities. Over time, most companies simply lose their discipline. But Dimon kept Primerica focused. His ability to make quick decisions became legendary during this period, and his underlings came to appreciate it. It saved them incredible amounts of time.

Because of its own inability to say no, the Travelers Corp., the Hartford-based insurance company, came on bended knee to Sandy Weill in late 1992. Founded in 1864, Travelers was in trouble not because of its insurance business, but because it had made bad bets in real estate. Travelers offered so-called guaranteed investment contracts (GICs) that acted like annuities and had specific maturity dates. The company had taken the proceeds from those sales and invested them in mortgages. When those mortgages came due, the real estate market was a shambles, and Travelers faced a rash of defaults. The problem: an obligation on one side—the GICs—and a default on the other. It was not a good position to be in. The company was close to insolvency. (Travelers' one-way bet on real estate prices could stand as a mini precursor of the troubles of insurance giant AIG in the 2007–2009 financial crisis. The executives of AIG also convinced themselves that real estate prices would not fall, a bad bet that resulted in AIG's requiring $180 billion in bailout monies in 2008–2009. They might have served themselves better by studying Travelers' own travails.)

At first, Ed Budd, chairman of Travelers, wanted Primerica to make an investment in Travelers, rather than merely taking it over. After a Saturday of due diligence in Hartford, Weill liked what he saw, and he was seriously considering Budd's offer of a $350 million investment for 15 percent of the company as well as two board seats.

Dimon wasn't overly excited. His longtime colleague Charlie Scharf recalls that Dimon was concerned that the firm was diving in too quickly without entirely understanding all the risks it would be taking on. Still, Dimon shared Weill's desire to expand, and eventually found a way to make the numbers work to Primerica's advantage.

It took a hurricane, however, to get the deal done. On August 24, Hurricane Andrew pounded Florida and exposed the already weak Travelers to a welter of new claims. That gave Weill and Dimon the chance to put the screws to Budd, extracting more control—27 percent of the company and four, not two, board seats—for $722 million. Still stinging from his $90 million payout to Tsai's team (the gift of the G4 notwithstanding), Weill also demanded that the executives on Budd's team give up their golden parachutes.

On September 20, the deal was announced, along with 3,500 job cuts. In December, both Weill and Dimon were named directors at Travelers. Bob Lipp was sent to Hartford as an emissary of Primerica. Weill also picked up a valuable executive trinket. Travelers was a sponsor of the Masters Golf Tournament at Augusta National Golf Club, a connection he later exploited to become a member of Augusta itself. Dimon, no fan of golf, couldn't have cared less about the sponsorship. (In fact, his career-long aversion to golf goes hand in hand with his lack of interest in being a member of the "club.")

With each new company that he and Weill bought, Dimon slowly built his own circle of allies. First, there had been Charlie Scharf at Commercial Credit. Then, with the purchase of Primerica, he met Steve Black. In 1992, he hired Heidi Miller, a Princeton graduate who had been working at Chemical Bank, as his assistant. And shortly thereafter, he brought on Jay Mandelbaum, a onetime consultant at McKinsey, to join the team at Smith Barney. His colleague James Calvano later reflected that those who worked with Dimon soon became the most desirable people in the organization, as they would have been schooled in discipline and direction. "If they survived with Jamie," he said, "they could survive with you."

Mandelbaum's hiring is particularly instructive about Dimon's methods. After deciding to leave the consulting business, Mandelbaum had earned the goodwill of enough people at McKinsey that partners called up both Weill and Dimon recommending they hire him. Forty-five minutes after being told that Dimon had been called, Mandelbaum's phone rang. "Can you meet today at 5:00 o'clock?" the typically impatient Dimon asked. Mandelbaum soon joined the team.

. . .

The purchase of Primerica and investment in Travelers brought most of the Commercial Credit team back to New York from Baltimore, but the next deal gave Sandy Weill a professional homecoming. Before that could happen, though, a few pieces of his past had to be reshuffled. In early 1993 Jim Robinson was removed as chairman of American Express. Harvey Golub, whom Weill had personally recruited to American Express to run IDS before he'd left, was made chairman and CEO of the company.

Robinson had come under fire owing to the underperformance of American Express's brokerage and banking subsidiary, Shearson Lehman Brothers, since 1990. A slew of McKinsey consultants, including Jay Mandelbaum at one point, had been camped out at Shearson for two years trying to put its house in order, to no avail. With the executive transition, Weill had a revelation. If there's something that almost all new CEOs like to do, it's to dump some underperforming division right from the get-go, allowing them to start their tenure with a clean slate and solidly performing businesses. Guessing that Golub might consider unloading Shearson, Weill called his old friend and offered to take both the Shearson brokerage team and the company's building in Tribeca— at 388 Greenwich Street—off Golub's hands.

Over the next few weeks, Weill and Dimon negotiated with Golub and his team to come to a mutually beneficial deal. It was their most complicated transaction to date, as Weill had no interest in the investment banking franchise at Lehman Brothers, and so they sheared Shearson right out of Shearson Lehman. Even so, at a cost of about $1 billion, it was the largest sale of a brokerage in history. (To that point, both Weill and Dimon remained uncomfortable taking on businesses that had balance sheets too heavily exposed to the gyrations of the capital markets. Shearson, with its brokers, had very little exposure. Lehman was another matter entirely.)

Although Zarb was technically in charge of Smith Barney, and was therefore responsible for integrating the two companies, hammering out the deal once again fell to Dimon. Zarb marveled as he watched Dimon almost single-handedly pull off the transaction. From the negotiations themselves to determining which parts of Shearson were worth keeping and which should be jettisoned, Dimon was Primerica's point person across the board. "That was by far the most meaningful contribution he made while I was there, given what a major consolidation it was," recalls Zarb. Dimon saw the transaction in medical terms. Severing the two companies, he told the *New York Times*, "was like splitting apart Siamese twins."

(An opportunity for Weill's two protégés—Peter Cohen and Jamie Dimon—to face each other across the negotiating table had been eliminated in early 2001, when Robinson had forced Cohen out of Shearson.)

Primerica stock surged 12 percent on news of the deal, as investors concluded that Weill would do a better job running Shearson—he'd built the company, after all—than Robinson and Cohen had done. It also made Primerica a major force to be reckoned with. Smith Barney had been small, with just 2,000 brokers. And although the combined Smith Barney Shearson still lacked a significant investment banking franchise, it now had 11,400 brokers, posing a serious threat to the industry leader, Merrill Lynch, which had 13,000. Primerica also doubled its mutual fund assets to more than $100 billion, making it the fourth-largest provider of funds in the nation.

The press once again focused on Dimon's superiors, the titular heads of Primerica and Smith Barney Shearson—Sandy Weill and Frank Zarb. When the *New York Times* ran a picture of Weill and Zarb with their hands clasped, in celebration of the deal, Dimon was infuriated that they had taken full credit.

He wouldn't have too much time to dwell on the unfairness of it all. After all, there was the business of the integration at hand. Dimon quickly went to work, overseeing the $250 million construction of five trading floors in a new building—390 Greenwich—next to the one that had been acquired. Steve Black, now head of capital markets at Smith Barney, took the responsibility of laying off a large chunk of the combined fixed-income division, impressing Dimon with his ability to make "tough decisions." (Dimon himself received credit in the press for managing the cuts, an irony considering his anger at not getting enough credit for the deal itself.)

It was at this point that Jamie Dimon's "list" started to become famous—or rather, infamous—around the Smith Barney offices. On a single sheet of 8½ by 11 paper, Dimon kept a number of smaller handwritten lists, including "Things I Owe People" and "Things People Owe Me." Even as computers began to take over most parts of day-to-day life in the financial industry, Dimon has continued with his crinkled list to this very day, systematically attacking every single obligation on it with his ruthless efficiency.

Theresa Sweeney, his assistant from 1993 to 2000, can't recall the number of times she was on the phone with one restaurant or another, asking someone to send the list he'd left on the table back to his office. "Poor Chip," she recalls, speaking of Dimon's longtime driver. "He always had to go back and pick it up somewhere. He probably still does." (There was never any concern about confidential information, as few people can decipher Dimon's handwriting.)

During a slow day—of which there are very few when you're working for Jamie Dimon—Sweeney recalls Dimon asking her to go through more than a dozen boxes of materials he'd collected over his career. The two spent hours going through the stuff, and when they were finally finished, she thought she could take a break. Then she heard a noise from Dimon. "What is it?" she asked. "My to-do list is missing," he sheepishly replied. And the process of going through every box started all over again. "I can't remember how many times I had my head in a Dumpster looking for that thing," she laughs.

(Dimon has kept almost all his papers since the beginning of his time with Weill, including scraps he'd scribbled on while doing deals for Commercial Credit. Clearly, this is evidence of a healthy ego—how many of us think it necessary to collect our daily notes for posterity? Yet Dimon seems to have understood that he and Weill were making history, and thus that the scrapbooks might serve as a useful historical record.)

It got to the point that when Sweeney emerged from Dimon's office with a certain look on her face, the assistants who helped Sandy Weill and Bob Lipp all knew what had happened. "Everybody would say, 'Theresa, I'm so sorry,' " Sweeney says. "Because he couldn't get any work done until the list was found." To this day, Jay Mandelbaum tries to steal the list from Dimon and hide it—or add something to it—just to see his laser-focused boss momentarily lose his bearings.

Dimon made one more critical addition to the team in 1993, adding Michael Cavanagh, a mild-mannered middle-class Catholic from Long Island who'd been to Yale and gone on to Shearson Lehman and then to law school at the University of Chicago. Cavanagh had experienced the same kind of revelation as Dimon had a decade previously. He appreciated the thrill of investment banking, but he also saw that the job was essentially that of an agent, helping others figure out what to do with *their* money. His brief experience at Lehman had been in the principal investing group, and he sought a similar opportunity, to be a "principal," working with the house's money and not someone else's. Having known Jay Fishman from Shearson, Cavanagh secured an interview with Dimon and soon landed a job reporting to Mandelbaum.

Dimon also did an old friend a big favor at the time. He had kept in touch with Jeremy Paul since their days at Browning and saw his friend once or twice a year. With two young children, Paul had landed a gig as a law professor at the University of Connecticut Law School, and his wife was taking courses at Yale. Strapped for cash on his professor's salary, Paul was concerned about paying the bills if his wife didn't land a job once she finished up at Yale. There had been discussions at Primerica about Dimon himself moving to Hartford to get more involved at Travelers, and he concocted the idea that Paul take a sabbatical and join the company as his assistant. The purchase of Shearson made that idea unfeasible, however, as everyone understood that Dimon would be better utilized in New York. But they found a solution. Bob Lipp agreed to hire Paul as *his* assistant in Hartford.

Before he reported to Lipp, however, Paul did get to shadow Dimon at Smith Barney for two weeks. He was shocked by the capabilities of his longtime friend. If Dimon had 10 meetings a day with six people at each meeting coming in to brief him on topics x, y, or z, Paul watched in awe as it became painfully clear that Dimon invariably knew more about every topic than anyone else in the room, including those presenting.

Dimon also gave Paul a piece of advice he didn't quite understand at the time but has since come to appreciate. "This might be counterintuitive for you," Dimon said. "But it's more important to do 10 things and get eight of them right than to do five and get them all right."

Even as he was building his own team from the ground up, Dimon was confronted with a serious culture clash between the merged companies. Although many Smith Barney and Shearson people knew one another, Wall Street's tribal attitudes made the integration a difficult one. During a gathering of senior Smith Barney executives, Dimon cracked a joke. "I'm tired of all the moaning and complaining," he said to the room. "I am going to let each and every one of you fire one Shearson person, and then I don't want to hear any more." The entire room snapped to attention, salivating at the prospect of such a bloodletting. Dimon was amazed that they thought he'd been serious.

· · ·

Even though Primerica was now one of Wall Street's largest companies, the executive team maintained an informal approach to planning and strategy. Weill held monthly meetings in an old stone mansion on 100 acres of wooded property outside Greenwich. The standard routine was a long day of presentations and discussion, followed by long dinners. After a few drinks, Dimon invariably made fun of Sandy in front of the assembled group, prompting a few laughs among the old guard and a nervous quiet among others.

Joseph Plumeri, the president of Smith Barney Shearson who had come over to Primerica as part of the Shearson deal, was amazed by the lack of structure at the very top of the firm. The first time he joined in an executive retreat, he asked Dimon if he needed to bring a presentation to make to the group. "No, just write it on a board," was the response. "Write some numbers, whatever you want to do." Although he was shocked by the informality, Plumeri nevertheless did as he was told, and no one gave him a sideways glance.

Plumeri marveled at Dimon's ability to seemingly be everywhere at once. Primerica's president did have a title, and some specific responsibilities, Plumeri noticed, but what he really seemed to do was *watch* everything. And "everything" especially meant costs. The operating model of Primerica was one in which managers were encouraged to get expenses as low as possible, while guarding revenues in the process. "Don't do anything stupid," Dimon told him. "And don't waste any money. Let everybody else waste money and do stupid things; then we'll buy them."

• • •

For a time, the executive team held an annual end-of-year retreat at The Point resort on Saranac Lake, a lush "camp" not far from Lake Placid. With below-freezing temperatures, there was invariably a roaring fire. One year, when Dimon threw an empty FedEx shipping box into the fire, it was sucked up into the chimney, which became blocked. Soot spewed all over the room. It took the staff about three days to clean out the room, during which time Lipp teased Dimon relentlessly about the stupidity of the move.

Following in the path of other legendary financiers, Weill eventually bought his own camp—Green Bay—on Upper Saranac Lake in 1990. Like the most famous Wall Streeter turned Adirondack outdoorsman, John Pierpont "Jack" Morgan Jr., Weill spared little expense on the property. With a sizable main lodge surrounded by green-and-white guest cabins, the camp included a winterized boat dock, a fitness room for Sandy, and a two-lane indoor swimming pool for Joan. Unlike Morgan's, however, it did not have two Steinway pianos on the premises.

Despite his devotion to cost-cutting at work, Dimon later would not deny himself some of the trappings of an oligarch at home. In November 2006, he paid $17.05 million for a weekend house in Bedford Corners in Westchester County, the highest sale price in Westchester for the year. Nestled on a 34-acre estate on the small Howlands Lake, the 1930s mansion has a guesthouse, tennis courts, and apple orchards. When asked why he didn't buy a house in Greenwich alongside his fellow titans of finance, he replied, "I don't want the same scene on weekends that I have when I'm here. The weekend house is for family. It's for us to hang out together, to go to the local restaurants—and not even the nicest ones at that. I want to go to the local Indian or Italian place. That's what I like."

5. HIS OWN MAN

By 1993, Dimon effectively had day-to-day control over Smith Barney Shearson, whereas Frank Zarb approached his role more from a 30,000-foot perspective. The arrangement worked for a while. But running an important business without explicit acknowledgment of his role soon began to grate on Dimon.

Weill later wrote that Dimon began pestering him about what he saw as Zarb's managerial weaknesses, and that Dimon soon began working hard to "annihilate Zarb." Others, including Steve Black, now head of capital markets at Smith Barney Shearson, also began telling Weill that it was time to make a change.

Movement at rival firms offered Weill a radical solution to the problem, albeit one in contrast to his well-honed reputation for fiscal prudence. Morgan Stanley's chairman, Richard Fisher, had recently embarrassed Weill's old pal, the investment banker Bob Greenhill, by demoting him from president to "senior adviser." Greenhill had an enviable roster of corporate relationships, but Wall Street gossip was that he couldn't stay focused on the more mundane issues of running an entire company.

Weill and Greenhill had been close for years. In Weill's darkest days after getting thrown out of American Express, Greenhill had stuck by him, even helping to try to orchestrate the Fireman's Fund buyout. More recently, Greenhill had worked with Weill and Dimon on the Primerica transaction, and Weill's instinctive loyalty kicked in. That, and his ambition. Seeing an opportunity to buy a one-man investment banking franchise, Weill floated the idea of bringing in Greenhill as Zarb's replacement.

Greenhill, known as "Greenie" on the Street, was respected for all-night negotiations and his almost total lack of human emotion in the thick of business combat. A Yale graduate who had served in the navy in 1960, he once kept an Al Capp cartoon on the wall of his office in which Fearless Fosdick was riddled with bullets. The caption: "Mere Flesh Wounds."

Some say Dimon was excited to have a first-class banker on the company's starting line. Others say he was lukewarm about the idea. Why, he mused, was Weill proposing to replace one ineffective manager with another? "The entire world knows the reason he was demoted was because he couldn't manage a lemonade stand," said one senior official at Smith Barney. "And we want to hire him to be CEO of our company?"

Weill ignored such concerns and forged ahead. He and Dimon negotiated with Greenhill, eventually agreeing on a $20 million yearly salary plus 2 percent of Smith Barney's profits over $50 million. In late June, they sealed the deal, and Weill "promoted" Frank Zarb to the role of vice chairman of Primerica. Weill seemed to try to camouflage the true intent of the move by also promoting Bob Lipp—whose talents were never in doubt—but few failed to understand what Weill was up to. The press soon called such a move "being Zarbed"—the Sandy Weill equivalent of being kicked upstairs.

Greenhill instantly got off on the wrong foot. Before meeting a single person at Smith Barney Shearson, he lined up a few dozen Morgan Stanley bankers to bring along with him—he ultimately hired 32, including his own trusted sidekick, Bob Lessin, who was tasked with running corporate finance, along with another young gun, Mike Leavitt.

The message to the Smith Barney team: you people are not top-tier, even though I've never even met any of you, and my people are. To the Morgan Stanley crowd, Smith Barney, for all its efforts, remained a mediocre outfit. But they were going to change all that. Mergers and acquisitions bankers were the studs of Wall Street, and brokers were just its rank and file. Greenhill and Lessin did big, exciting deals, and they promised to do more of the same at Smith Barney.

For a time, it was a believable proposition. Morgan Stanley's chairman, Dick Fisher, at least, must have had reason to second-guess Greenhill's demotion in the months ahead. On one occasion, when the CEO of one of Morgan Stanley's clients was leaving Fisher's office, Fisher asked where he was headed. "To Smith Barney," was the response. Fisher asked if he knew how to get there. The CEO's deadpan reply: "I presume I go down the elevator and follow the groove."

And at first, Dimon tried to be as accommodating as he could be. Whereas Smith Barney had become accustomed to operating on a tighter budget than most investment banks—its people flew coach— the Morgan Stanley people demanded the same perquisites they had received in their old jobs: personal refrigerators, orthopedic chairs, town cars to take them home at 7:00 P.M. instead of at Smith Barney's 10:00 P.M. cutoff. "Don't worry about it," Dimon told those who were wondering about the double standard, even though he was worrying about it himself.

In a serious miscalculation, however, Greenhill lost the support of one potential ally from the get-go: the head of capital markets, Steve Black. Concerned about his friend Black's reaction to Greenhill's hiring, Dimon had personally assured Black that his position at the firm was safe: he was going to be made a vice chairman of Smith Barney Shearson along with Lessin. Black would run all of Smith Barney's capital markets businesses, and report to Greenhill.

Just a few days later, however, Greenhill informed Black that he planned to have him oversee only the equity side of the business, and that he was bringing in another Morgan Stanley veteran, Jack Lyness, to run fixed income capital markets. Also, Lyness was going to report straight to Greenhill, not to Black. Insulted, Black called Dimon and threatened to quit, along with his deputy Jim Boshart.

Completing the circle, Dimon then called Greenhill and read him the riot act. Greenhill still got his way about hiring Lyness, but it was an inauspicious start. Before he'd even begun working, he'd run up against the phenomenon known as Jamie Dimon. It was the first time, but it would not be the last.

Greenhill had demanded, in his negotiations with Weill and Dimon, that he be given the entirety of Smith Barney Shearson to run, not just the investment banking division. Weill agreed, but as an insurance policy encouraged Dimon to spend as much time as possible keeping an eye on operations.

It wasn't long before Dimon concluded that Greenhill was spending excessive sums on people who weren't worth the price—he regularly doubled Morgan Stanley bankers' pay in order to lure them to the firm, in addition to giving them substantial signing bonuses. More worrisome, though, was the growing anger among the unit's gigantic brokerage force about the new crowd's diverting a disproportionate amount of the company's profits. Greenhill, a career investment banker, was focused merely on the top line—bringing in revenues—while Dimon was, as usual, focused on the bottom line, the return on shareholders' equity; and thus the two men were on an inevitable collision course.

Worse, it seemed that the institutional arrogance bred at Morgan Stanley prevented the new hires from adapting to their new organization. Instead of seeking any way to put together a blended culture, they built a mini–Morgan Stanley within Smith Barney. Lessin, in particular, surprised the old guard with his presumption. He saw himself as equal to Dimon, a view shared by precisely no one. (One jarring difference: Lessin was prone to walking around the office with no shoes on, a habit that would be inconceivable to Dimon.) In any event, the question became moot shortly thereafter, when Lessin suffered a stroke and was forced to downsize his role at the firm.

Greenhill might have worked out if he had been able to deliver where it mattered: with market share and on the bottom line. Yes, he was throwing around huge sums of money, but if he succeeded in building an investment banking franchise, the thinking went, everybody would come out ahead. And he started off with a bang, landing an advisory role on the $8.2 billion takeover of Paramount by Viacom in 1993 that brought the firm $33 million in fees. That was followed by advice to Viacom on its purchase of Blockbuster Entertainment in 1994. The firm, which had come in twenty-second in mergers and acquisitions advisory rankings in 1992, vaulted to sixth place for 1993. By 1995, however, it was down to eleventh place, and the grumbling about Greenhill's spending grew louder.

Dimon could tolerate Weill's getting all the credit in the press for the company's success, but what he could not countenance was being saddled with partners who made a job he could easily have done himself a little more difficult. Coworkers came to see in Dimon a man both impatient to get the job done and able to relax when the time was right. "He worried a lot about substance, not so much about form," recalled Plumeri. "He always used to say, 'I just need to know the facts. I don't want to hear some long story. Just give me the facts.'" And then, at the end of a long day, Dimon might invite a few junior analysts into his office on the thirty-ninth floor of 388 Greenwich Street to share a nice bottle of wine. He was still only in his mid-thirties.

• • •

At the same time that he was engaged in the audacious experiment with Greenhill, Weill decided that the time might be right to propose to Ed Budd at Travelers that they fold the remaining 73 percent of the insurance company into Primerica. In addition to consolidating control of Travelers' operations—which would allow the Primerica team to truly do a number on its finances, instead of merely exerting influence at the board level—there was also the lure of the Travelers name and the company's well-known logo, its red umbrella.

Although the Primerica people had helped Ed Budd and the Travelers' team whittle down the insurance company's real estate exposure over the past year, Weill sensed that Budd was sick of heading the still sluggish company and would be ready to do a deal if the terms were right.

Negotiations lasted just two days in September 1993; Budd accepted Weill and Dimon's offer of a $4.2 billion stock swap. (Representing Travelers in the negotiations was First Boston's Gary Parr, a man whose path would cross Dimon's innumerable times over the next 15 years.) The combined company assumed the name Travelers Group, and the deal doubled Primerica's assets to $100 billion. The transfer of power was also complete. Weill was named chairman and CEO of the parent, Dimon president and chief financial officer, and Bob Lipp CEO of the insurance group. Budd was named chairman of the executive committee, a role with no actual responsibilities.

With the completion of the deal, Weill told anyone who would listen that he was finally back. In an article in *Business Week* in October, "The Contrarian—While Others Retrench, Sandy Weill Builds a Financial Services Empire," he called out his former employer. "Travelers is bigger than American Express," he told the magazine. (Travelers would do its own retrenching, cutting 4,000 jobs by the end of the next year.)

When Joe Wright, a friend of Weill's since the 1970s and longtime board member, cautioned Weill that Primerica might be ceding some of its terrific reputation in the financial markets by changing its name to the more consumer oriented Travelers, Weill was even more blunt. "Be clear," he said. "I am the one who had the reputation in the financial markets, not Primerica." Regardless of this moment of megalomania, Weill also knew enough to give credit where credit was due. In November, he bestowed on Dimon yet another title: chief operating officer of the Travelers Group.

. . .

In addition to trying to prevent Greenhill from blowing millions on his Morgan Stanley cronies, Dimon had to deal with another top executive who was giving him headaches: the company's head of brokerage operations, Joseph Plumeri. A motivator in the Sandy Weill mold, Plumeri was the kind of guy who could bring himself to tears rallying the troops; but the voluble Italian-American was an erratic manager. He had been unable to properly integrate the Shearson and Smith Barney units, and brokers were whispering to the press that the computer systems didn't always work and the bureaucracy was stifling.

Plumeri was also prone to making promises to brokers that he could not deliver on—such as guaranteed compensation—and resorted to petty threats when called on the carpet for them. A constant refrain, to either Greenhill or Weill, was that Plumeri was going to quit and take his 9,000 former Shearson brokers with him. Hearing of the threats, Dimon sat Plumeri down one day to put the older man in his place. "Joe," he said. "Just so you know, the first time that you say that to me, I am going to fire you. But you should know that you can raise any issue." Plumeri's response: "Perfect. We'll have a great relationship."

In the end, it didn't really work out. But Dimon wouldn't need to fire Plumeri. When they'd finally had enough, Greenhill and Weill called Plumeri into Greenhill's office in the summer of 1994 and told him he was being made a vice chairman of Travelers. From that point on, Dimon directly oversaw the brokerage force. He had never been busier. Theresa Sweeney, his assistant, felt as if she never sat down during this time. "In the beginning, I never asked him how he was; he never asked me," she recalls. "I walked in there at 7:00 A.M. and walked out at 10:00 P.M. I was working more hours than my husband, who was an investment banker. For a time, I never even knew if Jamie and I were friends. I've never worked so hard in all of my life."

Plumeri might have suspected he was being Zarbed. He might have been, but Weill had another idea. Realizing that the company's insurance business could use a hot-blooded leader like the exiled Art Williams, he put Plumeri in charge of overseeing Primerica Financial Services.

The media came to the conclusion that yet another addition to Dimon's portfolio made it certain he was being positioned as Weill's heir. Dimon's comment to *Business Week* on the issue was politic. "Sandy's got plenty of time, and that's something he needs to decide when the time is right," he said. "If it's not me, then so be it."

Two years into the Greenhill experiment at Smith Barney, it was becoming painfully clear to everyone involved that things weren't working out. Even though Weill had given Dimon official powers in early 1994, naming him chief operating officer of Smith Barney Shearson, it had proved difficult to rein in Greenhill's excesses.

Expansions in Hong Kong and Beijing the year before had been an expensive disaster. After initial success, Greenhill's team proved largely incapable of luring a meaningful number of their old clients from Morgan Stanley. Investment banking is all about personal relationships, and the idea that they'd raid not only Morgan Stanley's personnel *but also its client list* had been a large reason for hiring Greenhill in the first place.

Greenhill and Dimon were also, more often than not, working at cross-purposes. The big spender and the tightwad were natural adversaries. Even as Dimon's viselike grip on expenses kept the company's return on equity in the top ranks of Wall Street, Greenhill's continued spending was causing a widening rift between the brokerage and investment banking divisions. (Knowing his own reputation, Dimon used to crack wise at his own expense, asking people if they were tightening toilet paper dispensers so as to dispense only one sheet at a time.)

Dimon was no mere penny-pincher, mind you. He did invest in the business. Following the merger of Smith Barney and Shearson, for example, he invested significantly in creating state-of-the-art broker workstations and building out an array of new products and services offerings. Broker productivity rose sharply, net negative investment flows turned positive, and revenues went up. Spending that resulted in growth was fine with him, but spending that did not most certainly was not.

While Greenhill continued to gallivant around the country, his inability to deliver compelling results at the end of the day had become the talk of the firm. "We used to call him Rain Man," recalls one colleague. "He thought that meant it was because he was a rainmaker, but we were referring to Dustin Hoffman. Zarb had been ineffective, but cleaning up after Greenhill was like cleaning up after an elephant parade."

In March 1995, both the *New York Times* and the *Wall Street Journal* blew the infighting out into the open, rendering judgment that despite its grandiose ambitions, Smith Barney remained a minor player in investment banking. Indeed, over the past year, a desperate Weill had approached both Jon Corzine at Goldman Sachs and David Komansky at Merrill Lynch about a possible do-over by means of a merger. Neither was interested.

Meanwhile, Dimon was wrenching control of the business away from Greenhill. In May, he forced the head of bond trading, Jack Lyness, and three colleagues out of the company in a move that was called the "Memorial Day massacre." Increasingly mired in issues at Smith Barney, in June, Dimon ceded the title of chief financial officer of Travelers to Heidi Miller. Like Dimon under Weill, she had quickly risen from the position of assistant to become the CFO of the entire company. (Jay Fishman, who'd been angling for the job of CFO for years, instantaneously transferred his loyalty from Dimon to Lipp as a result. "Fishman could barely remember Dimon's name from that point on," recalls an executive.)

Increasingly frustrated, Dimon began openly criticizing Greenhill in meetings. Weill later wrote that he began to worry about Dimon's inability to get along with any number of people—Frank Zarb, Joe Plumeri, Bob Greenhill. "Somehow, it seemed as though Jamie had a problem with anyone with whom I shared a close relationship," Weill wrote in *The Real Deal*, "as though it amounted to a personal threat. I understood the legitimacy of many of Jamie's points, but it bothered me that he couldn't operate more collegially." Even so, Weill could see for himself that the results were not quite what he had hoped.

By the end of the year, Greenhill knew his time was up, and he took a $34 million severance package in January 1996. Dimon was named chairman and CEO of the company. His father, an employee of the firm, called and congratulated him. ("May I still call you directly to complain?" he joked.) One of Dimon's first moves was to apologize to the bank's staff for the expensive experiment gone awry. "We made a mistake, and I'm sorry," he said to the brokerage force. "Let's move on."

(Subsequent events would suggest that Greenhill's failure to take Smith Barney to greater heights was an issue more of corporate culture than of talent. He founded his eponymous investment banking boutique, Greenhill & Co., in 1997, and by 2009 had methodically built it into a $2 billion company that had 55 managing directors. He continued to rope down big-ticket advisory deals, and although the firm saw its results in 2008 decline along with the rest of Wall Street, its revenues were still $222 million.)

The first quarter of 1996 was an improvement for Smith Barney. With tightened cost controls, the firm delivered the highest return on equity on Wall Street. That was on top of a 30 percent return on equity in the fourth quarter of 1995, when Dimon had already effectively seized control of the firm from Greenhill. Later that year, in an interview with *Business Week*, Dimon even accepted responsibility for what most people perceived as Greenhill's failings. "We tried to do too much too fast," he told the magazine. "Blame it on me, not Bob."

. . .

It was during this period in Dimon's career that the seeds of an eventual falling-out with Weill were planted. As much as Weill was willing to let Dimon do behind the scenes, he was not prepared to share the limelight. When a picture of the two men appeared in the *New York Times* in July 1995 showing Dimon in the forefront with Weill standing distantly behind, Weill was outraged.

The headline of that article in the *New York Times* was "Becoming His Own Man: At Travelers, Weill's Protégé Is on the Move." Despite the fact that Weill had endorsed the idea of the story, many viewed the seemingly innocuous celebration of Dimon's talents as a critical turning point in his relationship with Weill. Weill came to see the article as an unforgivable transgression, even if Dimon obviously had nothing to do with the choice of photos in the story. "It's not good for Jamie to be getting this kind of publicity," Joan Weill mentioned to Themis Dimon in passing.

But that, of course, was a matter of opinion. The article was little more than a recognition of the obvious, that Dimon had been shouldering an ever-expanding workload for more than a decade. Insiders thought he deserved it, too. After all, he really was everywhere at once, whether it was negotiating the next big deal or focusing on even the smallest of tax-related issues. Colleagues teased him for walking around the floor at Smith Barney at 6:00 A.M. to see who was already in; they called this habit "bed check."

Although Weill himself made several glowing remarks about Dimon in the *Time*'s piece, he was taken aback by the suggestion from a board member implying that Dimon—not Weill—was the central figure at Travelers. Joseph Califano, a director at Travelers, had actually said exactly that: "He runs Smith Barney," said Califano, adding that

Dimon was more and more the driving force at Travelers as a whole. It seemed to many around Weill that his insecurity kicked in, and he increasingly came to view Dimon as a threat, not an ally.

(Weill had never lost—and would never lose—the joy of what one former colleague called "seeing his face on the cover of *Fortune*." Even in retirement, his offices are a shrine to the cult of Sandy Weill, corporate executive and philanthropist.)

Several people told Dimon that the story was going to cause him problems. They were right. Weill barged into a meeting the next day. "Who the fuck told Joe Califano to say that? And who chose that photo?" Still, Dimon initially failed to recognize the shift in his boss's perspective. "I was still a little bit of a kid," he recalls. "Weill's PR people orchestrated it. He knew about it. He knew better, and I didn't. But I don't think it was really about the picture. He looked more like a proud father in it than anything else. It was about Califano's quote. All of a sudden there was the question: 'Is Jamie really running this place?' I think that was what got to him."

The fact that the two men began to directly repudiate the press's characterizations of a "father-son" relationship was further evidence of the strain. Dimon pointedly told the *New York Times* in July, "I've got my own father, thank you." On the other hand, they gave so many interviews that it could also have been a natural reaction to being confronted with the same pat simplication once too often.

If he'd been more inclined to pay better attention, Dimon would have noticed growing angst emanating from the CEO's office. Weill came to believe that Dimon was deliberately keeping him out of the loop at Smith Barney during this time. On one occasion, Weill later wrote, when he suggested that the company purchase Aetna's property-casualty business in late 1995, Dimon said in front of the room, "You're making a mistake. You, Sandy." What some had admired as youthful self-confidence now took on a note of arrogance. "He'd always respected his own intellect," one former colleague recalls, "and reasonably so. But this was something else entirely."

The antithesis of the smooth backroom operator, Dimon came to be seen by some colleagues as more brutish than brilliant. Although he and

Weill had been swearing at each other since Baltimore, Dimon grew increasingly comfortable challenging his boss, and the resulting fights unnerved a number of colleagues. Whether or not he knew it, he might have been unconsciously expediting his own exit from the firm. He would find it extraordinarily difficult—if not impossible—to resign from the firm he helped build, but the growing realization that Sandy Weill wasn't going anywhere anytime soon put the ambitious Dimon in a bind. Judy Dimon recalls thinking she wouldn't have minded if her husband got a new job, considering the stress he was bringing home with him each day.

Dimon, though, chose to continue playing with fire. Ignoring what had happened a decade earlier when George Vonder Linden asked Weill to stay away from the Smith Barney meeting in Pebble Beach, Dimon began to do exactly the same thing. Weill wrote in *The Real Deal* that he "hit the roof" when Dimon's lieutenant Charlie Scharf told him that he was not authorized to provide Weill with certain information. (Scharf himself has no recollection of this, and has called the idea that he would try to withhold information from Weill preposterous.) Dimon was risking inflaming Weill's still simmering anger over having been frozen out of Shearson in the 1980s by Peter Cohen.

Weill goes on to write in *The Real Deal* that Dimon's "mafia" was stoking the younger man's ego—that Black, Boshart, Glucksman, Scharf, and others were constantly telling Dimon he was better equipped than Weill himself to run Travelers.

In an attempt to finally address the issue head-on, Weill invited Dimon and Judy to have lunch with him and Joan during a company off-site in early 1996 at the Dorado Beach hotel in Puerto Rico. Weill later wrote that after pleading with Dimon to stop cutting him out of the information loop, he was shocked by Judy Dimon's response. "But Sandy, you're not giving Jamie enough credit," she said, according to Weill's retelling. "He's been working incredibly hard, and you don't appreciate him. He doesn't even own as much stock as you!"

And so two large egos collided with full force. Weill later wrote of his surprise that his "junior partner" had "somehow . . . come to see himself as my equal." In a remarkable example of the pot calling the kettle black, he added, "It had become clear that Jamie's self-image had rushed ahead unchecked to the point of fantasy." Weill seemed to be talking as if Dimon were still an 18-year-old summer intern. Just to make things painfully clear that day in Puerto Rico, he added one final patronizing chastisement for the younger man: "You need to behave. If you do, all of this can be yours one day."

Judy Dimon calls the claim that she would suggest Dimon and Weill deserved equal stock onwership in the company "ridiculous." What she does admit, however, is feeling like a referee between the two men, explaining how Weill felt to Dimon and how Dimon felt to Weill. What she tried to explain to Weill, she recalls, was that her husband was under extreme pressure. "The situation was taking a huge toll on Jamie," she said. "And by the end everyone was upset with each other. And for what?"

• • •

At that time, Sandy's son Marc was the company's chief investment officer, in charge of a $3 billion portfolio. Originally, Dimon had been protective of Marc, as he had been with his own brother in high school—helping the younger Weill navigate the razor-sharp shoals of Travelers' politics.

In 1994 Dimon welcomed Weill's daughter, Jessica Bibliowicz, to Smith Barney as an executive vice president in charge of sales and marketing in the company's $55 billion mutual fund division. Bibliowicz would report to Dimon, not to her father. She had previously worked at Prudential Mutual Funds for two years and in Shearson Lehman's asset management division for the eight years before that.

In January 1995, Dimon named Bibliowicz chairman of the company's mutual fund operations, then the ninth-largest in the country. He'd even pushed her ahead of a candidate favored by Jeff Lane, the company's head of asset management, taking some political heat in the process. In reality, Bibliowicz ran only mutual fund sales, a department with a mere 18 people. Despite the loftiness of the title, she didn't oversee money management, operations, or finance for the fund group.

Dimon and Bibliowicz had been friends since childhood, but their relationship began to fray the next year, when Dimon pushed for the company to sell no-load mutual funds in response to the success of Vanguard and other no-load fund companies. Bibliowicz resisted the idea, arguing that the company should stick to its own internal funds—brokers were far more motivated to sell them, after all, because of the commissions—and Weill himself sided with her in discussions on the subject. Dimon eventually won the debate, and in July 1996 Smith Barney was the first Wall Street broker to sell no-load funds. In the end, the move proved to have been a smart one.

In August, the *New York Times* picked up on the tension, which Bibliowicz called "perceived" and not a "conflict." Whatever the case, there was a conflict soon enough. Dimon became convinced that Bibliowicz's strengths were restricted to "soft" skills like marketing and that she lacked a thorough enough understanding of the numbers of the business. He began to criticize her openly, alienating her and irritating Weill. At least some of the results seemed to support his claim. In 1996, for example, Smith Barney's mutual fund division brought in just $288.3 million in net new assets, compared with $3.1 billion at Merrill Lynch.

Soon, too, Lane found himself in Dimon's crosshairs. With Dimon repeatedly calling for his reassignment, Weill ultimately agreed, but at the same time suggested Bibliowicz as a candidate to be Lane's replacement. Dimon vetoed the idea, saying she was not yet qualified. After some deliberation, he instead promoted Robert Druskin, the onetime chief financial officer of Shearson Lehman Brothers and later co-CAO of Smith Barney Shearson. Druskin had known Weill since 1969, when he joined Shearson Hammill in the management training program, so Weill could hardly call the choice inappropriate.

Still, it rankled. And not long afterward, in February 1997, Dimon again subjected Bibliowicz to what Weill regarded as ignominy. Dimon named three executives to the Smith Barney planning committee—including Smith Barney's general counsel Joan Guggenheimer—and excluded Bibliowicz. Weill's daughter felt that this was a message directed squarely at her: a woman, yes, but not *you*. Guggenheimer, it should be pointed out, managed hundreds of people, compared with Bibliowicz's 18. (She was also a top-shelf legal mind who served as one of Dimon's closest advisers at three different companies before her premature death from cancer in 2006.)

From Weill's perspective it was an unforgivable slight. His reaction was near-hysteria. It was a staggering misapprehension on Weill's part, considering that there were numerous people within the company who deserved such a spot more than his daughter. Weill was also upset that Dimon did not inform Bibliowicz personally, even though she did not technically report to Dimon.

The final, irreconcilable breach in the relationship came when Dimon actually acceded to Bibliowicz's ambition. When she asked him how she could get ahead in the company, he asked what she aspired to. "Well, I'd love to run Smith Barney one day," she replied. Dimon told her that if that was ever going to happen, she needed experience in the retail side of the business. He then called Mike Panitch, who oversaw the retail branches, and asked him to find a spot for Bibliowicz to learn the ropes. Panitch initially replied that he would offer the boss's daughter a single Smith Barney branch. Dimon balked, and asked Panitch to put her in charge of one of the company's four divisions—East, Midwest, Southwest, or West.

Panitch offered her California, with the rationale that the other three states in the West division—Nevada, Montana, and Idaho—would add too much travel and too many headaches for someone settling into a new position, and assigned the other states to another division head. Dimon signed off on the arrangement, thinking that it wouldn't be a comedown for Bibliowicz, because California had 2,100 or so brokers out of the 2,700 for the four states combined. He was wrong. Bibliowicz felt slighted. Weill exploded when he found out. "You insulted her!" he raged.

Weill beseeched Dimon to reach out to Bibliowicz and somehow make things right, for fear that she was about the leave the company, and to his recollection Dimon agreed to do so. Then, after returning from a two-week vacation in France, Weill found to his displeasure that Dimon had done no such thing, and his daughter had decided to resign. In the midst of it all, the Travelers Group reached another milestone: in

March, the stock was added to the Dow 30 Index. But Weill, for once, was in no mood to celebrate.

Dimon told Bibliowicz she was doing the right thing. "Honestly, Jessica, you're not going to be treated properly around here anymore," he said. "Not everyone is telling you the truth. Not everyone is telling your father the truth. He's gotten too involved. You need your own life outside this company." When Weill chose to tell reporters that he had known nothing of the issues, Dimon was shocked. "That was the first time I saw him not being completely honest with the press," he recalls.

When Dimon's friend from Harvard Business School, Stephen Burke, who had gone on to work at ABC, read in the *Wall Street Journal* about Bibliowicz's departure, he called Dimon. "Jamie, did you miss the class at Harvard when they said you never fire the boss's daughter?" he asked. After a fifteen-second pause, Dimon replied, "I had to tell her she wasn't going to get a job she wanted, she didn't like it, and she left the company. I couldn't do something I didn't feel was right."

Others thought Dimon had placed inordinate importance on his own greatest strengths—analysis of financials—and overlooked the fact that Bibliowicz was indeed a marketing talent. "But in Jamie's mind, it would have been a compromise, that he risked losing credibility with his own people," recalls Bob Willumstad. "If it were me, I am guessing I would probably have found a way to make that compromise. It wasn't like she was incompetent."

According to Monica Langley, a member of Travelers' board, Arthur Zankel, also thought Dimon had lost sight of pragmatism at a crucial moment in his relationship with Sandy Weill. "This isn't your finest hour," Zankel told Dimon. "It was your prerogative as Smith Barney president to pick your own asset chief last year, but you could have put Jess on the executive committee. As businessmen, we all have to live with this stuff occasionally."

Most observers blame Weill, though, for putting Dimon in an untenable position. If Dimon had promoted Bibliowicz as fast as she'd wanted, it would look have looked as though he was sucking up to the boss. When he didn't, the boss became mad. But that was classic Weill.

Despite his well-deserved reputation as a visionary, he had blind spots when it came to what *he* wanted.

Bibliowicz later told the *New York Times Magazine* that her leaving had more to do with her father than with Dimon. "I couldn't be open with him because I had to go through channels," she said. "I didn't leave because of Jamie." Dimon, too, denied any irreparable damage. "Sure, we disagreed, but we worked it through," he told a reporter. "She was a friend before she got here. She was a friend while she was here, and she's a friend now."

His relationship with Weill, however, had just slipped down another notch, writes Monica Langley. "You drove her out," Weill accused the younger man. "It might be the right thing for your daughter and the company," was Dimon's curt response. When asked by reporters whether Jamie had thrown his status as heir apparent into doubt, Weill was pushed to even greater heights of annoyance. "I have never made it clear to anybody that Jamie is my successor," he said. "I have no plans to leave this company."

In August, Weill hired Thomas Jones from the asset manager TIAA-CREF and put him in charge of the company's asset management business. Weill had stripped this unit out of the Smith Barney infrastructure and made it a separate division reporting directly to him. When the *Wall Street Journal* asked if this was a retaliatory move, Weill denied it. "If I wanted to retaliate, I would really retaliate," he said.

Years later, Weill still stews over how Dimon handled the situation. "I've said this to him in the past, and he doesn't like me to say it," recalls Weill. "I think Jamie built terrific loyalty from some people and developed a group of people who he really had great relationships with. Others bumped into that, and those that bumped into that, their fate was not great."

It is amazing that when two men joined forces in a display of empire building for the ages, their relationship started to come undone over nepotism. What's more amazing is that each man had a critical shortcoming that did not allow him to find a way out of the situation. Weill could be so single-minded about his own needs and wishes that he failed to consider the position he put others in. And Dimon, ever the moralist, could not bring himself to bend in the one instance that nearly anyone would have given him a pass on. (On the other hand, maybe he was looking over his shoulder. If you have an inkling that you're about to engage in a power struggle with your boss, it's probably smart not to promote his kids.)

Bibliowicz landed a job as president of John A. Levin & Co., and later National Financial Partners (NFP), an insurance company roll-up that went on to buy 180 smaller life insurance firms. She had a decade of success, but in a jarring display of symmetry, NFP slipped below $1 a share in 2008 just as Citigroup, her father's creation, also teetered on the edge of the void.

• • •

Fortunately for Dimon, Smith Barney was cruising, and this had the effect of blunting Weill's anger. Buoyed by a new issue market that set records in 1995 and 1996, the bank was taking a larger chunk of Wall Street business, and Dimon's focus on the bottom line meant that the firm achieved profitability ratios—if not actual gross revenues—exceeding those of nearly every other bank on the Street. Smith Barney's return on equity reached an astounding 36.7 percent in the second quarter of 1996.

"Jamie was demanding. He was relentless," remembers his assistant Sweeney. "And he always wanted the one thing I hadn't done. I'd walk in there with my pad of paper and he'd give me 10 things to do. I'd go back to my desk. An hour later, he'd call me and I'd have already done nine of them. And he'd ask for the tenth. And he pounded and pounded and pounded until you got it done. By the third time he asked for something, you better have been at a funeral, because that was the only acceptable excuse for not having it finished."

Dimon refined a tactic Weill had long utilized: skipping several layers of reporting to find the exact person who might have the number or answer he was looking for. While it was efficient—why ask person A for something if you knew A would merely turn around and ask person B, when you knew perfectly well who person B was yourself?—it also caused consternation in the ranks. It was not uncommon for an executive to walk by Dimon's office and see one of his own reports in there talking to the Travelers president. "What's *he* doing in there?" the executive would ask Sweeney, fearful of insurrection. "Why is *she* in there?"

It was a lush time for all. In the second half of the 1990s, stock and bond underwritings doubled in number, along with the total market value of firms listed on the New York Stock Exchange. Investors' appetite for stocks fueled the largest bull market in history, pushing financial institutions to record levels of profitability. Travelers' stock climbed from $21 in 1994 to $53 in late 1996. This was the dawn of the cable network CNBC, along with real-time stock tickers that scrolled across the bottom of its screen.

But not all the news at Smith Barney was good. With Greenhill's departure, the firm ceded back all the progress it had made in mergers and acquisitions. Scores of bankers had followed Greenhill out of Smith Barney, and some who didn't leave were pushed out. Dimon showed Greenhill's deputy Bob Lessin the door in early 1997, and recast the goals for the investment banking division to more moderate levels. He told *Business Week* that instead of "elephant hunting"—aiming for a piece of the biggest deals—Smith Barney planned instead to make the middle market its specialty.

Dimon continued grooming a few of his best employees, particularly Mike Cavanagh, Heidi Miller, and Charlie Scharf. (A colleague later referred to one of the three as "Jamie Dimon's Jamie Dimon." When asked about it, the executive jokingly dismissed the label, adding that they had yet to have the opportunity to fire their boss's daughter, thus making any such comparison premature.) Dimon utilized management tactics similar to those Weill employed, including shifting the most promising underlings around to ensure the broadest learning experience, even if it was not entirely clear to a lawyer such as Cavanagh why, at 26 years old, he should be mired in the budgeting process for the retail brokerage system at Smith Barney when most of his friends could already lay claim to much more obvious career paths.

In August 1996, Dimon worked with three CEOs—Daniel Tully of Merrill Lynch, Phil Purcell of Dean Witter, and Jon Corzine of Goldman Sachs—to hammer out a $100 million settlement with regulators over price-fixing on Nasdaq. Only 40 years old—the youngest CEO of a major securities firm—Dimon emerged from the negotiations with an even higher profile than before. His confidence, too, grew along with the fortunes of Smith Barney. *Business Week* ran a lengthy profile in October 1996, "Whiz Kid."

(In an amusing coincidence, two colleagues independently gave Dimon the book *All I Really Need to Know I Learned in Kindergarten* at this time.)

Several colleagues noticed that Dimon began to morph from being a "Sandy guy" to being a "Smith Barney guy" during this period. As a result, his and Weill's public fighting continued even as Travelers was enjoying solid financial results. "I can still hear Jamie saying 'But Sandy!' with his arm up in a meeting," recalled Marge Magner in a 2008 interview. "Without any fear. For the right reasons."

As the tenth anniversary of the Commercial Credit takeover neared, Dimon's frustration spilled into the open with greater frequency. "Sandy feels like he did all this by himself," he told one colleague. A constant refrain from Dimon was, "What about us?"—and it was the source of ever-increasing tension between him and Weill. He could hardly contain his growing resentment.

6. THE BOILING WITHIN

By the late 1990s, Wall Street worshipped at the altar of Alan Greenspan, the chairman of the Federal Reserve. Greenspan, who had been given the nickname Maestro, had ushered in a new golden era. Weill knew the Maestro well. In the early 1970s, he'd hired the wonky economist to speak to Shearson's research department, and they had engaged in long-running debates about the economy ever since.

Greenspan had taken over the Fed in 1987, succeeding Paul Volcker, who had crushed inflation in the early 1980s by dramatically boosting interest rates. The cost of that rise in interest rates, however, was plunging the economy into what was then the most severe recession since the 1930s. The early going was tough for Greenspan—the stock market crashed in the fall of 1987 and the national economy sputtered for most of the first half of the 1990s—but by the latter half of the decade, things were humming along.

A disciple of the objectivist philosopher Ayn Rand—author of *Atlas Shrugged* and *The Fountainhead*—Greenspan was a vocal, if often convoluted, proponent of free-market ideology and laissez-faire capitalism. Famous for his intentionally incomprehensible testimony in front of Congress—he was legendary for saying nothing in a complicated way—he was nevertheless widely trusted for his market acumen. Bankers particularly adored him. By relaxing the Glass-Steagall Act, he opened the door for banks to become major deal makers and create new financial empires.

Passed in 1933 in response to the crash of 1929, Glass-Steagall was intended to prevent deposit-taking banks from incurring too much risk. Specifically, they could no longer speculate in the stock market. Major firms, including the august House of Morgan, were cleaved into one of two kinds of entities: commercial banks and investment banks. Also, no nonbank company would thereafter be allowed to own a bank. The effect was to make banking an exceptionally dull business, like a utility.

The law held up for a long time, but by the 1980s, American banks considered themselves to be at a competitive disadvantage. Large foreign institutions were expanding, unhindered by such restrictions. For years, banks lobbied for the Glass-Steagall to be repealed, or at least defanged. According to Ron Chernow's *The House of Morgan*, in 1984, when Greenspan himself had been a director of J.P. Morgan, he'd helped circulate a document prepared by the bank, titled "Rethinking Glass-Steagall." Six years later, J.P. Morgan became the first bank to receive permission from the Federal Reserve to underwrite securities, managing a $30 million bond offering for the Savannah Electric and Power Company.

As Fed chairman, Greenspan was not entirely laissez-faire. When the stock market went on a wild tear in 1996, he gave his famous "irrational exuberance" speech, which had a somewhat calming effect on investors' excitement. But when it came to regulation, Greenspan pushed to give banks a great deal more latitude in their operations. He relaxed the limits on banks' ability to own securities businesses (they had previously been allowed to earn no more than 25 percent of their total revenues from this source). Another arm of the government, the Comptroller of the Currency, decreed that banks might engage in securities underwriting and the sale of insurance if they did so through subsidiary companies.

The end result: after more than 50 years, Greenspan effectively dismantled Glass-Steagall with assistance from Weill, President Bill Clinton, and Secretary of the Treasury Robert Rubin. (Clinton signed a bill in November 1999 that demolished any remnants of Glass-Steagall.) By the time Congress moved to formally repeal the act, it was as good as gone. Greenspan went further—joining forces with Rubin, he blocked an effort by the Commodities and Futures Trading Commission to impose greater regulations on the derivatives market. Among others, E. Gerald Corrigan, who'd been president of the Federal Reserve Bank of New York from 1985 through 1993, had raised alarms earlier in the decade about the headlong growth of the derivatives market, but Greenspan had sided with the industry and its argument that it was "self-policing." The owner of *Forbes* magazine, Steve Forbes, later accused Greenspan of believing himself a "monetary philosopher king with Louis XIV 'I am the state' proclivities."

Banks started to make a flurry of big deals. In early 1997, Bankers Trust bought Alex Brown, becoming the first U.S. bank to acquire a securities firm, and Morgan Stanley merged with Dean Witter Discover & Co. in a $10 billion deal. Chemical Bank also bought rival Chase Manhattan, for $9.8 billion in 1996, but chose to keep the latter's more prestigious name.

It was under Greenspan's auspices, then, that the Wall Street juggernaut, the creation of giant, financial supermarkets that offered every money-related product under the sun, began. The wholesale clearance of regulatory hurdles made it possible for firms to assemble themselves into conglomerates that were too big to fail, a paradoxical situation that led managers to ignore traditional risk controls and make audacious bets with their capital.

Sandy Weill and Jamie Dimon were early and enthusiastic participants in this movement, a somewhat dubious legacy. On the one hand, banking CEOs can reasonably argue that they needed scale (and leverage) to squeeze sufficient profit from businesses that were largely based on low-margin commodity products. On the other hand, it is also clear that the deals that built these giants were like a party drug, blinding Wall Street to their long-term implications. Everybody wanted to seize the moment and grab a share of the fees, the associated risks be damned.

Although both Weill and Dimon will, to this day, swear by the efficiencies and profit-making potential of mega-institutions, the truth is that the majority of the big-time deals did not work. Perhaps the theory is sound, but the practice is another story. A sprawling conglomerate in the wrong hands (see Chuck Prince at Citigroup) is a disaster waiting to happen.

Greenspan also later came to be known for the "Greenspan put." (A put option gives the buyer the right, but not the obligation, to sell an asset at a predetermined "strike" price. If prices rise, you don't sell. If they fall, you sell at the strike price and minimize your losses.) With aggressive interest rate cuts in the event of any kind of crisis—the Mexican crisis, the Asian currency crisis, the Long-Term Capital Management crisis, the bursting of the Internet bubble, or 9/11—his Federal Reserve created the impression that investors essentially had a "put option" on asset prices, and in the process arguably encouraged excessive risk-taking. His successor Ben Bernanke continued the tradition, resulting in the notion of the "Bernanke put." The financial crisis in 2007–2009 ended any thoughts that these puts actually existed. When it came to crunch time, there was no one on the other end of the theoretical contract, and investors watched their portfolios evaporate.

. . .

At this point, Weill and Dimon were bickering so much that many colleagues believed some kind of awful climax was inevitable. But in those heady years, personal friction could be overridden by pursuit of the next big deal. As it turned out, however, a major disappointment was on their immediate horizon.

Weill had correctly sniffed out the possibility that Greenspan might be amenable to a deal that was, on its face, a direct repudiation of Glass-Steagall: Travelers acquiring a commercial bank. The law did allow for such a possibility, provided the insurance operations were spun off within two to five years. But Weill had an audacious idea. He would try to buy J.P. Morgan. The bank was no longer a powerhouse, but its name still evoked a power and prestige that Travelers entirely lacked.

His reading of Greenspan aside, Weill's confidence also stemmed, in part, from the increasing acceptance of corporate America in the national psyche. In the early 1980s, corporate profits were just 3 percent of GDP. By the end of the next decade, they accounted for 10 percent. Business leaders were profiled glowingly and uncritically in *Fortune* and

Business Week; Jack Welch of General Electric was a national treasure. Even Wall Street was enjoying a brief (though fleeting) period of public approval. The insider traders and junk bond kings of the 1980s had been forgotten. Wall Street titans were considered innovative geniuses; how could Congress justify preventing the smartest people in business from doing as they saw fit?

Weill contacted J.P. Morgan's head, Douglas "Sandy" Warner, and the two men apparently found enough common ground to put together two three-man teams, one each from J.P. Morgan and Smith Barney. (J.P. Morgan would effectively be merged with Smith Barney in the event of a deal.) For Weill, it would be another feather in his Travelers' cap. For Warner, a deal might help establish J.P. Morgan as a full-blown investment bank with a more diversified set of businesses, particularly by adding Smith Barney's brokerage force. Dimon was on Smith Barney's three-man team, and gave his counterparts from J.P. Morgan a daylong presentation on Smith Barney's brokerage capabilities. (One member of the Morgan team, Jes Staley, would eventually find himself working for Dimon, but not for another seven years.)

Weill, thinking the merger discussions with Warner were farther along than they actually were, called Greenspan to see if he could give the green light for such a deal. Greenspan replied that he was "open to the logic" of such a combination. But negotiations stalled as Warner made two demands that Weill considered unthinkable. First, the 50-year-old Warner wanted a hefty $30 billion for his company. Second, he wanted the 64-year-old Weill to retire within 18 months of a deal. If Weill thought he might find a way to wiggle out of the retirement condition, the price was beyond ridiculous. Sandy Weill never overpaid for anything, not even for one of the most iconic brands in finance. The talks collapsed. According to journalist Roger Lowenstein, Weill later complained to a colleague that Morgan "would never sell to a Jew."

Despite the fact that the combination of Travelers and J.P. Morgan was not to be, Weill gained something valuable out of the flirtation—Greenspan's implicit endorsement of such a deal—which eventually inspired him to come up with an even more ambitious idea. In the meantime, another deal came knocking in just a few weeks.

. . .

Wall Street is merciless. Companies that are the toast of the town on one day can become pariahs in an instant. So it was with Salomon Brothers in the late 1990s. The famous investor Warren Buffett had stepped in to take 20 percent of the company in the wake of a 1991 Treasury bond scandal that had cost Salomon's chairman John Gutfreund his job—and the company $290 million in fines—but it was commonly understood that Buffett did not see himself as a long-term owner and had been seeking an "exit strategy" for some time. Salomon had become one of his most troubled investments, and he was ready to be done with it. Rumors of the company's sale had been circulating since 1995.

Buffett's handpicked replacement for Gutfreund, Deryck Maughan, had succeeded in stabilizing Salomon, and a recent run of strong trading profits had Buffet thinking the time was right to sell. Maughan had been an adviser to the British treasury from 1969 to 1979 and had run Salomon's Tokyo office from 1986 to 1991, after which time Buffett had tapped him for the CEO slot. Weill had brought Maughan on to the board of trustees of Carnegie Hall that same year, and the debonair Englishman reached out first to Weill when he decided to test the waters for a sale of Salomon in August 1997.

On paper, the deal made a lot of sense. For starters, Salomon's international operations could complement Smith Barney's more domestic franchise. Although Salomon didn't offer much in the way of investment banking, the combination of the two firms' fledgling efforts would make them stronger than they might otherwise have been. And Salomon's position as the market's strongest player in bond trading would be a perfect addition to Smith Barney's relative strength in equities.

On the other hand, such a deal violated a number of Weill's cherished precepts regarding acquisitions. In the first place, he would be buying a company on an upswing—a more characteristic approach would have been to buy when Buffett had bought, *not* when Buffett was looking to sell. Most glaring, though, was the notion that Weill was even considering buying a firm with a penchant for letting its traders make outsize bets with the firm's capital.

Weill and Dimon loved brokers for the stability and profitability they provided. But *traders* were something else entirely. A heavy reliance on trading profits was antithetical to everything these two cost-conscious micromanagers stood for. Robert Greenhill might spend $10 million on an overrated investment banker, sure. But an unsupervised trader could lose *$100 million* in a single day. A botched risk arbitrage trade had recently cost Salomon just that.

Salomon, in fact, was a big player in the emerging realm of derivatives trading, and it was difficult, if not impossible, to get a real fix on the attendant risks of that business. Some months earlier, in fact, Weill himself had referred to Salomon's trading outfit as a "casino," and now here he was thinking of buying that casino outright. (Sandy Weill, it can be argued, was somewhat cavalier in his choice of Salomon as the investment bank that would take Travelers to the next level. Building a top-tier investment bank is more difficult than merely making a turnkey purchase.)

Finally, there was the issue of culture. Salomon's "Big Swinging Dicks" had been lampooned in Tom Wolfe's popular 1987 book *Bonfire of the Vanities* (in which Wolfe coined the term "Masters of the Universe") and in Michael Lewis's 1989 insider account *Liar's Poker*. Both books had painted a culture in which the client was viewed more as prey than partner, and the Treasury bond scandal had revealed a moral vacuum at the top levels of the firm. Weill and Dimon had only recently rid themselves of the overweening personalities of Greenhill and Lessin. In Salomon, they were quite possibly buying an entire firm of such characters.

But Sandy Weill was nothing if not an opportunist, and spurred in part by the failure of the J.P. Morgan deal, he pressed ahead in his quest for Salomon, figuring he could solve the in-house problems once he got his hands on the firm. After a few weeks of due diligence, he pushed the board and audit committees toward a deal. Dimon, the board member Joe Wright recalled, was inclined toward the deal as well, although by his very nature he was more focused on the risks they'd be taking. And there was no question that this was a departure from their plain vanilla heritage. Plain vanilla is just fine with Jamie Dimon. A business doesn't have to be sexy to get him excited; it just needs to be reliable, profitable, and growing.

Good times make for good results, Dimon knew, even if a company wasn't on the perfect path. But if the good times were to end, Salomon's enormous risks posed a threat to Travelers' overall health. Awareness of any potential downside was one of Dimon's most ingrained character traits, and although he eventually came around to the merits of the deal, he obsessed over its risks much more than Weill. This is not to say that Dimon was risk averse. But he was a numbers man to the core, and he needed to able to calculate as best he could what the risk was before he could be comfortable taking it on.

Warren Buffett liked the idea of a deal with Travelers. Maughan had been a sensible choice to run Salomon because in 1991 he'd been in the firm's Tokyo office and was untainted by the trading scandal. But Maughan was incapable of the powerful leadership that Buffett sensed Weill and Dimon could provide. Salomon, rife with fiefdoms, had resisted Maughan's efforts at wholesale change; a principled attempt on his part to tie compensation more closely to performance had blown up in his face. But both Weill and Dimon were by that point legendary for their intolerance of fiefdoms, and Buffett saw an opportunity to finally put the place right.

After just a month of negotiations, a deal was struck. On September 24, 1997, it was announced that Travelers was buying Salomon Brothers for $9 billion. The market read it as a good deal for Buffett and Salomon, sending Salomon's shares up several points. But the judgment was different when it came to Travelers. Investors wondered whether Weill and Dimon understood the kinds of risks they were taking on with the fast-and-loose culture of Salomon. Travelers fell 4 percent.

Buffett wrote a note, which was included in the press release for the deal, praising Weill for showing "genius in creating huge value for his shareholders," a fact many observers pointed to while second-guessing the rationale for the deal itself. It was known that Weill disliked arbitrage. So what was he doing buying a firm that lived and breathed on just that? Did he just want to do a deal with Buffett, to show he was now operating in the highest spheres of financial deal making? He'd been denied the chance more than 10 years before with the Fireman's Fund, and it appeared that he wasn't going to let the opportunity pass him by again. "Sandy spent nine billion dollars to get a piece of paper from Warren Buffett saying what a great investor he was," an insider later told the journalist Roger Lowenstein. "He was running around showing it to people like a kid in a candy store."

Still, the deal did push Travelers a little higher up the Wall Street food chain, at least in terms of market value. By October, the company's market value was $55 billion, far exceeding that of Merrill Lynch ($24 billion) and even Morgan Stanley Dean Witter ($44 billion). The deal also vaulted Smith Barney up in the investment banking league tables. But the announcement of the deal did nothing to bridge the widening chasm between Dimon and Weill. When the two men joined a few Salomon executives at The Four Seasons for celebratory drinks after the announcement, they were at each other's throat within minutes.

• • •

As if he needed another one, Jamie Dimon also had a new bone to pick with his boss. Although he'd been effectively running Smith Barney by himself since Greenhill's departure, the Salomon deal brought Deryck Maughan along with it, and Weill told Dimon that he had decided to make Maughan a co-CEO of the unit alongside Dimon.

Dimon was enraged. He reminded Weill that in previous negotiations with Salomon, Weill had indicated that Dimon would have complete control. But now, with the deal done, Weill refused to budge on the matter. Weill later wrote that he considered the co-CEO arrangement an insurance policy against his deteriorating relationship with Dimon. He may actually believe that. But from Dimon's perspective, it looked more like another way that Weill, after elevating him to the level of a near-equal, seemed intent on undermining him and limiting his power.

(When Travelers had flirted with the idea of buying Salomon the previous year, Weill had told associates that he would fire Maughan if the deal was completed. To view Maughan now as the answer to his problems was a stunning about-face.)

Dimon was not the only one who thought he was caught in a

Groundhog Day nightmare. The financial press jumped on the issue, asking Maughan on the day of the announcement how he thought the power sharing would work out. "We will agree," responded Maughan, diplomatically. "For the sake of the firm, we are obligated to find agreement."

This was not a situation that could be dealt with privately. In October, *Business Week* published a story titled "How Long Can These Two Tango?" Both men dutifully gave the answers that were expected of them. "We want to operate as a team," said Maughan. "The idea of partnership is not foreign to us." Dimon chipped in with a perfunctory, "There's plenty of work for both of us to do here."

Within Travelers, there was a long-running joke about Sandy Weill's fickleness. If you walked by Weill's office and saw a new face, you might be moved to ask, "Who's that?" The answer: "That's Sandy's new best friend." For a long time, that had been Dimon, but Weill kept finding new supplicants. There had been Greenhill and now there was Maughan. But while Greenhill's talents as a deal maker were unimpeachable, Deryck Maughan was something else entirely—a product of a culture whose values and priorities were the antithesis of Travelers'. Forget whether or not Dimon could get along with Maughan. Could Dimon even trust him?

Weill might have been impressed by Maughan's European polish, but there were aspects of his personality—and his wife's—that did not portend well for his relationship with the no-nonsense Dimon. A scathing 1995 piece by Suzanna Andrews in *New York* magazine made the case that Maughan had been in over his head at Salomon yet had a tendency to say things like, "I am the hardest-working man at Salomon Brothers." Most top executives also thought he put politics ahead of the interests of the firm, a conclusion arrived at after he seemingly forced the star trader John Meriwether out of Salomon—Meriwether had gone on to found Wall Street's hottest hedge fund at the time, Long-Term Capital Management. A stream of talented partners had also left during Maughan's tenure.

Then there was the issue of Maughan's wife, Va. A onetime Pan Am reservation agent who had changed her name from Lorraine

Hannemann, Va Maughan was a gossipmonger's dream. Stories floated around that it was she, and not Maughan, who had negotiated his pay packages at Salomon. She reportedly once refused to allow a Salomon executive the use of her car and driver to take his sick baby to the hospital, and she also was said to have bragged about a relative in the Japanese mafia. Shortly after the merger, at a 1997 company retreat at the Phoenician in Scottsdale, Arizona, Va threw a fit when she found out that Jamie and Judy were in a room across from the Weills, whereas the Maughans were in a different building. The Dimons switched rooms to keep the peace, but the event foreshadowed an ugly and career-changing confrontation the next year.

· · ·

There was no honeymoon after the Salomon deal. Just a month later, on October 27, the Dow Jones skidded 554 points—7 percent—when investors panicked over a developing crisis in Asian currency markets. After a decision by the Thai government to cut the "peg" of its currency to the U.S. dollar, the Thai baht itself collapsed, and the region's currencies fell like dominoes, with similar collapses in both South Korea and Indonesia. Salomon lost $50 million in the process.

Weill and Dimon also received a quick lesson in the kinds of risks they'd taken on by bringing a bet-the-farm culture under the Travelers umbrella. Salomon's equity risk arbitrage unit suffered a loss of $100 million betting that British Telecommunications would purchase MCI Communications. Steve Black disbanded the group, but the firm's much larger fixed income arbitrage group remained intact.

Although the losses only intensified Dimon's distaste for Maughan and the whole Salomon culture, the two men briefly found common cause, in a surprising situation. They combined to block another attempt at inappropriate nepotism by Weill.

Just as Weill had argued in 1996 for his daughter's advancement against Dimon's wishes, in early 1998 he pushed to have his son Marc, then 41, placed in charge of the firm's fixed income arbitrage group. Dimon and Maughan were united in their conviction that the division was a potential powder keg in the wrong hands—and that Marc Weill's were definitely the wrong hands.

When Marc was hired, Dimon had seen the possibility that Weill might mishandle his son. Accordingly, Dimon had insisted that Marc report to him, not to Weill. Dimon even had a conversation with Weill's wife, Joan, and had pleaded with her to make sure her husband left Marc alone to do his job. Still, Dimon knew Marc's limitations, and categorically refused to put him in charge of Salomon's arbitrage desk. Weill backed down. In the future, when Dimon was no longer in his way, Weill pushed his son into roles beyond his capabilities, with far more money to manage—he ultimately oversaw $60 billion as well as the firm's private equity initiatives—and even added him to the firm's management committee. At that point, the pressure was too much, and he left the company in 2000. He later formed his own venture capital firm and focused on hobbies including collecting mineral specimens and flying radio-controlled helicopters.

The year did end on a somewhat high note. Travelers stock was the top-performing member of the Dow Jones industrial average in 1997, soaring 78 percent. Dimon earned $23.1 million plus another $37 million in stock options. To outsiders, it might have even seemed that he and Weill had pulled off another daring deal. At a Goldman Sachs investment conference in November, Weill said of himself and Dimon, "I'm Batman; he's Robin."

Behind the scenes, however, the trading losses at Salomon had put everyone on edge. Dimon and Maughan continued to circle each other warily, and Weill continually turned up unannounced at meetings. Dimon found the intrusions frustrating and disruptive, because the focus was usually the intricate details of the business that Weill was uninterested in—so that, invariably, Weill threw the meeting off course. As a result, Dimon sometimes scheduled important meetings for times when he knew Weill was out of town. Insecure about losing control, as had happened with Peter Cohen at Shearson, Weill resolved that he wouldn't stand for such insubordinate behavior, even if that subordinate was named Jamie Dimon.

7. A BRIEF VIEW FROM THE TOP

In 1998, Jamie Dimon and Sandy Weill completed their 16-year climb to the top of Wall Street. But Dimon wouldn't have long to admire the view. By the end of the year, he was facing the end of the partnership that had defined his career.

At Travelers' regular planning group meeting in Armonk in December 1997, the topic was pure Weill: What next? Mike Carpenter, Travelers' head of corporate planning, took the group through a number of possible merger candidates, including American Express, Goldman Sachs, J.P. Morgan, and Merrill Lynch. At some point, the name Citicorp was tossed into the ring, resulting in a chorus of incredulity. Citicorp was simply out of Travelers' league—too big, too powerful.

Dimon remembered the idea for what it was—"the mother of all deals." Conceptually, a merger made all the sense in the world. Citicorp was the global leader in virtually every banking product that existed, from credit cards to checking accounts, and Travelers was strong in almost every financial product outside banking itself, with Travelers' insurance, Salomon Smith Barney's brokerage and investment bank, and Primerica's financial advisers.

But there was a glaring problem. Despite the reputation of Weill and Dimon as deal makers par excellence, Citicorp loomed high above them as the Tiffany of financial services companies. Travelers, by comparison, was a deal maker's concoction, an agglomeration of parts. Although the deal might make sense in terms of complementary businesses, there was hardly any reason for the highly regarded, patrician CEO of

Citicorp, John Reed, to consider ceding the top post to Sandy Weill in the event of a merger. And it was hard to see how Weill would accept anything less than being the boss.

But in raw numbers, Weill noted that Travelers' market capitalization was not too far from that of Citicorp itself. His company's brand might not be as respected as the global bank's, but a decade of delivering for investors had pushed Travelers' value to such a high level that the suggestion of such a deal could not be laughed off.

• • •

John Reed was a standout in the world of commercial banking. Considered the most visionary banker of his time, he saw the power of technology before most of his peers, giving Citicorp a leg up in the ATM business as well as in the use of databases to ferret out new business opportunities with current and prospective customers. He was a pinstriped banking man to the core, and he sat atop one of the world's most admired companies, with $21.6 billion in 1997 revenues and $3.6 billion in net income.

A professional character, Reed also liked to hide in his office and communicate with his staff by memos. In this, he was the opposite of Sandy Weill, a relentless backslapper who liked nothing more than being in the trenches, among his employees. "Reed did not like people," recalls a longtime colleague. "Give him a whiteboard and an office where he didn't have to associate with humans and he could lecture for hours. Mind you, if he did run into you, he'd try to prove to you every day that he was smarter than you were."

But the man *was* smart, smart enough, in fact, to realize that in a fast-consolidating financial services landscape, he had to remain open to any and all ideas about how to keep the company competitive. He realized that the bureaucracy of the giant bank he and his predecessor Walter Wriston had built was stifling the firm, that it needed a dose of adrenaline, and that it could do with a bit of balance. Despite its size and reputation, the company occasionally stumbled in a very big way. Ten years before, for example, it had endured the largest loss in corporate history as a result of the Latin American debt crisis.

Word had gotten out that Reed had recently spoken to Harvey Golub at American Express about combining the two firms, and although nothing came of the discussions, the episode showed an openness that Weill found encouraging. In December 1997, when Weill called Reed to suggest that they get together for a chat, Reed proposed meeting in Washington on February 25, when they would both be attending a Business Council meeting of prominent CEOs.

Reed didn't quite know what he was in for. When he knocked on Weill's hotel door at 9:00 P.M., he thought Weill was going to ask him to spend $25,000 for a table at a charity dinner, or something of that sort. Instead, Weill had his sales pitch all ready to go. Reed was barely through the door when Weill launched into his vision of a merger of equals, a combination of the two firms that would sit powerfully atop the financial world. He proposed sharing the leadership role as co-CEOs, and splitting the board 50-50 with directors from both companies.

Reed did not reject the idea out of hand, and the next morning at 7:00, Weill was on the phone with Dimon. Monica Langley recounts their conversation. "You won't believe it!" Weill said. "This could be the greatest deal of all time!" Although he'd been kept in the dark about the meeting with Reed, Dimon knew what his boss was talking about. "The mother of all deals?" he asked. "Yeah, the deal to beat all deals," Sandy replied.

Dimon was floored. This was the dream they'd been talking about for the better part of a decade. From their modest beginnings in Baltimore—indeed, from the listless days in the Seagram Building in 1985—they had somehow managed to get to this point, the absolute pinnacle of their industry. The mother of all deals was no longer just a joke to be bandied about during bullshitting sessions.

Upon reflection, Reed found the idea compelling enough to suggest that Weill continue discussions with Citicorps' vice chairman Paul Collins, and a second meeting was scheduled for March 2. By this time, Weill felt it important enough to bring both Dimon and the head of corporate planning, Mike Carpenter, into the loop, and the two men joined Collins and Weill on March 5 at Weill's apartment to continue figuring out how such a combination might work. Over the next few days, Dimon himself fielded most of Collins's financial questions about a deal.

· · ·

The two companies' teams agreed to meet in Armonk on March 20 and 21, once Reed had returned from a trip overseas. In advance of that, however, Weill invited Reed to a private meeting on the evening of the nineteenth, and it was over dinner that he secretly dropped the first of several bombs designed to curtail his protégé's ambitions.

Having noticed that Reed had taken a liking to Dimon, Weill later wrote, he told Reed not to view Dimon as the eventual CEO of the combined firm. "Don't do this deal in order to get Jamie as a successor," Weill said. "You'll have to see for yourself, but there are issues here you aren't aware of." Little more was said on the issue, but an inexorable process had begun. (James Robinson had dispatched Sandy Weill in part by co-opting Peter Cohen. Weill would be damned if that was going to happen to him again. This time, he wasn't going to go "up and out.")

Over the next two days, the teams hashed out much of the conceptual framework for a merger, including a name—Citigroup—and a plan that the company would have three main divisions: the corporate investment bank, the consumer business, and asset management. Dimon quite reasonably assumed that he would be put in charge of running the corporate investment bank, the same job he had shared with Maughan at Salomon Smith Barney.

What he did not consider, given his place on the boards of Travelers and its predecessor companies for several years, was the possibility that he would not be on Citigroup's board. And that's when Weill lobbed bomb number two. In mid-March, while the two men went over details of the deal at Weill's apartment, he turned to his longtime lieutenant and said, "Jamie, you're not going to be on the new board."

This statement marked the final and irreconcilable breach in a relationship that had once been closer than the bond between most fathers and sons, even if the two men chafed at such a notion. It was not just another disagreement. Weill was telling Dimon that he was never going to become CEO of Citigroup. This was the end, albeit at this point more figuratively than literally.

In the fairy-tale version of Dimon's career, he succeeds his mentor and leads Citigroup to greater glory. In the fairy tale, Citigroup is not on the verge of extinction 10 years later, while Jamie Dimon is leading one of its only healthy competitors. The future of American banking, in other words, was shaped by this very moment. How much different history might have been had Sandy Weill done what Dimon fully expected him to—assure him that the job would soon be his. But Weill was not yet ready to think past his own career. He was living in the present, and he was sick to death of Dimon's thinking they were equals. Dimon was his *junior* partner. And he didn't need a junior partner on the board when he had an equal one in John Reed.

Dimon was dumbstruck. "Sandy, I've been building this company for 15 years with you—please don't do that to me," he sputtered. Weill then launched into a tortured rationale to explain why it wasn't possible for him to do what most people assumed was a fait accompli. He had agreed with Reed that no insiders other than the co-CEOs would be on the combined board, he said. Dimon didn't buy it, arguing that his place on the board could be justified by putting another Citicorp executive such as Paul Collins on it as well. Weill countered with Bob Lipp. What would Lipp think if Dimon were appointed and not he? "Sandy, go ask Bob," Dimon replied. "Bob will tell you to put me on the board."

What's more, Dimon said, there was a point of pride. There had already been much discussion about his being president of the combined company, and he pointed out that in the event he did have the title, he would be one of the only presidents of a major public company not on its board. In other words, it was an embarrassment, a snub. But Weill was resolute. "We've decided." At that point, Dimon couldn't take it anymore, and left.

Shell-shocked, he later told a friend, "My God. I helped build Travelers." Frustrated as he was by what he saw as the unfairness of the situation, Dimon somehow failed to grasp the larger implication of Weill's remark. Sandy Weill had begun to dismantle what had been corporate

America's longest-running, best-known, and most widely lauded succession plan.

. . .

The next few weeks were filled with phone calls and meetings to make sure the deal went off without a hitch. Weill called Alan Greenspan to make sure they'd at least get preliminary approval from the Federal Reserve. He called Secretary of the Treasury Robert Rubin, who actively lobbied for repeal of Glass-Steagall, ultimately making the transaction legal. (Rubin subsequently resigned from the government and joined Weill at Citigroup. He earned $115 million from Citigroup over the next decade before resigning under a cloud of criticism in early 2009.)

On Saturday, April 4, 1998, the two companies' boards approved the merger. By Sunday afternoon, Weill couldn't contain his excitement anymore, and called John Reed to suggest that the two of them call President Bill Clinton. There was no reason they needed to do so, but Reed went along. Weill, after all, had just completed the greatest roll-up in history, culminating with the largest merger of all time—a $70 billion combination.

The deal was announced Monday, April 6. *Fortune* magazine wrote, "We are at ground zero of one of the most fascinating business and management stories ever to come along." As astonishing as the deal itself was the ability of the two management teams to keep it a secret for as long as they did—further testimony to Weill's prowess as a deal maker. As a result, his fame rose even higher. In a story in the *New York Times*, Peter Solomon, the onetime vice chairman of Lehman Brothers, paid Weill the ultimate deal maker's compliment. Weill, he said, "has the audacity to merge up."

It was more than just one huge transaction. The die was cast for a new model of banking, and competitors had to get with it or get left behind. The industry soon convulsed with deals. NationsBank and BankAmerica merged in a $64.8 billion deal. First Chicago and Banc One entered a $30 billion Midwest marriage. And Bank of New York made a play for Mellon Financial. None of those, however, excited investors and the press as much as the Citigroup story. That creation, after all, was complete. Advertisements promoting the creation of Salomon Smith Barney had included the line, "We're just getting started," Now, in a presentation announcing the Citigroup deal, Dimon flashed a slide that simply said, "We're done."

• • •

It was only a few days after the ink had dried on the merger agreement signed by Weill and Reed that Weill launched bomb number three.

Shortly after the announcement of the merger, Weill and Reed met in Bermuda to develop executive roles at the combined company. They were joined by two lieutenants from each side—Dimon and Bob Lipp from Travelers, and Paul Collins and Bill Campbell of Citicorp, that company's vice chairman and head of retail, respectively. (Campbell was a marketing legend. A Canadian, he'd helped create the Marlboro Man campaign during a 28-year career at Philip Morris.)

Monica Langley writes that when the absence of the four men was noted, they were labeled "the Untouchables," on the assumption that their attendance at the session practically guaranteed that they would be given the most senior sub-CEO roles in the combined firm.

And at first, that's what it seemed would happen. Reed, who had demonstrated respect for Dimon's intellect and drive, had no problem elevating Dimon above other Citicorp executives in the combined company. "I've only met two men who can carry a bank balance sheet in their head," Bill Campbell later observed: "John Reed and Jamie Dimon." Dimon also felt he had something in common with Reed. "He could be a cold-blooded analytic, and so could I," he recalls.

Given Dimon's nearly sterling reputation on Wall Street, no one on the Citicorp side seemed to find the prospect unsettling. In addition to whatever operating role he held, he would be president of Citigroup, right underneath the co-CEOs.

And the first pass at a management structure reflected just that. The men also agreed that Dimon would be chief executive officer of Citigroup's global corporate unit, which would include both Salomon Smith Barney and the company's corporate banking business. Beneath him on the organizational chart were Victor Menezes of Citicorp, head of commercial banking, and Deryck Maughan, chief of Salomon Smith Barney. Satisfied with their work, Lipp, Reed, Collins, and Campbell flew back to New York while Weill and Dimon stayed behind for a meeting with a contingent of brokers. A draft announcement had even been written up, ready to be put through the company's legal and public relations processes.

There are two competing accounts of what happened next. Weill says that Maughan flatly refused to report to Dimon, and demanded a different arrangement. Langley says the opposite, that Maughan voiced no objection whatsoever. Weill's version is probably the truth, as it seems unlikely that the proud Englishman would cede authority to Dimon without at least token opposition. Still in thrall to Maughan, Weill more likely than not agreed to a new arrangement without putting up much of a fight. On Tuesday of the week following the retreat in Bermuda, he told the reassembled group that he had rethought his original position, and that instead of having Maughan report to Dimon, the two men should be co-CEOs of the global corporate unit.

To this day, Weill will argue that he brought Deryck Maughan over to Travelers in the Salomon deal *in case* something ever happened between him and Dimon that resulted in Dimon's leaving the company. "I did it in case of a blowup with Jamie," he said in an interview in his office in December 2008. "So there would be someone else who knew how to run that business." But there was Weill, proposing a management structure that was itself very likely to precipitate the blowup. (Dimon's supporters call the explanation revisionist thinking. "Deryck's a nice guy," says one. "But Deryck was not capable of running the company and Sandy knew that. So he's full of shit when he says that.")

It wasn't just Dimon who was baffled by the about-face. Reed, too, was curious as to why a co-CEO structure was necessary. Weill insisted that Maughan would quit. Reed reportedly replied, "Who gives a shit? Let him leave." But Weill wouldn't budge, and offered a mealymouthed litany of reasons why his hands were tied.

"You guys are crazy," Dimon said in a meeting with Weill and Reed. "It's an outrage. It will destroy the company. I'm shocked you would even think about something like this. The day you announce it, the troops will be lining up ready to go to war. This will be trench warfare. And by the time you two figure it out, everybody will be so discredited, people won't know what to do about it." Sandy countered that he and Reed had agreed to be co-CEOs, to which Dimon responded that having co-CEOs over operating units was a different matter entirely.

From there, things proceeded to get more complicated. Worried that if two former Travelers executives—Dimon and Maughan—were put in charge of the global corporate bank there would be disenchantment among the Citicorp crowd, Reed proposed a third structure: not co- but tri-CEOs, with Victor Menezes raised to equal rank with the others. Weill immediately agreed to Reed's suggestion. When he saw Dimon about to explode, writes Monica Langley, he turned to him and said, point-blank, "Shut up."

Dimon was still named president of the combined company, a title implying that he was senior to his co-CEOs at the global corporate bank, a nod to the heir apparency all observers still believed existed. All except Weill, that is. Weill withheld the title of chief operating officer, repeating the ignominy forced on him when he joined American Express in 1981. Adding insult, the only senior executive who would report directly to Dimon was Heidi Miller, the CFO. The rest would report to Weill and Reed.

Deep down, Dimon knew things had taken a very wrong turn. Despite Weill's trying to sweet-talk him into believing that the title of president meant he was well positioned, Dimon saw the empty title for what it was. "I said, 'I don't have the job, I'm not on the board, but you're going to give me a title?' I should have realized it when he told me about the board. I should have left the company at that point. You'd think by then I might have figured it out, but I didn't. I accepted that too, didn't I? Sandy knows exactly how far he can go. I loved the company. It was my family. I couldn't leave them. But Sandy doesn't always think about just right or wrong; he thinks about his options down the road. The board decision was the sign, and I should have known better. But look, you live and learn."

Things then proceeded according to Weill's grand plan. At a meeting with Alan Greenspan, chairman of the Federal Reserve, and other Fed officials later in April, Weill was given a "positive response" to the merger. Although Weill continued to push to have Glass-Steagall changed, Citigroup was given two years to divest itself of the Travelers insurance unit.

On May 6, Weill and Reed unveiled the new management structure to the public. In addition to the arrangement at the global corporate bank, Bob Lipp and Bill Campbell would run the company's consumer business, and the Travelers veteran Tom Jones would run asset management.

. . .

Perhaps if the markets had stayed calm, all the players within Citigroup might have been able to maintain their composure as they struggled to complete not one but two mergers—the Citicorp deal as well as the still unfinished Salomon integration. But the summer of 1998 proved anything but calm.

Salomon's fixed income arbitrage group, which used quantitative modeling to profit from temporary pricing anomalies between similar securities, had long been the company's crown jewel. But in the spring of 1998, it began suffering increasingly frequent losses as the markets remained skittish and relatively illiquid. By the end of April, in fact, it had already lost $200 million for the year.

Although Salomon had for years delivered outsize profits on its arbitrage bets, Dimon and Weill began to sense that maybe the jig was up. With a number of defections from Salomon, most prominently John Meriwether and his team at the powerful hedge fund Long-Term Capital Management, other firms were using similar if not identical strategies, with the inevitable result that the arbitrage opportunity was shrinking. This, in turn, meant that the risk-return trade-off on the unit's big bets was heading in the wrong direction.

The arbitrage group's members had also done a surprisingly poor job of ingratiating themselves with their new bosses. In his insightful indictment of financial innovation, *A Demon of Our Own Design*, Richard Bookstaber recalls a series of meetings in which the heads of Salomon's proprietary trading—Rob Stavis, Costas Kaplanis, and Sugar Myojin—were tasked with making Weill, Dimon, and Travelers' CFO Heidi Miller comfortable with their strategies and positions. At the end of a meeting in the anteroom between Weill and Dimon's offices on the thirty-ninth floor of the Greenwich Street building, Stavis for some reason took it upon himself to demand that everyone—Sandy Weill and Jamie Dimon included—return the presentation books he'd used, given the proprietary nature of the information within. Dimon turned and threw his on the table with a dismissive shrug. But Weill ignored the request and walked out of the room. The Salomon swashbucklers weren't dealing with Deryck Maughan anymore; they were dealing with Sandy Weill and Jamie Dimon.

Their new masters weren't sure they even trusted the group. At the turn of the year, for example, both Weill and Dimon were getting nervous about Russia—its lawlessness, its nuclear threat, and the prospect that it might default on its debt. But their exhortations to draw down Salomon's Russian exposure never seemed to be put into action. In a meeting with the arbitrageurs in June, recalls Bookstaber, Dimon was more forthright. Holding his hand up, thumb and forefinger nearly touching, he barked, "By our next meeting, I want our Russia exposure down to this." (His instructions were followed, and it proved a prescient decision. In July, Russia nearly defaulted, saved only by a $22.6 billion bailout organized by Secretary of the Treasury Bob Rubin, and on August 17, Russia actually defaulted on its domestic ruble debt.)

The last straw came soon thereafter, when the fact emerged during a risk management meeting that the unit had somehow found itself with an outright bet on the direction of the yen worth $1 billion. Dimon had previously told the group it was forbidden to make outright bets, and was to restrict itself to relative value trades—buying one security while selling short a similar one simultaneously—and he was understandably furious. At this point, the group's fate was sealed. The group members were completely ignoring their boss's orders, or they were incompetent. Either way, they had lost the faith of Travelers' top management.

On the Monday of the July Fourth weekend, Dimon summoned the arbitrage group and informed its members that it was being disbanded. According to Bookstaber, Dimon was succinct. "The following will be released to the press in five minutes," he said, before reading a press release announcing the group's dissolution. Members of the unit had one month to decide if they wanted to stay on at the company or take a severance package. And then he left. The headline of a column by Floyd Norris of the *New York Times* put it simply: "They Bought Salomon, Then They Killed It."

Dimon offers a nuanced explanation of the decision to close the unit down. He and others realized, he says, that the firm was duplicating trades in different business units. One trade on the government bond desk—so-called "on the run versus off the run Treasuries"—was replicated by the proprietary traders. Likewise in mortgages. Likewise in municipal bond arbitrage. And the proprietary desk was taking far larger gambles with the duplicate trades. "You get the guys in the other businesses that are working 60-hour weeks and the guys on the prop desk working 35 hour weeks," he recalls. "But who got preferential access to our balance sheet? The guys in arbitrage. Who got to use the shorts? Who got to use the hard-to-borrows? Who got the cheap financing? But it was the same trade over here. The other flaw was that the prop desk was motivated by the structure of their compensation deals to maximize their bets. Thank God we closed it. We lost more than $700 million, but it could have been multiples of that."

(Contrary to the image of Dimon as a perpetual cost-cutter, at the same time that he was reeling in the *fixed income* derivatives exposure, he was aggressively investing in building out Salomon Smith Barney's *equity* derivatives business. According to Bob DiFazio, cohead of the company's equities business, the business went from virtually zero revenues in the beginning of 1998 to a $400 million annual run rate shortly thereafter. Though Dimon wasn't around to enjoy the fruits of his labor, the unit was up to a $1 billion run rate by late 1999.)

The unwinding of the fixed income unit's positions contributed to the market's instability that summer, especially at Long-Term Capital Management (LTCM), which, having been founded by Salomon veterans, had on its books many of the same positions that Salomon was now vigorously selling. In fact, Dimon recalls, the Salomon arbitrage unit had only 10 material trading strategies it played around with. "With all the bullshit around it, there were just 10 trades," he recalls. "And they were the same 10 trades that LTCM had." (LTCM, in fact, was jokingly referred to by the Travelers crowd as "Salomon North.")

Long-Term Capital Management wasn't just any old hedge fund. Through the magic of leverage, it had turned $5 billion of capital into a $100 billion giant, and its sudden shakiness posed a threat to the entire market.

John Meriwether, the head of LTCM, called Dimon on August 25, proposing that instead of continuing to sell its positions, Dimon might continue combining the remnants of Salomon's arbitrage group with LTCM. He was rebuffed, in part because Sandy Weill wasn't partnering with any hedge funds, let alone the teetering LTCM. The result was ironic. By avoiding doing business with LTCM, for fear of the hedge fund's instability, Weill and Dimon destabilized the entire market, endangering their own firm in the process. All of Wall Street was about to find out what traders meant by the well-known maxim that relative value funds "eat like chickens and shit like elephants."

· · ·

Dimon and Maughan, who had been openly hostile before the summer, were now engaged in full-scale warfare. Salomon was getting destroyed in the bond markets, and Dimon criticized Maughan at every turn. Although he himself had long enjoyed a special status as Sandy's favorite, Dimon disparaged Maughan's apparent attempts to ingratiate himself with both Weill and Reed.

Dimon also avoided Weill as much as possible during this time, choosing to stay primarily in his downtown office at Salomon Smith Barney in Tribeca, instead of the Citigroup Center headquarters in midtown. When Weill showed up in the Salomon Smith Barney offices, Dimon showed his resentment of Weill's presence. Maughan, on the other hand, was often found hanging around Weill's office in the Citigroup building, even though he had no role in the corporate group.

"Maughan jumped in Weill's back pocket from the get-go," recalls one staffer.

According to Weill, Reed also began to see Dimon in an increasingly negative light. Reed had once viewed Dimon as more of an intellectual peer than Weill—going so far as to invite Dimon and Judy to his home for dinner, as well as giving the younger man books and inviting him on a business trip—but now he began to be increasingly put off by Dimon's "constant carping."

In late August, when concerns over LTCM were on the front burner, Weill was worried that the company's exposure to hedge funds might put the merger—which had yet to close—in jeopardy. Weill demanded a meeting at Salomon Smith Barney to review the company's lending to various hedge funds. He wanted to reduce the number the company did business with from 500 to just 20. After originally trying to avoid a meeting altogether, Dimon reluctantly agreed to one in his own office, which was attended by Weill; Travelers' senior vice president of global development, Todd Thomson; and Salomon Smith Barney's fixed income head, Tom Maheras, and its chief risk officer, Dave Bushnell.

While the other four sat at a conference table in his office, Dimon purposely stayed behind his desk, a move one participant interpreted as "an obvious 'fuck you'" to Weill. Maheras led the group through a number of the firm's exposures, but when he declined to address the specific LTCM exposure—probably at Dimon's behest—Weill went ballistic, and appropriately so. With much of Wall Street exposed to LTCM, the fund's failure could prove catastrophic. "But Jamie was so caught up in the idea that Sandy was in his shorts, he couldn't have made a sensible judgment," remembers the participant. (Dimon's supporters say that this wasn't the case—that Weill didn't even understand the details and was just being difficult.)

It was then clear to most that the professional marriage had reached the breaking point. Each man had his own list of 50 or so grievances about the other. Dimon was warned by several colleagues, including Bill Campbell, Bob Lipp, and Arthur Zankel, that he needed to tone it down, that he was dancing too close to the edge. Dimon told all three men that he would make an effort to dial back his behavior, but he proved unable to do so in the end.

Making matters worse, the company's missteps were piling up. Despite its early selling, Salomon was taking a beating with the rest of the market, and had experienced about $360 million in trading losses through August. Travelers stock stood at just $30, about 40 percent below the price on the day the Citigroup deal was announced.

• • •

In the short term, however, Weill and Dimon's personal issues took a backseat to the crisis brewing at LTCM. John Meriwether, who just a few months before had been one of Wall Street's favorite clients— doling out fees of more than $100 million annually—couldn't find a shoulder to cry on. As Roger Lowenstein points out in his riveting account of LTCM's fall, *When Genius Failed*, "When you need money, Wall Street is a heartless place."

In a series of meetings at the Federal Reserve Bank of New York— meetings eerily foreshadowing those that would accompany the failure of both Bear Stearns and Lehman Brothers a decade later—Wall Street's top bankers tried to find a way to save LTCM, or at least save themselves in the ensuing market carnage. Weill attended one meeting, but Dimon and Maughan were the company's representatives in the final hours.

On September 23, 1998, 14 banks agreed to a capital infusion of $3.625 billion to keep LTCM from collapsing. All of Wall Street, it seemed, was on the hook—Bankers Trust, Barclays, Chase, Credit Suisse First Boston, Deutsche Bank, Goldman Sachs, Merrill Lynch, J.P. Morgan, Morgan Stanley, Salomon Smith Barney, UBS, Société Générale, Lehman Brothers, and Paribas—save for one glaring exception: Bear Stearns. Phil Purcell, then head of Morgan Stanley, is said to have blurted out, "It is not acceptable that a major Wall Street firm isn't participating." Merrill Lynch's chief, Herb Allison, agreed with this sentiment, asking Jimmy Cayne, the macho head of Bear Stearns, "What the fuck are you doing?" Cayne responded bluntly, "When did we become partners?"

The Federal Reserve was second-guessed for intervening in the capital markets, but it did stick to its historical prohibition against lending to nonbanking institutions. The Fed didn't bail out LTCM; the rest of Wall Street did. But it nevertheless crossed a line that had lingering ramifications a decade later, when Wall Street once again teetered on the edge. Orchestrating the bailout of LTCM was the original sin when it came to so-called moral hazard. The government had stepped in to facilitate the rescue of a bunch of capitalists gone mad. The next time that happened, Jamie Dimon would play a central role.

In retrospect, one can argue that by shutting Salomon's fixed income arbitrage desk, Weill and Dimon shot themselves in the foot; the unit's liquidation made it nearly impossible for LTCM to find buyers for many of the same positions in that summer's turbulent markets. "Who," points out Richard Bookstaber in *A Demon of Our Own Design*, "wants to buy the first $100 million of $10 billion of inventory knowing another $9.9 billion will follow?" In other words, in trying to trim its risk, Travelers just might have sent the *entire market* into a tailspin. Worse, once LTCM began begging for help, it was forced to open up its books to competitors, some of whom proceeded to ramp up their trading against the fund's positions, further crippling the market.

Then again, the pervasiveness of LTCM was really a result of long-term creep, as the hedge fund had extended its tentacles into nearly every firm on Wall Street, setting up, with practically any dealer of note, derivatives contracts that came to total a staggering $1 trillion of exposure. That is, it was everybody's fault for not paying attention soon enough to the possibility of a "fat-tail" event—the unlikeliest of outcomes that nevertheless do occur, usually with traumatic results.

(At the height of its power, LCTM had also demanded of its Wall Street patrons that it be required to post no collateral whatsoever on its trades. The competition for LTCM's business was so intense that almost all its customers agreed to this stipulation. Warren Buffett did the same thing in 2008, and many of the same firms once again lined up to violate principles of fiscal prudence. Wall Street does not learn its lessons easily.)

"If Long-Term defaulted," observes Lowenstein in *When Genius*

Failed, "all of the banks in the room would be left holding one side of a contract for which the other side no longer existed." Excessive monetary liquidity had pushed LTCM to ever-greater risks, and when the market slammed into reverse, a classic liquidity crisis resulted—all sellers and no buyers. Dimon later admitted to *Fortune* magazine, "We simply missed it." The result of that miss was a $1.33 billion fixed income trading loss in the third quarter of 1998 for Salomon Smith Barney. It might have been much worse: the bank had successfully dodged the Russian mess and had also pulled back from LTCM-related exposures earlier than it otherwise might have. Still, a $1.33 billion loss is a pretty convenient excuse if you're looking to fire someone, and that is exactly what Sandy Weill was looking to do.

Regardless of what he felt as mistreatment at the hands of Sandy Weill, Dimon did not allow May 1998 to pass without making a magnanimous gesture. That year was his fifteenth wedding anniversary, and he gave his wife a full third of his net worth as a present. At dinner with both her and the children, he handed her a rolled-up stock certificate, saying, "You deserve this; it's yours." Whereas many of her friends still needed to go through their spouses to buy or do something, Judy Dimon was now free to do as she pleased. Long used to treating his wife as an equal, Dimon had (nearly) made her his financial equal as well.

(The Dimons give generously from their family foundation as well as from their personal accounts. Jamie also gives gifts above and beyond annual bonuses to the people with whom he works closely, including his driver. And just like Sandy Weill, he has tried to spread stock ownership through every company he's run, from top to bottom, driven by a desire to see his colleagues get rich along with him.)

• • •

The events of the fall exacerbated the conflicts between the tri-CEOs at the corporate bank. By September, it became increasingly clear that Dimon and Maughan were unable to work together, let alone with Menezes, who had become relegated to a virtual sideshow. Maughan had begun deriding the setup as a "hydra," and Dimon increasingly found decisions made by Maughan, Weill, and others around him to be "stupid." "It was a sorry spectacle," Weill wrote in his autobiography. The men practically begged Weill and Reed to make a change, any change, just as long as it altered the status quo.

This history of shared power arrangements on Wall Street suggests that in their inability to get along, Dimon and Maughan were hardly unique. Jon Corzine and Hank Paulson were unable to do it at Goldman Sachs. Phil Purcell and John Mack likewise failed at Morgan Stanley Dean Witter. Before he died in 2008, Primerica's founder Gerry Tsai told a reporter about one of the favorite maxims he'd learned from the president of Fidelity, Edward Johnson II: "Do it by yourself. Two men can't play a violin." And here was Dimon, who along with Weill had excepted up the detritus of Tsai's career, facing nearly the same issue, only worse. He was being asked to play a violin as part of a trio.

Although Dimon quite possibly assumed that he would eventually work his way through this predicament and reclaim his position as Weill's heir, he was clearly playing with a weaker hand now than in years past. In any event, he was ordered to come up with a plan to share power, but he, Maughan, and Menezes consistently reported back that they could agree on nothing of the sort. In other words, they were refusing to do their masters' bidding.

Dimon had a number of fundamental problems he failed to recognize. He and Weill had always proved capable of somehow finding their way to conclusions that worked to the advantage of the company, but in recent years Weill had acquired the dreaded CEO disease, which made him unable to hear anything but what he wanted to hear. Maughan easily grasped that, but Dimon couldn't adjust to it. Worse, Sandy had other courtiers, including the general counsel Chuck Prince. (Mary McDermott, Weill's longtime head of public relations, remembers Prince as "the quintessential ass-kisser" during this time.) Finally, Dimon's constant nay-saying also hurt him in Reed's eyes, especially considering the nonconfrontational ethos Reed had so meticulously instilled at Citicorp.

Trouble would come, but first, there was celebration. On September 23, the Federal Reserve approved the merger of Travelers and Citicorp, which closed on October 8. Although the combined Citigroup's earnings fell 53 percent that quarter from the year before, the LTCM bailout had seemingly staved off a market collapse. Their creation would live to fight another day.

But perhaps Dimon would not. During Sandy Weill's annual apple picking day at his Greenwich estate that year, Frank Bisignano, head of operations and information technology for the corporate and investment bank, noticed that Dimon was forced to leave early, as he was flying somewhere that evening but had forgotten a pair of shoes. "Why doesn't he just borrow a pair of dress shoes from Sandy?" Bisignano wondered. And then it hit him—because Sandy wouldn't lend them if Dimon had asked. "This thing has reached DEFCON 5," he realized,

8. EVERYTHING BUT KILIMANJARO

At the moment of their greatest triumph, the 15-year partnership between Jamie Dimon and Sandy Weill collapsed in a way that almost nobody could have predicted. After repeatedly proving himself to be a man with judgment and intellect beyond his years, Dimon was shown the door for behaving like a petulant teenager. Not that it was entirely his fault. In the immediate aftermath of the merger of Citi and Travelers, Weill openly tested his protégé, as if all their years of working closely together had meant nothing. Perhaps if Dimon had been able to consider this a momentary phase in their relationship—as perhaps it was—he might have been able to restrain his worst instincts. But that's not what happened.

Shortly after the merger closed, Sandy Weill and John Reed convened a management meeting in Armonk, New York. The topic was supposed to be about integrating the two companies, but the subject that dominated the proceedings was the same one they had been hung up on for months: how to split one job, the head of the corporate investment bank, among three men—Jamie Dimon, Deryck Maughan, and Victor Menezes. Weill handled it poorly. Like a scolding parent, he ordered the three men into a conference room and told them not to emerge until they had a solution. This worked out about as well as can be imagined. The only thing they managed to agree on was that a tri-head structure simply could not work.

On the weekend of October 24, 1998, the combined company held a five-day retreat for 150 top executives and their spouses at Greenbrier, the luxury resort in White Sulphur Springs, West Virginia. There was serious business to be conducted—they were attempting the largest corporate integration in the history of financial services—but it was also intended to be a festive occasion, a celebration of the record-breaking deal. However, there was almost no good cheer among the Salomon Smith Barney crowd, and much of the event was marked by quarreling. At one meeting, Smith Barney's capital markets chief Steve Black openly quarreled with Maughan about how best to manage the company's corporate and investment bank unit. At this point, Dimon played the peacemaker, stepping in to quell heated emotions.

During presentations by various business heads, Weill recalls being struck by the difference between a polished presentation by Maughan and an "incoherent" one by Dimon, including "a strange analogy with the Peloponnesian War." Weill felt that Dimon's apparent lack of preparation was insulting and that as a result Dimon seemed anything but "presidential." Dimon's memory about the quality of his presentation is hazy, but the suggestion that his career could be judged on one presentation at an executive retreat rankles. "Maybe I didn't give a good presentation," he says. "But do you think it's acceptable to judge a 15-year career on one presentation?"

Rather than take command of the deteriorating situation and pull everyone together, Weill seemed to purposefully dial up the tension. At a group dinner, he asked those attending to name the persons who would succeed them in their roles at Citigroup. Neither Dimon nor Maughan mentioned the other; and, even more pointedly, Weill himself didn't offer an answer. Steve Black showed the most visible signs of the growing unease. Dimon had long ago told Black that he planned to embrace the Salomon people come hell or high water, because he wanted to make the merger work. In turn, Dimon had asked Maughan to "put his arms around Steve and make him comfortable." Instead of doing that, Maughan did the opposite, once inviting Black out for dinner only to tell him that he didn't give a damn about Black's future, that the only people who mattered were Dimon and Maughan. Black, Maughan made clear, was a fool for hanging around. Then, during a black-tie ball on Saturday, October 24, Dimon and his wife, Judy, sat with Steve Black and his wife, Debbie. In a gesture that could have moved things in another direction entirely, Black turned to Debbie and told her that as a peace overture he was going to ask Maughan's wife, Va, to dance. The couple went over together to where the Maughans were dancing, and he politely cut in. Maughan, however, failed to return the gesture, leaving Debbie Black standing alone on the dance floor. Embarrassed, she began to cry.

As if that weren't sufficiently "high school," the situation quickly degenerated further. After comforting his wife, Black lost his temper, marching over to Maughan—who is not a small man, standing about six foot three—and seized him by the flesh of his arm. "You fucking asshole," he said. "You can do whatever you want with me, but if you ever do something like that to my wife again, I will drop you where you stand." Expecting a fight, Black was surprised when Maughan simply turned and walked away.

Black had momentarily forgotten who wore the pants in the Maughan family. Moments later, an enraged Va Maughan—a healthy Hawaiian with Samoan ancestry who was nearly as large as her husband—came steaming across the dance floor headed right for him. Sticking her finger in his chest, she said, "Don't you ever talk to my husband like that again. You can't talk to my husband like that."

At this point, Dimon tuned in. "What was that all about?" he asked Black after Va Maughan had retreated. After hearing Black's side of the story, Dimon himself became enraged and went off to find Maughan. "Deryck," he said, upon tracking Maughan down, "if you snubbed her by accident, explain it. If you did it on purpose, that's a whole different thing." Once again, Maughan responded by turning away, at which point Dimon grabbed him and spun him around, tearing a button from his jacket in the process. "Don't you ever turn your back on me while I'm talking!" he shouted.

"You popped my button!" was all Maughan offered in reply.

Weill writes that he and his wife, Joan, had been sitting in the bar with Bob Lipp and Jay Fishman and their wives when the Maughans entered and explained what had just happened. Va Maughan said to Sandy, "This is no way for people to behave. How are you going to react to this? If this company doesn't think this sort of stuff is important, it may not be the kind of place at which we want to work." (Va Maughan did not work at Citigroup, but she apparently thought she did.)

Nobody came out of the night's events looking good—not Black, not Dimon, not Maughan. And all three paid a steep price. (Judy Dimon looks back on the entire weekend as something of an out-of-body experience, the kind of thing you can't bring yourself to believe is actually happening.)

Later that evening, Weill had Bob Lipp, Jay Fishman, and Mike Carpenter come back to his cabin to review the incident. The question was one nobody had ever dared consider before, let alone verbalize. Was it time for Dimon to go? Lipp, who'd worked with Dimon and Weill the longest, tried to defend his friend, to no avail. He was outnumbered. Weill was sick of Dimon. Fishman, once a Dimon acolyte, had never forgiven him for making Miller CFO. And Mike Carpenter, though no enemy of Dimon's, had only recently joined the company.

Weill wrote in *The Real Deal* that only at three o'clock that morning, when he was alone with Joan, did it finally dawn on him that Dimon must leave. But his retelling lacks credibility. Weill had played a Machiavellian game with Dimon for several years; the appointment of Maughan as co-CEO was merely the last in a series of moves that, if not explicitly designed to frustrate Dimon, had the effect of fraying their relationship. Weill simply refused to acknowledge how his own behavior had provoked Dimon.

The next morning, most Citigroup executives still did not know what had happened. When Charlie Scharf and his wife showed up in the lobby, happy and chipper, he couldn't get a read on the mood. "It's like a morgue in here," he told his wife. Once the two were in a car on the way to the airport, he was told about the near-brawl.

• • •

Once he had decided on a course of action, Weill moved expeditiously. He called Reed, who was flabbergasted at hearing of Dimon's behavior. The two men finally accepted what their tri-CEOs had been trying to tell them for months, that something had to give. On Monday, October

26, Weill and Reed asked Citigroup's general counsel Chuck Prince to conduct an "investigation" into the incident and to report back by the end of the week. On Monday and Tuesday, Dimon remained in his downtown office at Salomon Smith Barney. He and Weill had a single, brief phone conversation, during which Weill determined that Dimon had no plans to apologize for his actions. But the point was academic. Prince, ever the yes-man, gave his new boss exactly what Weill had wanted, concluding that Dimon had been in the wrong.

Equally important, the spectacle of his executives fighting like schoolchildren was all a man like John Reed needed to entirely change his opinion of someone. Reed is a man for whom cordiality, no matter how phony, must be maintained at all costs. Any misgivings he had about the merger with Travelers were precisely about the possible coarsening of the Citicorp culture. The last thing he wanted to do was turn over the institution he had nurtured to a bunch of hooligans. "Jamie has become an impediment to making this merger work," Weill said to Reed. "We've got to ask him to leave." Reed, never known for his warmth, delivered a stone-cold response: "You're absolutely right. Jamie's got to go." Weill had the backing he needed. (Lipp told Weill that he was acting rashly and that he should give the situation six more months. But Weill overruled him.) Weill later wrote that his relationship with Reed reached its zenith at this moment. Reed, after all, had given him the support he needed to make one of the biggest decisions of his life. A less charitable interpretation is that Weill, the master manipulator, had used Reed as a pawn in his endgame with Jamie Dimon. For all his intelligence and drive, Dimon was also predictable. Push the right button—such as giving him *yet another* co-this or co-that—and he would get angry. For Dimon, the co-CEO positions were an annoyance not just because he had to share power, but also because he believed them to be an inefficient way to manage. Push another button—like Weill's asking his executives to name their successors—and you have a man ready to crack. And crack he did.

Remarkably, Dimon failed to see it coming. He did not grasp that his time at Citigroup was coming to a close. On Friday evening, October 30, he sat in his office with his assistant Theresa Sweeney and asked her what changes she thought would come out of a management meeting in Armonk on Sunday. It was his belief that at the meeting the management structure would finally be adjusted to his advantage. Still, while a part of him assumed that things would work out as they always had, with Dimon getting his way and another incompetent partner removed from his orbit, another part of him was concerned. The previous week had been a conspicuously quiet one. Sweeney told him she hoped Weill would make him sole CEO of the corporate investment bank, so that he could get on with the work that needed to be done. Dimon seemed to hope the same. Unaware that his own ouster was in the works, Dimon invited 100 Salomon Smith Barney brokers to his Park Avenue apartment on Sunday for brunch on his expansive terrace. As the brokers trickled in, he sat around in a Smith Barney tracksuit. Then Weill called, asking him to come up to Armonk early. Dimon replied that because of the brunch, he couldn't leave at the very moment, but that he would be there as soon as he could.

Dimon eventually drove up to Armonk and walked unwittingly into his own execution. Weill and Reed sat him down in a small conference room. "We've done a lot of thinking about the organization just as you want and John and I have decided to make the following changes," said Weill. "Deryck is going to move to a strategy job, Victor will take the Global Bank, and Mike Carpenter will run Salomon Smith Barney." That last one threw Dimon for a loop, as that was *his* job. But Weill wasn't quite done. "And . . . we want you to resign."

Dimon offered only a one-word reply: "OK." Weill asked him if he wanted to know why. "Nope," replied Dimon. "I'm sure you thought it through." Reed was stunned. "Is that it?" he asked. "Well, yeah," replied Dimon. "You've obviously decided."

Despite his shock, Dimon agreed to stick around, and sat down in a larger conference room with Prince to finalize the press release announcing his departure. (Prince would also negotiate his severance agreement.) While they were waiting for the other executives to show up, Bob Lipp came into the room with tears in his eyes and gave Dimon a hug. Dimon also took a moment to call his wife. "Judy, I'm going to tell you something and please, please, don't tell me I'm making a joke," he said. "They asked me to resign, and I resigned." He then told her he'd be home as soon as he could. Leaving the conference room, according to *Tearing Down the Walls*, Dimon bumped into Maughan, who had just been told of his own fate. "Best of luck to you," Dimon said. "And to you," Maughan replied.

At about 2:00 that afternoon, Theresa Sweeney's home telephone rang while she was mowing the lawn. Her husband told her that Judy Dimon was on the phone. When Sweeney said hello, Judy Dimon said gravely, "Theresa, they've gotten rid of him." Sweeney's response: "Well, Deryck Maughan really needed to go." When Judy Dimon corrected Sweeney, her face went white, and her husband had just enough time to shove a chair beneath her to prevent her from falling to the floor.

Back in Armonk, once the entire executive team had gathered, Reed got to the point. "Jamie is resigning," he said. Sandy Weill didn't say a single word. (Dimon interpreted this as Weill's attempt to have former Travelers executives think it was Reed's decision and not his own. If so, it was not successful.)

Monica Langley writes that Dimon then addressed the assembled group. "Look, I've been with this company for fifteen years," he said. "I put my heart and soul into it. I want to tell you it's a fabulous place. Keep on making yourself proud." No one knew what to say, and so no one said anything. "I am sorry it didn't work out," Dimon continued. "I know that I have some blame for it. If I can help anybody, that's what I'm here to do. I still love this company. It has an incredibly fantastic future. You are all friends of mine, and I wish you the best." He was given a standing ovation.

He then walked out of the room. Weill followed. "You've been very gracious and nice," he said. "I still respect and love you." To which Dimon replied, "Look, Sandy, I don't know what to say."

"I'm sorry it had to come to this," Weill said, and moved to hug him.

"No hugs, please," said Dimon, recoiling. He walked from the room and went home.

After pulling off one of the largest mergers in history with Weill, Dimon set a dubious record of his own. His was, quite possibly, the shortest tenure on record of a president at a Fortune 500 company. He'd held the title for less than a month. He was only 42 years old. (In 2009, a questioner at a presentation to investors referred to Dimon's having "been present at the gluing together of Citigroup." His response: "I'm not sure that was glue. Maybe it was gum and paper clips. And I should remind you that I was fired 30 days after that deal was completed.")

For the first time in his career, Dimon had lost a power struggle. In an article the previous year—"How Long Can These Two Tango?"—*Business Week*'s writers had said that in the event of conflict, "the betting is that Dimon will ultimately prevail." This conclusion was based on his historical ability to remove those he felt were holding the company back—Zarb, Plumeri, Greenhill. But the journalists at *Business Week*, like almost everyone else at the time, had failed to understand the complexities of Dimon's and Weill's relationship. For all his deal-making prowess, Weill was a deeply insecure man who was not ready to share his moment at the top, not even with his most trusted soldier.

• • •

According to a later story in *Fortune* magazine, Dimon arrived home about 5:30 P.M. Judy, in tears and in a state of shock, met him at the door. "What did you do that was so bad?" she asked.

The couple gathered the girls in the kitchen. "Girls, I resigned today," Dimon told them. Then he corrected himself. "I was fired."

Kara, then nine, the youngest, asked the first important question: "Will we have to move?"

"No," her father said.

Laura, 11, the middle daughter, was next: "Will we be able to go to college?"

"Yes," her father said.

Then Julia, 13, cut to brass tacks: "Can I have your cell phone?"

At 6:00 P.M., Dimon participated with Weill and Reed in a conference call with the press. The three men explained that problems integrating the corporate businesses at Salomon Smith Barney and Citicorp had resulted in a need for a new management structure. It was one, however, that didn't give Dimon the authority he desired, and so it was mutually agreed that he would leave the firm. Even in defeat, Dimon loved the company he had helped build so much that he allowed its officers to lie about his reasons for leaving.

• • •

The stock market didn't take the news well. Whether because of concern that the merger wasn't going well or merely as an affirmation of Dimon's value to the firm, the stock price fell 2 percent that day, even though the Dow Jones industrial average climbed 114 points. At $46.13, the stock now sat 36 percent below its summer peak of $72.63. (Shares of J.P. Morgan jumped 10 percent that Wednesday, owing to rumors that Dimon was about to join the company.) By December, the value of the combined Citigroup had fallen from $165 billion to $108 billion.

Equity analysts were shocked by Dimon's ouster. Thomas Hanley of Warburg Dillon Read downgraded Citigroup's shares to "hold" from "buy" because of "increased organizational risks." Two other analysts also downgraded the stock, and still others voiced concern while maintaining their existing ratings.

The brokerage force at Salomon Smith Barney wasn't happy about the outcome, either. Weill anticipated this, and had buttonholed Jay Mandelbaum the next morning and asked for his advice on how to break the news to the company's brokers.

Weill was right to be concerned. After giving Dimon a standing ovation as he walked off the trading floor on November 2, brokers soon started leaving the firm in droves. In the immediate aftermath of the merger, there had been more departures on Citi's side than on Travelers' side, but after Dimon left, that switched. For all his brusqueness, Dimon engendered a fierce loyalty among those who worked for him. (Dimon's father, curiously, stayed on at Citigroup for several more years. But he laughs at the idea that he continued reporting to Sandy Weill even after Weill had fired his son. Ted Dimon Sr. reported to no one.)

The most prominent departure following Dimon's was that of Steve Black. In addition to being angry with Weill over the treatment of Dimon, Black was also steamed that he hadn't been given Carpenter's job. The very afternoon Dimon was fired, Carpenter informed Black that unless he got on board with the decision, he might as well start packing his bags as well. But Weill had a much subtler message for the 25-year veteran. Unless Black was prepared to tell colleagues that he *agreed* with the decision, he was no longer a welcome member of the team. "I'm not going to be disruptive," Black told Weill. "But if you're telling me that in order to stay here, I have to stand up in front of a large group of people and lie, I'm not going to do it. So maybe it's time for me to go as well." Realizing that Black was serious, Carpenter backtracked and spent the next several days trying to convince Weill that even though he had the knife out, he didn't have to get more blood on it. Maybe it was best to keep Black around. But Weill was adamant. A notorious worrier, he called Black late in the afternoon on Friday, November 6, clearly hoping to settle the matter so that it wouldn't ruin the weekend. "Twenty-five years is a long time, but if you can't get fully behind everything we're doing I think its time for you to go," he told Black.

Black replied that he thought Weill had fired Dimon for all the wrong reasons, and that he couldn't possibly stand in front of his colleagues and condone the move. Weill didn't budge. "Then it's time for you to go."

"Fine, I'm out. I'm done," Black retorted. On November 10, he resigned. Once again, Chuck Prince oversaw the severance negotiations.

On Monday, November 2, nearly 100 Salomon Smith Barney employees had gathered in a Tribeca establishment known as "Ponte's"— the Italian restaurant F. Illi Ponte, which called itself the "home of the angry lobster"—to bid Dimon adieu. The night of November 10, the same people reconvened for Black's good-bye. When the owner of the restaurant asked Theresa Sweeney how things were going at Salomon Smith Barney, she replied, "If you see us here next Monday, it's not going very well." (Sweeney chose to leave the firm along with Dimon.)

Dimon felt horrible that Black was in some sense collateral damage of his own battle with Weill. "I respect Steve's loyalty, but I told him to do what was right for himself," he recalls. "I felt terrible for him. I didn't want him to lose his job and career out of thinking he was protecting me, because there wasn't anything I could do anymore."

On December 29, the financial website TheStreet.com awarded

Dimon third place in its list "Top 10 Bad Byes of 1998." His award was called "The Son I Never Had."

. . .

Speculation erupted all over Wall Street about just what exactly had led Weill to make such a monumental choice, one that has, over the years, come to seem ever more rash and ill-conceived.

Weill ultimately came to view the conflict in very simple terms: Dimon was ready to be CEO, and Weill wasn't ready to retire. Weill's wife, Joan, said much the same thing in Weill's autobiography. "The problem was that Sandy was too young to step aside, so the mentoree couldn't get past the mentor," she told Weill's collaborator, Judah Kraushaar. Unable to resist another twist of the knife, she went on to say, "There's a reason that people like Frank Zarb and Bob Greenhill left the company. They all complained about Jamie being headstrong." Asked whether that was a fair assessment, Zarb responds, "Not true at all."

Dimon also saw the conflict between him and Weill in uncomplicated terms. "I stuck my finger in Sandy's eye," he told the *New York Times Magazine* in 2000. More than a few colleagues see the situation as resulting from an escalation of a certain pattern. Jamie did the work, Zarb got the glory; Jamie did the work, Greenhill got the glory; then along comes Deryck Maughan, and Dimon is asked to share once again, not only with Maughan but also Victor Menezes of Citicorp. "I don't know how many times you can go to that well before the well rebels," says one executive.

In his autobiography, Weill tries to argue that Jamie Dimon was never his heir apparent. Most knowledgeable sources consider that revisionist history. "He should have been a Soviet," one said after reading the passage. "You sit there and go, 'What? Are you kidding?' But Sandy says some things enough times that he actually starts to believe them."

Weill steadfastly maintained that the fallout over his daughter's departure had nothing to do with Dimon's firing. But he also suggested that Dimon had lost Joan's backing as a result of the way Jessica had been treated. In the end, though, Weill maintains that he simply could no longer put up with Dimon's flagrant displays of disrespect. "Jamie had annoyed me to no end over the last three years, and our relationship had gotten so dysfunctional that it plainly was hurting others in our company," he wrote in *The Real Deal*. "Still, I felt sick given all that we had accomplished together. Jamie had wanted me to treat him as an equal partner, a desire for recognition [that] I understood but was unwilling to satisfy. I was nearly twenty-five years his senior and . . . his demands for equal treatment were disproportionate with what he deserved."

Weill went on to chide himself for nothing more than a failure to teach. "I brought Jamie along quickly and in doing so probably gave him a sense of entitlement which discouraged him from building a consensual management style," he wrote. "My real mistake, though, was that I repeatedly missed the chance in our early years together to curtail his aggressive behavior and mentor him into becoming a team player." Weill was not alone in that sentiment. There were many who thought that Dimon might not have what it took to be a true leader, in large part because of his temper. (Dimon would suggest that his problem was not that he was not a team player—he worked extremely well with the likes of Bob Lipp, Bob Willumstad, Marge Magner, and even Chuck Prince—but that the relationship between him and Weill was the issue.)

Eight years later, in late 2008, Weill had begun to voice regret. "I had no doubt what Jamie could achieve," he said. "I loved working with him. I loved the relationship we had and I feel terrible that it's not what it could've been. I am very proud of what he's doing."

Mary McDermott, Citi's communications chief, was on vacation in Italy when she heard of the firing. Sitting in the Grand Hotel in Florence, she found herself crying her eyes out. Weill later asked her to call *Fortune* magazine's influential columnist, Carol Loomis, to say that it was the hardest thing he'd ever done in his life. Loomis's blunt reply: "But he did it, didn't he?"

Both men should have faced up to their issues earlier. Weill might have stood up to Dimon more forcefully earlier than he did. Having been unclear about succession, he must have known the frustration he was causing his protégé. It was entirely reasonable that some loyalists fed Dimon's ego, in hopes of plum roles when the succession actually came to pass. Dimon might also have come to terms with Weill's inability to let go and perhaps left the firm to strike out on his own before he was forced out.

To some colleagues, it seemed as if to Dimon it was all about Dimon, and nothing more. "When we got to the point of how Citigroup was going to be organized, the whole process was put on hold for three weeks because of Jamie," said one Travelers executive. "He wanted to be president. He wanted to run the corporate investment bank. He could be one or the other, but not both. And he held out for both. It had a lot to do with his ego, and his relationship with Deryck. 'I want this job! I want that job!' Everybody was thinking, 'Jesus Christ, man, we have just done this huge merger and all you are focused on is you?' It ground on him so much because he thought *he'd* made Sandy, so he didn't understand how this was happening to him." (Dimon categorically denies this account, and insists that he didn't even want the title of president of the parent; he thought it a dumb title, especially when he had a real one running Salomon Smith Barney.)

In retrospect, what happened is simple enough. Dimon was endangering Weill's ability to successfully integrate the two companies and to add to his ever-growing reputation. And when it came to the short strokes, Sandy Weill was always about himself—all the way back to Cogan, Berlind, Weill & Levitt—and no one, not even Jamie Dimon, was going to stand in his way. Dimon was only the latest, and most prominent, in a long line of Sandy Weill casualties. The only differences were that Dimon had more talent and capability than anyone Sandy had ever roughed up before, and that they had shared the longest and deepest relationship. In the process, Weill lost the last person who worked for him who stood up to him, costs be damned. "I always think of Jamie at Citigroup," recalls Bob Willumstad, "as being the guy who would say what everyone else was thinking."

From Dimon's perspective, it's important to understand that his confidence in his own instincts made it nearly a given that he wasn't going to be satisfied with being a great assistant coach. Yes, Sandy Weill did have the vision. And yes, Jamie Dimon was the operations guy. After the Citicorp merger, though, there was nothing left to do but integrate the two companies. Dimon could be forgiven for coming to the conclusion that the company was no longer in need of Weill's particular skills but desperately in need of his own. And if that had been the case, why shouldn't the title have come along with the job?

Richard Bookstaber, author of *A Demon of Our Own Design*, considers the move one for the history books. "If somebody were to list the most costly single business decisions in the history of time, one would be the purchase of AOL by Time Warner," he says. "That destroyed more value than anything else. Another thing was Sandy firing Jamie. I can't envision that Citi would be in the problem it was in right now if Jamie had stayed there. That probably cost $200 to $300 billion. It's pretty amazing."

· · ·

What lessons Jamie Dimon took from Sandy Weill is a question that has preoccupied a lot of market commentators since Dimon's exit from Citigroup. Even though more than a decade has passed since they worked together, the business press never tires of rehashing the issue. It's an obsession best characterized by a post on the website Marketwatch.com in 2006: "Before Brad and Jen, there was Sandy and Jamie."

There has never been much debate as to whether Weill or Dimon possesses more raw intellectual firepower; it is Dimon, no question. Sandy Weill, on the other hand, is proof that you should never underestimate the man who overestimates himself—at least not when all the stars are aligned in his favor: cheap financing, a rising market, and a fawning business press.

That said, Weill surely passed on a number of crucial rules of running a business. The first: when you're doing M&A, do it quickly and efficiently, with no uncertainty. Weill could be ruthless in starting to clean house virtually the instant a deal was done, but it was an effective way to get everyone moving forward at once. "That's Sandy's drill," says Marge Magner, who stayed on at Citigroup until 2005. "It comes out almost automatically."

Weill also showed Dimon the benefits of taking the long view. As Weill showed in both phases of his career, when you worked with him it was almost impossible to view something as a stopping point. He was always thinking about what things *could* be. "Sandy gave him that whole concept of looking out and being opportunistic and knowing where you're going," recalls Joe Wright. Dimon, too, remains in awe of Weill's audacity. "To do the deals that we did?" he recalls. "I look back at those and think, 'God, Sandy, you had guts.' "

Weill also impressed upon Dimon the importance of getting your *entire* house in order, not just the shopwindow that customers see. When you're in a commodity business, the only way to thrive is to be a low-cost producer. And when you're selling money, you're in a commodity business.

Another long held Weill principle: know when to be capital rich. Both the economy and Wall Street have cycles, and he who is capital rich when the competition stumbles will see opportunities abound. Weill used this strategy to great effect in both stages of his career, and it allowed him to take over much larger companies with his smaller but more financially secure organizations. Too many discussions of both Weill and Dimon paint the two as risk averse. Neither is anything of the sort; rather, they have eschewed financial risks so that they might embrace strategic ones.

It's reductive, but the secret to Sandy Weill's success was no secret. As Dick Bove, at that time an analyst with the securities firm Ladenburg Thalmann, put it, "Buy businesses with significant cash flow, preferably at a discount, prune their expenses without sacrificing revenues, and then use that additional cash flow from those cuts to buy more companies until you end up owning Citigroup."

Dimon later said that he "learned a lot from Sandy Weill—including what not to do." Among the things not to do: hogging the spotlight so much that your senior team feels underappreciated. Heidi Miller told *Business Week* in 2005, "The Sandy mythology is so large that it often obscures the contributions that other people made."

"Sandy wasn't a mentor in the traditional sense," Dimon recalls. "In the sense of people giving you advice and sitting you down. That's what most people mean. I got none of that. Sandy was much more sink or swim and he just shed people left and right who didn't meet his standards, but it wasn't really a mentoring thing. He had a tremendous work ethic, and he was always thinking about how the world was going to change. He was brave and bold. I learned a tremendous amount from him."

"Jamie is the smartest man I ever worked with," recalls Dimon's former colleague Mary McDermott. "But Sandy had the best instincts. I guess that's why they worked so well together." Brian Posner echoed that sentiment. "Jamie is really about precision and knowing everything about everything," he says. "Sandy is much more conceptual, about the big picture."

Even if your business is your life, it's important to keep some distance between your work life and your home life. For Sandy Weill, there was no distinction, and that lack of clarity clouded important issues in the office, particularly when it came to his children. Although Dimon is both friends and friendly with his subordinates, he does maintain more distance than Weill ever did. And therein lies a profound difference between the two men. Sandy Weill *needs* to be liked. Jamie Dimon doesn't really care if you like him or not. Dimon will ask one or two employees to join him for drinks. Weill asks 300 people to his farm to pick apples.

"Throughout his career, Sandy could engage people in a way that was unique and made them feel good about themselves and what they were doing," recalls Jay Mandelbaum. "But Jamie has a different leadership approach, which is based more on his abilities, fairness, and directness. Sandy's a smart guy, but his success was often based more on how he related to people." Weill, was, and remains, a bit of a goofball. At a birthday party planned for him at The Four Seasons, the crowd listened to "I Heard It through the Grapevine" sung by a bunch of people dressed as grapes. That is not Dimon's style.

Asked in late 2008 what other rules of thumb he practiced in his career, Weill responded succinctly: "Don't fuck up." But that's precisely what he did in the fall of 1998.

• • •

Dimon wasn't exactly forced into penury when he was fired. He eventually reached a $30 million severance agreement, which included a three-year, three-phase noncompete that went far above and beyond the norm. (Black received $20 million.) Dimon was rich enough never to work another day in his life, but at 42, he was certainly not contemplating retirement. This was a man who, over the course of his 16 years following business school, had spent about 75 hours a week at work.

He was, however, completely demoralized by the turn of events. The weekend after his firing, Dimon and Judy attended a party at the home of their college pals Peter and Laurie Maglathlin in Darien, Connecticut. "He was devastated," recalls Laurie Maglathlin. "And totally blindsided. I really do believe that when he walked into that office he had no idea he was going to walk out without a job. And it wasn't about being humiliated, even though he had been. It was more about him being hurt and betrayed and saddened by it all." Jamie Dimon, friends say, is a man who *engages* in the project at hand, with all the focus he can muster. Tear anything away from him, and you'll throw him for a loop. Tear his life's work away, and you have done much more.

In a bizarre move, his former employer agreed to give Dimon temporary space in the Citigroup building itself. (He used a separate entrance from the Citigroup executive team.) For the next several weeks, all he and Theresa Sweeney did was respond to well-wishers—all manner of people called, up to and including Senator Charles Schumer—before transitioning into preparing and sending out the Dimon family's annual Christmas card and responding to hundreds of the same. "We were drowning in a sea of paper," recalls Sweeney, who estimates that they spent about eight weeks thanking people for wishing Dimon well.

Commuting to the building that Sandy Weill worked in did not sit well with Dimon. It didn't sit well with Sandy Weill, either. On a weekday in mid-January 1999, Theresa Sweeney picked up the office phone to hear Dimon on the other end. He told her to stand up and walk to the Park Avenue window. "You see that green patch between the lanes on Park?" he asked. "That's where we're going to be on Friday if we don't find a place to go." After just two months, he was being tossed out of the Citigroup building once and for all.

They didn't move far, only across the street. Dimon was going to set up shop in the Seagram Building, just as Weill had done after being tossed from American Express in 1985. (Dimon's wife noticed the irony in the move, but she kept the thought to herself.) He decorated his office with a white board, a boxing dummy, and a pillow that said, "My Next Boss Will Be Normal." He also had a pillow that said, "The Best Is Yet to Come." (A tough man with a lot of pillows.) Shortly thereafter, he and Weill found themselves in The Four Seasons at the same time. The two did not speak.

The firing sobered Dimon, taking him off the frenetic, overachiever's treadmill he'd been on since college. It was a position very similar to Weill's after his own ouster. "It was a strange time for him," Dimon had told Jon Friedman of *Business Week* in 1989, regarding Weill's time in the Seagram Building. "He had been running nonstop his whole working life." Dimon might have been speaking of himself in 1999.

The break gave Dimon more time to spend with his children, as well as time to talk with Judy about his firing. If Dimon was hurt at being cast aside, Judy was furious. "Even though Jamie was at peace with himself, I was a raging maniac because of the way he'd been treated," she recalls. Dimon constantly reminded his wife that it was his net worth, not his self-worth, that had been tied to the company. The latter, he said, was something Sandy Weill could never take from him. (Nor, for that matter, could Weill take his net worth, which by that point was quite substantial.)

Dimon leaned on Judy during his time off, and by all accounts, she was the right person at a tough time. Considered by friends the glue that holds the family together—a Harvard MBA herself, she willingly took over the role of head of household so Dimon could pursue glory with Weill and beyond—Judy Dimon was as important to Jamie Dimon as Joan Weill was to Sandy over the years.

Another rift opened between Dimon's mother, Themis, and Joan Weill. They'd been friends for 25 years, but following Jamie's departure from Citi, Themis did not speak to Joan for more than a year. Affection eventually returned to their relationship, but they would never again be as close as they had been.

Dimon cast himself as the victim in a Shakespearean tragedy, the prince who died because the king did not understand his own destiny. He told friends that he was stunned by his firing, that although he was certainly aware of the problems between him and Sandy, it had never occurred to him that they could outweigh his value to the company. "I never saw it coming," he later told the reporter Roger Lowenstein. "I thought one day we'd have a drink and work it out."

In February, Dimon filed with the Securities and Exchange Commission to sell 800,000 shares of Citigroup worth some $42.5 million—his participation in the blood oath had come to an end, and the separation was complete. Dimon also severed ties with most people he considered Weill partisans.

A board member of both the Mount Sinai–New York University Medical Center and the Center of Addiction and Substance Abuse (CASA), he spent some months during his forced sabbatical negotiating a bond sale for CASA when it was looking to purchase permanent headquarters in midtown Manhattan. The former Primerica board member Joseph Califano, head of CASA, watched with admiration as Dimon played two banks—Chase Manhattan and J.P. Morgan—off each other in the debt negotiations. Dimon extracted an all-in financing cost of just 3 percent annually over 20 years for CASA.

In his career, Jamie Dimon has been on the board of only one public company for which he did not work at the time. In 1999, when Andrall "Andy" Pearson, the chairman of Yum! Brands, asked him to join its board, Dimon accepted. "Andy is one of the truly exceptional businessmen I ever met," recalls Dimon. "He's in a category with Jack Welch and Warren Buffett. Andy was talking about some of the stuff Jack did at General Electric way before Jack did it. Stuff like training people, about discipline, about honesty."

(Dimon also puts Merrill Lynch's former CEO Daniel Tully in that group. When he and Tully traveled back and forth to Washington in 1996 during the settlement negotiations in the Nasdaq price-fixing scandal, Tully offered Dimon some words to live by that he's repeated on many occasions. "Son," Tully told the 40-year-old CEO of Smith Barney. "It's not just whether you tell the truth. It's whether you even *shave* the truth.")

Ever the disciplined goal-setter, Dimon made a list of things he wanted to do during his time off. One thing he did was read what he wanted to—not what he had to read for work—something he'd had little time for in the past decade. He began to do so voraciously, knocking down about two books a week, primarily history. "History is humbling and inspiring," he later told a reporter. "It puts you in your place." He read biographies of Caesar, Alexander, Napoléon, Nelson Mandela, and ten U.S. presidents, including George Washington and Abraham Lincoln.

(Dimon's reading taste runs to both business and history, but he'll read just about anything, from the memoirs of Ulysses S. Grant to Bill Bryson's 2003 best seller *A Short History of Nearly Everything*. He admires Grant particularly, he says, for the lucidity of the man's thinking. "They say his success on the battlefield boiled down to the sheer clarity of his orders," Dimon says admiringly. If he were making a list of books for the aspiring CEO, he would start with Shakespeare, adding *Built to Last* by Jim Collins and Jerry Porras, *Only the Paranoid Survive* by Intel's Andy Grove, Warren Buffett's annual letters, and Graham and Dodd's *Security Analysis*.)

Next on the list: boxing. Dimon had been a longtime runner and tennis player, but to work out some of his frustration, he began taking boxing lessons. More generally, he wanted to get back into shape. When asked if he was successful, Judy smiles and says yes. He also traveled. He took a trip to Denmark to visit his brother Peter, who spent eight years there. He took his daughters on an expensive, luxurious trip across major cities of Europe, including Paris, London, Rome, Florence, and Venice.

(Despite his hectic career, Dimon had made a point of going on vacations with the family on a regular basis. Over the years, he took three RV vacations with the girls to the Shenandoah Valley; up the east coast; and from Yellowstone to Yosemite through Sequoia National Forest, ending in Los Angeles. "People in the office seemed shocked that I knew how to drive an RV," he recalls. "I asked them, 'What do you think? That I bring my driver with me?'" As a family, they took weeklong vacations to Vail every year, as well as the Grand Canyon, the Green River, South Africa, and Greece's Turquoise coast.)

Under the list item "do things with Judy" he also agreed to try out a week at a Canyon Ranch spa in the Berkshires. He lasted three days. "I'd get up at 6:00 A.M., read the papers, go for a 10-mile run, come back, have a massage, and it would only be 10:30 in the morning," he recalls. "I lost like three pounds while I was there, but there was nothing else to do." Judy Dimon stayed the whole week.

James Long, Dimon's Harvard classmate—the two men were in each other's weddings—talked to him and heard about the list. When Dimon told him that one of the items on it was driving the Lewis and Clark trail, Long jumped at the opportunity to join him. Dimon flew to Billings, Montana, alone and drove to Portland, where he met up with Long. The two men then drove down the coast to San Francisco. In the end, Dimon accomplished everything on his list but climbing Mount Kilimanjaro.

He also made new friends. On a trip to Israel with a few U.S. executives, Dimon met Greg Brenneman, the young president and CEO of Continental Airlines. The men spent some time in the Knesset—the legislative branch of the Israeli government—with the president and prime minister, and also visited the king of Jordan. Dimon and Brenneman became fast friends, and have been available to each other as sounding boards over the years.

Dimon surprised not a few friends during this time with the thoughtfulness of his deliberations. Here he was, a lifelong workaholic, taking more time than anyone expected to plot out how best to spend the next decade or so of his career. Judy Dimon insists that her husband is not a workaholic. "He's just one of the most efficient men alive," she says. He might be one of the most thorough as well. He would not take a job until he had reviewed *all* his options.

• • •

The day after Dimon left Citigroup, Weill addressed Salomon Smith Barney's staff over the "squawk box," the intercom used on Wall Street trading floors. During the address, he opined that though he himself had been unable to find a job for 10 months after his ouster from American Express, he was sure that Dimon would be overwhelmed with job offers and would quickly find a new gig. Weill was right about the offers. By the time Dimon left Citigroup, he was one of the most celebrated executives in the country, and interest in hiring him was palpable. But Weill was wrong about the new job. It would be 16 months before Dimon made a decision about what to do next.

The list of companies that took a shot at luring Dimon is a lengthy one. For starters, there were the financial services companies—AIG, American Express, Deutsche Bank, Goldman Sachs, J.P. Morgan, and Barclays Bank in London. He turned down the last one, he said, because he didn't want to move his family to London. (He also told the Maglathlins that he preferred to work for an American company. Dimon was and remains a patriot.) The legendary hedge fund manager George Soros called.

Jon Corzine, who had recently been ousted from Goldman Sachs by Hank Paulson, called and asked if Dimon had any interest in perhaps buying the core of LTCM and using it as a platform to build a company in the spirit of the Blackstone Group, a financial services firm for the new millennium. "I'm either going to do this with you, Jamie, or run for a Senate seat in New Jersey. I haven't made up my mind yet."

"You're kidding me!" Dimon replied. He was intrigued, but it wasn't quite the right thing for him, either. "I always thought that was funny, though," Dimon recalls. "Because he did run, and he won."

The interest did not stop there. Starwood Hotels & Resorts was interested. Jeff Bezos tried to lure Dimon to Amazon.com, a tempting opportunity in early 1999, with the Internet frenzy still ongoing. "For a minute there, I had this fantasy of moving the family to Seattle. I was dreaming of being Tom Hanks on a big houseboat and I would never wear a suit again," he recalls. "But it just wasn't me. I like Jeff Bezos, but I'm a finance guy. It's like taking someone who has played tennis their whole life and telling them from then on they had to play golf. You have to relearn all these new skills. Plus, I wasn't sure I wanted to do that to my family, to move out to Seattle on a bit of a gamble." Priceline.com also came calling. So did Webvan. During his time off, Dimon looked at no fewer than 100 Internet companies, and concluded that only about 10 would survive. He decided the space wasn't for him.

Arthur Blank, the cofounder of Home Depot, also inquired. Despite not knowing his way around a toolbox, Dimon took the idea very seriously. (Over dinner with Dimon, his Harvard classmate Stephen Burke teased him about even considering the idea. "Have you ever even been in a Home Depot?" he asked the lifelong New Yorker. Judy Dimon felt the same way. "He felt like a foreigner in there," she recalls about a visit to a store.) He was offered the position of national finance chairman for Al Gore's 2000 presidential campaign, but turned it down.

Dimon made another list during his time off: potential occupations. It included teaching, politics, investing, sitting on boards, and retiring. And banking. (Speaking of banking, every day that he and Sweeney sat in their office in the Seagram Building, they looked out the window at Citigroup, the company he had helped build. They amused themselves by throwing rubber darts at the window.)

In April, four months after Dimon left Citigroup, Bill Campbell followed him out the door, frustrated by the same issue—too many chiefs—and rented his own office in the Seagram Building, a few floors beneath Dimon. Campbell often joined Dimon, Brian Posner, and Peter Freund (who had formerly been a derivatives expert at Bankers Trust) in Dimon's office to spitball about new ideas.

Dimon also kept in touch with a number of colleagues at Citigroup, but to a man they were actually afraid of provoking Sandy Weill by being seen with Dimon. The result was a lot of skulking around when it came time to see old colleagues like Jay Mandelbaum, Heidi Miller, and Charlie Scharf.

Dimon also thought a lot about a vision he had for melding discount and full-service brokerage. Although he came from a full-service background, he could not deny the success of Charles Schwab's discount operation, and he had his eye on earning the same kind of valuation from the stock market for a new kind of firm. After long bull sessions, the group at the Seagram Building opened a bottle of wine and stared at Dimon's whiteboard, envisioning the future. Over long dinners at the Della Femina restaurant in the Helmsley Building at 230 Park Avenue (now Bobby Van's), they did more of the same.

One day Posner found Dimon scribbling meticulously away on a single 8½ by 11 sheet of paper and asked him what he was doing. It was the list Dimon had kept for years, and he kept it still, despite not having a lot to do at that point in time. To this very day, he redoes the list every two days, once he runs out of space on the page.

Dimon gave Posner a piece of advice. "Rule number one," he said. "Return every phone call, every e-mail, within 24 hours. Especially now. Especially when you're out of work." Posner found Dimon religious about such things, about the necessity of conducting oneself in a certain way, and it made an impression on him that resonated for years.

Meanwhile, the honeymoon between Weill and Reed came to a swift end. By July 1999, the two men admitted that they were not getting along, and decided to split duties atop Citigroup. Reed took the "soft" ones—technology, legal, and personnel—and Weill maintained control of the company's financial and business operations.

On October 22, the Glass-Steagall Act was repealed. Reaching perhaps the height of his megalomania, Weill thought it prudent to issue a statement "congratulating" Congress and President Clinton for having done so. A mere three days later, Secretary of the Treasury Bob Rubin resigned his position and joined Citigroup as an adviser to the co-CEOs. Dimon, by this point, had found enough distance in the year since his firing to hit the lecture circuit. In a guest lecture at Columbia on the topic "The Trusted Lieutenant," he used more Shakespearean analogies. In a thinly veiled shot at Deryck Maughan, he told the students they must be vigilant about spotting the Iagos in their midst. Moving from *Othello* to *King Lear*, he also advised that the earl of Kent might have been more diplomatic while still being honest in his criticism of the king. In a later lecture at the 92nd Street Y, he told the audience he had every intention of returning to the financial services industry, and that he hoped to find a job he could focus on for the next 10 years.

That same month, *Fortune*'s Carol Loomis wrote an echo of a story she'd written 13 years before. The headline: "Exp'd Mgr, Fin'l Svcs, Seeks Position; Jamie Dimon Waits for the 'Fat Pitch.'" Loomis went on to call Dimon the most famous unemployed person in the country.

• • •

A year after his dismissal, Dimon was also ready to put his anger at Weill behind him. One morning in December, Theresa Sweeney noticed him shuffling around the office, walking back and forth in front of her desk. "What's going on? You're as nervous as a cat," she said. Dimon asked her to take a seat in his office. "I'm going to ask you to do something, and I don't want to hear one word about it again," he said. "I want you to get Sandy Weill's office on the phone. I want to talk to Sandy. I'm asking him out for lunch."

Like her boss, Sweeney had no love for Weill, but she did as she was told. She didn't want to speak to Weill, however, so when his assistant said that she would get him, Sweeney told Dimon to wait on hold himself. When Weill got on the phone, Dimon was brief. "Isn't it time we break bread?" he asked. Weill accepted the overture, and the two agreed to meet at The Four Seasons for lunch on December 16.

After hearing Dimon hang up, Sweeney picked up her purse and headed for the office door to go grab a coffee. She was enraged that he'd decided to make peace with the man who'd betrayed him so profoundly. Dimon was right behind her. "Aren't you going to say anything?" he said. "I can't believe you're not going to say anything." Not even bothering to remind him that he'd made her promise not to do that very thing, Sweeney replied, "Make sure the press knows that *you* initiated the call."

At lunch, Dimon opened the discussion by telling an obviously nervous Weill to relax. He then said that he wanted to talk about the past for two minutes, and two minutes only. "Sandy, I would never have done what you did," he said. "I don't think that you firing me was in the best interests of the company. But I want you to know that I share a lot of the blame. It doesn't make sense to apportion the share 60-40 or 40-60. I'm not sure it matters." Dimon then offered a list of his own mistakes. Weill's reply: "Thank you very much for saying that." A moment later, a half admission: "It takes two to mess up a relationship like we did." And that was it. The conversation turned to Dimon's job search and the state of the world.

The Four Seasons is a place to be seen, and seen they were. The next day, the *Financial Times* told the world of the rapprochement, under the headline "Season of Good Weill as Feud with Dimon Ends." ("It was pretty funny," Dimon recalls. "The front page of the paper said 'Heavy Russian Casualties in Chechnya, Record U.S. Trade Deficit, and . . . Dimon Has Lunch with Weill.")

Much of the credit for the thaw in relations was Dimon's. Even though he has always maintained that Weill did the wrong thing, he chose to swallow his pride and apologize to the man who fired him, a man, it should be pointed out, who could not bring himself to express an apology in return.

Still, at the start of 2000, it wasn't clear yet that Dimon would find that next job he sought in financial services. In January, he was among a consortium of investors who put $33 million into Lions Gate Entertainment. He invested with the former Goldman Sachs banker Christopher Flowers in Japan's Shinsei Bank—an extremely lucrative move. He briefly considered spending his time merely investing his own substantial fortune, but his heart wasn't in it. Dimon needed action, the ebb and flow of a real company doing real business. In the meantime, though, he was hanging around the Seagram Building, writing and erasing plans for the next great financial services company on his whiteboard with Campbell and Posner.

Then, one day, Dimon started apologizing to Campbell for wasting his time. "I'm not sure we're going to be able to do our little dream of creating a next-generation financial services firm right away," he said. "I think I'm going to take a job." Campbell laughed. "Jamie, stop apologizing," he said. "You're a young guy. Operating companies is totally different than doing deals. And you want to operate a company. It's a completely different undertaking. And you get a completely different payback."

9. THE OUTSIDER

During his hiatus, Jamie Dimon had been courted by some of the most respected companies in the country, but when it finally came time to commit, he went for a familiar type: another boring bank in another financial services backwater. As he had done with Sandy Weill 15 years before, Dimon had sniffed out a financial institution in distress that could be the platform on which to build an empire. Jamie Dimon had found his own Commercial Credit. It was called Bank One. And it was in Chicago.

Though it had austere roots going back to 1863, Banc One had evolved into a rather unsightly beast—a decentralized collection of regional banks built through a decade-long string of deals, the last significant one being the $29 billion combination of Banc One of Columbus, Ohio, and First Chicago NBD of Illinois. That deal had been completed in 1998, when the Travelers-Citicorp union set off a wave of consolidation in the industry. But neither institution had wanted to entirely cede its identity, so a compromise had been reached. The headquarters would be in Chicago and the partner from Ohio would provide the name (albeit with a *k* instead of a *c*).

Before Dimon arrived, the merger had largely failed to take. Though the institution ranked as the fourth-largest bank in the country, the combined operations were beset with problems from the start. The Ohio side had been a hodgepodge. Run by John McCoy, whose family had taken over City National Bank in Ohio in 1935 and had proceeded to make 130 acquisitions in 20 years, it had been built by means of a strategy that was as laissez-faire as any. Banc One's modus operandi had been the "uncommon partnership": competitors were bought up with the promise that they'd be allowed to just keep on doing what they were doing, so long as they signed on the dotted line. It was an attractive proposition to sellers, but the unfortunate result was that the company failed to take advantage of synergies or scale. It was the antithesis of the Weill/Dimon acquisition model.

First Chicago NBD, still struggling to complete a 1995 merger between First Chicago and Detroit-based NBD, wasn't in much better shape. Although it predated the great Chicago fire, the bank, which was primarily focused on corporate customers, had a shabby reputation for serving consumers. It desperately needed to get a leg up in the retail game, and its board saw a merger with Banc One as a means to that end.

To the banking community, the combination looked akin to two drunks leaning on each other to stay upright. In an increasingly competitive national landscape, for example, Banc One had a certifiably random collection of geographical strengths—Illinois, Louisiana, and Arizona—as well as disparate and incompatible systems. Then there was a pronounced clash between the entrepreneurial culture of Banc One and the buttoned-down tone at First Chicago. There had been a lot of turnover in the executive ranks. These problems were manageable as long as the numbers held up, but just a year after the union, the company fell short of Wall Street's earnings expectations for what would be the first of four quarters in a row.

The troubles were concentrated in First USA, the credit card unit which Banc One had bought for $8 billion in 1997 and which was in the process of imploding. The unit had mistreated its customers in the wake of the merger, jacking rates from 4.5 percent to 19.9 percent, for example, if they paid one day late more than once. Customers complained about rude service and being incorrectly docked for late payments— First USA was the worst-rated bank in terms of complaints in 1999, with three times as many as number two, which was Citigroup—and customers started to leave en masse. That year, a whopping 16 percent of them canceled their cards. Once the driving engine of the company's earnings, First USA had become a serious drag by the summer of 1999,

forcing McCoy to surprise investors with a preannouncement of negative earnings in August. The company's consumer lending and credit
card division, he told analysts, was likely to earn $500 million less than
expected.

McCoy's management style, much lauded by Wall Street when he
was on the way up, was now seen as a liability. His nickname became
"Fly-By McCoy." After the earnings surprise, he refused to cancel a European vacation, and the situation ultimately came to a head in November, when the company had to preannounce yet again. With the stock in
free fall—it tumbled from a high of $63 in May to half that—the board
ousted McCoy and replaced him on an interim basis with Verne Istock
from the First Chicago camp. Two board members—John Hall and
James Crown—became interim cochairmen and leaders of the search
for someone with a proven record of providing stability and coherence
to a company built by acquisition.

* * *

In his farewell speech to the company, McCoy said he hoped that it would
be able to attract a replacement such as Marc Shapiro, who had built and
then sold Texas Commerce to Chemical Bank, or Jamie Dimon. So even
though the executive search firm Russell Reynolds was hired to formally
conduct the process—it contacted some 150 people about the position—
Dimon's name was on the short list from the very start.

The only questions for the search committee: Was it prudent to hire
a man who'd just been fired by the reigning emperor of finance? And if
they could get past that, how on earth could they persuade the native
New Yorker to move his family to Chicago? Dimon's response when
he was first contacted about the opportunity wasn't encouraging:
"Chicago? . . . Chicago?" Contrary to the popular version of the story—
in which he showed up and wowed his prospective employer from day
one—Dimon had an initial meeting with the board of Bank One in Chicago for which he admits he was unprepared, a rare occurrence and
evidence of his noncommittal outlook at the beginning of the discussions. Luckily for him, his energy impressed the board, which kept the
discussions ongoing.

The first issue was settled in a series of meetings that began in November 1999, when Dimon first met with Charles Tribbett III and Andrea Redmond of Russell Reynolds, and culminated in a two-hour presentation Dimon made to the board in Chicago in late February. He had come to town with a list in his pocket of what he would do in his first 100 days on the job, much of it revolving around vigorous cost-cutting that included write-downs and layoffs. At this point, the board members understood that they needed a leader willing to do the deferred dirty work of integrating all their acquisitions, and Dimon blew them away with his focus and attention to detail.

James Crown, who had come back to Chicago to work for his family's investment business in 1985 after working for Salomon Brothers, called his own connections in New York for the "book" on Dimon—an extremely demanding boss, white-hot intelligence, did not suffer fools gladly, a strong leader who wanted a strong team. Although Dimon was known to be combative, Crown heard that he also welcomed being told he was wrong. Finally, and perhaps most important, Dimon refused to play office politics. He didn't give a whit where people came from and cared only that they had the ability to do the job at hand. For an institution paralyzed since its inception by two hostile camps, this was a major draw.

On the other question—whether Dimon would actually move to Chicago—the board members faced a challenge. He was already rich enough never to work another day in his life, so they couldn't necessarily tempt him with money. And although Chicago has its charms, asking any longtime New Yorker to move anywhere is a notoriously difficult proposition.

The board members understood that they might win by appealing to Dimon's strong desire to be his own boss and prove to the world that he was no mere Sandy Weill apparatchik. The question they put to Dimon was simple. What other major U.S. bank would be ready to bring in an outside CEO within the next five years? Citigroup was obviously off the list, and there didn't seem to be imminent job openings at the top of Bank of America, Wachovia, or Wells Fargo. If Dimon wanted back in the game, Bank One was his best shot. Dimon was sold.

Still, the board members had reservations. They were concerned about the effect of a hardened New Yorker on their proudly midwestern institution. And they certainly didn't want to be a mere vehicle for Dimon's larger ambitions, which would surely take him back to New York in due course. Dimon insisted that he was prepared to make a total commitment to the bank, but the board had heard that before. In the 1980s, First Chicago had hired Barry Sullivan as CEO, only to see him keep his residence in New York and commute to work. Midwesterners didn't much care for that.

Meanwhile, Dimon had to deal with his own family. Asking three teenage daughters to move to Chicago was no small request. In this, he proved to be as shrewd a manager as he was in the office. As the parent of three children, Dimon had discovered that it was important to spend chunks of time alone with each one, in order to bond. And so, when his daughters started complaining that they didn't want to move to Chicago, he proposed that the eldest of the three, Julia, then 15, accompany him on his next trip to see the board. They spent several days in Chicago; Julia even came to the Bank One office and attended the press conference announcing his hiring. Judy Dimon remembers a phone conversation in which Julia said, "Mom, we have two choices for school, but I think we should go to the Latin School of Chicago. I spent a day there, and I have the applications filled out for all three of us, but I need to fill in the 'parents' comments' section. So . . . what do you want to say about us?' "

The board was split, with the 10 members who came from the First Chicago side supporting their own man, McCoy's interim replacement, Verne Istock, who had been with the company since 1963. But they were at a mathematical disadvantage. Eleven members came from the Banc One side. The unemployed Dimon ultimately beat out four other outsider finalists, including Lewis Coleman, then chairman of Bank of America's investment banking arm, as well as Marc Shapiro.

Dimon told the board he believed in "eating his own cooking" and rewarded their confidence in him by purchasing 2 million shares of stock at $28.37 a share, for some $57 million, the day before his appointment was announced. The move showed he was all-in and from that day forward, nobody questioned his commitment to the job. On March 27, the press conference was held, and Bank One shares promptly rose 12.2 percent, giving Dimon a paper gain of $7.25 million. By the end of the week they were up 30 percent. In interviews with reporters, he joked about his departure from Citigroup, saying that he hoped it would be the last time in his career that he exited a job in such a way. But when asked how he'd fare without Weill by his side, he was curt. "I couldn't care less," he replied. "That's not me. I want to be happy and do the best thing for my family."

· · ·

Jamie Dimon might have been unemployed for more than a year after leaving Citigroup, but he understood the value of his own talents. So he drove a tough bargain when negotiating, hiring the New York lawyer Joseph Bachelder to negotiate a generous pay package. They ultimately came to a five-year deal with the board that included a $1 million base salary and a bonus of $2.5 million in the first year and up to $4 million a year thereafter. Dimon received 35,242 shares of restricted stock, options on another 3.24 million shares, and a guarantee that he receive at least $7 million in annual stock grants. He won the right to cut the size of the board, as well as install himself as chairman, in addition to CEO. Dimon, at long last, was his own boss.

Three early moves showed a political astuteness for which he had not been known. First, he called John G. McCoy, who had run Banc One from 1958 to 1984 before handing over the reins to his son. "Your son has built a fabulous institution," Dimon told him. "And I hope what I do makes you proud of me." When asked who his model would be for turning around Bank One, he didn't hesitate: "Sandy Weill." He also went to meet Chicago's mayor, Richard M. Daley, the day after his appointment, and said he planned to be a good citizen of Chicago.

Dimon decorated his office with a vintage 13-star U.S. flag, a four-star general's helmet given to him by the former U.S. Army brigadier general Pete Dawkins, and a sign that said "No Whining." He also put mounted magazine covers documenting his career on the walls, a self-aggrandizing custom he would give up later in his career.

Jamie Dimon spent his earliest days in this modest house in East Williston, New York.

Jamie and his brothers with their grandparents, Panos and Theonia Dimon.

Themis Dimon loved dressing up her boys in the same outfits, as seen here in 1962. From left to right, Jamie, Teddy, and Peter.

Jamie and the family's beloved sheltie, Chippy, in 1969.

Ted and Themis Dimon in 1962.

A star athlete in high school, Dimon played soccer, basketball, and baseball.

Jamie Dimon and his future wife, Judy Kent, at Harvard Business School.

Dimon and his groomsmen on May 21, 1983.

Jamie and Judy in 2008.

Dimon is extremely close to his daughters, Laura (l.), Julia (m.), and Kara (r.), seen here at the Bat Mitzvah of a family friend in Washington, D.C., in 1995.

The Dimon family at President Obama's inauguration in January 2009.

Jamie Dimon worked with Sandy Weill for more than fifteen years. In 1986, the two men parachuted into Baltimore's Commercial Credit and turned it into the platform on which they would eventually build Citigroup.

Bill Winters, co-CEO of JPMorgan Chase's investment bank.

Steve Black, Winters's counterpart, in Anguilla just before the dinner during which Dimon called to alert him to the impending sale of Bear Stearns.

JPMorgan Chase obtained Bear Stearns's headquarters at 383 Madison Avenue as part of the purchase of the investment bank in March 2008. Some JPMorgan Chase executives urged Dimon to buy the company if only to acquire the building—thus preventing a much longer commute to a proposed new site for the JPMorgan headquarters at the southern tip of Manhattan.

By the late 1980s, Dimon had already earned a reputation as one of Wall Street's sharpest minds, even though he was barely in his thirties.

For all its internal problems, Bank One remained a giant, the fourth-largest bank holding company in the country, with $36 billion in market value, $265 billion in assets, 1,800 retail branches, and 56 million credit card customers. Dimon flew to Columbus, Dallas, Detroit, Phoenix, and Wilmington in April to visit employees, and began restructuring the executive ranks. Several top managers departed, including the heads of corporate banking, middle market banking, and capital markets. Within a year, Dimon replaced all but one of the 13 executive committee members, with seven of the new hires coming from Citigroup, and followed through on his intention to reduce the board from 22 to 13.

The board had actually tried to make Dimon agree to keep Istock on as president indefinitely, but Dimon had balked, saying that the solution to infighting between the Banc One and First Chicago factions wasn't to create two new competing factions atop the company. He also explained that if he was to be CEO, it would be he and not the board who would choose his executive team. It was hard for anyone to make the argument that Istock had done a bang-up job in the role anyway, he argued, considering the disarray at the bank. Dimon ultimately agreed to have Istock stay on for three to six months, with no one reporting to him, so that the two men might get to know each other. When that probation period was up, Istock left the company and its board, albeit with a healthy exit package. Dimon did not replace him.

Dimon refilled the board with his own allies, including Bob Lipp; Stephen Burke, the president of Comcast, who was a friend from Harvard Business School; and David Novak, Andrall Pearson's successor as chairman and CEO of Yum! Brands. (Dimon was still a board member of Yum!)

Under the separation agreement he'd signed, Dimon was forbidden to solicit his former colleagues at Citigroup; but nothing prevented Bank One from hiring those who came to him. And come they did. In May, Mike Cavanagh, who had risen to be chief administrative officer and managing director of Salomon Smith Barney Europe, joined Bank One as senior vice president of strategy and planning, a new position. In June, Charlie Scharf, the CFO of Citigroup's global corporate and investment bank, signed on to be CFO. In September, Jim Boshart came on board as head of commercial banking; and Dimon named Heidi Miller, who had left Citigroup in February to become chief financial officer of the Internet travel outfit Priceline.com, to the Bank One board.

He also hired the Citigroup veteran William Campbell as a consultant, tasking the longtime branding expert with the question of what to do with Wilmington-based Wingspan.com, the company's ailing Internet banking operation. (It had accounted for $150 million in losses in the previous year.) The unit was being formally offered for sale, but Dimon wasn't convinced that there was any "there" there to sell. He also brought his pal from the Seagram Building, Peter Freund, on board for a time.

(Sandy Weill can—and should—be given credit for the 12-year vision that took a tiny company called Commercial Credit and somehow ended up swallowing Citicorp. Once his creation was complete, however, he managed to gut the top ranks of the company in a remarkably short time. By the end of 2005, a dozen crucial colleagues who'd helped him build the company had left—Jim Calvano, Mike Cavanagh, Jamie Dimon, Bob Lipp, Marge Magner, Jay Mandelbaum, Heidi Miller, Joe Plumeri, Charlie Scharf, Joe Wright, Bob Willumstad, and Frank Zarb. The only person of note left from the Baltimore days was Chuck Prince, who held on long enough to be made CEO. Had those other people remained with the company, it is unlikely that Prince would have even been a top-five candidate for the job.)

The arrival of the New Yorkers raised concerns in Chicago that Dimon was merely creating Citigroup West. There was also concern in New York. Weill called to complain about what he perceived as excessive poaching, but Dimon was unmoved, telling his former boss that every single person who had joined him in Chicago was coming to a much worse company for a much smaller job and a lot less money. Dimon guaranteed his hires just a one-year contract at two-thirds of their previous salary—much the same approach Weill had taken at Commercial Credit. How could top talent be attracted by that? For the potential of sharing in the upside.

"If I were you," Dimon told Weill, "I'd be looking *inside* to see why your people are leaving."

The number of defections did suggest discontent inside Citigroup. Weill's allies had been quietly pleased when no one except Black had initially followed Dimon out the door. But now it looked as if that was only because they were waiting until Dimon was in a position to hire.

The media were split on Dimon. Some coverage seemed to reflect a Weillian point of view. The trade publication *US Banker* published an article titled "Is Anyone Monitoring Jamie Dimon?" *Business Week* was even more blunt in its April 18, 2000, issue, asking, "Jamie Dimon: The Wrong Man for the Bank One Job?" and including a vague, unattributed criticism—"A dealmaker is a different personality than a leader." *CBS Marketwatch* posted a report about how Citigroup was on top of its game at the same time that Bank One was on the bottom.

Other coverage was more complimentary, sometimes embarrassingly so. In June, *Fortune* published an article titled "Dimon in the Rough: The Problem Solver." *Bank Investment Consultant* headlined its story "Boy Wonder."

What no one grasped at the time was one of several ironies that mark Dimon's career. The union of First Chicago and Banc One was, at least in part, a response to the creation of Citigroup just two years before. In effect, Dimon and Weill had scared the midwestern banks into a merger that failed to cohere, giving Dimon an opportunity to parachute in and play the hero. The specter of Citigroup, in good ways and bad, was still hanging over him.

• • •

Dimon confided in his old friends that his time off from work had mellowed him—that he was going to do it differently this time around. He wanted to buy a boat, he said, and take them on cruises around Lake Michigan. Plus, they would all go on vacations in Greece together. But the new Jamie Dimon never quite took hold. Within weeks, he was back to working long hours. "I'm still waiting for that cruise," Mike Cavanagh recently mused.

(When Cavanagh's wife, Emily, visited Chicago to scope out the housing market, Dimon asked her to join him for dinner at The Four Seasons hotel. When she told him how much the Cavanaghs were planning to spend on a house, he replied that her husband was lowballing her and that she should spend more.)

In late summer 2000, Judy and the kids made the move to Chicago. After taking care of school arrangements—the girls did end up at the Latin School of Chicago—Judy went into a funk for months. "I really missed close family and friends," she recalls, "and wasn't able to be immediately responsive to the open and welcoming ways of the Midwest."

But she began to acclimate. In October, the Dimons paid $4.68 million for a mansion on Chicago's "gold coast," a 15,500-square-foot, 26-room pile with eight bedrooms, 11 baths, a game room, an exercise room, and a 900-square-foot roof terrace. The family had been living quite well for years, but this was something else—a trophy house that had been redesigned by the well-known Chicago architect Marvin Herman. One longtime colleague of Dimon's described it as "like an embassy." The Dimons had numerous parties at their home, including one on Halloween that was attended by several hundred people. True to his philosophy of no perquisites, Dimon neither asked for nor received assistance from Bank One in purchasing the residence.

(Although the entire family had moved back to New York by 2007, the Dimons still owned the house in Chicago in 2009. It was listed for sale for $10.5 million, a tough price for another young family to cough up during a recession. "We loved living there," recalls Dimon. "But it's just not going to sell and there's nothing I can do about it.")

Dimon achieved a personal milestone in Chicago. He bought his first new car. (The family's Volvo wagon had been used.) But the financial wunderkind realized that he had a problem—he didn't know how to play the car-buying game. He called Jim Boshart and asked Boshart to accompany him and show him how the negotiations were supposed to go. He ended up buying a Lexus.

Every Friday night, Dimon and Judy went to Mario's Gold Coast Ristorante, a neighborhood favorite—and Sunday night was dinner with the family. When their daughter Julia introduced her parents to Luol Deng, a classmate from Duke who made the roster of basketball's Chicago Bulls, they became fans of the team and attended a few games. Dimon even took up the guitar.

Dimon says he came to love Chicago and got involved in civic causes, joining the boards of the city's Civic Committee, the Economic Club, and the University of Chicago, where his brother Peter had received a PhD in physics. After a lunch with one of his daughters at a South Side fire station, where they heard about the problem of finding victims in smoke-filled rooms, Dimon personally gave $1.2 million to the city's fire department so that it could buy 120 thermal imaging cameras—one for every firehouse in the city. (Bank One also paid for 10 firemen to go to New York after 9/11 to help with the cleanup in lower Manhattan. Upon returning, one of the firemen presented Dimon with the boots he'd worn at Ground Zero. Dimon still keeps them in his office.)

For her part, Judy Dimon expanded on the work she'd been doing in education in New York City's inner-city schools. She helped put together the Campaign to Expand Community Schools in Chicago, working alongside Arne Duncan, then deputy chief of staff to Paul Vallas, CEO of the Chicago public schools. (Duncan became Barack Obama's secretary of education in 2009.) She also cochaired a $50 million fundraiser so that her daughters' school could add facilities. "Serious arm bending," is how she remembers the effort. "But a lot of fun." The Dimons hosted about 15 different fund-raising cocktail parties at their house for various graduating classes of the school. She also cofounded another $50 million public-private partnership that transformed 150 of Chicago's toughest public schools into community schools with extended operations, programs, and services.

Still, the city never entirely believed that the Dimons were there for the long haul. Jamie was dogged by questions regarding when he was going to move back to New York. In an interview with the *Chicago Sun-Times*, Dimon voiced frustration at not being taken at his word. "If I work here for 20 years, I die and they send my ashes back to New York, they're going to say, 'See, he wasn't going to stay here.' "

There was at least one good reason to be suspicious. The Dimons somehow never got around to selling their Manhattan apartment. Both of Jamie's brothers used it a bit during the family's time in Chicago. At this point, Dimon was wealthy enough that he didn't need to sell one house in order to buy another. But keeping a multimillion-dollar apartment as a crash pad for your brothers doesn't exactly fit the profile of a man known for fiscal prudence.

• • •

The first six months at Bank One were not easy. Dimon says he was surprised at the extent of the company's problems, as well as the severity of the measures they called for. After he held his first conference call with analysts on April 5, three kept their "hold" ratings on the company's stock, while another reiterated a "sell." There were serious doubts about the safety of the company's dividend in the face of a pronounced weakness in earnings.

(Despite the chaos in 2008 and 2009, Dimon still calls 2000 the toughest year he's ever had professionally, by a wide margin. As the new boss with a reputation for aggressive cost-cutting techniques—read: layoffs—he was a man people hesitated to be around, for fear of slipping up. "I was pretty much alone that whole year," he recalls. "Working seven days a week.")

Dimon faced the company's shareholders at its annual meeting on May 16. In previous years, some 100 to 150 people had attended the proceedings; but more than 500 piled into an auditorium in 2000 to see their new superstar CEO, while another 100 watched on monitors in adjacent rooms. When one shareholder complained that service had deteriorated to a point where it was nearly impossible to get a live person on the phone, Dimon offered his own number. (Nine years later, when he and other executives had been hauled in front of Congress to answer for the sins of their industry, Dimon was told of one congresswoman's constituent who had complained to her about being mistreated at the hands of JPMorgan Chase. He offered his number once again.)

The complaints did not stop there. Questions were raised about the company's recent sale of $2.15 billion in real estate loans to Household International, about increased interest rates, and about the increasingly troubled credit card unit First USA. Dimon responded that he hoped First USA would return 1.5 percent on assets in the next year—versus just 0.6 percent in the first quarter of 2000—and adjourned the meeting after only 25 minutes. It wasn't exactly the blockbuster performance that some observers had been hoping for.

Three months after Dimon's arrival, the stock was back where it had been before he started, under $27 a share. Nineteen of 24 analysts who followed the company rated it a "hold" or a "sell." Mike Mayo of Credit Suisse, long-considered the "ax" of the industry—the analyst with the most pull—maintained a "sell" he had initiated more than a year previously at $60. This was despite a note he had published after Dimon's hiring: "Bank One got a home-run hitter in getting Jamie Dimon. . . . That's a real coup for the company."

Dimon let Wall Street know that Bank One would not be giving guidance on earnings until further notice. He then set about solving problems and did not issue bold pronouncements. There was a lot of sorting out to be done, and grumbling was inevitable. That summer, *Barron's* talked of increasing pessimism among analysts about the bank's prospects.

In his July call with analysts, Dimon established the guideposts by which the whole world could judge the company's performance. He emphasized execution over grand strategic goals. He showed no inclination to go on an acquisition binge, preferring to focus on the most granular details—systems conversions, reporting structures, risk management, and financial controls. ("I always like to point out that I didn't do a deal for four years in Chicago," Dimon recalls. "Doing deals isn't fun. The fun thing is actually building things.") He also demonstrated the basic conservatism that he believes is the foundation of banking. Several years later, the companies that experimented with exciting but dangerous new concepts—Citigroup, which became obsessed with "operating leverage"; Merrill Lynch, which decided to hoard complex mortgage products—were the first to stumble when the credit bubble burst in 2007.

The analysts were, incidentally, right to be worried about the company's dividend and earnings. Dimon concluded that the dividend needed to be cut in half. Such moves are obviously wildly unpopular with shareholders, especially those who own a lot of stock, and Dimon took grief for it. But there was no question in his mind that it had to be done. "We need the capital, we're paying out too much, I'm not confident things are going to get better anytime soon," he told one large shareholder, with his customary bluntness. "We're going to cut it. It's the right thing to do." He went ahead and did so on July 19, freeing up some $1 billion in annual cash. (He did the same thing in 2009 at JPMorgan Chase in an effort to preserve capital in the midst of continued market turmoil. By then, the market knew enough to trust Dimon, and the stock rallied in response.)

Bank One's problems, it turned out, ran a lot deeper than the credit card fiasco at First USA. With seven different deposit systems and five different loan systems, reconciliation problems emerged week after week. Corporate and middle market credit underwriting were disasters. The company had taken on too much credit risk, and wasn't earning nearly enough on the capital it had deployed. From 2000 through 2003, the company wrote off some $15 billion in bad loans.

To cut costs, Dimon did as was feared and laid off 12,000 employees. He also spent hundreds of millions of dollars to merge the computer systems, a move that quickly paid for itself. He introduced more than 2,000 new profit-and-loss statements, including one for each of the company's 1,800 bank branches, and initiated a program in which retail employees could share profits if their branch hit its own targets. He installed a rigorous new risk-management system that was aimed at helping the company avoid excessive credit exposure in any particular industry, a decision that helped the bank fare better than many of its competitors in the technology and telecom meltdown of 2000.

Dimon turned the bank upside down, not only slashing expenses but also installing new incentive structures. Branch manager compensation was overhauled. Previously, all branch managers had received bonuses ranging from 5 percent to 12 percent of their salary. Henceforth, the top 10 percent of branch managers were to receive a bonus equal to 100 percent of their salary; the next 10 percent received 50 percent; the next 10 percent received 30 percent; and the bottom 30 percent would receive no bonus at all. This was an old trick Dimon had learned from Weill in his days at Commercial Credit. He also made a number of what he called "battlefield promotions" during the first year, promoting people before he would have in more normal circumstances because he felt he had no choice.

He and his senior team turned McCoy's old office into what was nicknamed the "Lava Lounge." They furnished it with old couches from bank branches and, yes, a bunch of lava lamps. This is where they brainstormed plans to change the culture of the institution. No issue was too small for their attention. When Judy told Dimon of a flickering Bank One ATM screen at a Walgreen's in Chicago, Dimon called the company's outside service vendor himself. When he was told that the problem had been "monitored" for six months, he fired the vendor on the spot.

He also changed rules he found ridiculous. At an early executive meeting, he walked into the conference room with a cup of coffee in his hand. The old First Chicago building was decorated with a lot of white carpets, and one executive told their new boss that no coffee was allowed in the conference rooms. Dimon couldn't believe his ears. "I looked at my coffee, I looked at him, and I said, 'Well, it is now.'"

This style took some getting used to for veteran Bank One executives. One compared speaking to Dimon to "drinking from a fire hose." This is not an unusual reaction. His is a manner of speaking that must be experienced to be appreciated. Dimon is not, as the Greek historian Plutarch might have observed, the kind of man who saves his breath to cool his porridge.

Dimon later said his most serious oversight during his first 18 months was that it took him precisely that long to realize that Bank One's branches were open, on average, for two fewer hours than its local competitors. With $10 billion and 35,000 employees invested in the retail business, he couldn't believe that he hadn't noticed such a simple fact. But what bothered him even more was that no one had bothered to tell him. That, he said, was a sign that the company's DNA was flawed.

When he issued a diktat that the banks stay open for longer hours, he was told that the move would kill morale. "Tough," he replied, "this is what we do." His new colleagues came to realize that although Dimon was sincere about open and honest debate, he was also unafraid to draw it to a close and make an unpopular decision. "You need people who will argue and fight but at one point, say, we're going to take the hill," he told an audience in late 2008. "Some debates are chicken or steak. It becomes time to eat."

Dimon disdained the chronic hiring of consultants, and cut the practice back to the bare minimum. James Crown—whose family had a significant stake in Bank One—remembers one instance when an accounting consultant gave a "long-winded and pompous and hard-to-follow presentation" that left him thinking, "Maybe it's just me. Maybe I'm the only one who didn't get it." But Dimon felt similarly. "That was a terrible presentation," he told the assembled group after the presenters had left. "This is why I hate consultants." He picked up the phone and called the partner who had just departed, leaving a message in which he said not to bother sending a bill, because the presentation had been a waste of time. A few minutes later, he called back and said, "The call I just made—I wasn't kidding. I'm not paying for it."

He eventually tossed out consultants from Trammel Crow, which at one point had had 50 people working in Bank One's offices. In 2002, he eliminated a $2 billion outsourcing deal with AT&T and IBM that McCoy had signed in 1998. Although he saw savings down the road, this move wasn't a decision driven by short-term financial gains. Dimon considers information systems one of the core competencies of a financial services company, and he thought the function (and any associated information technology strategy) belonged in-house.

(Dimon is vocal about his antipathy toward much of the consulting used by large corporations today, with the notable exception of McKinsey & Co. "It's substitute management," he says. "A Good Housekeeping seal of approval. It's political, so if you make a decision you can say, 'It's not my fault, it's their fault.' I remember at Citigroup when we hired a consulting firm to do a study about how our capital was deployed. I thought, 'What is wrong with us? Shouldn't this be the job of management? Shouldn't we understand capital?' I do think consultants can become a disease for corporations, and I don't say that lightly, because I really do believe it. We do still use smart people to do consulting for us. But it has to be with a very senior person and there is no phase two. By that, I mean at the end of the project, I have the brain and they have the money. I don't need anyone to *implement* anything. That's a joke. You can't have outside people implement stuff inside companies. It doesn't work. And by the way, if that's going on, what the hell are your own people doing?")

Dimon knew how to play hardball with customers, too. He told nearly 1,000 corporate borrowers that Bank One would no longer serve them if they didn't broaden their relationship with the bank beyond loans. Partly as a result, the corporate loan portfolio shrank by about $50 billion. He disliked lending money for rapidly depreciating assets like cars, and largely took Bank One out of the auto lease business. He took $4.4 billion in write-downs and loan loss provisions in 2000, and the company ended up posting a loss of $511 million for the year.

Ever the conservative, Dimon boosted the company's allowance for credit losses to 2.4 percent, up from 1.4 percent in 1999. While Bank One's tier 1 capital ratio—the most-watched measure of a bank's balance sheet strength—slipped from 7.7 percent to 7.3 percent that year, Dimon had it back at 10 percent by the end of 2003.

He also introduced what he referred to as "waste-cutting" initiatives, his preferred term for cost-cutting. Employees were paid $1,000 for money-saving ideas. He cut executive perks to the bone, including country club memberships, car services, auto leases, supplemental pension programs, matching gift grants, and even magazine subscriptions. A story in *Money* magazine in 2002 reported that the number of newspaper subscriptions paid for by the company incensed him, and that he told one executive, "You're a businessman. Pay for your own *Wall Street Journal*." This was yet another "Weillism" that dated from Commercial Credit. But Dimon also did things that Weill never would have done, such as cutting the company's annual entertainment junket at the Masters Golf tournament because of the famous golf club's refusal to admit women. (At Bank One and later at JPMorgan Chase, he also cut funding for the Boy Scouts because of that organization's ban on gay scouts.)

He assured executives that getting rid of these entitlements would eventually make them all better off when the company started to do well again. It was a brave move, one that risked more defections than Dimon could handle in the short term. But it had the desired effect of disrupting the company's complacent culture. "Leaders emerged," Dimon said in late 2008. "Although some people hate your guts for the rest of your life." He also restructured the bank's options so that they expired in six years instead of 10—a classic Dimon move. If you wanted to be part of his team, the message went, you needed to be invested in the here and now.

The first annual report that Dimon wrote at Bank One, in February 2001 (for the year 2000), was a laundry list of problems identified and solutions implemented. Writing about the need for a fortress balance sheet, the necessity of keeping risks reasonable relative to capital deployed, and the benefits of performance-based compensation, he also laid out a grab bag of management philosophies that made him sound like the Warren Buffett of banking.

"Problems don't age well; denying or hiding them guarantees that they will get worse" was one. "Bureaucracy, silos, and politics are the bane of large corporations; they must be combated vigorously and continually" was another. And then an example of a heresy with regard to the modern religion of excessive executive compensation: "This company cannot and will not pay the senior people more when the company does worse."

Buffett himself wrote Dimon a note congratulating him on the letter, and saying it was "just about the best I've ever witnessed." To this day, Dimon keeps a framed copy of that note in his office.

"Jamie writes a great letter," says Buffett. "He writes it like he would write it to me if I owned 100 percent of the bank. It's a very sensible and literate letter from a manager to his owners. You can't find many like that. You particularly don't find them in financial services."

• • •

Back at Citigroup, there was high drama in the executive suite. On February 27, 2000, the company's board met to consider the long-term leadership of the company. Reed asked the board to force both he and Weill to retire—as per the agreement he claimed the two men had made— and to choose a new CEO to run the firm. Weill denied having made such a deal, and pushed for Reed to be shown the door. Bob Rubin, who had been brought on board by Weill, backed—guess who?—Weill. After eight hours of debate, Weill was appointed sole CEO of the firm.

The next day, Citigroup announced that Reed would retire in April; he was the latest of Weill's "partners" to be liquidated. Weill himself committed to retire in two years. Because Jamie Dimon was still nominally a free agent at this point, speculation erupted that he might return to the company he had helped build. But Dimon's deal just a month later with Bank One scotched that possibility.

Although relations between Dimon and Weill had thawed since their reconciliation at The Four Seasons, the two families had yet to bury the hatchet. But the two men soon showed that they could swallow their pride when it came to important women in their lives.

Over drinks in New York one day in late 2000, Weill told his erstwhile protégé that Joan missed Themis. The next night at dinner, Langley writes, Dimon's mother told her son that she, too, missed Joan. Dimon decided to call Joan the next day and urge a rapprochement. The two women soon exchanged letters, followed these with lunch, and then had a double date with their husbands, just like old times. Except that it wasn't, really. Yes, they were back on speaking terms, but the family-like closeness they once shared would never be resumed.

Weill held tightly to his new throne. In 2001, he was named to a three-year term on the board of directors of the Federal Reserve Bank of New York. But the subject of Jamie Dimon remained a sore spot. In 2001, when Thomas Hanley, an analyst at Friedman, Billings and Ramsey, postulated that Citigroup might buy Bank One to bring Dimon back as Weill's successor, Weill was not amused. He told his board that they were not to consider anything of the sort.

• • •

Making his new job at Bank One that much harder was the fact that Dimon was working in the midst of an economic bust. In April 2000, less than a month into his tenure, the Internet bubble popped. A sharp falloff in business investment followed, slowing economic growth by half a percentage point. Still, the economy shrank by only 0.03 percent during the ensuing recession. That's because the Federal Reserve hastily cut interest rates from 3.5 percent to 1 percent to revive the economy, a move that is now commonly seen as one of the major contributors to the credit bubble that finally exploded in 2008. But back then, the dot-com fallout, combined with the 9/11 terrorist attack, had most observers lauding the Fed's chief, Alan Greenspan, for his actions.

At Bank One, though, financial results rebounded—the company posted net income of $2.6 billion during 2001, versus its loss of $511 million the year before. Dimon's moves had impressed the market, which now expected a transformative deal. Known alternatively as the "Jamie premium" and the "Dimon effect," the sheer force of Dimon's reputation added value to the company.

The analyst Mike Mayo later called Dimon the "$7 billion dollar man," his estimate of the effect of Dimon's personal popularity on the company's value. But could it be sustained? Some analysts speculated that the continuing problems at First USA might make the stock a "value trap"—one that appears cheap but is actually indicative of a company that's falling apart.

Consolidation in financial services continued apace. In January 2001, Chase Manhattan bought J.P. Morgan for $28 billion. In April, Wachovia purchased First Union for $13 billion. Dimon played small ball by comparison; his only significant deal of the year was a completely unexciting purchase of $6.2 billion in credit card receivables from Wachovia. In June, he closed Wingspan.com, the company's sputtering Internet banking unit.

The September 11 attacks affected Dimon as much as any American. He established a disaster relief fund at the Bank One Foundation, promising to match all employees' contributions up to a total of $1 million.

Then, in December 2001, came Enron's bankruptcy, which spurred a new wave of popular resentment against the financial community, picking off big firms one by one. In 2002, investigators concluded that JPMorgan Chase's bankers had gotten into bed with Enron, helping the shysters in Houston to disguise about $2.6 billion in loans through the use of off-balance-sheet entities. In July 2003, the company paid a $135 million fine to settle charges of aiding and abetting Enron's scams. Citigroup confronted its own Enron in June 2002, with the collapse of WorldCom and the subsequent revelations that Citigroup's analyst Jack Grubman and Sandy Weill had exchanged a series of messages implying that Grubman would maintain a "buy" rating on WorldCom, despite his reservations, if Weill helped get Grubman's children into the prestigious 92nd Street Y nursery school on New York's upper east side. In Wall Street parlance, Grubman had breached the "Chinese Wall."

Weill denied making any such deal with Grubman, and in September he sacrificed Mike Carpenter on the altar of WorldCom. The tabloids weren't accepting any of Weill's denials, however, and continued to have a field day with the 92nd Street Y story—the first of a number of cracks in the foundation of Weill's reputation. Despite the arrival of a hagiography about Weill—*King of Capital*—in May 2002, and the fact that *Chief Executive* magazine, purveyor of puff pieces for the narcissistic CEO, named him "CEO of the Year" in July 2002, the more august *Wall Street Journal* ran a story in October 2002 suggesting that his interests had "diverged" from Citigroup's and criticizing him for lax oversight.

Dimon, incidentally, had negotiated Grubman's $20 million-a-year contract in tandem with Steve Black and Deryck Maughan before leaving the firm. They had been nervous about a partnership offer Goldman Sachs had been dangling in front of Grubman, and they had decided to keep him despite the ridiculous pay package and the possibility of abuse. But both Black and Dimon insist that the "Chinese Wall" remained unbreached during their tenures at Salomon Smith Barney, and that things got fuzzy only after they left. (Their protestations notwithstanding, Salomon Smith Barney was no paragon of high-minded principles in the 1990s. As was true of every investment bank at the time, the company's research analysts got cozier with their investment banking counterparts than one might wish.)

Still, once the two men were gone, some internal discussion revolved around the idea of having the research department *report to* the investment bank, a discussion Dimon says never would have happened if he had still been around. Weill also attended a number of meetings between Grubman and the firms he covered, another no-no that Dimon says he would not have considered.

The Citigroup board began considering a future beyond Weill, and pressed him on his retirement plans. In *The Real Deal*, Weill is surprisingly forthright about his reaction to hearing rumors than Dimon had put out feelers about a return to the firm, either on his own or through a merger with Bank One—rumors Dimon himself emphatically denies. "I adamantly opposed [it]," Weill wrote, "and reminded the succession committee that he had long ago burned his bridges."

Interesting words, coming from the man who lit the match that set those bridges on fire, but not very surprising. "With Sandy, you don't return," mused Frank Zarb in 2008. "People who leave Sandy Weill are never invited back. I mean, look at the history. Try to find another one, other than me." It's also hard to see which bridges Dimon himself had burned, save the one between him and Weill. Dimon is a friend of and friendly with the majority of his former colleagues, one exception being his old boss.

Later, the emergence at Credit Suisse First Boston of the so-called "friends of Frank"—a list of more than 300 people and institutions who received preferential allocations of pre-IPO shares in hot technology companies from the hotshot banker Frank Quattrone—evoked a similar mini-scandal from the 1920s, when such a list of "preferred" friends came to light at J.P. Morgan and Company. The practice was known as "spinning," and the investigation ensnared Citigroup as well. Quattrone was ultimately cleared of any actual crimes in federal appeals court in New York, but the extralegal conclusion was inescapable: Wall Street remained a rigged game.

Throughout 2002 and 2003, New York's attorney general, Eliot Spitzer, and his crusading investigators were knocking on nearly every door on Wall Street. Merrill Lynch, for its part, paid a $100 million fine to shake the monkey of Henry Blodgett and his duplicitous Internet ratings off its back. Citigroup paid a $300 million fine in April 2003. In all, 10 investment banks paid $1.4 billion in fines to the state to remove the threat of public trials.

Dimon remained largely silent on most of the scandals, save for a few public pronouncements decrying laxness in the United States' rules for disclosure and accounting. When Bank One's name came up in the mutual fund trading scandal in 2003, Dimon removed the head of mutual funds, Mark Beeson, and then called Spitzer himself and apologized, against the advice of his counsel. Dimon told the attorney general that if anyone at Bank One stonewalled him, he should let Dimon know personally. In 2004, Spitzer allowed the bank to pay a fine of $100 million to settle all charges. Dimon's distance from New York certainly didn't hurt. And so, unlike most of his peers, his reputation suffered nary a scratch during the period. As Arthur Levitt, former chairman of the SEC, later told *Fortune*, "Jamie Dimon is the un-Enron."

• • •

By 2002, Bank One was on firmer footing, and Dimon was back in the hunt. "A weak economy creates opportunities for strong companies," he wrote in the 2001 annual report. "I believe we are in a position to take advantage of emerging opportunities." By the end of the year, $1.5 billion had been slashed from the company's cost base. He continued to write down poorly performing assets, taking $5.81 billion in charges for the year. Dimon had refused a bonus for his work in 2000, but he accepted $3 million in 2001. Along with a restricted stock award and options, his pay package came to $18.1 million.

Those who knew him well also saw an emerging personal maturity. Dimon had always been highly regarded for his intelligence and drive, and had served as CEO of one business or another at Travelers, but he had always been the number two person. Sandy was the one going out and spending time with other CEOs. Sandy was the one coming up with the strategic vision. Of course, he would throw 10 ideas against the wall and Jamie would be the one to tell him which ones were smart. But that's very different from doing it all yourself. At Bank One, Dimon learned what it is to be a real boss.

He also continued to surround himself with ex-colleagues. He hired Heidi Miller away from Priceline to be Bank One's vice president of strategy and development in early 2002, and then lured Jay Mandelbaum from Citigroup to work in corporate strategy—the eighth executive he had snagged from his former firm. (By this point, the no-solicit portion of his separation agreement had expired.) Although Miller told an interviewer that Dimon "can be a pain in the ass," she also said that working for him could be exciting. (Her tenure at Priceline.com had not been a success, so Miller was also probably happy to return to Dimon's fold.) Within two months, Dimon promoted her to CFO, and moved Charlie Scharf over to run Bank One's retail banking unit.

There was one Citi veteran he tried but failed to hire during this time—Frank Bisignano, the chief administrative officer of Citigroup's corporate and investment bank. Dimon had just about landed Bisignano when Weill, in a fit of competitive madness, offered Bisignano a pay package worth more than $15 million over the following two years. When Bisignano broke the news to Dimon that he had, sensibly, decided to stay put at Citigroup, Dimon responded, "I got it. I got it. But you're going to end up working with me by the time we're done."

By mid-2002, rumors were swirling about what company Dimon might be prepared to buy. Bear Stearns came up in an article in *American Banker*, and that rumor was at least partly on the mark. Dimon, Jim Boshart, and Charlie Scharf had spent some time speaking to Bear's executives, including its copresidents, Alan Schwartz and Warren Spector; and its chief financial officer, Sam Molinaro. The problem: James Cayne, the egomaniacal head of Bear Stearns, told his board that he would take nothing short of a significant premium to Bear's share price to accept an offer from Dimon.

No matter that an offer hadn't been made in the first place. "He wanted $100 a share," recalls Dimon. "I said, 'Jimmy, there's no way we could pay a price like that.' The logic of the price wasn't even what the company was worth, by the way. It was based on some formula of what Jimmy would have made if he stayed there five more years. I told him a deal could make sense for both sides, but that the price couldn't be remotely close to that. Keep in mind, too, that this is the same stock we ended up buying for $10 a share in 2008."

An article in *Forbes* in May ("Rough Cut Dimon") rattled off a list of just about all the commercial banks Dimon might consider buying, including Commerce Bancshares, Fifth Third Bancorp, Golden State

Bancorp, KeyCorp, National City, SouthTrust, and UnionBanCal. All Dimon would say was that he had his eyes open. "We have the capital, we have the management. . . . At some point, something will come along that makes sense for us.

"People expected me to come in and start doing deals," says Dimon. "But that's not me. I'm different. You can't start a war until you have an army, and we couldn't even run our own business well. I said, 'No, we're going to get this thing fixed and from that strength, if something makes sense, we'll do it.' You have to earn the right to do a merger." Dimon has consistently referred to his first few years at Bank One as "boot camp," and he meant what he said. His army needed to get its basic skills in order before it would be ready to set out on some sort of conquest.

Fortune threw in its two cents in July, with the article "The Jamie Dimon Show"—documenting a particularly showy performance for bank employees at which Dimon shouted, "What do I think of our competitors? I hate them! I want them to bleed!" For all his new maturity, Dimon was still capable of a burst of over-the-top enthusiasm. At a dinner organized in New York by Citigroup's Bob Rubin in 2002, when all the talk was of Enron, David Swenson, head of the Yale endowment, mused about the need for reforms in research and structured products. Dimon responded angrily, telling Swenson, "Maybe someday you can run a big company yourself!" Rubin and the other guests were mortified. Jamie Dimon was still a hothead.

In October, speculation surfaced about a possible deal with JPMorgan Chase. With Bank One's shares surging and JPMorgan's under pressure because of its overexposure to bad telecom loans, the idea had legs.

Bank One's business was stabilizing. By 2003, the company was on a single technology platform with a single brand. First USA was again profitable, but it was no longer called First USA. It was all Bank One now. Bank One was now a partner of the likes of Amazon, Avon, Disney, and Starbucks. That year, the company added 434,000 new checking accounts, versus just 4,000 the previous year. Dimon had even eliminated the fees for using a live teller. Credit card sales surged 83 percent, and home equity loans 29 percent. The bank earned $3.5 billion, its best year to date. Dimon had also diversified the company's business, boosting non-lending revenue to 64 percent of the company's large corporate banking business, up from 45 percent in 2000. The company's tier 1 capital ratio, a widely watched measure of strength, was 10 percent, up from 7.3 percent in 2000. Dimon had delivered on his promise of a fortress balance sheet.

Not that there weren't missteps. The bank took a $100 million hit in 2002 for making the wrong call on hedging interest rates. And a credit card partnership left the company dangerously exposed to the bankruptcy of United Airlines in 2002–2003; Dimon was forced to lend $600 million to the faltering airline, the first time that the bank had ever lent to a bankrupt company. (Dimon tapped his new friend Greg Brenneman—who had by that point left Continental Airlines to start his own private equity firm—for advice on handling the United Airlines exposure. He also spent a lot of time on the phone with JPMorgan Chase's Jimmy Lee. Dimon had finally become a CEO, but he was not afraid to ask others for input.) When United came out of bankruptcy, the bank was repaid in full.

• • •

As solid as Bank One's business had become, Wall Street saw something else entirely: a ticking clock. Dimon had often said that until the company's systems were integrated, there was no sense in talking about acquisitions. But now, the integration was done. And still no deals. By May 2003, the "Dimon effect" was waning. An article in *Barron's* reported that investors were getting antsy, waiting for Dimon to make a move.

That summer, Citigroup announced that its longtime general counsel, Chuck Prince, was taking over the role of CEO from Sandy Weill. Dimon's chances of ever getting that job seemed increasingly remote, but it hardly mattered. Given the rot that was already being revealed within the far-flung Citi empire, it no longer seemed like an enviable position, despite Dimon's known reputation as a "mess manager," a boss who actually liked to clean up other people's mistakes.

With Bank One, Dimon proved he could take a wounded beast and nurse it back to health. He could get his arms around a complex business, reset expectations, make sure that the financial statements reflected the fundamentals, and hire and focus good people. What his critics never stopped pointing out, however, was that he still hadn't proved he was anything more than a cost-cutting zealot. "The blueprint for turning around a company is to make an assessment, stabilize it, get rid of excesses, and grow it," Tom McCandless, a bank analyst at Deutsche Bank, later wrote. "He got all the way up to the last step." From 2000 through 2003, Bank One's revenues rose just 17 percent while those at San Francisco-based Wells Fargo jumped 44 percent. Dimon's defenders say that's ignoring the obvious, including the significant in-branch improvements. Branch revenue rose by $600 million in two years while he was there, despite the fact that he shut down a number of underperforming branches and dropped a number of low-margin products.

Dimon was sensitive to this criticism. In his 2000 annual report, he'd written, "No company has ever had much of a future by cutting costs alone. Success is measured by top- and bottom-line growth." He was in no way opposed to growth, spending hundreds of millions of dollars to open dozens of new branches, but he was obviously more effective at removing excess costs than at adding new revenues. Return on equity, a measure of operating efficiency, climbed from a negative 2.1 percent in 2000 to 15.6 percent in 2003. Even so, more than half the analysts who followed the company still rated it a "hold" or a "sell."

Still, the stock did well, climbing 59 percent in Dimon's four years there, nearly triple the growth of the S&P 500. More than anything else, Dimon proved himself up to the task of being number one. Some CEOs are prone to boast of their achievements, but Dimon is programmed the other way, talking of what work remains unfinished, of the challenges that still loom. This tendency is known as "managing expectations" on Wall Street, and Dimon showed at Bank One that he knew how *not* to disappoint people. Having promised $2.2 billion in annual cost savings at Bank One, he delivered $3 billion by the time he was done.

The chattering classes were convinced that Dimon would snap up another company in short order. In 2001, he had told a reporter that he "would like to be back in a position where we can be predator, not prey.

You have to earn the right, and we're not quite there yet." By the summer of 2003, Wall Street was telling him that he was there. Then in October, Bank of America agreed to buy FleetBoston for $48.2 billion— a 43 percent premium to that bank's value the day of the announcement. Investors were experiencing another one of their periodic convulsions of enthusiasm, in which a 43 percent premium could be negotiated with a straight face. (Why not 40 percent?)

The pile-on began. Big deals were all over the news, but Jamie Dimon stayed on the sidelines. "Big Bank Merger Dulls Dimon's Edge," a story in *Crain's Chicago Business* suggested. He had a twofold problem on his hands. If Dimon was going to be a buyer, the price of any potential acquisition had just skyrocketed beyond anything a guy with his sense of value could contemplate. If he'd thought of being a seller, there was now one less major buyer in the market. Did Dimon lack Weill's signature gift, the ability to sniff out opportunity and pounce on it? That question would be answered soon enough.

10. THE RETURN

If asked to predict Jamie Dimon's next dance partner, not many would have suggested William B. Harrison, Jr., the CEO of JPMorgan Chase. Harrison and Dimon were a study in opposites—an old-style gentleman banker and a brash young CEO who didn't much stand on ceremony.

Harrison and Dimon had first met when Commercial Credit had been a client of Harrison's at Chemical Bank. Harrison had even been to Baltimore. Although they had run across each other from time to time in the intervening years, they didn't get to know each other well until Dimon took over Bank One and their paths started to cross at industry events.

A native of Rocky Mount, North Carolina, and a onetime high school basketball star (he also played for Dean Smith at the University of North Carolina), Harrison was a third-generation banker who'd worked his way up the ranks at Chemical Bank under Walter V. Shipley. Starting in 1987, when Chemical bought Texas Commerce Bancshares for $1.2 billion, Shipley had been a driving force in the industry's consolidation, purchasing Manufacturers Hanover in 1991 for $2 billion and then Chase Manhattan for $10 billion in 1995. Shipley held on to the CEO slot at the combined bank until 1999, when he ceded the role to Harrison.

While trying to put his own stamp on Chase, Harrison was widely criticized for overpaying in a flurry of acquisitions at the top of the bull market of the late 1990s. His timing was lousy. He snapped up the technology investment bank Hambrecht & Quist in September 1999, just a few months before the technology bubble burst, paying an overblown $1.4 billion. He followed that with the $7.7 billion acquisition of the London-based merchant bank Robert Fleming Holdings in April 2000, and then paid $500 million in July for the mergers and acquisitions boutique Beacon Group. With the last deal, he committed one of the cardinal sins of the M&A game—buying an entire company to secure the services of a single individual. In this case, it was Beacon Group's senior partner, Geoffrey Boisi, a former Goldman Sachs hotshot. Boisi stuck around for just two years, making the deal exceedingly expensive in retrospect.

But one hire turned out to be quite savvy. In mid-2000, Harrison secured the services of Steve Black, who had been out of the job market for 18 months, to run Chase's burgeoning equities business.

Harrison wasn't done. He kept making deals. In September 2000, he and Douglas "Sandy" Warner, CEO of J.P. Morgan, shocked the industry by announcing a $34 billion union of their respective companies. The deal evoked memories of Shearson and Lehman, a marriage of high and low finance. Chase Manhattan had a powerful consumer brand, but it paled beside the century-old prestige of J.P. Morgan, which catered to ultra-wealthy individuals and corporate chieftains.

In doing all this, Warner and Harrison were playing catch-up to Weill, who was setting the agenda for the entire industry. Size was everything, the thinking went, and the two men figured they could compete better in a potentially problematic marriage than on their own. Warner was named chairman of the combined firm; Harrison would be president and CEO.

Like many colossal deals, the merger of J.P. Morgan and Chase struggled to live up to its potential. Integration was painfully slow, and management couldn't figure out how to run the thing effectively as a single entity. The firm's private equity unit got crushed at the end of the 1990s bubble. Too many telecom loans led to more pain, and trading results were erratic. The company's 2001 return on equity was a puny 0.24 percent. By 2002 the stock was trading for 70 percent of its book value, a pitifully low ratio at the time. Then it got worse. The Enron debacle had cost the firm $135 million in fines in July 2003, but there was an even greater cost. The once august institution was now just another Wall Street firm on the make.

Fifty-nine years old at the start of 2003, Harrison began to focus on identifying a capable successor. In assembling a platform that gave JPMorgan Chase a shot at future greatness, he'd been criticized for both the timing and the expense of his moves. But he'd built the platform nonetheless, and was ready to spend more time relaxing at his Greenwich estate. The board of the company was ready for a change as well. The problem was that Harrison didn't feel any internal candidates were strong enough to run the company. The job required both vast technical skills and leadership skills. To succeed in banking tended to mean specializing in one particular area, and that left most talented executives knowing very little about the rest of the business. But there was an outsider who seemed to have all the right ingredients.

· · ·

Harrison and Dimon began informal talks in January 2003. Then in May, Dimon called to say he was in New York and would love to meet Harrison. The two men had lunch in Harrison's dining room at JPMorgan Chase, and then did so again in July. After that, things started to get serious, and secrecy became a concern. They began meeting in a suite that JPMorgan Chase kept at the Waldorf-Astoria on Park Avenue. Dimon also joined Harrison one night at Harrison's home in Greenwich.

As a matter of course, Dimon has always kept a one-page piece of paper that includes companies his firm might buy, merge with, or sell to, developed with the help of his management team and shared with the board. "You have to be careful, though," he says. "I've seen too many boards or management when their own businesses are doing poorly, they start to bullshit about M&A. People just fall into that. So we separate it. We review our businesses and what we're doing well organically. That kind of growth will get you a higher value for your shareholders, by the way. M&A is risky and tough, so the discipline is different. You really need to think about the landscape, to ask yourself what's changing." In any event, at the time, JPMorgan Chase stood out as having the strongest business logic with Bank One. (FleetBoston had been number one in a theoretical merger of equals before it was sold.)

In this era of intense consolidation, the two CEOs spent a lot of time discussing "what ifs" about the future of industry. The fit between the companies seemed solid on paper. JPMorgan Chase could expand its branch banking business in the process, reducing its dependency on its volatile trading and investment banking franchises. And Bank One would be transformed from a regional player into an international powerhouse, the second-largest bank in the country after Citigroup. Dimon and Harrison also predicted $2.2 billion in cost savings, in part from some 10,000 layoffs.

Harrison knew by May that this was a deal he wanted to do. He just needed to bring Dimon around. After all his overpaying, Harrison was convinced that the market would pummel his stock if he paid a big premium, so he began by insisting that JPMorgan Chase pay no more than the market price for Bank One shares. Dimon countered with a demand for 35 percent on top. Someone was going to have to give a lot if the negotiations were to have any chance of success.

When the deal between Bank of America and FleetBoston, with its 43 percent premium, was announced, it appeared that Harrison would be forced to give more in the negotiations. But he dug in his heels; he knew this was the last big deal of his career, and he would be damned if he was going to solidify a reputation for being an easy mark. Besides, JPMorgan Chase was enjoying a resurgence—profits jumped from $1.7 billion in 2002 to $6.7 billion in 2003, with the investment bank under David Coulter given much of the credit. Coulter had joined the firm in 2000, when Harrison purchased The Beacon Group. For what it's worth, he was considered the top in-house candidate for CEO, but Dimon beat him to it.

Dimon later told a group of Bank One employees that upon hearing of the Fleet deal, he'd called Harrison and said, "Bill, at 40 percent, I'll drive your car." Harrison's response: "At 15 percent, you could be president."

Before the Bank of America deal, Harrison felt he'd been making headway in convincing Dimon that anything close to a 30 percent premium would result in stock market carnage, which wouldn't have been good for either of them. But Dimon's overriding duty at this point was to Bank One's shareholders, who would rightly howl if they suspected he was accepting too little from JPMorgan Chase in exchange for advancing his own career. So he pushed for a 20 to 25 percent premium.

Harrison was in tight spot, too. The industry was in the grip of merger mania, and if Harrison didn't snap up Bank One, someone else surely would. It wasn't just the company that was attractive—it was Dimon himself. Harrison desperately wanted Dimon as his successor, and started sweetening the terms. Upon completion of a transaction, the two men agreed, Harrison would remain chairman and CEO for two years, while Dimon would be president and chief operating officer of the company, with compensation equal to 90 percent of Harrison's. After that, Harrison would relinquish the title of CEO to Dimon, while still remaining chairman of the board.

Dimon extracted further concessions. Despite the fact that JPMorgan Chase was much larger than Bank One—with $793 billion in assets to Bank One's $290 billion—the board would be made up of seven outside directors from each side plus Harrison and Dimon. Two-thirds of the directors would have to vote against Dimon to deny him the top spot when the time came. The minnow was swallowing the whale.

In November, Dimon enlisted Gary Parr of the investment bank Lazard Frères as an adviser. The two men had known each other since 1993, when Parr had sold part of the insurance company Allegheny Corp. to Dimon and Weill. Harrison relied on his own in-house bankers. The two teams had their own code words for the deal. Bank One called JPMorgan Chase "Park" in its documents (the bank's headquarters were on Park Avenue) and called itself "Clark" (its own Chicago head office was on Clark Street). JPMorgan Chase referred to itself as "Jupiter" and called the smaller Bank One "Apollo." (Lazard made $20 million in fees for the deal; the JPMorgan Chase bankers were paid $40 million in an intracompany transfer.)

(Dimon's go-to investment banker in 2009 was JPMorgan Chase's own Doug Braunstein. But he's not averse to using outside bankers if they earn their keep. "I have enormous respect for Gary Parr," he says. "And if someone outside the firm brings us an idea, they will be compensated for it. I think it's important that you're open-minded to other people's ideas. Braunstein was on the other side of the deal and I almost throttled him on three separate occasions. Ultimately when a guy's on the other side you learn how good they are and you kind of want him on your side at one point.")

By the close of the year, both men had made sure their boards were comfortable with the deal. The Bank One board, in particular, was happy with the succession plan, as it didn't want a repeat of First Chicago and Banc One's infighting. "We had shown that having a good CEO makes a huge difference," recalls Bank One's board member James Crown. "And with the company finally moving back up in terms of earnings, we didn't want to put shareholders back at risk with a leadership that might reverse the gains that had been made."

Early in 2004, Dimon reached out to his old friend Steve Black, who was now deputy co-CEO of the investment bank under its chairman, David Coulter, at JPMorgan Chase. He asked Black to dinner with him and Jim Boshart, as sort of a final check on the various issues and personalities involved in the potential combination. Black had already told Harrison what he knew about various people at Bank One. But Harrison was his boss. This was the guy on the other side of the table. After making sure Harrison and Coulter didn't view such a dinner as inappropriate, Black and Boshart had a four-hour meal with Dimon on Saturday, January 10, at Aretsky's Patroon on East 46th Street.

The next morning, a Sunday, Black's phone rang at 7:00. It was Bill Harrison, anxious to know how dinner had gone. "These guys are close to getting this thing done," Black thought to himself after hanging up the phone.

(Dimon had tried to hire Black at Bank One, but it was a very short conversation. Despite the fact that Dimon had already lured James

Boshart—Black's best friend—there was no way Black was packing his bags and relocating to Chicago. "I'm not moving," he had told Dimon. And that was that.)

Black was right about things moving fast. After negotiating in earnest for about four months, the two men finally came to an agreement early that week. Harrison broke the logjam by offering a 10 percent premium, giving Dimon himself a paper profit of about $44 million on his Bank One shares. In a matter of days, the two made a $58 billion stock-for-stock deal, which was announced on January 14. The combined company had $1.1 trillion in assets (just below Citigroup, with its $1.3 trillion) and 2,370 branches in 17 states. It was also the second-largest credit card issuer in the country, with $123 billion in credit card loans outstanding. Bank One's stock jumped 10 percent in after-hours trading while JPMorgan Chase's slid a modest 4 percent.

(No one complained when Dimon moved back to New York, despite all the hullabaloo about his long-term plans when he'd taken the job at Bank One. He'd made money for his shareholders, and he'd turned a Chicago bank into a global player. It was enough.)

JPMorgan Chase stock wasn't down for long. The influential analyst Mike Mayo—by this point at Prudential Securities—liked the deal and upgraded the shares. The stock bounced, pushing the premium up over 12 percent. At that point, Harrison called Dimon and said that if the stock climbed much further, Harrison would be forced to renegotiate. There was ultimately no need for this, and the transaction got done at a 14 percent premium. At a subsequent meeting with employees in Chicago, Harrison praised Dimon's negotiating skills. "It's been, without question, the most stressed kind of time a CEO can go through when you're negotiating one of the deals. Particularly with Jamie. That's also why I look older today."

Dimon admitted a slight hesitation. "Two or three times, I felt deep anxiety about this deal," he said. "It's terrifying. Do you push the button or not? If you don't, and this opportunity is gone when you want it later, you've made a horrible mistake. So I pushed the button."

A group of shareholders later sued J.P. Morgan, Harrison, and Dimon, maintaining that Dimon had offered to sell his company for $7 billion less than the deal price if he could have the top job immediately. The accusation was that Harrison had thus overpaid—again—just so that he could hang on to his job for two more years. Both Harrison and Dimon denied any such thing, but the deal's premium nevertheless raised eyebrows—not because it was big but because it was so small. In March 2004, Wachovia purchased SouthTrust for a 20 percent premium. Among the recent deals, Bank One had somehow sold out for the smallest premium of all.

Dimon later admitted that although he'd briefly considered selling the company to the highest bidder, he never tested the waters, not even bothering to gauge the interest of other potential acquirers, such as Wells Fargo. He justified the deal with JPMorgan Chase as the best fit for Bank One. (Others would snipe that it was also the best fit for Jamie Dimon.)

No matter what the terms were, the deal paved the way for Jamie Dimon's triumphant return to New York, to go head-to-head with Citigroup. "We'll give Citi a run for its money!" he told the press when announcing the deal. (Fans of bloodsports lamented that Weill had largely passed the reins to Prince by that point.) The irony was that for the second time in a row, Dimon had found opportunity at a company that had been scared into an ill-fated merger by the fear he and Weill had struck into the hearts of the competition while building Citigroup.

Dimon later revealed that the first person to call and congratulate him about the deal was none other than Sandy Weill. They had taken aim at J.P. Morgan & Company together almost 10 years before, and Weill couldn't help celebrating the occasion, even if it meant more formidable competition for Citigroup. One word during the phone call was unclear to Dimon, however. Weill had said either, "*You* finally got J.P. Morgan," or "*We* finally got J.P. Morgan." There was no more "we." It was a warm exchange, however, and the two men shared a laugh, as in old times.

Harrison's last deal was his finest. The staid southerner had snagged the most sought-after man in the industry as his successor. After spending the prime of his career in the huge shadow that Sandy Weill had cast, Harrison ultimately bested his rival in the last, most important decision a CEO makes—whom to turn the company over to. Weill had Chuck Prince; Harrison had Jamie Dimon. Harrison also bested Weill when it came to graciousness on the way out the door. Whereas Weill clung to power as long as he could, eventually fumbling the succession process as a result, Harrison identified Dimon, persuaded him to come aboard, and then let go in exactly the manner he had promised.

The usual litany of articles followed. *Time* magazine: "Dimon's Jewel." *Newsweek:* "The Kid Stays in the Picture." *BusinessWeek:* "Jamie vs. Sandy: An Epic Grudge Match." *Fortune:* "The Deal Maker and the Dynamo." *Fortune* best captured the mood with the following observation: "At last J.P. Morgan's William Harrison has made a deal the market loves. Why? Because in buying Bank One, he's bringing Jamie Dimon back to the big show, where he belongs."

. . .

Despite all the carefully negotiated succession planning, Jamie Dimon still had a reputation for being somewhat difficult in the presence of anyone else's authority. And two years is a long time for a man in a hurry to wait. How long before he and Harrison clashed? As one person close to Dimon put it quite clearly, "Jamie likes to take over." Dimon had been unable to control his anger while working with Sandy Weill, with whom he'd shared an especially close relationship. But he barely knew Bill Harrison. For the previous four years, Dimon had been in total control, which was how he liked it. How would he bring himself to share power again?

Though Harrison had critics, almost everybody who's ever worked with him or for him praises his character. Comfortable in his own skin and far less insecure than Weill, Harrison was able to let the 48-year-old president and CEO-designate have his customary bursts of passion without being threatened by them. Judy Dimon even asked her husband why he couldn't be as patient and mature as Bill Harrison, a remark Dimon repeated at a number of leadership meetings with JPMorgan Chase's employees.

What helped in the transition was that during their months of negotiations, the men had planned very carefully how they would jointly run the bank, and had determined which people were best suited for which roles. They had sketched out an organizational structure three or four levels deep in most places.

Dimon told his direct reports that if they felt they had a legitimate disagreement with a decision he'd made, they could go and visit Harrison together. His intention was to eliminate politics at the level beneath the CEO and president, for fear that politics would otherwise destroy the company. In return, he got nothing but cooperation from Harrison. "We both wanted it to work," recalls Dimon. "He really wanted a successor, so he wasn't fighting me. It was mature. We talked about everything. We weren't competing."

No big merger goes off without casualties, and at JPMorgan Chase there were a few, including those who had seen themselves in line for the job of CEO. Don Layton, who'd been a vice chairman in charge of all the Chase-related businesses and had spent 30 years at the company, quit when he found he'd be reporting to Dimon, with the result that Dimon was then in charge of finance, risk management, and technology, in addition to being president and COO. David Coulter, who had arranged to continue reporting directly to Harrison while sharing the office of the vice chairman with Dimon, was effectively demoted from chairman of the company's investment bank in September 2004, when he agreed to become chairman for the company's west coast business. (He left the company the next summer.)

That same September, Dina Dublon, JPMorgan Chase's chief financial officer since 1998, announced her resignation. Dimon's longtime lieutenant Mike Cavanagh, who had been running middle market banking, replaced her. (In a classic example of his occasional tone-deafness, Dimon announced at Dublon's retirement party, "If you paid one dollar for Texas Commerce Bank, you paid a dollar too much!" Dublon had overseen the $1.2 billion deal, and several executives from Texas Commerce were in attendance.)

Dimon also sent the head of human resources, John Farrell, packing after the two failed to see eye to eye. In a lot of large companies, human resources tends to take on a life of its own, introducing new programs and acting as if it were a business in and of itself. Not so in Jamie Dimon's world, where HR is about helping people get what they need, *period*. On the other hand, Dimon significantly expanded the company's finance division, whose members would be put to work counting virtually anything that could be counted.

One person he did keep around was Jimmy Lee, the legendary J.P. Morgan banker who had pioneered the use of syndicated loans. A larger-than-life personality, Lee was also known for backroom politicking and front-room confrontations, but Dimon knew a valuable asset when he saw one. The Rupert Murdochs, Sumner Redstones, and Sam Zells of the world asked for Lee by name when working with J.P. Morgan. He also hosts an annual confab in Deer Valley that draws an enviable roster of heavyweights, including DreamWorks' Jeffrey Katzenberg, General Electric's Jeffrey Immelt, Microsoft's Steve Ballmer, and the NBA commissioner, David Stern.

(Shortly after the deal, Dimon asked Lee to join him for dinner at the Post House, a steak house in the Lowell hotel on East 63rd Street. Moments after sitting down, Lee pulled a piece of paper out of his pocket and put it down on the table next to him. Dimon looked at Lee and said, "What's that?" Lee replied, "It's the list of things I needed to do today. I wanted to make sure I covered all the topics I wanted to talk to you about." Dimon looked incredulous. "Let me see that," he said. After a quick scan of the sheet of paper, Dimon threw it back at Lee dismissively. "That's not a list," he said. "Do you want to see a real list?" He then pulled his own out of his pocket. The two men laughed at their shared, antiquated approach to scheduling.)

As time passed and he handed more and more power over to Dimon, Harrison's one disappointment was finding out that when you hire the most confident man in finance, it's unlikely he's going to ask for your advice very often. Harrison used to seek his predecessor's counsel out of respect, even if he'd already made up his mind. Dimon didn't bother with such pretense. "But if you understand that, you're OK," says Harrison. "He doesn't waste time like that."

The transfer of power from Harrison to Dimon stands as one of the cleanest and most orderly in recent financial history. In stark contrast to the disastrous handoffs that have characterized Wall Street—David

Komansky to Stan O'Neal at Merrill Lynch, Jon Corzine to Hank Paulson at Goldman Sachs, and, worst of all, the vicious civil war between Phil Purcell and John Mack at Morgan Stanley—it is a model of clarity and execution.

· · ·

In Bank One's last annual report as an independent company, Dimon noted that the company's share price had risen 85 percent during his tenure, versus a 25 percent decrease in the S&P 500 and a 24 percent increase in a relevant index of banking stocks. Touching on an issue close to his heart—financial strength—he also trumpeted the fact that on the day the merger was announced, the bond-rating agencies had put both banks on "positive watch."

He called out an old foe, Prudential Securities' analyst Mike Mayo. On a conference call with analysts, Dimon said, "Mike Mayo has had Bank One for sale since the day I got there. And yesterday he made it a buy. The first [thing] he wrote about [Bank One] was something like, 'Even Hercules couldn't fix that mess.' I want the next one to say, 'I was wrong.'" A minute later, a voice came on the line. "Jamie Dimon . . . it's Mike Mayo. Since you got to Bank One, I was wrong." Dimon's response: "Thank you."

(Mayo actually stewed over being called out in public, especially as he didn't consider that his rating of Bank One was a failure. He'd actually downgraded Bank One stock to "sell" in 1999, when it was trading for $60 a share. Even though he'd been wrong about it during Dimon's tenure, this was still one of the best calls he'd made in his career. But he took the high road and said nothing. Two years later, though, when Dimon made another crack at his expense during a presentation to investors on January 31, 2006, Mayo thought the criticism of his record had gone too far, and issued a report defending his stock picks, as well as pointing out certain errors in Dimon's remarks. The *Financial Times* picked up the controversy, and on the day of its report, Mayo's phone rang. It was Dimon, calling to apologize to him.)

Mayo had been right about one thing, though. Despite Dimon's capable restructuring of Bank One, he did have trouble juicing the company's revenues. Even in 2003, the firm's top line actually fell 3 percent, to $16.2 billion. He was undoubtedly the Mr. Fix-It of banks. But did he have the vision to take one to the next level without a jumbo-size acquisition? His defenders argue that he was shrinking the bank by shedding underperforming businesses in order to have a solid core from which to grow, and he sold to JPMorgan Chase before that strategy came to full flower. Critics respond that it's impossible to know what *might* have happened, and that Dimon sold the company for fear of not delivering.

In one last burst of enthusiasm, Dimon said in an employees' meeting that even if Bank One had forgone a few billion in the deal, it didn't matter; if they did a good job, JPMorgan Chase's stock could reach $100 in five years—the equivalent of adding $200 billion in market value. Nearly five years later, in the midst of the credit crisis, the stock was treading water at $35 a share. "I didn't say I'd eat my hat if it didn't get to $100," he recalls. "But that's taken on a life of its own." Sitting on a bookshelf in his office was an Australian leather hat under glass. Beneath it, a clock was counting down to zero, with only 150 days remaining—a gift from the JPMorgan Chase executive Blythe Masters. "That's going to be hard to chew," he laughs.

Dimon stepped down from the board of Yum! Brands when he became president of JPMorgan Chase. At the time, corporate governance experts and the media had begun shining a spotlight on the issue of interlocking directorates—evidence of the clubbiness atop large American companies—and both Dimon and David Novak—the CEO of Yum!—decided they didn't need the trouble. "I told David, 'I need you on my board more than you need me on yours,' " Dimon recalls. "And he said, 'You're right.' " (Interestingly, Dimon now agrees with Weill's position at Citigroup that there be no insiders on the board. "But at that point in time there were lots of boards that had them," he says. "I agree you shouldn't have any. But that wasn't the issue for Sandy. He wasn't saying, 'We're going to do this for corporate governance reasons.' That wasn't the issue at all.")

A few months after the merger, Dimon and a group of JPMorgan Chase's senior executives were having a dinner in a private room at Le Bernardin, when Ina Drew, then head of the bank's treasury group, walked into the room and announced that Sandy Weill and Ken Bialkin were eating in the main room with their wives. Jay Mandelbaum and Bill Harrison decided to go downstairs and invite Weill up to say hello to the team.

Weill did come to say hello, and Dimon went down to visit Joan Weill. A number of longtime JPMorgan Chase executives had never met Weill before, and were excited to meet the banking legend. They peppered him with questions about, for example, his opinion of their own performance, and the rumor that Weill had been on the verge of buying Deutsche Bank. He had been, he replied to the latter, but the German company's CEO, Josef Ackerman, had backed out at the last minute.

His defenses down, Weill spent forty-five minutes with the JPMorgan Chase team before graciously taking his leave. Word came back the next day that upon returning downstairs, Weill had told his dinner companions that the team had shown him more respect than Chuck Prince had offered since Weill had made him CEO of Citigroup.

One important constituency wasn't thrilled about the merger: the Dimon family. Dimon had moved three young girls to Chicago at a challenging age, and here he was, four years later, proposing to move the two who were still in high school back to New York. "There's been a lot of crying in the household these last two days," he told reporters when the deal was announced. Judy Dimon, who had taken nearly a year to adjust to Chicago, wasn't ready to pack her bags yet, either. (This is not to say she didn't support the move. When he asked her opinion, Judy told her husband, "We're not getting any younger. And this is your chance to do something great.") The decision was made for Judy to stay put until the youngest daughter, Kara, graduated from Chicago Latin in 2007. "Women would say to me, 'Don't you even dream about making Kara move and go to another high school,'" recalls Dimon. "So I commuted for two and a half years. That was painful. I had no idea how hard it was going to be, being away from home four days a week. Leaving home on Sunday night to come back to New York was depressing. I hated it."

The family eventually purchased a second apartment on Park Avenue for $4.875 million in December 2004, combining it with the one they already owned. Built in 1929, their apartment building is one of the few left in Manhattan with a grand courtyard in the middle. The triple-arch entrance suggests opulence within.

Still, the Dimons' apartment somehow manages to be understated despite its oversize footprint. "For a long time, most of our furniture was hand-me-downs," Dimon recalls. "Sure, we could afford better stuff, but the kids were there and we had a dog and I never wanted to be the kind of parent who was always worried about the kids spilling something. I still don't. But when we came back, we renovated it." That said, it is still a place where you can entertain 100 brokers on the terrace on a Sunday.

• • •

When Dimon stepped into Harrison's shoes at JPMorgan Chase, he was, for the first time in years, in an unfamiliar role. Unlike Sandy Weill and Chuck Prince, Dimon had yet to run a global mega-bank, with innumerable moving parts.

His first move was to expand the company's profit centers from five to six—the investment bank, retail financial services, credit cards, commercial banking, treasury and security services, and asset management. The first three were the largest in terms of revenue and profits, but the last two had demonstrably superior returns on equity.

The merger actually *was* a good fit, as there had been little overlap among the two companies' business lines. In the first quarter of 2004, for example, JPMorgan Chase earned 57 percent of its net income from its investment bank and 22 percent from retail banking and credit cards, whereas 59 percent of Bank One's earnings came from retail banking and credit cards, 31 percent from corporate loans, and 10 percent from asset management.

In strong markets, the combined company hoped to see a disproportionate share of earnings come from investment banking and trading. When the market was choppy, the retail and commercial banking divisions might provide stability. And the treasury and asset management divisions were money machines requiring very little capital.

Specific roles took several months to be determined, but Dimon's core posse from Bank One remained with the merged company—Mike Cavanagh, Jay Mandelbaum, Heidi Miller, Charlie Scharf, and his adviser Bill Campbell. Whereas Cavanagh, Miller, and Scharf went on to carve out well-defined roles as CFO, head of treasury services, and head of retail, respectively, Campbell became a part-time adviser. Dimon's Praetorian guard stayed largely intact.

Dimon swears he doesn't use consultants unless they are absolutely necessary, but he continues to use the services of Andrea Redmond, the recruiter who helped get him in the door at Bank One. (What better endorsement of an executive recruiter than the one who finds *you* for the job?) Redmond introduced one of the more recent additions to the company's operating committee, its credit card chief, Gordon Smith, to Dimon in 2007. (Smith had been a high-level executive at American Express.)

Mandelbaum found himself with the most amorphous job, head of strategy and business development. Heritage JPMorgan Chase's head of asset management, Jes Staley, had been concerned that Mandelbaum—having run asset management at Smith Barney—would be gunning for his job but the mild-mannered Mandelbaum instead settled into a role as one of Dimon's most trusted sounding boards. The other was the firm's general counsel, Joan Guggenheimer, the woman Dimon had long ago elevated over Weill's daughter Jessica Bibliowicz. Both stood out for their ability to tell Dimon when he was wrong. "Whenever I have really complicated stuff, I give it to Jay," Dimon has said.

("Jamie is either in agreement with you or he's going at you," says one JPMorgan Chase executive. "With one exception. He will sit down and reason for hours with Jay. If something is really going wrong, you watch, the person who is behind him is Jay Mandelbaum.")

When Dimon rolled into JPMorgan Chase, his reputation was largely unchanged from that he'd had before decamping for Chicago: a cost-cutter and systems integrator; a man who got excited by finding ways to collapse 10 different credit card processing technologies into just two or three. But Bill Harrison quickly realized that the Jamie Dimon who returned from Chicago was different from the one who had left New York. Mergers take their toll on institutions, and if people aren't happy, they will leave, raise hell, or rebel, and Dimon seemed to understand that. "A merger exposes how good a leader is very quickly," recalls Harrison. "And Jamie got his hands around things very quickly."

Two things surprised Dimon out of the gate. The first was a practical issue. The company's technologies were far less integrated than he'd thought. The second was about the enduring nature of a powerful brand. "We could get off a plane anywhere in the world and the prime minister would want to see us," he recalls. "I knew the name was good, but I didn't know how good that calling card still was." (The bank, for example, has been doing business with Saudi Arabia's national oil company, Saudi Aramco, for 70 years.) If he could get everything moving in the right direction, he would have something he never had at Bank One or at a pre-Citi Travelers: a gold-plated corporate name on which he could capitalize.

As always, Dimon stamped out internal politics wherever he could. In early executive meetings at JPMorgan Chase, a few people thought it in their best interests to try to pull him aside afterward and whisper their thoughts about this person or that one. He quickly made it clear that he was uninterested in such grade-school tactics. "If you can't say it in the room, don't say it at all," he told more than a few executives. (He later elaborated to *Fortune* on his irritation with obfuscation. "In a big company, it's easy for people to b.s. you," he said. "A lot of them have been practicing for decades.")

He also sought out people he refers to as "culture carriers"—those who might give him insight into the way the old JPMorgan Chase had worked, and where there was room for improvement. He took these people out, one-on-one, for a drink at the Helmsley Palace bar, the Lowell hotel, or the King Cole lounge in the St. Regis hotel, just to chat. One executive, who is gay, found Dimon's forthrightness so disarming that he quickly came out to his new boss. "It took me five years to come out to my previous CEO and 10 years to come out to the one before him," he recalls. "But Jamie Dimon has no bias. He's only biased against dishonest, game-playing people."

Dimon occasionally revealed his soft side. At a "town hall" meeting he held with secretaries in the company's London office, one secretary stuck up her hand. "Mr. Dimon," she said. "Yesterday my boss had me work for three hours—half of my afternoon—researching and booking a cruise for his mother." Thinking she'd just busted her boss, she waited for Dimon's temper to flare. "For his mother?" asked Dimon. "Yes," she replied. "Well, if it was for his *mother*, that's OK." Dimon's reports are nearly unanimous in pointing out what they consider to be the sincere, warm man hiding behind his relentlessness. When he smiles, they say, he is actually smiling, and not offering up a crocodile smile, what the old hands of Wall Street refer to as "grin-fucking."

He also won over most members of the JPMorgan Chase management team who hadn't yet worked for him. "He's really smart and cerebral, with an incredible capacity for retaining facts and information," says the commercial bank head, Todd Maclin. "But he's also really good with people. If you looked at our operating committee, what you have is a bunch of people that aren't very much alike. But every single one of them will just go to the wall for the guy, and for very unique reasons. He's got an extraordinary ability to connect with people, help them do what he wants them to do, and also feel good about working for him."

Early on, Dimon made a valuable connection to Bill Winters, a low-key J.P. Morgan veteran who ran the investment bank with Steve Black. Winters and Dimon had never met before the merger. Although J.P. Morgan had been viewed over the past half decade as a second-rate collection of talent, Winters was a standout. After the deal had been announced but before it was formally approved, he flew to Chicago to meet his new boss. Winters was blunt. "You have a reputation for not liking two things—complicated derivatives and proprietary risk-taking," he told Dimon. "But I can tell you that's a lot of what we do. So why would you want to merge with us?"

"It's not that I don't like derivatives," Dimon replied. "It's only when I don't understand them. So I want to spend some time getting to know them." Dimon meant what he said. He spent his first year at JPMorgan Chase understanding markets he hadn't been exposed to, and became supportive of the company's derivatives business. "Nor do I have a problem with risk," Dimon continued. "But what I can't stand is when proprietary risk takers in a company have preferential access to the balance sheet and compensation in relation to other parts of the firm."

Dimon explained to Winters that his problem with the Salomon arbitrage desk in 1998 was that Salomon's traders did have preferential access to the company's balance sheet and also got paid more, with the result that many of the firm's smartest people wanted to work on that desk, siphoning intellectual capital away from the rest of the business. And when something went wrong for the prop desk, it did so catastrophically.

Winters promised Dimon that no such preferential access would be permitted. Dimon had made a strong impression on him, so much so that instead of looking for a new job, Winters decided to stick around. Black and Winters were named co-CEOs of the investment bank in March 2004, just over a month after Dimon's arrival.

Dimon largely left the two men alone for the time being. The bank had suffered a large brain drain after the merger with Chase; according to one estimate, 80 of the top 100 people at the firm were gone within 18 months of the deal. But Black and Winters were rebuilding, and put together a revamped management team—hiring a trading standout, Matt Zames, from Credit Suisse; putting Carlos Hernandez in charge of equities; and moving the J.P. Morgan veteran Blythe Masters from the position of chief financial officer to overseeing commodities trading. They removed a number of management layers to enhance decision making and also revamped the company's credit systems in the hope of more effectively controlling their exposures.

Winters focused primarily on the company's credit and trading businesses out of the London office, while Black oversaw investment banking efforts from New York. The company made heavy investments in building out its energy trading capabilities as well as its mortgage-backed securities business. Co-CEOs tend to be a recipe for disaster in almost any industry, but Black and Winters struck a workable balance. They also told Dimon that if either of them appeared to be trying to stab the other in the back, he should fire them both.

One area that needed no rebuilding whatsoever was the company's derivatives business. JPMorgan Chase had long held a dominant position in all manner of derivatives—in 2004, the company was the top player in interest rate options, interest rate swaps, and credit and equity derivatives—and at the time of the merger it held $37 trillion in notional derivatives contracts, more than half the derivatives held by U.S. banks and trust companies. A lot has been made of this fact, but Dimon had by that point come around to the argument that derivatives were a good business for the firm, provided the risks and exposures were monitored rigorously.

For starters, the "notional" amounts were almost irrelevant numbers when collateralization and netting between JPMorgan Chase and its customers were accounted for. The company's net derivatives receivables at the time were actually far smaller, at $66 billion. That was still a large number, but not an outsize one compared with the rest of the industry. Morgan Stanley, for example, held $67 billion in net receivables at the time, and Goldman Sachs $62 billion. Both had far smaller balance sheets, as well, so JPMorgan Chase was actually taking on less risk, relatively speaking. (Still, the assumptions used in getting to that $66 billion were fraught with possible risk. If the investment bank's risk managers were off on that $37 trillion by just 1 percent, that's the equivalent of $370 billion, or three times the value of the entire company in early 2009.)

Much had been made by that point about Warren Buffett's letter to the shareholders of Berkshire Hathaway in 2002, in which he wrote, "In my view, derivatives are financial weapons of mass destruction, carrying dangers that, while now latent, are potentially lethal." But as he also wrote in the letter, he agreed it was true that derivative securities allowed for dispersion of risk by market participants not inclined to shoulder it. Dimon saw both sides of the argument as well, and considered it a valuable business for his company to be in.

(Six years later, Berkshire Hathaway revealed substantial derivatives holdings on its own balance sheet, positions Buffett had personally established because of what he saw as mispricings in the market. "I'll continue to say that used widely, derivatives pose systemic risk," says Buffett. "But that doesn't mean they're evil. We're holding $7 billion or $8 billion of cash attributable to ours. And I think these will work fine for me and not so well for the other guy." In his 2008 letter to shareholders, Dimon showed that his own position had not changed, either. "With proper management, systemic risks created by derivatives can be dramatically reduced without compromising the ability of companies to use them in managing their exposures," he wrote.)

Never one to lack swagger, Steve Black had told anyone who would listen after the merger between J.P. Morgan and Chase that he was going to build world-class capabilities in parts of the business where they were deficient. He'd been convinced that many of the previous decade's mergers had been nothing more than "stacking doughnuts"—the holes in the business that had existed before were still there. In 2001, Black boldly predicted JPMorgan Chase would take its equities underwriting business to the top five within three years and to the top three in five, a claim that was scoffed at on Wall Street. At the time, the firm didn't even appear in the "league tables," the year-end rankings of underwriters. But in 2003, it grabbed the number four position, up from eighth the previous year. And in 2004, it cracked the top three, ahead of schedule. Dimon knew to leave well enough alone.

Dimon charged into his work much the same way he had at Bank One in Chicago, with both elbows out. After he had been at the firm about a month, the new board of directors held a risk committee meeting. A number of division managers came before the board to make presentations about trading positions and other exposures; Dimon surprised most in attendance by showing that he was already familiar with most of their numbers. When one manager was unable to answer a particular question and said that he would report back to the board in a month, Dimon exploded: "No, I want to know tomorrow." As the blood drained from the executive's face, Bob Lipp thought, "Some of these people won't last long."

Lipp was right. Dimon swiftly removed managers who didn't have the answers when he wanted them, and replaced them with people like John Hogan, a veteran from Chase Manhattan who took over as the firm's chief risk officer in 2006.

Dimon went after "waste-cutting" with his usual zeal, shutting down 15 corporate gyms in the United States and Europe, removing fresh flowers from the company's offices, and ending all use of executive coaches. ("We have to be clear that managing is the job of managers, not outsiders," he deadpanned regarding the last move.) When he found out that a preponderance of high-level executives at JPMorgan Chase had their own chiefs of staff, he terminated the practice. Any consulting projects that cost more than $100,000 had to be personally approved by Dimon. Consulting costs plummeted. Staffers came to respond to certain queries by saying, "That's going to be a Jamie decision."

He gutted executives' benefits, eliminating country club memberships, first-class airline travel, 401(k) matching, severance plans, golden parachutes, deferred compensation, and change of control provisions. Performance would thereafter be rewarded solely with generous stock grants and options. Higher-paid employees were told that their health insurance premiums would be increased in order to subsidize those of lower-paid ones. He also instituted a "blood oath" similar to one he'd participated in at Commercial Credit so many years before. Members of the company's executive committee were required to hold on to 75 percent of their restricted stock awards, even after they vested. Just as the rumors had flown at Smith Barney about toilet paper, rumors flew about Dimon at JPMorgan Chase. Did he really go down to the street and ask the drivers of parked Lincoln town cars in front of the building what executives had called for them? No. But in the view of many, this was the kind of thing their new leader was entirely capable of doing.

(One thing about Dimon that was no myth: when he said "casual dress," he meant it. The first off-site meeting of the company's operating committee after his arrival was in Nantucket. For the two-day retreat, executives had been advised to dress "casually." When the team showed up in "office casual"—khakis and collared shirts—they were surprised to find Dimon wearing vintage tennis shorts that barely covered his thighs, and sneakers with no socks.)

In an attempt to make divisional managers more responsible for their bottom line, Dimon also pushed expenses that had somehow made their way into the "corporate" division back down to the units themselves. If there's anything Dimon hates, it's unallocated expenses. Sitting down with divisional managers in the summer of 2004, he explained that the profit and loss statements would need to be redone so that the results would better reflect the reality of their business. "OK, but we can't do it for the 2005 budget, so we'll do it for the 2006 budget," one executive suggested. "Oh, no," Dimon replied. "We're going to do it right now. We're going to get in this room and do it ourselves."

JPMorgan Chase had been a longtime sponsor of the U.S. Open tennis tournament in New York City, and senior employees had long enjoyed the perks of taking clients to the company's box at Arthur Ashe Stadium. But they didn't account for the cost of these tickets in their divisional results. Dimon recognized the sponsorship as a valuable piece of branding for the company but also thought that individual units should "pay" for tickets out of their own budget, rather than have corporate simply cover the entire cost. As a result of this and other initiatives, corporate's share of expenses plummeted from $5.3 billion in 2005 to just $1.1 billion in 2006. In 2008, a manager had to be prepared to take a $2,400 hit to his or her budget for a single U.S. Open ticket, making an invitation to a client a far more serious consideration than it had been in years past.

Dimon didn't stop there. After finding out that regional bank managers at Chase made five times as much as their new colleagues from Bank One, Dimon slashed compensation at hundreds of staff positions by as much as 50 percent over the next two years. He also took aim at the company's large outsourcing contracts, just as he had done at Bank One. In 2005, he canceled a $5 billion contract in which IBM was managing computer systems—in the process nullifying the largest outsourcing contract in history. "We want patriots, not mercenaries," he told *Fortune* magazine.

Around the same time, Dimon gathered the firm's top information technology people and told them they had six weeks to decide on a single computer system, covering the company's retail deposit platform, general ledger, credit card processing, and customer identification systems. He told them that if they didn't make the choice, he'd do it for them. In early summer, he cut matching programs for charitable gifts.

These moves did not endear him to his spoiled colleagues. "He's going down like cod liver oil," one banker told *Business Week* magazine. Another told *Euroweek*, "The news that Jamie is flying in is similar to being told that Ivan the Terrible is coming for tea."

It wasn't all just cost-cutting and reprimands. In short order, Dimon put his stamp on the company's strategic considerations, including whittling down Chase's auto leasing business and eliminating a program to lend to owners of manufactured housing. In December, the firm took a majority stake in the hedge fund Highbridge Capital, a $7 billion outfit based in New York City. Jes Staley, head of asset management, had to convince a skeptical Dimon of the merits of investing in Highbridge, a move he'd been pushing for despite a lack of support from his own management team. But his boss had come around in the end. By the end of 2007, the unit was managing $44.7 billion in capital and was the largest hedge fund operation in the world. (In June 2009, JPMorgan Chase purchased the rest of Highbridge, making it wholly owned.)

Staley also decided to take Dimon on regarding an issue that struck several of his colleagues as a dangerous one—whether the company's asset management group should stick with its proprietary offerings and not sell other firms' funds. Just as he had done at Smith Barney, Dimon advocated a so-called "open architecture" in which the firm's brokers were allowed to offer any number of funds, not just those from JPMorgan Chase. Staley insisted that they use only outside money managers to complement a core offering of in-house products. Colleagues referred Staley to Monica Langley's book *Tearing Down the Walls*, showed him the part where Jamie and Weill's daughter had quarreled over this same issue, and asked: did Staley want to suffer the same fate as Jessica Bibliowicz? "But that wasn't Jamie's way at all," says Staley. "He once said to me in the middle of a disagreement, 'Don't change your mind unless you change your mind.'"

Staley ultimately convinced Dimon by appealing to Dimon's own thinking on another issue. Dimon had shut down the IBM outsourcing contract because he believed that in financial services, controlling core technology and data was crucial to winning. Staley pleaded with Dimon that outsourcing asset management was in essence doing the same thing.

"If you outsource it, you're just going to be average," Staley said. After battling for nearly a year on the issue, Dimon finally relented. "He wants to understand your business," says Staley. "And he'll give you his views. But it is *your* business unless you don't perform."

(Staley's one concern was that Dimon would be unable to resist buying a brokerage firm to bolster the company's equity unit. Staley felt that the brokerage business conflicted with that of the private bank. His concern was not unfounded. Dimon had even said in a speech that if Smith Barney were to go up for sale, he would be an interested buyer. "My biggest worry was that Chuck Prince would call up in the middle of the night in 2007 and say, 'Jamie, here's Smith Barney,'" recalls Staley. "How could Jamie have said no?" Luckily for Staley, in early 2009 Citigroup agreed to merge its Smith Barney brokerage unit with Morgan Stanley's. The idea was officially off the table.)

With Charlie Scharf overseeing retail at Chase, he and Dimon instituted their policy of eliminating across-the-board bonuses for branch personnel and redeploying some of that money to top performers. Before they came, half of branch managers earned a bonus of $8,000 to $18,000. In the new system, the top generators of revenues and profits could earn as much as $65,000 in bonuses, whereas the poorest would earn nothing and quite possibly lose their jobs. (This was the same strategy they had implemented at Commercial Credit's branch offices back in the 1980s, and then at Bank One in Chicago.)

True to his initial promises, Harrison did not try to impede Dimon from taking power out of the gate and making large-scale decisions about the company's future—despite the fact that Dimon wouldn't officially be CEO until January 2006. "It's clear that Dimon has taken control," the analyst Dick Bove of Punk Ziegel told *Fortune* in October. Not that Harrison minded some of the fringe benefits; when you hitch your wagon to a superstar, people notice you a little more. In October, the two men joined Charlie Rose for an interview at the Economic Club of Chicago.

The company's 2004 annual report showed the extent to which it was now the Jamie Dimon show. The letter to shareholders, which had been four pages the previous year, now stretched to seven, and a number of Dimon's mantras had found their way into its pages. The company strived to use just one set of numbers—both internally and externally—to bring clarity to performance. He gave the same presentation to analysts and investors as he did to the board. The term "fortress balance sheet" was now part of the official management lexicon. Harrison and Dimon also set a goal of 20 percent return on equity through the economic cycle, with the idea that they might achieve 30 percent in good years and maintain a minimum of 10 percent in bad ones.

These grandiose plans aside, the company still struggled to deliver on its bottom line. In the third quarter, with earnings down 13 percent, Dimon didn't try to sugarcoat the situation. "These are terrible results," he said. "We don't feel good about it." That left little for anyone else to say. If you admit your mistakes, Dimon's theory went, you save yourself the hassle of having your critics point them out to you.

By the end of the year, 6,500 jobs—4 percent of the workforce—had been cut, and merger-related cost savings totaled $400 million. But lousy trading results sank the company's overall earnings, which fell 34 percent, from $6.7 billion to $4.47 billion. The heads of stock and bond trading were both fired. As unimpressive as those results were, Citigroup was in much worse shape, still embroiled in all manner of controversies, including continuing fallout from the Jack Grubman debacle.

In an awesome display of the Dimon effect, the analyst Dick Bove interpreted the poor results as a positive, in that they would allow Dimon to continue to make changes at the company going forward. Bove was not alone. *American Banker* named Dimon Banker of the Year for 2004, in large part owing to the merger. On December 20, he was named to the *Time*/CNN list of 25 "business influentials." He earned $7.9 million for the year, versus Harrison's $8.9 million.

Still, the nagging question about Dimon refused to go away. Did he have the vision to drive growth without acquisition? There were only so many banks one could buy, after all, and the integration problems could very easily overwhelm any inherent benefits of a deal. Dimon could bring costs down; that was indisputable. But for the stock market to take a real shine to JPMorgan Chase, he would have to show that he could raise revenues more quickly than the competition. And that wasn't happening. The combined companies' revenues rose a meager 2.8 percent in 2004. Worse, the return on equity was a paltry 10 percent, well below that of the competition.

. . .

As 2005 began, the media were cheering Dimon on from the sidelines. *Business Week* named him one of its "managers to watch" in January, and followed that with an article titled "Dimon's Grand Design" in March. But the stock market was still holding back its approval. The merger had been one of three major bank deals in 2004, and Bank One's former shareholders were lagging in returns—their stock was worth 9 percent more now than at the time of the deal, versus a 36 percent gain for shareholders of SouthTrust (which had been bought by Wachovia) and 58 percent for shareholders of FleetBoston (which had been purchased by Bank of America). Much of the differential had to do with the lower premium Dimon had accepted to get the deal done, but it was a third-place showing nonetheless.

Dimon's new colleagues had by now experienced his insatiable appetite for detail—there were no numbers or statistics that he wasn't interested in, whether it was the number of tickets bought for a Billy Joel concert or the number of phone calls people made each day. "Sometimes, all that matters are the details," he told *USA Today*. "Sometimes details will sink you. CEOs should drill down." By drilling down, Dimon meant sitting down and spending three hours or more every month going through 50-page books prepared for him by every division head, with the numbers from the prior month. "One thing Jamie brought with him to the company is the commitment to understanding a basic fact," recalls the commercial banking chief, Todd Maclin. "And that's that every single risk you're taking can be broken down to its smallest components and therefore be better understood. All it takes is time and effort."

Dimon also brought the painful and laborious tradition of sitting down with the operating committee for eight hours each year to go over the rationale behind the compensation of *every single one* of the firm's top 500 earners. Upset with the idea that other executives would have input into how to compensate their direct reports, some managers complained to Dimon. "Don't they work for me?" he was asked. "No, they work for the company," he replied. "How can you decide what to pay people if you don't know how other people think about the job they're doing?"

Despite the seeming sense in such practices, Wall Street—including much of JPMorgan Chase before Dimon arrived—usually tends in the opposite direction, toward secrecy and hoarding information. "If you'd asked someone else for their profit and loss statement before Jamie instituted this stuff, they would have told you to go jump in a lake," says Todd Maclin. "It would be like asking to see their hemorrhoid scars. 'That's personal stuff!' they'd say. 'How dare you ask me to see my P&L?' But now, it's like they're all posted somewhere on the company's intranet. There's just so much transparency."

People were also becoming more familiar with his tendency for debate-driven decision making. When you worked for Jamie Dimon, he expected you to speak your mind. If you didn't, he'd just as soon replace you. "I don't care if we do the trade or don't do the trade," he told a reporter. "I care that we do it right. . . . If you work in a company where you can't walk in the room and say what you think, you create an atmosphere where you don't do the best you can and where people don't disclose things."

"Jamie brought a level of communication and consistent analytical rigor to the operating committee that was familiar to me from the old J.P. Morgan but that had gone missing between 2001 and 2004," recalls Winters. "And he brought the fortress balance sheet mantra. The old J.P. Morgan had done some things right and some things wrong. A fortress balance sheet had been one of our tenets, but we lost it after we sold the company to Chase. Jamie brought it back."

The emphasis on openness extended to what senior executives felt free to say to the media. Whereas, in later years, Sandy Weill did not tolerate outright criticism, Dimon's reports at times seemed to be trying to one-up each other regarding how much they could get away with in terms of the backhanded compliment. "I'm not going to say he's perfect," Steve Black told *USA Today*. "[But] when you're yelling and screaming and sticking your fingers in each others' eyes, you're treating Jamie as one of your partners, not as the CEO." Heidi Miller, CEO of JPMorgan Chase's treasury and securities services, voiced a similar point of view. "He's not a saint," she said. "He makes mistakes, but he lets you talk back." And again, more about the yelling: "The yelling is never personal," Miller added. "He doesn't yell that much anymore."

He would, however, get directly involved in any issue that he thought was hampering the bank's ability to execute. Never having lost the taste for a profitable cross-sell, Dimon was incensed when the commercial banking head, Todd Maclin, told him investment bankers were preventing his people from contacting prospective middle-market clients. A heated meeting subsequently took place, during which Dimon relieved angry investment bankers of a number of clients, giving them to Maclin's team. "The room was filled with hollering and yelling," Maclin told *Fortune*. But Dimon did not back down.

What mattered to Dimon was that people got paid for performance and that the right people were doing the right jobs. That's about it. "That's why Americans love sports," he told a reporter. "There's a purity in it—you win or you lose—but in corporate America when you strike out, there's always some excuse. . . . Leaders should step down when a company does poorly, not be given increased pay."

As many years as he'd been in the business, Dimon had not yet grown bored with old-fashioned relentlessness; he was like a football coach content to stick to a dominating ground game. "He just pounds through and pounds through and pounds through, as opposed to someone who tries really clever plays," says Richard Bookstaber, author of *A Demon of Our Own Design*.

He was also investing for the future. In 2005, the bank invested $300 million in its retail branch network, opening 150 new branches and making strategic moves such as putting 270 ATMs in Duane Reade drugstores in New York and 200 ATMs in Walgreen's in Arizona. The company also rebranded 1,400 Bank One branches under the Chase identity, and converted the remaining 560 in 2006. It also completed the largest credit card conversion in history, putting 30 million Chase and Bank One customers on a single technology platform.

Winters and Black, meanwhile, had focused on reducing the volatility of the firm's trading through a number of initiatives, including their own investments in technology. They instituted tighter "stop losses," triggers for bailing out of a losing trade. Trading results were less volatile in 2005 than in 2004—even as revenues were rising significantly—and that trend continued in 2006. The company also continued to make progress in the league tables, moving into the top slot in convertible bond offerings, high-yield corporate bonds, and leveraged loans in 2005.

Much of 2005 was taken up by pushing through the completion of the merger. The company spent $2.9 billion on information technology during the year, including $1 billion on technology platform conversions, more than its major competitors. Analysts were impressed with Dimon's commitment to the drudgery of making the company's in-house systems talk to each other. "Someone sneezes in their mortgage division, and someone in credit cards catches a cold," observed the CIBC Oppenheimer analyst Meredith Whitney.

Merger savings rose to $1.9 billion, and by the end of the year most of the targeted 12,000 layoffs were complete. In recognition of the power of technology to position the bank for the future, Dimon named the chief information officer, Austin Adams, to the firm's 15-member operating committee. "Technology is to us what manufacturing is to General Motors," he told a reporter, explaining that good information systems are a "moat" that protects a business from rivals.

Dimon finally managed to lure Frank Bisignano away from Citigroup. It wasn't easy, as Bisignano had been running one of Citigroup's largest business units, the global transaction services group; Dimon wanted him to take on a distinctly less glamorous role as chief administrative officer. Luckily for Dimon, Bisignano had always wanted to work with him again, and now that Dimon was back in New York, the time was finally right. "I'll do whatever job you want me to do," Bisignano told him. "As long as I have a voice, I'll play whatever position you want."

The slow disintegration of the Travelers culture at Citigroup was certainly on the minds of many who attended a reunion at Armonk that summer; Chuck Prince invited Dimon, Bob Druskin, John Fowler, Bob Lipp, and Joe Plumeri to join some old friends, including Willumstad and Weill, as well as new Citi employees such as the wealth management chief Todd Thomson and the chief financial officer Sallie Krawcheck. Dimon didn't feel uncomfortable at all returning to the place where Weill had fired him seven years before. While the old hands were telling stories and cracking wise about their time together, neither Thomson nor Krawcheck seemed inclined to rib their boss, Prince, along with everyone else. The camaraderie and bonhomie that had once existed at Travelers was no more.

Earlier that year, in July, Dimon and Harrison had dinner at The Four Seasons, and Harrison said he would step down at the end of the year. And again, he was true to his word. On December 31, Dimon became CEO and president of JPMorgan Chase. At his first investors' conference as CEO, his parents were sitting in the front row. "It was cute on one level," recalls the analyst Meredith Whitney. "But also totally unorthodox." (Shortly thereafter, Dimon eliminated any company spending at the Masters Golf Tournament in Augusta, Georgia, as he had done at Bank One. He'd had to wait at JPMorgan Chase, however, as Harrison was a member.)

Dimon wrote the letter to shareholders in the 2005 annual report, and it was as evocative of Warren Buffett as ever. (Todd Maclin says Dimon looks at writing this annual letter as the president does at writing the State of the Union address.) He stressed the need for "honesty," "integrity and honor," and doing "the right thing, not necessarily the easy or expedient thing." This was writing for an audience, not just reporting results. And for good reason. Everyone *was* watching Jamie Dimon, waiting to see what he'd do now that he was completely in charge at JPMorgan Chase.

11. WINNING BY NOT LOSING

Friendly foreign ministers notwithstanding, Dimon inherited a company that had been losing its world-class cachet for decades. The merger with Chase Manhattan had done nothing to resuscitate it; in fact, it had the opposite effect. In *The House of Morgan*, the financial historian Ron Chernow writes that executives at J.P. Morgan had rejected entreaties from Chase as far back as 1953, out of fear that a merger would endanger the firm's reputation for "haute banking." Those fears proved valid.

This is not to say that Chase Manhattan had no pedigree of its own. Its earliest predecessor company actually predates J.P. Morgan & Company itself by nearly a century. After Alexander Hamilton founded the Bank of New York, the nascent state's first commercial bank in 1784, he had the playing field to himself until 1799, when his political rival Aaron Burr founded the Bank of Manhattan. That bank's predecessor, the Manhattan Company, had been one of the island's first water companies; it used hollowed-out pine logs as its pipes. Burr took advantage of a legal loophole that allowed the company to invest its excess capital outside its primary business, and in the process founded the bank. Hamilton and Burr eventually settled their differences in a duel, and JPMorgan Chase owns the pistols they used. They're displayed on the fiftieth floor of the Park Avenue headquarters and are worth an estimated $25 million.

A banker named John Thompson founded the Chase National Bank in 1877. He named his firm after Salmon P. Chase, who'd been

President Lincoln's secretary of the treasury as well as chief justice of the United States. Chase came to be called "the Rockefeller bank" because of its extensive ties to industrialist John D. Rockefeller. His grandson David joined the firm in 1946 and eventually took over as CEO. In 1955, after being spurned by J.P. Morgan, he and the chairman, John J. Mc-Cloy, merged Chase with the Bank of Manhattan, creating Chase Manhattan. In 1960, Rockefeller oversaw the construction of the bank's downtown headquarters at One Chase Manhattan Plaza (technically, Liberty Street). At the time, it had the largest bank vault in the world.

Chemical Bank swallowed Chase Manhattan in 1996. Chemical had been on an acquisition tear of its own under the leadership of Walter V. Shipley, purchasing Texas Commerce Bank in 1986 and Manufacturer's Hanover in 1991. (As with Chase, its roots predate that of J.P. Morgan & Company; it was founded in 1823 as a producer of chemicals including camphor and saltpeter.) Bob Lipp later served as a historical bridge between the Commercial Credit crowd and those he'd worked with at Chemical in the 1980s.

J.P. Morgan & Company had its roots in the "gilded age" of American finance. Founded in 1871 by J. Pierpont Morgan and the Philadelphia banker Anthony Drexel, the bank dominated the country's burgeoning railroad industry, and soon became the most influential and powerful bank to corporate interests in the country. It went on to save the U.S. Treasury with an infusion of gold in 1893 and then save the New York Stock Exchange—and New York City itself—with an eleventh-hour deal that put an end to the financial panic of 1907 by assembling a syndicate to purchase $30 million in bonds from the city. At the company's offices at 23 Wall Street at the corner of Broad and Wall (also known as "The Corner"), J.P. Morgan himself was more monarch than banker. According to Chernow, the creation of the Federal Reserve in 1913 was in part motivated by a desire to free the government from reliance on the House of Morgan. Nevertheless, just two years later, in 1915, the company made the largest international loan—$500 million—to the allies in World War I.

Never the largest bank in total assets, J.P. Morgan & Company distinguished itself by its influence and reputation as the lender of last resort. It was also the bastion of "first class banking in a first class way"—epitomizing the notion that bankers were not mere moneygrubbers but gentlemen.

By the time Dimon arrived, however, gentleman banking was an anachronism, and the institution seemed to have a much greater history than it did a future. JPMorgan Chase trailed both Citigroup and Bank of America in retail banking, and its investment bank was an also-ran to Goldman Sachs, Merrill Lynch, and Morgan Stanley. (The last of these, it bears noting, was the securities business spun off from J.P. Morgan & Company in 1935, following the passage of Glass-Steagall.)

"There is no way in which Dimon can sit back and say, 'I want to be as good as Goldman Sachs in investment banking,' " wrote *Euroweek* at the time. "Except, of course, in his dreams." Indeed, when Dimon took the reins of JPMorgan Chase, few expected him to restore the company to anywhere near its former dominance. His job was more widely seen as fixing a busted institution. In January, the *Wall Street Journal* ran an illustration of him carrying a ladder, hammer, and blueprints. It didn't seem possible at the time that he might achieve the former by doing the latter.

• • •

The fuel of Wall Street is part hope, part reality. The market is driven not just by what's actually happening but also by expectations of what might happen. When it comes to the future unknown, one of Wall Street's favorite parlor games since Dimon first took over at Bank One is: What will Jamie buy next?

As 2005 came to a close, with the transfer of power from Harrison, the game began anew. In October, *Fortune* suggested Dimon had "the urge to merge" despite the fact that he told the magazine just the opposite. "I would be extremely reluctant to do a deal with our current stock price," he said. "Our people aren't ready either. We need our 101st Airborne to do an acquisition, and they're still on the ground putting together the mergers we've already done."

Despite repeated denials, the chatter continued. Rumors centered on Bear Stearns and Morgan Stanley, either of which would plug gaps in JPMorgan Chase's portfolio—both had substantial brokerage units as well as prominent prime brokerage businesses that serviced hedge funds.

But there would be no deals, and Wall Street turned its attention elsewhere, particularly to the booming housing market. Lenders all over the country were throwing money at homebuyers, and underwriting standards were in free fall. From just $492.6 billion in issuance in 1996, the mortgage market had grown to $3.1 trillion in 2003. Between 2001 and 2007, $15 trillion in mortgages was issued. If it seemed as though every other person was a real estate agent or a mortgage broker in 2005, that's because they were. Just a few years after the dot-com debacle, America had embarked on yet another gold rush, but this time it wasn't just in California—it was everywhere. Refinancings had climbed from just $14 billion in 1995 to nearly $250 billion by 2005. As Daniel Gross suggests in his book *Dumb Money*, "Houses were the new tech stocks, valued not so much for the income they could produce as for their rapid growth potential."

In January 2006, Alan Greenspan stepped down as chairman of the Federal Reserve. He was given a send-off befitting a heroic general. Never mind that at the tail end of his 18-year tenure, an asset bubble of historic proportions was looking as if it would pop any minute. That was a problem for later. President George W. Bush appointed the Fed governor Ben Bernanke to be Greenspan's replacement. One of Bernanke's first significant moves was to lift the restrictions on Citigroup that prevented it from making further acquisitions until it had upgraded its "compliance culture." He also actively resisted the regulation of hedge funds in May 2006, saying it would "stifle innovation."

Wall Street extracted profits from the housing boom largely through securitization—firms bought all the mortgages they could get their hands on and then bundled them into packages of bonds that they sold to investors. As the most successful version of financial alchemy in history, securitization also planted the seeds of the housing market's eventual implosion, by removing any reason for a lender to care about whether the borrower would be able to repay the loan, as the lender would have sold the loan off into the secondary market anyway. But it took time before that problem would become manifest. Buoyed by rising home prices—by 2006, 86 percent of refinancings included home-owners borrowing even more money than they had previously owed—Americans spent widely, boosting the stock market in the process. By mid-2006, stocks had climbed more than 50 percent from the market bottom in 2002. It was a self-reinforcing cycle of borrowing and consumption.

Many of JPMorgan Chase's competitors were focused on growth for the sake of growth, and the market was rewarding them for it. Citigroup, which had yet to find its footing since its scandals earlier in the decade, found its new motivating principle in a concept known as "operating leverage"—the ability to grow revenues faster than expenses, thereby increasing profits. This concept is sound in theory—profitable growth is the goal of any manager—but CEO Chuck Prince's obsession with the notion led Citigroup to start growing its balance sheet indiscriminately, with managers piling on new assets that earned the bank even the slightest of "spreads," or profit. In rising markets, such a strategy can seem brilliant. But if capital should become scarce and your debt can't be rolled over, the results can be disastrous.

Although JPMorgan Chase was in the game on several fronts—it aggressively grew its mortgage business, its home equity lending, and its leveraged loan book (in which it syndicated giant loans to finance private equity deals)—Dimon remained preoccupied with preparing the bank for a time when the froth came to an end. "You don't run a business hoping you don't have a recession," he liked to say; and he spent countless hours on scenario planning, with an emphasis on bear-market possibilities. He remade the company's information systems so that he could get the reports he needed when he needed them. This allowed him to make rapid strategic decisions, and also gave him another way to hold his people accountable. At Citigroup, accountability was in short supply, but at JPMorgan Chase, it was getting more abundant. "What you could see was a consistency to performance, rather than someone chasing the flavor of the month," recalls Marge Magner, Dimon's former colleague at Travelers. "That, and a respect for the balance sheet that's unwavering."

In nearly all respects, the paths of JPMorgan Chase and Citigroup diverged. In 2005, Chuck Prince effectively forced out both Magner and Willumstad. A short time later, they launched Brysam Global Partners, a private equity firm that would invest in retail financial services companies. Their biggest seed investor was Jamie Dimon, via JPMorgan Chase. Firing people is one thing; driving them into the arms of your closest competitor is another. When he retired from an active role at JPMorgan Chase in 2008, Bob Lipp joined Magner and Willumstad at Brysam.

"We think [the business] should be prepared for adverse times," Dimon told analysts in a conference call. "In fact, we think if you're strong in adverse times that that puts you in the position where you actually can do more interesting things, either hire people or buy other companies that are having a tough time." Dimon and his team were constantly modeling what might happen if there were 10 percent unemployment, for example, or a 10 percent move in currency exchange rates. "Run your business knowing it might be sunny, it might be stormy, or in fact it might be a hurricane," he said. "And be honest about how bad a hurricane might be." The goal was not only to earn high returns at the top of the cycle but also to avoid giving them back at the bottom.

The media responded to the message, at least in part. In April, *Fortune* magazine's authority on Dimon, Shawn Tully, wrote a cover story headlined "The Toughest Guy on Wall Street" that extolled the virtues of a certain kind of anal micromanagement. In the article Steve Black pointed out, "He jumps into the decision-making process. If you just want to run your business on your own and report results, you won't like working for Jamie." (Inside JPMorgan Chase, there were snickers at the suggestion that Dimon was really all that tough. "My secretary wouldn't stop giggling about it," he recalls.) *Time* magazine followed up by putting him on its 2006 "*Time* 100" list of the world's most influential people.

(On balance, the coverage of Dimon in the press over the years has been overwhelmingly positive—the *Wall Street Journal* has called him "reliably quotable." That's due in large part to the fact that reporters find his candor refreshing. "When I talk to the press, I may not answer all their questions," he says, "but I'm accessible. I may tell them that something is none of their business or that it's privileged information. But one thing I don't do is lie to them.")

Analysts and investors, however, weren't quite so jazzed by the company's cautious tilt. The chief financial officer, Mike Cavanagh, recalls being harangued by investors demanding a reason why they should bother with JPMorgan Chase stock when they could own "best-in-class" competitors like Goldman Sachs in investment banking or American Express in credit cards—companies that were two to three times as leveraged as JPMorgan Chase. And analysts were losing interest in merely watching costs go down. They craved big news, like an acquisition or significant gains in market share. "He told us to expect big progress in 2005," the CIBC analyst Meredith Whitney told *Fortune*. "Now we won't see major improvements until 2007."

JPMorgan Chase's quarterly calls became known for their regularity. The presentations to investors, used during quarterly conference calls, have been largely the same since the beginning of 2006, right down to the fonts and colors used to highlight the company's results. Mike Cavanagh, who presents the company's financial results along with Dimon, admits that little effort is put into making them entertaining. "The routine is nice and boring," he says. "The information isn't boring but the way we go about it is painfully monotonous, even to me. We set up the presentation so people can compare profits brutally to natural competitors in each of our businesses. It causes us to need to fall on our sword when it's obvious that the numbers say so. We're not trying to figure out how to tell the story differently every three months."

Still, the company's stock was stuck in neutral, while other firms' stocks were on the move. From the beginning of 2005 through mid-2006, JPMorgan Chase shares rose just 7.7 percent, while Goldman's had rocketed 44.6 percent. Shares of Morgan Stanley were up 13.8 percent, while Wells Fargo—which could claim no "Dimon effect"—had edged out JPMorgan Chase with a 7.9 percent gain. Wall Street was bored with Jamie Dimon.

. . .

By the fall of 2006, the U.S. housing and mortgage markets had gone off the rails, but Wall Street seemed not to notice or care, shrugging off some analysts' warnings of impending disaster. The bull market in real estate had essentially unshackled itself from the underlying reality. No one wanted to hear the bad news, so few did.

Much of Wall Street, in fact, doubled down just as the real estate market was reaching its peak. In September 2006, Merrill Lynch paid $1.3 billion to buy the subprime lender First Franklin Financial. A month before, Morgan Stanley had spent $706 million for Saxon Capital, another subprime lender. Subprime loans had risen from $145 billion annually in 2001 to $625 billion in 2005, accounting for 20 percent of all issuance. Wall Street was paying little attention to where loans came from—firms just wanted the raw material for their mortgage securitization assembly lines.

In the summer of 2004, Bill Winters had persuaded Dimon to unload a so-called structured investment vehicle (SIV) that had come onto the company's balance sheet as part of the Bank One deal. (Despite his skill at micromanagement, Dimon had apparently not noticed this potentially explosive asset.) Essentially arbitrage vehicles that borrow short-term to finance investments in longer-term debt—including mortgage and bank securities—SIVs were, in times of easy credit, perfect fee generators for banks, which typically managed them for investors. Banks held these entities off their balance sheets, since they were not technically the owners of the assets themselves. But should credit ever become scarce, as it inevitably does in a slowing economy, they could be obligated to step in and cover losses.

Winters helped Dimon to realize that the fees didn't offer a high enough return to offset the implied risk, and they unloaded the sole SIV, worth $8 billion, that sat on their books to the London-based bank Standard Chartered. "We sold it to someone who thought the best way to manage the risk was to take on twice as much of it. Scale is the answer every time except in the tail," Winters later said, referring to how concentrated risks in SIVs worked out just fine until they instantaneously blew up in their sponsors' faces. Citigroup, true to form, was moving in the other direction, piling into SIVs just as JPMorgan Chase pulled out.

Winters also reduced the credit lines the bank was extending to other banks' SIVs from $12 billion to $500 million.

With regard to structured products, Winters was no neophyte. He had been part of the J.P. Morgan team that had revolutionized credit derivatives in the late 1990s. The first innovation came to be known as a "credit default swap" (CDS). In looking for a way to reduce exposure to their client Exxon—which had recently tapped a multibillion-dollar credit line with the bank in anticipation of having to pay substantial fines for the *Exxon Valdez*'s oil spill—Winters's colleague Blythe Masters had found another investor willing to insure the debt for the bank in exchange for an annual fee. In the process, J.P. Morgan was able to reduce its exposure to Exxon without having to sell the loan, thereby keeping client relations strong. (No corporate borrowers want to see their bank unloading their loans.) It was nothing short of revolutionary. What the J.P. Morgan team had done, writes Gillian Tett in *Fool's Gold*, was to "overturn one of the fundamental rules of banking: that default risk is an inevitable liability of the business."

The Federal Reserve later ruled that banks could reduce the required level of capital reserves by using credit derivatives. From that point, it was clear that there would be no shortage of buyers of CDS. Nearly every bank in existence had loans it would like to get off its books. There would surely be no shortage of sellers, either, whether these sellers were hedge funds making outright bets or insurance companies thinking their expertise in traditional forms of insurance could easily extend into the realm of credit.

To turbocharge the market for credit derivatives, the J.P. Morgan team eventually created a product called a broad index secured trust offering (BISTRO). Complex in its details and accounting, the product was nevertheless simple in essence—it aggregated the odds of default on a whole package of loans, not just on a single credit. Collateralized debt packages had long been around, but BISTRO represented a whole new segment—synthetic collateralized debt obligations (CDOs). Wall Street has an endless ability to slice and dice, though; and as soon as it was created, BISTRO was separated into various "tranches" that carried different levels of risk and return. Investors in the junior tranche would eat the first losses due to any defaults, and therefore earn the highest return. The mezzanine tranche came next, and after that was the senior tranche.

The credit rating agencies agreed that the different tranches deserved different credit ratings, and convinced themselves that even if a CDO was made up of low-rated credits, the senior tranche might actually have a higher rating than any of the individual loans. Even if every single credit in the CDO had a 30 percent risk of default, the thinking went, the odds that most of them would default at once were arguably infinitesimal. If you held the senior tranche, therefore, you were actually holding something whose probability of default was less than 30 percent. Thus, it had a higher rating.

Although both rating agencies and investment banks were pilloried in 2007 and 2008 for what was eventually reduced to a joke about filling a bag with crap and calling it gold, the intellectual argument behind the tranche ratings wasn't dishonest or entirely flawed. It just failed to properly take into account the low-probability scenario in which most of the loans *did* default at once. And it's not as if bankers weren't aware of the possibility. Because J.P. Morgan had agreed to step in and guarantee BISTRO in the event that its funding was wiped out in some sort of über-default, they gave *that* risk its own name—super-senior. Better yet, they found a buyer of that risk (or, more precisely, a seller of insurance against it)—the insurance giant AIG. Joseph Cassano, head of a unit called AIG Financial Products, figured he was getting something for nothing with the transaction. It was like selling insurance against the end of the world. Why not take the money now, especially considering that if the end did come, you probably wouldn't be around to have to pay the bill anyway? A decade later, AIG would pay a colossal price for Cassano's cynicism.

(What Cassano and many others missed was the auto-synchronous relationship of many loans. Buy 12 different loans, and you're pretty diversified. In principle, this is true. Unless, that is, those loans are all mortgages for houses sitting next to each other on a beach in Charleston, South Carolina. One strong hurricane, and the portfolio would be decimated. And the global real estate crisis hit like the mother of all hurricanes.)

Although the company occasionally kept a portion of that hived-off risk on its own books, the members of the BISTRO team considered themselves financial intermediaries as opposed to investors in the product itself. They saw it as a way to reduce their corporate lending risk, as opposed to taking on more. As the author of *Fool's Gold*, Gillian Tett, pointed out in the *Financial Times*, however, Wall Street turned the product inside out. "As often occurs with Wall Street alchemy, a good idea started to be misused—and a product initially devised to insulate against risk soon morphed into a device that actually concentrated dangers." Money was still cheap in the first half of the decade, and investors were clamoring for higher yields. Wall Street responded by creating newer flavors of synthetic CDOs that added leverage and delved into riskier asset classes, including subprime mortgages. The only conceivable problem for investment banks was that tranches for which they couldn't find a buyer had to be held in inventory.

Demand for synthetic CDO product was so high that the yields on these newer, far riskier structures were pushed downward, raising doubts about whether the market was properly pricing the risk. That was especially the case, as a pioneer in collateralized mortgages, Lewis Ranieri, told *The New Yorker* in 2008, because by this point banks were lending to almost anyone who wanted to borrow, to buy whatever house they wanted, for no money down, no matter what their financial wherewithal. "They had created the perfect loan," said Ranieri. "They didn't know what the home was worth, they didn't know what the borrower earned, and the borrower wasn't putting any money into the purchase. The system had gone completely nuts."

By late 2006, Winters had concluded that it was no longer worth the risk to underwrite or hold any such product on the company's books. At the time, CDOs were yielding just 2 percentage points more than Treasuries. To hedge the CDO risk, JPMorgan Chase needed to buy credit default swaps, but the cost of those was rising. (In this, at least, the market was getting it right. Investors in CDOs might be taking too little yield, but sellers of insurance on those CDOs were starting to demand more money, even though it ultimately proved to be nowhere near enough.) Winters had no problem convincing Dimon of his concerns, and the bank began to pull back from all asset-backed CDO underwriting, while also selling the majority of subprime mortgages originated by the bank during the year. "I'd love to say we saw what was coming," Winters later said, referring to the housing collapse that crushed the value of these securities. "But that would be a lie. We just couldn't see the return in them."

Merrill Lynch's CEO Stan O'Neal, among others, disagreed, and revved up his firm's production of the complex securities. In 2006, Merrill underwrote $44 billion in CDOs, three times its 2004 output, collecting $700 million in fees. It created another $31 billion in 2007. O'Neal had personally intervened to set the company on this course, providing all the necessary capital to take the firm from fifteenth place in CDO underwriting in 2003 to first place in 2005. In mid-2006, he fired three executives who had warned that the firm was becoming dangerously overexposed in CDOs.

Wall Street firms issued $178 billion in mortgage- and asset-backed CDOs in 2005 and almost twice that in 2006. They effectively overstuffed the pipeline, and an increasing volume of the securities stayed in-house. At first, that didn't worry executives such as O'Neal. The idea that Wall Street functioned merely as intermediary was officially out the window. Wall Street firms were acting like drug dealers who forgot the cardinal rule of the trade: don't start taking the junk yourself. By mid-2007, Merrill owned more than $32 billion worth of CDOs.

In keeping only the highest-rated portions of the CDOs on their books, Wall Street executives looked at it as the perfect double-dip: fees for underwriting and profits from owning the least risky component of a package of debts—the probability that everything would default at once. Most of the stuff they kept on their books was AAA-rated, top-notch stuff, as good as the debt of Johnson & Johnson or General Electric. The world would have to come to an end before the strategy backfired. This was an echo of the flawed perspective at Long-Term Capital Management in the late 1990s. "The source of the trouble seemed so small, so laughably remote, as to be insignificant," Roger Lowenstein wrote about LTCM in *When Genius Failed*. "But isn't that always the way?"

Investment bankers were well compensated for ignoring the risks.

Huge bonuses were paid from CDO deals, even though large pieces of these deals ended up sitting on the companies' own balance sheets. It was a salesman's nirvana. If no one wanted to buy the product you created, your own company would buy it from you, paying full commission.

Analysts responded by giving JPMorgan Chase what one insider calls "a world of shit for our fixed income revenues." In 2006, the company was ranked nineteenth in asset-backed CDO issuance, well behind Citigroup, Merrill Lynch, Lehman Brothers, Bear Stearns, and UBS. Instead of wondering whether those other firms were being lazy with their own capital, chasing the so-called "carry trade" on CDOs, critics said that JPMorgan Chase was being too cautious. "One of the toughest jobs of the CEO is to look at all the stupid stuff other people are doing and to not do them," says Bob Willumstad, Dimon's longtime colleague at Travelers. "Maybe you're the stupid one."

But Dimon became more cautious yet. JPMorgan Chase had a reputation before he arrived for a tendency to get overexposed to Wall Street fads, such as telecom loans and technology private equity. He was determined not to repeat these mistakes by diving into the subprime and securitized debt fads. He remained vigilant about improving what he referred to as the "productivity" of the firm's risk capital—more bang returned for every buck risked. He had already scaled back the firm's proprietary trading activities in 2005, and he wasn't about to reverse course and pile on risky assets less than a year later. "Everyone was trying to grow in products we didn't want to grow in," he later told a reporter. "So we let them have it." Included among those products were so-called negative amortization and option adjustable-rate mortgages, which enticed undercapitalized home buyers to take on huge debts.

In October 2006, at a meeting with executives of the company's retail bank, Dimon was told that subprime loans made by the retail bank were deteriorating dramatically. At the same time, the numbers showed an even greater deterioration among the loans made by competitors such as First Franklin (which Merrill Lynch had just bought) and Lehman Brothers. The credit card division, too, was seeing a decline in the quality of its own subprime lending. Dimon came to the conclusion that it was time to *really* dial back the subprime exposure. He called Billy King, then chief of securitized products. "I've seen it before," he told King. "This stuff could go up in smoke." Within weeks, the bank sold more than $12 billion in subprime mortgages it had originated. Dimon's intuitive grasp, which his friend Jeremy Paul had seen in high school, was serving him in his role as CEO—while his managers handled their own patches, he monitored the bigger picture and realized that something was amiss.

In moving his bank out of the way of the oncoming subprime train, Dimon proved to be an exception to the great economist John Maynard Keynes's cynical observation that a "sound banker . . . is not one who foresees danger and avoids it, but one who, when he is ruined, is ruined in a conventional and orthodox way along with his fellows, so that no one can really blame him." Dimon would not be ruined along with his fellows.

If there's one thing that even Dimon's supporters will criticize him for, it's that he willfully circumvents traditional chains of command, thereby complicating his managers' relations with their own subordinates. He might ask 10 people for the same piece of information, just so he gets it as soon as possible. But his meddling is tolerated because of the results. In fact, some people see the meddling as one of his more valuable assets. "All the great CEOs that I've ever seen have this characteristic," says his longtime adviser Bill Campbell. "They spend a lot of time at 50,000 feet, they spend significant time—although hopefully not too much—on the ground, and not much time in between. The 50,000 feet stuff is obviously incredibly important in terms of strategy and all that sort of stuff. The ground stuff is really important too. It helps the people that are on the ground because they believe they have a leader that understands them, can talk to them, can touch them, and understands their problems. But it also throws the middle management off because they go, 'God, he knows *that*.' Or 'He knows *her*.' It's very good for middle management to have a leader that's kind of bipolar in that way."

JPMorgan Chase's head of strategy, Jay Mandelbaum, points out another unique trait that has allowed Dimon to excel in the role of chief executive. When making decisions, he is extremely adept at looking at all the available information and quickly isolating the few issues that matter. "He won't overanalyze a thing to death either," says Mandelbaum. "At some point, you've got to go with your instincts."

The company's investment bank reported a 0.1 percent decline in profits in 2006, a year in which the likes of Goldman Sachs, Morgan Stanley, and Merrill Lynch reported 76 percent, 61 percent, and 44 percent increases in profit, respectively. Earnings at the top five independent investment banks, in fact, had tripled between 2002 and 2006, to more than $30 billion. And bonuses totaled $23.9 billion, more than $136,000 per employee. JPMorgan Chase's historically volatile trading results had been tamed, but in other regards the analyst community was disappointed. "We entered 2007 thinking we were slipping," recalls Winters. "We were missing a few things, that's true; our commodity business was very small. But in retrospect it would become clear that we just weren't booking a lot of revenues on business that would end up proving very expensive. If you could go back and take out of our competitors' earnings what was later attributable to disasters, I think we probably did very well."

• • •

While investors clamored for a big deal, Dimon actually shed assets, selling Brown & Co., the company's deep discount brokerage business, to E*Trade for $1.6 billion, and selling its life insurance and annuity underwriting business to Protective Life Corporation. JPMorgan Chase did acquire 339 bank branches (and their associated commercial banking business) from the Bank of New York, but that wasn't stuff to excite anyone.

"People are always saying I'm going to rush in somewhere and do a deal," says a frustrated Dimon. "But that's not me. We did a lot of small little buys and sells, usually driven by the outline of the business, until Bear Stearns. I certainly don't need to do a deal that adds some seventh leg to our business unless it has some strategic imperative."

On a call with analysts in May, he tried, once again, to make explicit his view of acquisition opportunities. "There are three things that have to make sense," he said. "And they are not in order of importance. One is the business logic. There should be clear business logic to it. The second is the price. Sometimes there is a price [at] which you cannot make it pay for shareholders. And the third is the ability to execute. [You have to be able to] see clearly getting done what you need to get done, whether it's management or systems or marketing or culture or something like that. If those things make sense, you can then weigh and balance them. Meaning, if you have exceptional business logic and an easy ability to execute, you could pay a higher price. And conversely, if those things are a little more complex, you want a margin of error by getting a lower price."

Of course, it doesn't always take a splashy acquisition to make a pile of money. In the summer of 2006, Dimon, Black, and Winters made their most audacious play of the year when they snapped up a portfolio of disastrous bets on natural gas prices that had been made by Amaranth Advisors, a $9.2 billion hedge fund that was facing collapse if it couldn't get the underwater trades off its books. On the weekend of September 16, Amaranth was desperately seeking a buyer for the trades. Goldman Sachs offered to do a deal for a portion of the total, but it demanded a $1.85 billion payment to relieve Amaranth of the positions.

Lacking that much cash, Amaranth turned to JPMorgan Chase, the hedge fund's clearing broker, and asked if the firm might return $2 billion of posted collateral so it could get the deal done. Steve Black and Bill Winters refused. When Goldman then backed out, Amaranth received a similar offer—"Give us cash and we'll take over the trades"— from the Chicago-based hedge fund Citadel, to take the entire portfolio off its books. But the problem remained. JPMorgan Chase wouldn't release the cash. The answer, in the end, was obvious. JPMorgan Chase and Citadel made a joint bid for the trades. (With JPMorgan Chase in on the deal, the question of releasing collateral somehow disappeared.) The company made about $725 million in profit on the positions, in part by turning around and selling many of those it had just purchased to Citadel. *Risk* magazine named JPMorgan Chase "Energy Derivatives House of the Year" in 2006, in large part because of its success on the Amaranth trade.

Amaranth later sued JPMorgan Chase for more than $1 billion, accusing the company of abusing its position as the hedge fund's prime broker to put the kibosh on the deals with Goldman and Citadel in favor of its own purchase. A number of counts in the complaint were thrown out—including allegations that Black and Winters spread rumors about Amaranth, thereby expediting its collapse—but the case was still alive in mid-2009. Critics suggested that Dimon, Black, and Winters saw the size of the potential profit on the deal, and plowed ahead regardless of the legal risk, knowing they could cover their legal costs with the profits in any event.

Dimon, who considers the lawsuit "silly," had no pity for the collapsed fund. "When you have outsize positions like they had in illiquid markets, that's life," he says matter-of-factly. "The Goldman deal would have let Goldman cherry-pick the pieces they wanted, leaving us with the rest. We weren't going to be left with the highly toxic leveraged stuff while Goldman bought everything else at a huge discount. They also wanted us to release our collateral early. But we had no obligation to— and weren't about to increase our exposure like that." JPMorgan Chase had the upper hand, in other words, and it would be damned if it wasn't going to use the situation to its advantage. Period. There is no "gentlemen's club" discount in Jamie Dimon's world.

(Jamie Dimon, it almost goes without saying, is not the kind of man who finds all babies cute. "I never noticed babies until I had my own, and then I suddenly realized they were all around me," he says. "But once mine weren't babies anymore, I stopped noticing everybody else's." Nor are all companies—or countries—created equal. He has a special spot in his heart for his *own* family, his *own* company, and his *own* country. He doesn't wish harm on anyone, but supplicants without a direct connection to him are best served by looking elsewhere for help.)

The hurt feelings weren't only at Amaranth. JPMorgan Chase's top two energy traders, George "Beau" Taylor and Parker Drew, soon left the company in an apparent dispute over compensation and credit surrounding the Amaranth trades. (David Puth, the onetime head of the firm's currency and commodity business, had left just a few months before. Black and Winters were continuing to clean house.)

At the same time that the firm was celebrating its gains from Amaranth, the executive team was mourning the loss of one of its own. Joan Guggenheimer, who had been general counsel at Citigroup, Bank One, and JPMorgan Chase, died on July 30 after a lengthy battle with cancer. She had taken a leave of absence just three days before, and her death had a great impact on Dimon, who personally wrote a memo that concluded with the remark, "We were privileged to know her." When a caller asked to speak to Dimon the evening of her death, one of Dimon's daughters told him that her father was closeted in his music room, with Frank Sinatra blaring at top volume. "He is the only CEO I've ever met who cries," says one executive.

In October, Dimon signed off on the $460 million sales of 5.3 million square feet of excess real estate to Toronto-based Brookfield Asset Management. The company agreed to long-term leases as part of the deal, and the sale freed up capital it could use to continue investing in growth businesses. With the real estate market gone mad, Dimon wasn't going to pass up a chance to let JPMorgan Chase take advantage of the insanity. This was another example of Dimon's classic approach to wastecutting. After arriving at JPMorgan Chase, he had made the team in charge of the company's portfolio of real estate walk every single floor of every single major building the company owned and report back how much excess space was on hand. The team found 5.3 million square feet.

In December, Dimon hired Stephen Cutler as the company's new general counsel. Cutler had been the enforcement director of the Securities and Exchange Commission during the debacles at Enron and Worldcom, for which JPMorgan Chase had paid $4 billion in fines. Deal making aside, Dimon had just turned a potential adversary into an ally.

• • •

Dimon was part of two transitions at the end of 2006. One of them was a true changing of the guard: he took over from Bill Harrison as chairman of the board. Dimon was now totally in control of the third-largest bank, by assets, in the country—after Citigroup and Bank of America. The other was more symbolic, but no less poignant. In November, Dimon replaced Sandy Weill as a director of the Federal Reserve Bank of New York.

In January, Dimon declared the merger with Bank One complete, and also reported a dramatic increase in return on equity, which had climbed from 8 percent in 2005 to 13 percent in 2006, driven in part by $3 billion in merger savings. Characteristically, he was unhappy with the results despite the improvement—the goal was a 20 percent return on equity. Still, in celebrating his taking on the chairman's role, *The Economist* described him as Tenzing to Weill's Hilary. Dimon was paid $63 million for his work in 2006: $27 million in salary and $36 million from exercising options. He was again named to the *Time* 100.

That summer, Dimon and his family headed off for a vacation in the Caribbean with the Maglathlins and their three children. Dimon spent half an hour a day on the telephone and the rest of the day enjoying himself with everyone else. He brought his guitar along, but few were eager to hear him play. ("He's OK," says Peter Maglathlin. "Although he'll tell you that he's good.")

When Weill's autobiography, *The Real Deal*, was released in October 2006, it contained what many considered a considerable degree of revisionism, particularly concerning his relationship with Dimon. (One longtime colleague refers to it as "the gospel according to Sandy.") Dimon was enraged by a number of remarks Weill attributed to him, criticizing other executives at Travelers and Citigroup. Dimon maintains that he did not say many of these things, and that it was Weill himself who made many of the remarks. A number of people, including Frank Zarb, were hurt by quotes attributed to Dimon. And in more than a few cases in which Weill's quotes were accurate, they were a breach of what Dimon considered strict confidence.

Dimon claims that he has not read the book, but that he has heard enough from others to know he need not have bothered. "Honest criticisms are fine with me," he says. "But he went too far." Friends and colleagues noticed that Dimon basically stopped making an effort to remain friendly with Weill after the book's release. While always respectful, he just doesn't go out of his way anymore.

• • •

Although he rarely appears in the social pages, Dimon did attend the $3 million birthday fete that the private equity kingpin Stephen Schwarzman threw for himself at the Park Avenue Armory in February 2007. The bash was seized on as a symbol of the new gilded age—Rod Stewart was paid $1 million to play for half an hour—and the city's financial elite turned out in full force to eat lobster and baked Alaska and drink 2004 Louis Jadot Chassagne-Montrachet. Along with Dimon were Goldman Sachs's CEO Lloyd Blankfein, Merrill Lynch's Stan O'Neal, Bear Stearns' Jimmy Cayne, and Lazard's Bruce Wasserstein.

Sandy Weill retired as chairman of Citigroup in 2006. A retirement party was held in the Egyptian Room at the Metropolitan Museum, and the guest list included the former president Bill Clinton and the Saudi prince Alwaleed. Dimon attended, but kept a low profile. Although a few dozen people spoke in tribute to Weill's lengthy career, Dimon was not among them. He wore a regular business suit to the black tie event, and though he did greet people beside Weill for a bit, he left before the party got going. "You know what they say about cars that have been in a wreck?" muses one executive about the relationship between two men. "You can send them to the body shop, but they're never going to be the same." (Then again, maybe for Dimon it's just a party thing. At a faux-retirement party in Armonk for Joe Plumeri when he left Shearson to work at A.L. Williams, Dimon showed up in shorts and running shoes. "He's bright, but different," observes a longtime colleague, "and loves to be viewed as a maverick.")

By 2007, the JPMorgan Chase brand had been largely refurbished, and strong numbers were posted by the investment bank. Not only was the unit bringing in record revenues; it also recorded a 30 percent return on equity in the first quarter. (It didn't hurt that nearly every asset was rising in value in 2006.) Whatever Wall Street thought of him, Dimon's stature inside the bank was also increasing. At one so-called "town hall" event in Columbus, Ohio, employees looking for pictures or autographs besieged him, and he took an hour to get out of the meeting after it had officially ended. "These events are now almost cultish," says one insider.

As much of a chiseler as he may be at heart, Dimon has continued to support JPMorgan Chase's corporate art collection, which comprises some 37,000 pieces largely collected by David Rockefeller during his tenure at Chase. Though it's not the largest corporate collection—both Deutsche Bank and Bank of America have larger ones—it is of extremely high quality, with a number of Warhols and Calders. Dimon's own taste in art runs toward what might be called the patriotic. For a time, he kept in his office a four-foot maquette of the Statue of Liberty made in the same foundry in Paris as the original. He also has a copy of James Montgomery Flagg's famous "I Want You" poster of Uncle Sam.

With the history of the franchise in mind, Dimon also had the bank's client dining rooms on the forty-ninth and fiftieth floors of 270 Park Avenue refurbished in 2007 and 2008. Spread across both floors are remarkable displays showcasing some of the company's extensive collection of financial artifacts, including the first greenback ever printed in 1862, one of Carlos Baca's famous paintings of J.P. Morgan himself, a snowy oil painting by Guy Carleton Wiggins, and a painting by Anton Schutz of the Bank of Manhattan's original headquarters at 40 Wall Street. (The one gap left in that history is a portrait of Dimon himself—a tradition at JPMorgan Chase. To date he has refused to sit for one.)

Even after he secured the additional title, Dimon's style continued to be more that of a CEO than a chairman, as he remained engaged in most facets of the business. As always, he was intensely focused on where the company could improve. One of his favorite mantras is "More, better, faster, quicker, cheaper."

He's been able to succeed with this approach in large part because of the tightness of his inner circle. Although Dimon is more than capable of hurting subordinates' feelings—often in the very same way for a second or third time—he is not mean-spirited. And he will apologize. As a result, his top managers have a genuine affection for him, which has helped him keep a stable core, unlike many of his competitors. Citigroup in the Chuck Prince era was a notorious hornets' nest. And it's no secret that few colleagues liked Merrill Lynch's Stan O'Neal.

. . .

By early 2007, it was no longer difficult to find a bear in or around Wall Street. Doomsaying commentators, including an economics professor at New York University, Nouriel Roubini, were imploring investors not to underestimate the obvious signs of weakness in subprime and how it could easily spill over into other areas. But Wall Street still found reasons not to take their concerns seriously. In January 2007, Michael Lewis wrote a column for Bloomberg News titled "Davos Is for Wimps, Ninnies, Pointless Skeptics," lampooning Roubini, the private investor Steven Rattner, and Morgan Stanley's economist Stephen Roach for daring to introduce pessimism at the annual global economic retreat in Switzerland. In bull markets, bears always get picked on.

While Jamie Dimon and his colleagues were having doubts about the housing market, most investors were chuckling right alongside Lewis, happy to see their portfolios gaining. Investment bankers continued to book fees and mark huge gains from their mortgage-related underwriting and investments.

Bear Stearns, the smallest of Wall Street's major players, had turned in a record fourth quarter in 2006, the result of a decision to focus on mortgages above all else. Bear was full of what its former CEO Alan "Ace" Greenberg called PSDs—those who were poor, were smart, and had a desire to get rich. Forget appearances; making money for the firm was all that mattered. Do that, and you were handed the keys to the kingdom. And the way to make money at Bear in those days was in mortgages. The firm was the leading underwriter of U.S. mortgage-backed securities from 2004 to 2007.

Ralph Cioffi was among Bear's most successful mortgage men. A former bond salesman who had been with the firm since 1985, Cioffi had been made a hedge fund manager in 2003, when the firm gave him $10 million to invest in subprime mortgage-backed securities. He launched what was called the High-Grade Structured Credit Fund, and out of the gate, it was profitable for 40 straight months, a record almost too good to be true. (Cioffi's comanager, Matthew Tannin, once compared the fund to a bank account.) Such success emboldened Cioffi to delve into even riskier strategies, and in 2006, the firm set up a second, more leveraged fund, the High-Grade Structured Enhanced Leveraged Fund.

Cioffi told investors that the leverage wasn't dangerous, because he was buying only supersafe securities, rated triple-A and double-A by the credit-rating agencies. According to William Cohan, author of *House of Cards*, Cioffi was lying. It wasn't just 6 percent of the funds that were invested in subprime mortgages; it was more like 60 percent. And the leverage was devastatingly high. The first fund was leveraged about 35 to one, and the second at a breathtaking 100 to one. At that level, a drop of 1 percent wipes out all the equity.

When the housing market stalled, as it did in late 2006 and early 2007, that's exactly what happened. Housing prices were not yet in free fall, but some securities had slipped to about 95 percent of their value by the spring. Cioffi took a huge paper loss and was unable to meet margin calls from his overnight lenders. (This is the lesson of leverage. If you pay only $1 for $100 worth of securities while borrowing the other $99, and those securities lose $5 in value, you're not only out your original $1. You now owe $4 just to get back to breakeven. Multiply those numbers by several hundred million, and you can appreciate the pickle Cioffi found himself in.)

In a move as brazen as it was cynical, Cioffi decided that the way out of the mess was to find a few patsies to take the toxic securities off his hands. In May, he put together a plan to create a company named Everquest Financial, and prepped it for an initial public offering. What would Everquest do? Overpay for Cioffi's underwater securities. (The name of the company—"Everquest"—was classic Wall Street, both portentous and meaningless.)

Unfortunately for Cioffi, a number of reporters at both the *Wall Street Journal* and *Business Week* sniffed out the scheme by early June, and he was forced to abort it. A total of $4 billion in securities had to be liquidated to satisfy redemptions and margin calls by the funds' creditors.

By this point, those creditors, including Merrill Lynch and JPMorgan Chase, were threatening to pull the plug and send both funds into default. In an attempt to head off the crisis, the copresident of Bear Stearns, Warren Spector, convened a meeting of the firm's lenders, including Merrill Lynch, JPMorgan Chase, Goldman Sachs, and Bank of America, at the company's offices at 383 Madison Avenue. The gist of his message was that everything would be OK; Cioffi was an expert in such things, and just needed some breathing room to put the funds back on a solid footing. John Hogan, chief risk officer for JPMorgan Chase's investment bank, attended. Hogan asked a question. Was Bear Stearns prepared to provide a capital infusion to help the funds meet their margin calls? When he was told the answer was no, he left the meeting and returned to the JPMorgan Chase headquarters.

After being debriefed by Hogan, Steve Black picked up the phone and called Spector. "You guys are out of your mind if you think we're not going to put you into default," Black told him. Spector replied that Black and Hogan did not understand the business, and that JPMorgan Chase was the only bank that was giving Bear Stearns a hard time about the loans. "I don't believe you," Black replied. "Don't call us again." And that was it. The call was over.

Black, who'd been a fraternity brother of Spector's copresident, Alan Schwartz, at Duke University, then called his old college buddy. "I don't want to speak to Spector again," Black said. "And just so you know, we're going to default you." That evening at 5:30, JPMorgan Chase sent a messenger with a default notice across the street to the Bear Stearns offices. (Security guards at Bear turned the man away, saying the office was closed for the evening. The next morning, at 6:00, the default notice was delivered.)

Merrill Lynch responded even more aggressively. In a public rebuke to Bear, the firm, which had exposure totaling $1.46 billion, seized $400 million in collateral and threatened to sell it; such a sale would push prices of the fund's remaining holdings down farther. JPMorgan Chase did the same, but less publicly. The firm ultimately sold $400 million of its collateral back to Cioffi for cash. (In its contracts with Bear Stearns, JPMorgan Chase had what was referred to as a "no dispute clause": Bear had no right to dispute the pricing of the collateral held by JPMorgan Chase. "That served us well," recalls Black. "We didn't have to waste a lot of time arguing about the value of collateral.") The combined efforts of its creditors ultimately forced Bear's hand, and on June 23, the investment bank injected $3.2 billion of its own money into Cioffi's funds, an eye-opening event for anyone not yet cognizant of the weakness in the

U.S. subprime mortgage space. The funds eventually collapsed entirely in July.

The stock market was taken by surprise, falling 186 points, or 1.4 percent, the day the bailout was announced. Still, not many took the funds' troubles as a sign of a financial apocalypse. When JPMorgan Chase held its own second-quarter conference call on July 18, Bear's financial services analyst David Hendler started a query with, "Just a question on . . ." but was interrupted by Dimon. "Actually, David, we have a few questions for you," he joked. It was funny, albeit in a morbid sort of way. Although the losses were huge, Bear Stearns was still standing, and people like David Hendler still had jobs. As Bryan Burrough later pointed out in *Vanity Fair*, the firm thought it had survived a near-death experience.

By August, Bear was putting out fires left and right. On Friday, August 1, the firm held a conference call, trying to calm investors' nerves about the collapsed funds. On August 5, the CEO of Bear Stearns, James Cayne, forced Spector to resign. (It later emerged that Spector had unilaterally authorized a late-game $25 million injection into Cioffi's funds, without telling Cayne or the board. The discovery of this prompted Cayne to issue the death sentence.)

The stock market itself had stabilized, but the world of high finance had a new, much more ominous problem on its hands. The availability of short-term credit had dried up overnight. When France's biggest bank, BNP Paribas, halted withdrawals of three funds on August 8, because it couldn't "fairly" value their holdings, panic set in. Despite a $130 billion injection of funds into the market on August 10 by the European Central Bank, a credit crunch had begun in which no one entrusted his money to anyone else anymore, and the normally fluid overnight lending markets evaporated. The Latin root of "credit" is *credere*, "to believe." Belief had been obliterated.

What comes next is common to all historical financial panics. Individuals who act rationally (i.e., they try to sell, in order to protect their own interests) have an aggregate effect that is ultimately irrational (i.e., with all sellers and no buyers, assets that do have an inherent value are nevertheless deemed worthless). In other words, if there's no price at which someone will take something off your hands, its value is necessar-

ily zero. And if you're a borrower who needs to sell *something* to pay back your debts, you're in deep trouble.

"Credit is the air that financial markets breathe, and when the air is poisoned, there's no place to hide," writes Charles Morris in *The Trillion Dollar Meltdown*. The start of the credit problems prompted CNBC's talking head Jim Cramer to unleash his now infamous rant beseeching the Federal Reserve to cut interest rates. Like Michael Lewis's sarcastic column about Davos, it seems naive in retrospect. The market's problems were far too complex to be solved by a mere rate cut. Morris was soon forced to change the title of his book to *The Two Trillion Dollar Meltdown*. (It may well have to be revised further.)

Although they were not desperate for capital, executives at Bear Stearns concluded that a vote of confidence from a prominent outside investor might quiet the critics. Over the next few months, they held discussions with the financier Henry Kravis of KKR, who considered ponying up a $2 billion cash infusion in exchange for 20 percent of the company. When the deal fell apart over conflict-of-interest issues, the company turned to several other possible investors, including the private equity firm J.C. Flowers, the hedge fund Fortress Investment Group, Berkshire Hathaway's Warren Buffett, and Jamie Dimon.

That summer, after several quarters of being ignored by analysts, Dimon and his team were the toast of Wall Street, as it became increasingly clear that Dimon's philosophy of the fortress balance sheet had positioned the firm to do just what he had promised—to be predator, not prey, when the environment got ugly. In a stark reversal, JPMorgan Chase was getting headlines for its strong positioning.

In October, the company announced $3.4 billion in quarterly profits, but also $1.64 billion in write-downs on its own credit exposure. The news sent JPMorgan Chase stock skidding nearly 10 percent. But only Goldman Sachs had fewer losses.

Had Bear been seeking to sell, say, its prime brokerage business, Dimon and his team would have been all ears. But swallowing the bank whole, including its vast subprime book, was not palatable. "We took a look and we weren't interested," Dimon recalls.

In September, news reports revealed that Bear's shareholder Joseph

Lewis had secretly been building a 7 percent stake in the firm, spending $860 million in the process. But that wasn't a cash infusion; he'd bought the shares on the open market, a move that did nothing to alleviate the firm's capital issues. In October, Bear announced a deal with the Chinese securities firm CITIC, in which the two companies agreed to invest $1 billion in each other. But investors saw the back-and-forth for what it was: an empty gesture. And then in November, all hell broke loose. The *Wall Street Journal* ran a front-page story about James Cayne, portraying him as a chronic dope smoker who spent more time playing in bridge tournaments than he did managing his floundering firm. (It had already been reported that he'd been playing golf the day the hedge funds were bailed out.)

Bear Stearns was now a symbol of risk management gone amuck, and on Wall Street, where reputation is everything, the *Journal's* article spelled the end for Cayne, if not the entire firm. Bear hung around long enough to place second in *Fortune* magazine's annual list of the most admired securities firms—behind Lehman Brothers—but it was now officially circling the drain. At the end of 2007, Bear Stearns reported $2.6 billion in write-downs, as well as its first-ever quarterly loss. Bear Stearns was the smallest firm of Wall Street's giants, and the first to go down. But its problems were hardly Bear's alone.

· · ·

Citigroup's former CEO Chuck Prince will go down in the annals of business as the guy who drove the once proud bank straight into a wall. (*The Economist* referred to him in May 2009 as "Citigroup's former bumbler-in-chief.") Never a verbose man, he will nonetheless also be remembered for what was one of the most ill-timed utterances by an executive in history. In July 2007, just before the world's credit markets seized up, he spoke of Citigroup's commitment to continue funding leveraged buyouts through the provision of so-called leveraged loans. "As long as the music is playing, you've got to get up and dance," he told the *Financial Times*. "We're still dancing."

Less than a month later, the roof fell in on the dance hall, and Citigroup found itself stuck with $57 billion of leveraged loans on its books

that it could no longer sell. And it was not alone. JPMorgan Chase, the longtime leader in the leveraged loan market, was sitting on $41 billion of its own. Eighteen months later, both banks were still writing down those loans, as investors' appetite for highly leveraged companies failed to come back. (The exposures were large, but providing loans is the business of banks, and neither bank suffered much criticism for getting caught flat-footed by the swift and brutal change in investor sentiment.)

Citigroup, however, had a more serious vulnerability exposed by the freeze in credit. In his relentless quest for positive "operating leverage," Chuck Prince had sponsored some $100 billion of SIVs as of the summer of 2007, making Citigroup by far the leading issuer in the $400 billion market. (Dimon, usually a stickler for detail, later admitted being taken off guard by the sheer size of the SIV market. He wasn't the only one.)

Because SIVs earned a mere estimated 0.35 percent or so on their investments, which the sponsor had to split with the equity investors (equity investors, of course, were not in the SIV for just a 0.35 percent return—leverage gave them returns of 8 percent or so), Citigroup earned an estimated $175 million a year from its SIV business, despite potentially ruinous risks to both its balance sheet and its reputation. When the market for short-term borrowing disappeared, the SIVs were effectively insolvent, exposing the equity investors to a wipeout unless Citigroup stepped in to save them.

In October, Secretary of the Treasury Henry Paulson—the onetime chief of Goldman Sachs—floated the idea of creating a so-called "super-SIV" that would take the underperforming SIVs off the books of firms whose balance sheets were buckling under this unexpected weight. JPMorgan Chase, Citigroup, and Bank of America would invest a total of $100 billion to create such a fund. Some CEOs might have balked at the notion of effectively bailing out their competitors, but Dimon was prepared to play the statesman. On a conference call with analysts in October, he talked of taking one for the team. "I think it's clear that there may be asymmetric benefits to different parties in the super-SIV idea," he said, "but it's also clear that it may ameliorate some of the pressure on some of the markets that is taking place today. If the system is helped, we think that's good for everybody. It's perfectly reasonable that J.P. Morgan take part in something like that."

The plan never got off the drawing board. After waffling for several weeks about whether or not it had any contractual obligation to provide liquidity or guarantees to the SIVs it said it merely "advised," Citigroup finally buckled in December and agreed to take $58 billion worth of SIVs back onto its balance sheet, thereby obviating the need for the super-SIV. By that time, Chuck Prince was gone; he'd resigned in November, just a few weeks after the *Wall Street Journal* had run an article with the headline "J.P. Morgan's Time to Grin." Dimon, however, steadfastly refused to publicly celebrate Citigroup's troubles.

"He's smart enough to know that Citigroup has embarrassed themselves enough and he doesn't need to gloat," says one of Dimon's former colleagues. Instead of dancing on the graves of Sandy Weill, Chuck Prince, and Citigroup, Dimon retreated from the press. JPMorgan Chase's own results were nothing to brag about. At a conference in November, however, he stated, "SIVs don't have a business purpose"—a clear swipe at Citigroup. In the company's 2007 annual report, he elaborated on the subject. "There is one financial commandment that cannot be violated: Do not borrow short to invest long—particularly against illiquid, long-term assets." "You know what sinks companies?" he asked an audience in late 2008. "Financing illiquid assets short."

The Federal Reserve chief, Ben Bernanke, took Jim Cramer up on his advice and cut rates in September and October 2007. Although the equity and credit markets rallied in approval, that relief was short-lived. Third-quarter results from Wall Street firms were a debacle, with Citigroup and Merrill Lynch leading the parade of losers. Stan O'Neal, who had elbowed his way to the top of Merrill Lynch in 2002, led his firm down the same primrose path as Bear Stearns, particularly in its embrace of subprime CDOs. Citigroup's earnings fell by 60 percent in the third quarter; Merrill's results dropped from a $2.2 billion gain in the third quarter of 2006 to a $2.3 billion loss in the same period in 2007.

It began to dawn on the rest of the country that Wall Street firms had at some point ceased to focus on their original function—putting people with money together with people who need money—and had turned inward, becoming, in John Brooks's words, "a mindless glutton methodically eating itself to paralysis and death." Brooks wrote that in 1973. Thirty-five years later, it was the same story all over again.

When Warren Buffett decided to sell long-term put options on the S&P 500 index—essentially a bet that the market would be higher when the options expire between 2019 and 2027—he refused to post any collateral whatsoever against the positions. The banks would just have to take him at his word, and everybody did—except Dimon. "We stuck to our knitting, we lost the business, and we moved on," he recalls. The last prominent investor to demand no collateral posting was John Meriwether of Long-Term Capital Management.

"I advise other companies' CEOs, don't fall into the trap where you go, 'Where's the growth? Where's the growth? Where's the growth?' " Jamie Dimon told Charlie Rose in early 2008. "They feel a tremendous pressure to grow. Well, sometimes you can't grow. Sometimes you don't want to grow. In certain businesses, growth means you either take on bad clients, excess risk, or too much leverage. Wall Street firms felt this pressure to grow, and they succumbed to it."

The strategy of piling on leverage to juice returns had pervaded Wall Street's executive suites. According to a study by the management consultancy Oliver Wyman, leverage appears to have driven almost half the growth in return on equity from 2003 through 2007. Ralph Cioffi of Bear Stearns wasn't the only one putting his equity at risk by loading up on debt; all of Wall Street was in on the scheme.

Warren Buffett thinks Dimon separated himself from the pack by relying on his own judgment and not becoming slave to the software that tried to simplify all of banking into a mathematical equation. "Too many people overemphasize the power of these statistical models," he says. "But not Jamie. The CEO of any of these firms has to be the chief risk officer. At Berkshire Hathaway, it's my number one job. I have to be correlating the chance of an earthquake in California not only causing a big insurance loss, but also the effect on Wells Fargo's earnings, or the availability of money tomorrow. Any big institution has a lot of risks that can be modeled reasonably well. Somebody at the top has to be thinking about that stuff every day. Jamie is the kind of guy you want to have running an institution like that. You have to have somebody that's got a real fear in them of what can happen in markets. They have to know financial history. You can't evaluate risk in sigmas."

Another contributing factor was that money had been too cheap— nearly free—for too long. It is only logical that Wall Street chieftains, with limited liability in their roles as executives at public companies, and unlimited access to capital, would take on so much risk. They shared in the upside and were protected on the downside. Chuck Prince received a good-bye present of $39 million for nearly wrecking Citigroup. Stan O'Neal of Merrill Lynch received $162 million for gutting Merrill to the point at which it was forced into a shotgun marriage with Bank of America.

In 2007, JPMorgan Chase announced $3.1 billion in market-related write-downs, versus $20.8 billion at Citigroup. And JPMorgan Chase's sales per employee, a measure of operating efficiency, were $349,000 in 2007, versus just $218,000 for Citigroup. The irony was hard to ignore. The promise of the so-called universal bank that had been the driving force behind the creation of Citigroup was being realized—but not at Citigroup. In March 2008, Weill issued something of a mea culpa, telling *Fortune*, "I get an 'F' for succession planning."

In November 2007, Dimon hired Barry Zubrow, formerly a partner at Goldman Sachs, to be the firm's new chief risk officer. Jon Corzine, the erstwhile Goldman CEO and current governor of New Jersey, had recommended his former colleague as someone who could talk to both the board and the company's traders without alienating either of them. At the same time that his competitors' risk-management processes were being revealed as woefully inadequate, Dimon was continuing to improve his own.

• • •

Although Dimon and his team were able to sidestep the subprime meltdown, they made a number of critical blunders of their own in the last days of the credit bubble. In home equity, the company ran with the pack, repeatedly loosening underwriting standards to keep market share. From a relatively conservative loan-to-value (LTV) ratio of 80 percent, Charlie Scharf and his team eased their standards to an LTV of 85 percent and then again to 90 percent. They also went along with so-called "no documentation" loans, in which the bank simply took borrowers at their word. In a remarkable display of cavalier lending, only 22 percent of home equity loans made by JPMorgan Chase in the first half of 2007 were supported by full documentation. That is not a figure any bank could be proud of. (Other banks went farther, issuing so-called NINJA loans—in which borrowers had "no income, no job, and no assets.")

That explains why in 2007 the company wrote off $564 million in home equity loans, and added $1 billion to reserves. "We could have known and we should have known," says Dimon. "Part of it was like the frog in boiling water, who doesn't know it's getting hot until it's too late. But that's no excuse. The fact is, it was bad underwriting. I'd like to write a letter to the next generation that says, 'Even if you see home prices go up 100 percent over five or 10 years, don't go past 80 percent loan to value!' "

In the rush to add mortgage volume, the company also embraced the wholesale "channel" in which outside mortgage brokers made loans and passed them on to the company. This was an added dimension of risk; the company had little control over underwriting practices that went on outside its own walls. Although such loans accounted for only 33 percent of outstanding prime mortgages at the end of 2008, they accounted for a whopping 78 percent of losses. Dimon had written in the company's 2006 annual report that the home equity division had maintained "its high underwriting standards." He was wrong about that, at least as far as its wholesale business was concerned.

Dimon considers the decision to use mortgage brokers the biggest mistake of his career. After a speech at the Chamber of Commerce in March 2009 in which he said just that, the National Association of Mortgage Brokers released a statement calling it a "senseless" attack. The bank made other grave mistakes as well, such as aggressively chasing market share in jumbo mortgages and credit cards even as the economy had begun to shrink, leaving it with billions of dollars in future write-downs. Dimon's vaunted ability to connect the dots failed him in these instances. The push to add market share in mortgages was successful—origination in the first quarter of 2008 increased 30 percent to $47 billion, doubling the company's share from 5 to 10 percent—but it also cost the firm more than $500 million. "We were too early," Dimon later said.

According to Scharf, he and his team made a serious miscalculation. "We didn't think housing prices were going to go up forever," he says. "We did say they could go down. But when we asked 'What's the worst it could be?' we got that one totally wrong." Dimon wrote in the company's 2006 annual report that credit losses "could rise significantly, by as much as $5 billion over time." He was off by several orders of magnitude.

Steve Black, cohead of the company's investment bank, has a joke he pulled out at the company's "investor days" in both 2008 and 2009. As the market leader in making loans for leveraged buyouts—so-called leveraged lending—the bank had a chance to look at nearly every big deal that came down the pike. "The good news is that we turned down five of the last 10 deals," says Black. "The bad news is that we took the other five." JPMorgan Chase lined up with everyone else to make loans to Boots, a retailer in the United Kingdom; to the electric utility TXU; to Chrysler; to Home Depot's supply unit; and to Sam Zell's takeover of the Tribune Company.

With $41 billion in outstanding leveraged loans when the market cratered in 2007, JPMorgan Chase saw that value plummet. Worse yet, the company had made the same mistake as it had in home equity, progressively loosening debt covenants and ceding an extraordinary amount of power to borrowers. It had, in other words, chased the market down when it should have held fast. By the end of 2007, it had its bearings again. JPMorgan Chase refused to finance the buyout king Steve Schwarzman's $1.8 billion bid for the mortgage arm of the New Jersey-based PHH Corp. (In January 2008, Schwarzman was forced to back out of the deal and pay PHH a fee of $50 million. After initially pointing a finger at JPMorgan Chase and suggesting that the bank should share in the breakup fee, Schwarzman reportedly apologized to Dimon.) Still, the company wrote the value of its leveraged loan portfolio down $1.8 billion in 2008.

One loan that the company did not make, but which still proved nettlesome, was financing for a buyout of a client, Dow Chemical, in early 2007. In April, it emerged that bankers at J.P. Morgan Cazenove—a joint venture half-owned by the firm—were working on a possible LBO of Dow Chemical without the approval of Dow Chemical's CEO, its CFO, or its board. Winters pulled the plug on the project when he found out that the bankers were working with what appeared to be a rogue contingent of Dow Chemical's executives.

"It's part of the job," Dimon says about the mix-up. "You can't expect to have a perfect batting average, and you can expect to make legitimate mistakes. When Bill Winters found out, as he puts it, we put our pencils down. Did that happen too late? Yes, it should have happened earlier. Our client did have a legitimate complaint." Dimon had dinner with Andrew Liveris, CEO of Dow Chemical, the next month, to try to smooth things over. He later told Liveris that Dow director and former chief financial officer J. Pedro Reinhard and another executive, Romeo Kreinberg, had effectively been mounting a coup. Liveris fired the pair a few days later.

Black and Winters are both irked that they saw the end of the credit bubble coming and talked about it incessantly, but failed to do enough to insulate the firm. "We missed it," says Black. "It's our fault. We did it. We said, 'This thing is coming to an end, and we're not going to be involved in these transactions,' and then we end up in five of the last 10."

Black likes to say the company was smart twice (in avoiding SIV and CDO exposure) and unlucky once (in its leveraged loan exposure). One could invert the construction, however, and say it got lucky twice and was stupid once. It was well known on Wall Street that for some time JPMorgan Chase had had two warring mortgage factions—origination (at Chase Home Finance) and securitization (in the investment bank)—that prevented the bank from mounting a competitive end-to-end mortgage effort. Dimon even replaced most of the Chase mortgage team in hopes of reducing the friction. (The executives later showed up at Washington Mutual, where they were eventually fired by Dimon a second time.) The company was also lucky because it wasn't competitive in big subprime markets such as California and Florida.

Instead of a deliberate decision to avoid CDO underwriting, critics say, Dimon just hadn't gotten around to knocking heads in his mortgage unit until shortly before disaster hit. "Jamie's been very good, and he's also been very lucky," said Sanford Bernstein's analyst Brad Hintz. "Was that a great skill, that he didn't address [the issue of those warring mortgage teams] until [it was] too late? Or was it luck?" In other words, JPMorgan Chase's good fortune in the summer of 2007 might have been an accident.

Those on Dimon's team reject this version of events, saying that although they had been overhauling their end-to-end mortgage capabilities, they didn't act because they *chose* not to. In late 2005, they noticed that default rates on subprime mortgages were starting to pick up, and they therefore decided—just as they had when selling the SIV in 2004—that it might be better to sit this one out. Instead of adding to their subprime risk, they began reducing it, particularly through the use of mortgage derivatives.

(One of the great ironies of the late stages of the mortgage bubble, Gillian Tett points out in *Fool's Gold*, is that demand was so high for subprime mortgage product that it outstripped actual supply. Derivatives, on the other hand, could be made out of whole cloth. The only issue: like any financial product, a derivative needs both a buyer and a seller. There was no shortage of people who wanted to own subprime risk, but they'd have nothing to buy if there was no one who wanted to sell it. By seeking to hedge their own subprime exposure through the use of derivatives, then, JPMorgan Chase and others inadvertently helped prolong the insanity longer than it otherwise might have been had investors been limited to buying actual loans.)

Then there's the $2 billion CDO that no one seemed to have noticed, and which ended up taking $1 billion out of the company's fourth-quarter earnings in 2007 when it lost half its value. Some executives at the company had proposed that the bank actually begin investing in subprime product, and while the decision was working its way through the appropriate channels, a unit of the bank went ahead and purchased a $2 billion subprime CDO. The proposal was ultimately rejected, but the CDO stayed on the books. Winters refers to the episode as "an outright control lapse" and "the biggest single mistake we've made in a long time."

• • •

The International Monetary Fund estimates that stock market bubbles happen about every 13 years, and that housing bubbles occur every two decades. That's what makes it so amazing that the majority of Wall Street firms were caught unawares by the credit debacle. Dimon's daughter Laura called him in the fall of 2007 and asked, "Dad, what's a financial crisis?" Without intending to be funny, he replied, "It's something that happens every five to 10 years." Her response: "So why is everyone so surprised?" (Dimon is fond of Mark Twain's wry comment that history does not repeat itself, but it does rhyme.)

One answer to Laura Dimon's question is that this time around it wasn't just one entity (such as Long-Term Capital Management) or one investment product (such as Internet stocks) that melted down. Almost every credit product out there collapsed—subprime mortgages, mortgage-related collateralized debt obligations, asset-backed commercial paper, auction-rate securities, SIVs, Alt-A mortgages, financial insurers, home equity.

Among the large commercial and investment banks, only Goldman Sachs and JPMorgan Chase seem to have been in any way prepared for the possibility of disaster. In March 2007, Dimon had written in the company's 2006 annual report, "Credit losses, both consumer and wholesale, have been extremely low, perhaps among the best we'll see in our lifetimes. We must be prepared for a return to the norm in the credit cycle. We do not know exactly what will occur or when, but we do know that bad things happen. There is no question that our company's earnings could go down substantially. But if we are prepared, we can both minimize the damage to our company and capitalize on opportunities in the marketplace."

And so, despite taking its own losses in leveraged loans and mortgage holdings, JPMorgan Chase reported record earnings in 2007 of

$15.4 billion on revenues of $71.4 billion. The bank had also delivered genuine operating leverage. Between 2004 and 2007, the company's top line grew by 67 percent, but income from continuing operations grew 260 percent. The cross-sell worked, too; gross investment banking revenue from commercial bank clients hit $888 million, up from $552 million in 2005. What's more, the company's return on equity more than doubled, rising from 6 percent to 13 percent. While that was still below average for the industry, the change was certainly in the right direction. The bank now operated in more than 100 countries, had more than $1.5 trillion in assets under management, and held $15 trillion in custody agreements.

Cost-cutting, too, continued apace. The company had shed 13 million square feet of excess office space since 2003. Since the acquisition of the Bank of New York branches in 2004, the number of computer applications used by the bank had fallen from 7,868 to 4,763. At the same time, the company's computing power and storage continued to rise. At the end of 2007, JPMorgan Chase had 9.8 petabytes of online storage capacity, enough to house the entire Library of Congress online.

A strong balance sheet, which used to be de rigueur among large U.S. banks, was now a major competitive differentiator. JPMorgan Chase's tier 1 capital ratio—the ratio of equity capital plus cash reserves to total risk-weighted assets—was 8.4 percent, well above that of its primary competitors, Bank of America, Citigroup, Wachovia, and Wells Fargo.

The company's investment bank was showered with accolades at the end of the year. *Institutional Investor*, the trade magazine of investment bankers, named J.P. Morgan the investment bank of the year. *Risk* magazine named it the best derivatives house of the year as well as over the past 20 years. The company took the top spot in overall investment banking fees for 2007, and its lowest showing in the underwriting tables was a fourth-place ranking in common stock. The company led in convertible securities, high-yield corporate bonds, loan syndications, and leveraged loans.

By carefully cultivating top talent from both the J.P. Morgan and Bank One teams, Dimon had largely avoided any meaningful conflict in the company's executive suite. At the end of 2007, of the 15 top executives at the company, six had come from Bank One or Citigroup (Dimon, Frank Bisignano, Mike Cavanagh, Jay Mandelbaum, Heidi Miller, and Charlie Scharf), five from J.P. Morgan (Steve Black, Bill Winters, Todd Maclin, the asset management chief Jes Staley, and the chief investment officer Ina Drew), and four had been hired since the merger (Steve Cutler, Barry Zubrow, the credit card chief Gordon Smith, and the head of corporate responsibility, Bill Daley).

And so Wall Street's favorite parlor game began anew. Dimon told analysts in July 2007 that he was sick of answering questions about possible acquisitions, but that the party line remained the same. "I get tired of saying this," he said. "But I'll say it again. It's got to have business logic, the price has to be right, and we have to have the ability to execute." By the end of the year, however, analysts and investors saw the blood on the street, and they knew Jamie Dimon did, too. "Dimon has been preparing for this type of environment for the past two years," wrote the UBS analyst Glenn Schorr in October.

Fortune magazine once said that Jamie Dimon wouldn't rest until he was recognized as "the world's most important banker." He was about to become just that.

12. ALL THAT HE EVER WANTED

At the start of 2008, Wall Street analysts had completely come around to JPMorgan Chase. Being boring was now a virtue. Although the company was facing the same gruesome economic environment as its competitors, it had suffered far smaller write-downs in 2007, and coverage of JPMorgan Chase practically demanded that the bank be "opportunistic" and on the watch to "scoop up some distressed assets or a distressed bank."

By one widely watched measure of financial stability—the amount of leverage on a company's books—Dimon and his colleagues looked downright judicious compared with their freewheeling competitors. At the end of 2007, JPMorgan Chase's balance sheet was leveraged 12.7 times, versus 19.2 times for Citigroup, 26.2 times for Goldman Sachs, 31.9 times for Merrill Lynch, and 33.5 times for Bear Stearns.

The new year brought two milestones for Dimon. The first was professional. On January 16, JPMorgan Chase eclipsed Citigroup in market capitalization. The event was widely remarked by Wall Street, though Dimon claims it meant nothing to him. "I don't look at market capitalization as a measure of success," he says. "You've never heard me say a word about it. You've never read it in a press release, and you've never heard Mike Cavanagh [the chief financial officer] talk about it. You've never heard anyone in this company say that size is good, and you never will. I don't want to be big and stupid. I want to be really good at what we do. Stock price is almost irrelevant to me, although I will admit I was surprised." (Although his argument is persuasive to some degree, it strains belief that Dimon does not focus on both what the company does and where its stock price is trading. Not only is his net worth tied to the level of the company's stock, but on Wall Street, stock price is the way the score is kept.)

The second milestone was a little more personal. Dimon cochaired the annual meeting of the World Economic Forum in Davos, Switzerland, in January. Wall Street had long known of Jamie Dimon, but the wider world had known him less. News reports also confirmed that Dimon had hired the former British prime minister Tony Blair as an adviser to the company. (Blair was being paid either $5 million or $1 million a year, depending on whom you believe. JPMorgan Chase had no comment on the issue.)

In the meantime, Barack Obama was catching up to Hillary Clinton in the polls for the Democratic nomination. As a board member of the Federal Reserve Bank of New York, Dimon was prohibited from making an outright endorsement, but his preference for Barack Obama was an open secret.

Although the bank had performed admirably in 2007, Dimon was concerned about weakening results in both the investment bank and the company's loan portfolios. The price of a barrel of oil had hit $100 on January 3, the U.S. dollar was cratering, and the Fed once again cut rates three weeks later in an effort to stave off the recession that had become all but inevitable. After all their work to keep the company's balance sheet strong, executives at JPMorgan Chase faced the likelihood that they might be the good house in the bad neighborhood, dragged down with the broader economy.

The turmoil had already claimed another victim. On January 8, the chairman and CEO of Bear Stearns, James Cayne, who had been at the firm since 1969, resigned from the CEO job, under pressure. (He held on to the title of chairman of the board.) Alan Schwartz, the company's sole president since the firing of Warren Spector in August, replaced him. The market was becoming increasingly skittish regarding the viability of Bear Stearns. By mid-January, the price on credit insurance for $10 million of Bear's debt had risen to 2.3 percent annually: $230,000—double that of Morgan Stanley and four times that of Deutsche Bank.

At JPMorgan Chase's "investor day" in February, the mood was mixed. The company had record revenues and earnings in 2007, yes, but the economy was looking grim. Also, the company sat on $94 billion of home equity loans, and delinquencies were headed skyward. Losses on the home equity portfolio had surpassed Dimon's stress-testing scenarios, and the CFO, Mike Cavanagh, said that in the future the company would be assuming a more conservative stance. He dropped a bomb on the audience by explaining that the firm could add as much as $450 million more to loan-loss reserves in the first quarter alone. "We did not see the magnitude of the housing crisis coming," he admitted. Though it had sold off much of its subprime portfolio, the company still owned $15.5 billion worth, and more than 12 percent of those home owners had been delinquent for 30 days or more.

The company also shifted $4.9 billion of leveraged loans from "held for sale" to "held to maturity" on its balance sheet; this shift allowed it to delay taking losses on the loans. "We are going to be cold-blooded economic animals on [these loans]," Dimon told his investors. "If we don't mind holding [them], we're going to put [them] in the portfolio." Cavanagh insisted that the company viewed the loans as good investments, but JPMorgan Chase nevertheless tacked on an additional $500 million to its loan-loss reserves. In 2008 alone, Cavanagh added, it had already determined to mark the leveraged loan book down another $800 million.

Dimon was his usual self—confident, vaguely dismissive, a little funny—and spent time after the presentation joshing with his lieutenants about the fact that Charlie Scharf's presentation had sent the company's stock down the most during the morning. (The sessions are broadcast over the Internet, and investors react to the presentations in real time.) During cocktails after the full day schedule, his penchant for analysis was again on display. He suggested to Steve Black, cohead of the investment bank, that they chart the day's presentations to see who inspired the market and who did not.

Earlier in the day, Dimon had voiced irritation with what he considered the overdone concern among investors about the state of the markets. "This is not the first crisis that ever happened," he told the assembled crowd. "We shouldn't be all atwitter over this stuff. Life goes on. Recovery will come . . . for most." He was right in suggesting that some would not recover. A few weeks later, the first major victim of the financial crisis was knocking on his door, begging for help.

. . .

The first week of March seemed quiet on the surface, but chaos reigned inside Bear Stearns. Even though the company was on track to report solid earnings in its first quarter, trading partners were increasingly skeptical that it was a reliable counterparty. Not only did Bear have its own substantial mortgage exposure; it was also a significant lender to a few hedge funds—Carlyle Capital, Peloton Partners, and Thornburg Mortgage—that were also looking wobbly because of their own bad mortgage bets.

When the end came for Bear Stearns, it came hard and fast. By March 5, the annual cost of credit insurance on $10 million worth of Bear bonds had risen to $350,000 and was heading higher. On March 6, the Dutch firm Rabobank told Bear's executives that it would not roll over a $500 million loan coming due the next week. At the same time, Moody's downgraded a number of mortgage-backed securities issued by Bear. The company's stock slipped to $62.30—less than half its October levels. On March 7, the cost of credit insurance rose to $458,000. By the next Monday, March 10, the cost was $626,000.

Remarkably, as Bear teetered on the edge, a key member of its leadership for some reason concluded that being out of town was acceptable. Alan Schwartz, then CEO, was in Palm Beach at the luxurious Breakers resort for the company's annual media conference, a confab at which he mingled with Time Warner's Jeff Bewkes, Disney's Robert Iger, News Corp's Rupert Murdoch, and Viacom's Sumner Redstone. He chose not to rush back to New York to take charge.

Schwartz issued a press release on March 10 claiming that the company's "balance sheet, liquidity, and capital [remained] strong." The company was sitting on $18 billion of cash, he told investors and counterparties; there was nothing to be concerned about. Not true. The firm was dangerously leveraged, with just $11.1 billion in tangible equity backstopping $395 billion in assets. Worse, trading partners were now leaving in droves.

On Tuesday, March 11, the Federal Reserve made an unprecedented move—it decided to open its discount window to investment banks for the first time, allowing them to borrow up to $200 billion in Treasury securities in exchange for any mortgage-backed collateral the banks might provide. The hitch: the program would not commence until March 27. Charlie Gasparino suggested on CNBC that the Fed's moves were clearly aimed at helping Bear. The only question was whether that help would come in time. Another Dutch bank, ING, told Bear it was withdrawing $500 million of financing. Rabobank, which had already done the same, signaled that it would also not renew a $2 billion loan coming due the next week. Adage Capital, a hedge fund, removed its money from Bear's prime brokerage arm that day, and other hedge funds were making noises about doing likewise. Fidelity Investments, which had been an overnight lender to Bear to the tune of $6 billion a day, pulled its funding during the week. Federated Investors, into Bear for $4.5 billion a night, also reneged.

William Cohan suggests in *House of Cards* that the "dirty little secret" of Wall Street firms was just how much they relied on such overnight "repo" funding. He was right. Although there was always the risk that a firm might lose its access to short-term funds instantaneously—and thus be left unable to repay its obligations—this hadn't happened to any major firm in memory, and the risk was therefore essentially ignored. Until it couldn't be.

That same day, the chief of the New York Fed, Tim Geithner, and the Fed's chairman, Ben Bernanke, hosted a luncheon in the Washington Room at the New York Fed on 33 Liberty Street. The CEOs of most of the top Wall Street firms were in attendance—Lloyd Blankfein of Goldman Sachs; Ken Chenault of American Express; Dimon; Dick Fuld of Lehman Brothers; Bob Rubin, chairman of the executive committee at Citigroup; and John Thain of Merrill Lynch. A few kingpins of private equity and hedge funds were also there, including Ken Griffin of Citadel Investment Group, Bruce Kovner of Caxton Associates, and Steve Schwarzman of the Blackstone Group. There was no one representing Bear Stearns in the room; Schwartz had not even been invited.

On the morning of Wednesday, March 12, Schwartz appeared on CNBC in an effort to deflect growing concerns about the company. "Some people could speculate that Bear Stearns might have problems, since we're a significant player in the mortgage business," he said to the anchor, David Faber. "None of those concerns are true." If this was not an outright lie, it was surely a twist of the truth. The previous day three banks—Credit Suisse, Deutsche Bank, and Goldman Sachs—had all received numerous "novation" requests from investors seeking to have someone take over Bear's side of various derivatives trades.

Schwartz returned to New York on the afternoon of March 12. That evening, he called the banker Gary Parr, of Lazard, who was watching Patrick Stewart in a performance of *Macbeth* in Brooklyn. Parr left at intermission and met the Bear executives at their offices to discuss their "strategic options"—Wall Street's code for a fire sale. Schwartz also called H. Rodgin Cohen, the chairman of the law firm Sullivan & Cromwell. After a brief discussion, according to the *Wall Street Journal*, Cohen dialed Tim Geithner and asked if there was any way the Fed might accelerate the timing of the opening of the discount window. "I've been around long enough to sense a very serious problem," Geithner told him. "If he's worried, Alan needs to call me."

Schwartz did call Geithner the next day to brief him, but maintained that he hoped to find a solution without the Fed's help. He was kidding himself. By this point things were moving so quickly that there was little for him and his colleagues to do but watch the money stream out the door. That morning, the hedge fund Renaissance Technologies took $5 billion out of Bear's prime brokerage arm. In the afternoon, another hedge fund, D.E. Shaw & Co., did the same thing.

At the day's end, Bear had just $5.9 billion of cash on hand, and the company's stock price was plummeting. Gary Parr was working the phones, trying to find what he called a "validating" investor—an outsider who could lend credence to the idea that Bear was still viable. One of the first people on his list was Jamie Dimon.

At the same time that Alan Schwartz's world was falling apart,

Jamie Dimon was settling into his comfort zone. While JPMorgan Chase had chased market share during the credit boom—by loosening loan covenants or adjusting pricing downward along with the rest of the herd—their relatively disciplined approach had left Dimon and his operating committee in position to pick off a weakened competitor or two if the turmoil continued. In January, JPMorgan Chase had bought $4.3 billion in reverse mortgages from the struggling U.K. bank Northern Rock at a steep discount. "We are one of the few people that everyone knows are open for business and ready to work on some of these things," Bill Winters said at the time.

On the afternoon of March 13, in fact, a number of executives, including the chief financial officer Mike Cavanagh and Charlie Scharf, sat in an eighth-floor conference room at 270 Park Avenue, getting ready to go to Seattle the following Monday. Washington Mutual, the Seattle-based bank, had run aground because of its own subprime mortgage troubles and had put itself up for sale. There was also the possibility that one of the Ohio-based banks might be on the block, and Dimon intended to bid aggressively for at least one of the two.

Around 6:00 p.m., Dimon stuck his head through the doorway of the conference room. It was his fifty-second birthday, and he was heading out for dinner with his wife, his parents, and his eldest daughter, Julia. The celebration was to be at Avra, a Greek restaurant that was a favorite of his parents. "I got another call from someone who wants us to consider buying their company," Dimon said, almost in passing. To no one's real surprise, the caller had been Gary Parr, on behalf of Bear Stearns. "But it didn't have a tone of *This is going to happen in the next 12 hours,*'" recalls Cavanagh. "It was more like we should spend some time to see if something would make sense between the two companies. All by itself, given the environment, it wasn't a strange or alarming bit of information."

An hour later, during dinner, Dimon's cell phone rang. It was Parr, asking him if he had a moment to speak to Alan Schwartz. As Dimon walked outside to the sidewalk, the CEO of Bear Stearns cut to the chase. "We really need help," Schwartz said. "How much?" Dimon replied. "As much as $30 billion," was Schwartz's response. "Well, the answer to that one is easy," said Dimon. "No."

But Schwartz was desperate. He asked if Dimon would consider a mere overnight loan. "I can't; it's impossible," said Dimon. "There's no time to do the homework. We don't know the issues. I've got a board." Dimon suggested that Schwartz call both the Federal Reserve and the Treasury Department, and told Schwartz he would be in touch. And then he hung up.

Dimon left dinner, went home, and was on the phone for much of the night. The first of his flurry of phone calls was to Tim Geithner, who urged him to help Bear. Despite the implied threat that regulators can hang over a Wall Street CEO's head, Dimon wouldn't be bullied. "Tim, look, we can't do it alone," he said. "Just do something to get them to the weekend. Then you'll have some time." The two agreed to continue the conversation later. Dimon also spoke to Secretary of the Treasury Hank Paulson and to the Federal Reserve chairman, Ben Bernanke.

He also called Steve Black, who was on vacation in Anguilla with his wife, Debbie. At dinner in a beachside restaurant, Black knew something was up when a man came striding urgently toward his table. "Are you Mr. Black?" he said. As had happened so many times before, an investment banker trying to enjoy a vacation had been tracked down by his boss. In short order, Black was on the phone in the restaurant's kitchen with Dimon. Black returned the next day to take control of the investment bank's efforts in New York; in the meantime, Bill Winters (who received another call) led the team by phone from London on Thursday night and Friday morning.

Yet another call was to Mike Cavanagh, who by that point was at home for the night. "Jamie rarely calls in off-hours and is pretty respectful of family and weekend time," recalls Cavanagh. "So I knew something was up." After a quick briefing, Cavanagh was on the phone with John Hogan, the chief risk officer of JPMorgan Chase's investment bank. He then spoke with the chief financial officer of Bear Stearns, Sam Molinaro, and its treasurer, Robert Upton.

The executives at JPMorgan Chase were surprised to discover how baffled the executives at Bear Stearns were about what was happening. Instead of presenting a crisp request—"Here's what we need, J.P. Morgan: x billion dollars"—Bear's executives tossed out numbers ranging anywhere from $5 billion to $20 billion in the span of a single conversation. "The mere fact that it was that wide of a range left us thinking that they really didn't know how bad it was going to be," recalls Cavanagh.

At 11:00 P.M., JPMorgan Chase dispatched a number of credit people to the beleaguered firm's offices at 383 Madison Avenue, the first of many teams to go to the Bear Stearns building that night, headed by the senior trader Matt Zames. He was joined at 2:00 A.M. by teams from both the Federal Reserve and the Securities and Exchange Commission.

At 3:00 A.M., Cavanagh received another call from Dimon. "I felt like a fireman at that point," recalls Cavanagh. Dimon said he was about to get on the phone with the Treasury and the Federal Reserve and needed Cavanagh in the office immediately. An hour later, a bleary-eyed Cavanagh walked into John Hogan's office, and into the middle of a conference call with Dimon, Tim Geithner, Bill Winters, and Matt Zames. The discussion was still theoretical at that point, as the men speculated blow-by-blow on the events that would occur if Bear Stearns couldn't open for business. Bear Stearns, after all, had trading positions with 5,000 firms and billions of dollars at risk. "It was a scary description of events that we all thought would lead to more dominoes falling in subsequent weeks," recalls Cavanagh.

Dimon essentially demanded all hands on deck on Thursday night. By 6:00 the next morning, he told his team to cut Bear Stearns into numerous slices. He wanted the teams looking at those slices to come back every three hours and give him a sense of their value.

Government officials had no playbook for this kind of event. They also lacked the power to lend directly to broker-dealers such as Bear Stearns. Somewhere in the wee hours of the morning, a plan began to take shape. Instead of lending directly to Bear Stearns, the Fed would lend $30 billion to JPMorgan Chase, which would turn around and lend that money to Bear.

The arrangement was termed a "conduit," though it was really nothing more than a circumvention of the Fed's own lending restrictions. "It was harebrained," recalls one executive at JPMorgan Chase. "It wasn't like we went to 'Section Five' of the 'Emergency Financial System Meltdown Manual' and found out what we should do." The outcome, however, was nothing short of profound. For the first time since the Great Depression, the Federal Reserve was going to backstop an investment bank.

In the four-sentence release announcing the conduit, Stephen Cutler, general counsel of JPMorgan Chase, included a line saying that the secured funding would be good for "an initial period of up to 28 days," followed by the statement that "JPMorgan Chase is working closely with Bear Stearns on securing permanent financing or other alternatives for the company." When Alan Schwartz and Bear's chief financial officer, Sam Molinaro, received the release in an e-mail from Cutler at 6:45 A.M., they thought this meant that they had 28 days to come up with a solution to their predicament. They were naturally relieved. They shouldn't have been.

. . .

When the stock market opened the next morning, Bear's shareholders appeared to be relieved as well. The stock floated around its close of the previous day, $57 a share, even climbing to $62 in the first half hour of trading. Steve Black, who'd been up all night helping to get the debt facility in place, was packed and ready to go to Miami with his wife, Debbie, on a 10:00 A.M. flight. At 9:30, he switched on CNBC. He couldn't believe that the stock hadn't plummeted.

Turning to his wife, he said, "The markets don't have any idea what's really happening here. Mark my words, by the time we get back to New York, and the market has digested the news, the stock price will have been cut in half." It didn't take even that long. When the couple arrived at the airport with their luggage, the stock was already trading at $31 a share. One hundred ninety million shares of Bear traded that day—17 times the daily average, and the stock closed at $30 a share, down 47 percent. The cost of a five-year credit default swap on the company's debt had risen to $772,000, nearly double that of Lehman Brothers' $451,000 and triple that of Goldman Sachs's $253,000. Clients continued to pull out their accounts.

Alan Schwartz was in a car on the way to his home in Greenwich that evening when Paulson and Geithner called. Geithner delivered the first surprise. The financing from the Fed would not be available on Monday. Paulson delivered the second. A "stabilizing transaction" had to be done by the end of the weekend—in other words, the firm would have to be sold in the next 48 hours. Schwartz later testified, "All the leverage went out the window when a deal had to happen over the weekend."

Ever since, many of Bear's former executives have maintained that Paulson and the Fed played dirty pool by "changing" the terms of a deal made only the night before. Dimon didn't see it that way. The original goal of the financing was to get Bear to the weekend, at which point he (or any other interested party) could consider buying the company.

Then there was the exact wording of the press release itself, about which there has been much consternation. It did not say "28-day financing." It said "up to 28 days." "I've always considered this a moot point," Dimon said after the eventual purchase of Bear Stearns by JPMorgan Chase, "because they were still having a run on the bank. The Fed had lent them $30 billion on Friday and we had to lend them another $20 billion on Monday. We wouldn't have done that had we not done the deal, and the fact that we'd done the deal wasn't even stopping money from continuing to head out the door. So they would have never survived Monday anyway, even if the financing had been for 28 days. It didn't matter. It was over."

What's more, the lending from the Fed was collateralized, which meant that Bear Stearns needed to have assets to pass on. "The Bear people seemed surprised," recalls Cavanagh. "But I have no idea why. They didn't have the collateral anyway."

By 8:00 the next morning, Schwartz and Molinaro were back at 383 Madison, meeting with bankers from JPMorgan Chase as well as representatives from the private equity outfit J.C. Flowers & Co., which would prove to be the only other interested party. Other firms had representatives in the building, but none of them mounted a serious bid. Citigroup, obviously, had its own troubles. Bank of America was busy completing a purchase of Countrywide Financial. Goldman Sachs had the resources to buy Bear, but had no reason to—the two firms overlapped too much. But JPMorgan Chase was diving headlong into the deal, dispatching 16 teams from various departments to meet with Bear's officials and combing through their books.

The members of JPMorgan Chase's team were still not entirely sure that they were interested. They were merely doing due diligence at breakneck speed. While several hundred top executives scurried around the company's own headquarters at 270 Park Avenue holding meetings— some 2,000 people had been called in to work on the deal globally—Steve Black was thinking to himself, "Didn't we just do this?" And they had. When Bear's hedge funds had run into trouble in the summer of 2007, executives at JPMorgan Chase had taken a pass on buying the firm. Six months later, things were even worse for the struggling investment bank. So what was the point of going through the motions again?

"We'd been through it the past summer," Black recalls, "and we'd told them that we'd be interested if they wanted us to make some sort of convertible investment in their prime brokerage business. Alan's response had been, 'Why would we do that? Wouldn't it make the whole franchise worth less?' I'd said, 'That's a fair point, but consider this us registering some interest if you guys get to that point.' We had done the work on whether we'd be interested in the whole bank and the consensus was it wasn't worth all the aggravation. Certain pieces fit well, but the rest of it would have been too time-consuming to integrate. Plus, at the kind of price Bear was likely to get, it wouldn't give us much in the end." The "certain pieces" he was referring to were Bear's prime brokerage operations—estimated to be worth about $3 billion—its clearing business, and its energy and commodities divisions.

There was also the building. Constructed at the height of the commercial real-estate market in Manhattan, Bear's headquarters at 383 Madison Avenue were worth an estimated $1 billion. JPMorgan Chase had recently announced, with Mayor Michael Bloomberg and Governor Eliot Spitzer, its plan to construct a new headquarters for the investment bank in downtown Manhattan, on the site of the old Deustche Bank building, which had been condemned after 9/11. If JPMorgan Chase could nab Bear's building, it would save itself a whole different kind of aggravation. "We could have taken five years and spent $3 billion to build a new building, or just said, 'Who cares about the rest of Bear Stearns, let's just get the freaking building,' " recalls one JPMorgan Chase executive. "I kept saying, 'Guys, we *have* to get that building.' " The Bear building is even shaped like an octagon, the symbol of Chase.

At 11:00 Saturday morning, Steve Black and Mike Cavanagh quizzed each of the due-diligence teams on how much downside they saw, even if JPMorgan Chase were to pick up Bear Stearns for a single dollar. Was there enough value in the Bear businesses, they wanted to know, to absorb the pain that would come along with unloading or hedging all the toxic and unwanted assets? The numbers thrown out were all ballpark estimates: $2 billion worth of losses here, $500 million there. The goal was to come up with a raw total of the de-risking costs and lawsuits that would undoubtedly come with the deal.

This approach was Dimonology: dwell on the downside of a potential deal before entertaining the upside. "He kept the board informed of every change in their thinking as well, and didn't get too far out ahead of us" recalls JPMorgan Chase's director William Gray. "He inspires great trust that way. What we read in the papers was old news for us. He raised every problem that could occur. We could never walk out and say he never told us about this or that."

By the afternoon, the team from J.C. Flowers had a contingent bid ready: $3 billion for 90 percent of a recapitalized Bear Stearns' equity— the equivalent of about $2.80 a share including the billion or so new shares that would have to be issued—provided that Flowers could line up $20 billion in financing to cover Bear's short-term cash needs. Rounding up that much in such a short time was a long shot, but at that point, it was all Bear had.

A few hours later, Steve Black and the head of investment banking, Doug Braunstein, walked over to Bear Stearns to speak to Schwartz and Gary Parr. Bear's stock had closed at $30 on Friday, but Black had bad news for the two men. JPMorgan Chase hadn't been able to do as much work as they'd hoped, said Black, and so there would be no "firm offer" that evening. But their work had led them to one obvious conclusion. "If you guys are thinking that we're going to be interested anywhere close to where you closed, or God forbid, a premium, then we should just send everybody home right now, because it's not even going to be close," he added. "You need to tell us now that it's worth the effort to keep working. We're thinking of somewhere from $8 to $12 a share." Schwartz, feeling that he was out of options in any event, told Black to keep working.

A short time later, Schwartz called Dimon. He wanted to know whether Dimon considered this a "hell or high water" deal. In other words, if Schwartz asked his board for approval, he needed to know that Dimon was serious about getting it done, and wouldn't start adding conditions after the fact. Dimon told Schwartz that he'd kept his own board apprised of the process and he would be surprised if they didn't give him their support when it came time to pull the trigger. Schwartz said he'd meet with his board and be in touch in the morning.

Schwartz and Parr updated Bear's directors on the progress of the negotiations. Although disappointed at the low level of the offers, the board members agreed to continue pursuing both. They knew that Christopher Flowers was unlikely to be able to line up $20 billion of financing overnight. Bear Stearns, after all, had been unable to do the very same.

At 6:00 P.M., the JPMorgan Chase executives held another round-table discussion to get updates from their due-diligence teams. Dimon slipped into the meeting every now and then, sat down, listened for a few minutes, and then left without interrupting. His casual weekend wear was black jeans and a black T-shirt. "Jamie was dressed like Johnny Cash," laughs one executive. "I guess he thought he looked cool. But he didn't."

The head of J.P. Morgan's mortgage business was forecasting $1 billion in losses from unwinding Bear's mortgage positions. "Fine," said Cavanagh, "call it $2 billion." A few hours later, with more information streaming in, sources say the number was at $4 billion and moving higher. (JPMorgan Chase's executives eventually estimated that the total cost of the deal beyond the purchase price itself would be $6 billion. They raised that number to $9 billion in May.)

At 9:00 P.M., the executives took a straw poll. Steve Black, Barry Zubrow, and Mike Cavanagh favored the deal. The asset management head Jes Staley and the general counsel Steve Cutler had reservations. The team decided to sleep on it and get back to work the next morning.

Even among those who supported the deal, there was strong sentiment that buying Bear Stearns on such short notice was crazy. Never in history had anyone tried to take over a $400 billion balance sheet in just a few days, especially one that was surely full of holes. What's more, the company's executives had earned a reputation for being cautious, and this deal was anything but. Not only was there the question of what Bear's assets were actually worth; there was also what might be termed the Heisenberg principle of market uncertainty. By the very act of stepping in to save Bear, JPMorgan Chase would change the value of the company and its holdings—and not in a positive direction.

Throughout the day, Cavanagh had tried to stay optimistic, telling himself that they needed to give the deal a serious shot at happening. But in the car on the way home, his spirits began flagging. "What are we doing?" he thought to himself. The next morning, his thoughts had solidified. "We can't do this," he told Dimon.

Bill Winters had finally found time to get off the phone and fly from London to New York early Sunday morning. He arrived to find that Cavanagh was not the only one souring on the deal.

The first issue was Bear's assets. Although Bear Stearns had told JPMorgan Chase that about $120 billion was "at risk" of further deterioration, the JPMorgan Chase team had concluded that the number was likely to be closer to $225 billion. And it wasn't just the sheer amount that scared the team. The fact that it was a continually moving target comforted no one.

Worse yet, an article in the Sunday *New York Times* by the influential columnist Gretchen Morgenson added another dimension to the deal. In this article, "Rescue Me: A Fed Bailout Crosses a Line," she called Bear Stearns "this decade's version of Drexel Burnham Lambert, the anything-goes, 1980s junk-bond shop." Morgenson wondered what the merit was in saving a firm that had given its competitors the middle finger during the LTCM bailout, had been convicted of aiding 1990s "bucket shops" that defrauded investors, and then had gone whole hog on subprime.

"It became a reputational issue for us," recalls one JPMorgan Chase executive. "She was basically saying if you're ever going to let somebody go down, these are the dirtbags that you should let go down. They had a completely different culture than ours. Alan Schwartz might tell you that the two places would really fit together, but that's just not the case. The two cultures were 180 degrees apart."

After discussing the *Times*'s story, Steve Cutler and Jes Staley repeated their concerns. This time, they weren't outnumbered; both Black and Cavanagh had switched sides. The executives convened another roundtable, and the result was a thumbs-down. A smaller contingent then went to inform Dimon that they considered it irresponsible to do such a risky deal.

Dimon agreed with his team, and suggested making a series of calls. Dimon would call Geithner and Paulson, Black would call Schwartz, and Doug Braunstein would call Gary Parr.

With Schwartz on the phone, Black was blunt. "Look, Alan, I know what we said last night, but we've got more information now and we're not going to do a transaction at the level we were talking about. More to the point, I'm not even sure we can even do a transaction at all. Whatever options you may have been pursuing, you should keep pursuing them and not count on us to be there." Black continued: "Alan, you know me well. I'm not bullshitting you; this is not a negotiating tactic. Do not count on us. It's not just a question of price anymore." Braunstein delivered a similar message to Parr.

Geithner stepped out of a meeting to take Dimon's call. The discussion was brief. Dimon explained to Geithner that the risks were too great for JPMorgan Chase to buy the company on its own. "This wasn't a negotiating posture," Dimon later testified in front of the Senate. "It was the plain truth." Geithner was in a pinch. Despite all the subsequent descriptions of him as a dapper young bureaucrat-in-training, he had nevertheless failed to rustle up any further interest for the failing bank, and was facing a botched rescue operation as the first notable moment of his career.

Whatever Black and Dimon said, it certainly seemed like a tactical move at the time. And when Geithner called back a few minutes later and urged Dimon to keep trying to get a deal done, he was essentially signaling to Dimon that he now had negotiating leverage over both Bear Stearns and the Fed, which both had their backs to the wall. At the same time, Geithner was making it clear that this was a deal that *had* to happen. Even Jamie Dimon knew it wasn't a smart move to say no to the government a third time. "At that point, I think people kind of knew that this was something we needed to do," says a member of JPMorgan Chase's operating committee.

With the Asian markets opening at 7:00 P.M., everybody knew that Bear had to announce *something* or risk an implosion of the firm—and conceivably of the financial system itself. Bear's plan B was a deal with JPMorgan Chase, and there was no plan C. "There just wasn't any other great alternative," recalls Mike Cavanagh. "In the end we had to figure out a way to facilitate us buying them."

A number of former Bear Stearns executives view the events that Sunday as brinksmanship on Dimon's part. Dimon chafes at the notion, pointing out that no one had ever had to carry out such a massive amount of due diligence with such haste: "We had literally 48 hours to do what normally takes a month." This was not, in other words, the kind of predator-prey situation that Dimon had been preparing for since he arrived at JPMorgan Chase. A thoughtful man who luxuriates in rigorous analysis, he was being asked to put his own company at risk because another firm had played too fast and too loose. Another firm, it bears repeating, that he'd passed on buying just six months before.

Recall Dimon's three components of a successful deal: business logic, the ability to execute, and price. In this instance, the business logic was a mixed bag. Buying Bear would give JPMorgan Chase a few assets it wanted but would also saddle it with some it most certainly did not. The ability to execute was totally unknown, especially on such short notice. Bear's customers could continue to bolt, as could valuable employees. In a business where relationships and human capital are paramount, both were critical issues. In any event, the situation certainly wasn't going to be easy. To get a deal done, then, the price was going to have to come down even more. And because Jamie Dimon was holding the whip hand in negotiations, that's exactly what it did.

In fact, the price came down on two fronts. A little after lunchtime, Black called Schwartz and floated the idea that JPMorgan Chase might come back to the table at $4 a share. When told of the new number, Cayne was enraged, and suggested filing for bankruptcy instead of suffering the indignity of such a meager offer. His board talked him down, however, and went back to debating the dwindling options while waiting for an official offer.

At the same time, Dimon was explaining to Geithner that unless he received a substantial guarantee of Bear's dodgy assets—$30 billion worth, to be precise—he could not do the deal. It was too much risk for his shareholders. Realizing that he had no other viable options, Geithner agreed to provide a $30 billion nonrecourse loan, collateralized by a pool of Bear's assets.

Late Sunday afternoon, Secretary of the Treasury Hank Paulson called Dimon in his office. Dimon told Paulson that JPMorgan Chase was mulling over a $4-a-share offer. "That sounds high to me. I think this should be done at a very low price," Paulson replied. "Why $4? Why not $1? The less you offer, the less it's going to look like a bailout." Paulson didn't want to anger the American people by seeming to rescue greedy bankers from their own mistakes. He also raised the issue of "moral hazard"—the idea that bailing out equity holders of Bear Stearns would encourage future reckless behavior. "Where there is intervention, I really believe that the shareholders need to lose," Paulson later told *Fortune* magazine. "Bear Stearns was a great old institution, but I don't know how you can put government money in there and protect the shareholders."

Dimon replied that he'd been thinking of the shareholders' vote that would be required at Bear Stearns, and that to go much lower would be to risk enraging the very people he needed to approve a transaction. "But at the end of the day, it wasn't that big a deal, so we changed it to

$2," he recalls. On the subject of moral hazard, however, he took a slightly softer line than Paulson. "I don't quite get the whole moral hazard argument, the whole 'We'll show them!' mentality," he said. "So a drunk friend of yours falls in a river. Do you let them drown? No, you save them. And after you save them, you deal with their problem. No, I don't think highly paid executives at any investment bank deserve to get bailed out. But at some point, you're just talking about various degrees of suffering."

According to William Cohan's *House of Cards*, Doug Braunstein was dispatched to relay the news to Gary Parr. "The number's $2," he said. "You can't really mean that," Parr replied. "Are you serious? You really don't want me to go back into the board and tell them this." Braunstein told Parr that this was the final offer. Parr then wearily relayed it to the Bear Stearns board. Again, Jimmy Cayne said he would refuse to do the deal. Cayne owned 5.66 million shares, and had watched their value fall from nearly $1 billion to just over $11 million in the past year. "Two dollars is better than nothing," Schwartz replied. After a heated 30-minute discussion, the board unanimously approved the transaction at 6:30 P.M. (When the *Wall Street Journal* broke the news online at 7:00 P.M., John Mack, CEO of Morgan Stanley, wondered aloud whether the $2 was a typo. Many Bear Stearns employees did the same. Alan Schwartz, long considered one of the best deal makers on Wall Street, was selling his own firm for a song. Mack would nearly be forced to sell his for nothing come September, before inching his way back from the edge of the abyss.)

Warren Buffett—who passed on making his own bid for the company—gives Dimon credit for making a gut decision based on limited information. "You don't have to understand it perfectly," he says. "You just need to know the outer limits. A guy can walk into a room and you might not know whether he weighs 300 or 350 pounds, but you know he's fat. I just felt I couldn't even categorize it to that extent. But you can act, and we do act, with imperfect information. If Jamie told me that the boundaries of value for Bear were x and y, I would feel he was right. I've seen enough of his judgment to know it's extraordinarily good. He knows what he doesn't know. But you have to be willing to step up and take a swing. He knows the pitches he likes. He knows what he can hit. He's not going to sit around waiting for the perfect pitch."

Buffett continued: "It wasn't shooting fish in a barrel, but if it didn't work out he could stand the downside. If it did work out, there were significant pluses. He is a very cool, rational thinker. I have never seen him make a decision based on emotion. He has got the background and the mental equipment to make good decisions. I like to think that he and I think the same way, but I'm probably flattering myself."

At 8:00 P.M., in a conference call with investors, Mike Cavanagh walked through a six-page presentation. As part of the contract, JPMorgan Chase retained the right to buy the Bear Stearns building even if the merger failed. This was as important to some executives at JPMorgan Chase as anything else about the deal. "During the negotiations," Dimon recalls, "some of our investment bankers came up and said if you need a little more money, we'll chip in so we don't have to commute downtown."

Later that night, Geithner convened a conference call for Wall Street CEOs. Some 60 or 70 people called in, and the broad strokes of the discussion—led at points by Geithner, Dimon, and the treasury secretary, Paulson—were that the deal was being done to stabilize the market, and that it just might have saved the system.

Vikram Pandit, the CEO of Citigroup, asked a question about the risk to Bear's trading partners in certain long-term contracts. "Who is this?" barked Dimon. "Vikram," was the response. "Stop being such a jerk," Dimon snapped, adding that Citigroup "should thank us" for doing the deal rather than look for the holes in it. Much ado was made in news reports the next day about Dimon's use of the word "jerk." But the focus should have been on the follow-up remark. Because Pandit had found a hole in the deal—and it was a huge one.

• • •

Dimon received more acclaim during the week of March 17 than most bankers receive in a lifetime. He was referred to as "Wall Street's banker of last resort," "the most powerful banker in the world," and "a senior financial statesman," and he was compared in numerous instances to J.P. Morgan himself. (Former Bear Stearns employees were not among those praising Dimon. One had sardonically taped a $2 bill to the front window of the bank. Others were busy selling company materials on eBay. Bear T-shirts sold for $151; stock certificates sold for $42 apiece.)

In one sense, at least, the comparison was apt. During the panic of 1907, when Morgan had saved a floundering bank, he had picked up its stake in Tennessee Coal & Iron in return—patriotism and the profit motive rolled into one. "With his peculiar bifocal vision, he saw the panic as a time for both statesmanship and personal gain," writes Ron Chernow in *The House of Morgan*. Likewise for Jamie Dimon a century later.

Behind the scenes, however, things weren't so peachy. The third page of the presentation Cavanagh had made to investors on Sunday night included the following line: "[JPMorgan] will guarantee the trading obligations of [Bear Stearns] and its subsidiaries effective immediately." The purpose of the guarantee had been to head off another run on the bank by assuring the market that Bear Stearns could make good on its trades. A number of questions were raised about what would come of the guarantee if Bear's shareholders voted down the deal, and the answers were not particularly clear, except for the fact that the guarantee would last a year.

When the stock market opened on Monday, Bear Stearns stock bounced between $3.50 and $5.50 a share, signaling that the market didn't think the deal was going to get done at $2 a share. One reason was the guarantee itself. Bear's shareholders looking for a higher price could continue to vote down the deal, leaving JPMorgan Chase exposed for up to a year guaranteeing Bear's trades. With about a third of the company's shares held by employees—who were in a state of righteous indignation—the chance of a "no" vote was considerable. JPMorgan Chase had, in other words, given Bear's shareholders a one-year "put" option on their company as part of the deal, without meaning to do so. By continuing to vote against the deal, they could buy themselves time in which the company might recover, all while JPMorgan Chase backstopped the business.

Andrew Ross Sorkin of the *New York Times* reported that when the error was discovered, Dimon lashed out at his firm's lawyers at Wachtell, Lipton. A partner at Wachtell, Ed Herlihy, who had worked with Dimon on both the Bank One–J.P. Morgan and Bank of New York deals, had somehow missed this. Dimon also called Schwartz to argue that the agreement be modified. "Don't you understand that we have a problem? Shareholders may vote this down!" Dimon asked him. Schwartz, however, savored the first bit of leverage he'd had since Friday: "What do you mean, *we* have a problem?" He told Dimon he'd need a higher offer to make any concessions on the terms of the deal. Sorkin reported that Dimon was outraged, and that he even threatened to "send Bear back into bankruptcy." But cooler heads prevailed.

The guarantee was giving Dimon fits in another way, too. In its original language, it guaranteed only Bear's "trading obligations." That term didn't cover all the company's products, customer relationships, and subsidiaries, and a number of customers continued to take their business elsewhere for fear of suffering losses if the deal fell apart. Even if he could clarify the issue of the deal being voted down, Dimon had to expand the guarantee if he wanted to stop the customer exodus.

Looking back at the conference call during which he called Pandit a jerk, Dimon is both unapologetic and conciliatory. "He made a very good technical point, and it was one of the things that started causing us a problem the next day. But even he would say that in hindsight it was probably an inappropriate forum. But I never said he was wrong. No one had ever guaranteed someone else's trades before—not that I'm aware of—so it was certainly one of the issues we were concerned about." (In other words, Pandit was right.)

Dimon told his senior staff on Monday that he wanted to go over to Bear Stearns as soon as possible and "talk to the troops." The response was that he was crazy. Emotions were still raw, he was told, and it might actually be dangerous. One executive even put in a call to Alan Schwartz, pleading with him to call Dimon himself and say it was too early. But Dimon argued that staying away would be disrespectful. By Wednesday, March 19, he had waited as long as he was prepared to wait, and scheduled a meeting with 400 managing directors of Bear Stearns in their second-floor auditorium. Standing with him on the dais were Steve Black and Bill Winters.

Dimon tried a peacemaking approach—a wise move, considering that most of the people in the room had just lost the majority of their net worth, not to mention their reputations. Wall Street's scrappiest firm had just been swallowed whole by one of the most plodding and predictable. "I don't think Bear did anything to deserve this," Dimon said. "I feel terrible sometimes when people think we took advantage. I don't think we could possibly know what you are feeling but I hope that you give J.P. Morgan a chance."

At least a few people weren't going to let him off easy. During a Q&A, when he referred to the merger as a "shotgun marriage," a broker stood up and said, "I wouldn't use that term. I'd call this a shotgun wedding to a rapist. Yeah, yeah, the girl was lying there naked on the ground when you found her, that's true, but you did it anyway." (He was shouted down and booed by his colleagues. A number of Bear Stearns executives apologized to Dimon afterward.)

Another Bear employee added, "In this room are people who have built this firm and lost a lot, our fortunes. What will you do to make us whole?" Leaving aside the absurdity of Wall Streeters wanting a "do-over" on their stock, this raised an interesting issue. Just what could Dimon do to satisfy people whom he needed to make the deal worthwhile? "You're acting like it's our fault, and it's not," he said. "[But] if you stay, we will make you happy."

At that point, though, there were few happy people at Bear Stearns. In *House of Cards*, Cohan cites an e-mail sent by Paul Friedman, chief operating officer of Bear's fixed income division, to another Bear executive, despairing at their predicament. "The (optimistic) view is that this was JP's plan all along: bid, pull the bid, string it out to the last minute to force the Fed to take all the risk and then steal us cheap AND risk free." When the deal was sealed, Friedman wrote an e-mail to another executive while drunk. "Getting less coherent, but no less angry," he typed. "Death of a family member. Loss of friends. Wouldn't work at JPM on a bet—which is good since they wouldn't want me." He was not alone in that sentiment. Ed Wolfe, a securities analyst at Bear, responded to a question about whether he'd quit by replying, "Well, I can't talk about that but I'm never going to work for those fucking assholes." These were the sounds of a defeated group of self-styled rebels lashing out at the man who not only had not caused their demise but had salvaged what equity—and jobs—he could. He had done what any of them would have done had they been in the same situation. But whom else did they have to blame but themselves?

(Dimon was concerned about a possible staff exodus, and offered both cash and stock incentives to employees to stick around at least until the deal was closed. He also called a number of rivals on Wall Street and pleaded with them not to poach Bear's employees. Even in the midst of the craziness of the time, this is a bizarre image, like a lion asking other lions not to eat his recent kill.)

The criticism didn't end in the auditorium. It had been drizzling when Dimon stepped out the door of JPMorgan Chase to walk across the street to Bear Stearns. A bodyguard standing nearby decided to do the thoughtful thing, opened an umbrella, and held it over Dimon's head at the very moment a photographer from the *New York Times* was taking a picture. When the photo appeared in the paper the next day, Dimon was vilified on all manner of websites for his monarchal appearance—he looked like he had a butler. The general tone: *Who does this guy think he is?*

Dimon called JPMorgan Chase's head of communications, Joe Evangelisti, in frustration. "I have never ever in my life had someone hold an umbrella for me," he said. "Can't you buy that picture?" Evangelisti couldn't quash the photo—it was used in another story a short time later—but Dimon soon found he could laugh at the absurdity of it all. "That's the last time that will ever happen," he says. "There are jokes about it now. If I walk outside when it's raining these days, they'll literally throw an umbrella at me while trying to get some distance between us at the same time."

By the end of the week, the haggling was down to two crucial points. First, Dimon wanted to shrink the time during which JPMorgan Chase would be on the hook for Bear's trades if the deal was voted down. Second, he needed more certainty that the deal would close, and to that end asked for the right to buy new shares of Bear Stearns equivalent to 53 percent of the stock. (The original deal called for only a 19.9 percent stake.) On the morning of Saturday, March 22, Schwartz called Dimon and said that his board wanted to go back to $10 to $12 a share to get the deal done. "There's a psychological limit here," he added. "Don't come back to me at $9.99."

Meanwhile, having taken a lot of heat in the press for guaranteeing $30 billion in toxic securities, the Fed came back to Dimon and asked to renegotiate its deal. It wanted JPMorgan Chase to take the first billion in those losses, and then the Fed would take the next $29 billion. The Fed also wanted JPMorgan Chase to guarantee its loans to Bear Stearns. In the span of a week, Dimon had gone from calling the shots on both fronts to making concessions on each.

Sullivan and Cromwell's Cohen, who worked for Bear on the deal, was impressed by Dimon's approach to negotiations. "It's not unique, but really good negotiators follow this kind of style," he says. "Most people try to figure out what they want and how to get it. Jamie is one of a small number of people trying to figure out what the other guy wants and how to give it to them. It's a mind-set. That sounds like a play on words, but it isn't."

Whereas Schwartz and the board demanded $10 a share, Paulson wanted the price to stay at $2. The deal was at risk of falling apart, bizarrely, over a number Dimon himself considered beside the point. "It was irrelevant to me," Dimon recalls. "The only number that mattered was how much money we were going to lose de-risking the thing, not the per share price we paid." (In other words, if the company saw $6 billion in costs associated with the deal, the *total* price it was paying was $2 or $10 *plus* $25 in costs per share, or $27 to $35. So the nominal price per share really didn't matter too much. By the end of the year, with the cost of de-risking approaching $15 billion, the comprehensive cost per Bear share turned out to be about $72.50.)

Paulson finally relented on Sunday. Freed to raise his bid to $10 a share—for a total of $1.456 billion—Dimon got the guarantee changed. He also bought 39.5 percent of the company without having to submit to a shareholder vote. (Like the earlier request of 53 percent, this significant portion actually violated the New York Stock Exchange rules. No matter. Dimon had the entire government on his side, and the rule was waived.) The same day the new deal was announced, JPMorgan Chase bought 11.5 million shares for $12.24 per share. By the time of the actual shareholder vote in May, the company owned 49.73 percent of Bear's stock.

At the time, Dimon didn't publicly admit that his team made a mistake in the original agreement with Bear Stearns. But he didn't have to. The renegotiated deal admitted it for him. "We didn't anticipate that we were leaving optionality in the hands of the shareholders," he recalls. In other words, those shareholders weren't facing a binary choice of $2 or $0 per share; it was $2 or *perhaps more*. "That they could just keep voting against the deal in the hope that things might recover. We didn't make the deal airtight. In hindsight we should have made that guarantee shorter."

Mike Cavanagh is also philosophical about having had to go back to the negotiating table. "We'd latched ourselves to Bear Stearns at that stage with the guarantee," he recalls. "So it was worth it to us the subsequent weekend to get more certainty around the outcome. The one risk the government couldn't help us with was the risk that shareholders would vote the deal down. So we got a pound of flesh extracted from us and took it to $10 a share."

. . .

On March 24, the day the new deal was announced, Standard & Poor's raised Bear's credit ratings. That same day, Jimmy Cayne sold his 5.66 million shares for $10.84 apiece, a total of $61.3 million. The final vote on the deal was to be in May, and Cayne had now ensured that he wouldn't have to bring himself to vote on a deal he would never have done had he felt he had any choice. His old boss, Alan Greenberg, who was still a broker at Bear, charged Cayne $77,000 to make the trade, instead of the $2,500 that would have applied under an employee discount. "If he doesn't like it, he should do his future business elsewhere," Greenberg said in an interview with the *New York Times*.

Admitting that the deal had not been charity—JPMorgan Chase had kept the interests of its own shareholders paramount in negotiations—

Dimon nevertheless continued to push the notion that he'd done what he'd done *for the good of the country*, that JPMorgan Chase was "a responsible corporate citizen." When he testified in front of the Senate Banking Committee on April 3, he wrapped up his prepared remarks in a sweeping conclusion about the benefits of the deal.

"Bear Stearns would have failed without this effort, and the consequences could have been disastrous. The idea that the Bear Stearns fallout would have been limited to a few Wall Street firms just isn't so. People all over America—union members, retirees, small business owners, and our parents and children—are now invested in the financial system through pensions, 401(k)s, mutual funds, and the like. A Bear Stearns bankruptcy could well have touched off a chain reaction of defaults at other major financial institutions. That would have shaken confidence in credit markets that already have been battered. And it could have made it harder for home buyers to get mortgages, harder for municipalities to get the funds they need to build schools and hospitals, and harder for students who need loans to pay tuition. Moreover, such a cascade of trouble could have further depressed consumer confidence and consumer spending, resulted in widespread job losses, and accelerated the current economic downturn."

Dimon gave a polished performance in front of the Senate, without a hint of the cockiness that he usually can't hide when he is asked obvious questions. Watching the testimony on television, Mike Ingrisani, his high school English teacher, thought to himself, "No question that's the Jamie I knew, albeit refined to the nth degree."

Wall Street and the financial media focused on who had been the chief beneficiary of the government intervention—Bear Stearns or JPMorgan Chase itself. JPMorgan Chase was a huge lender to Bear and was also its clearing bank. A default by the investment bank would have cost it dearly, regardless of the response of the broader markets. If Bear's demise had started a cascade of defaults, as some analysts had feared, JPMorgan Chase, the largest player in the $45 trillion market for credit default swaps, could have seen any number of trading partners go bust. So even if saving Bear had saved everyone, the thinking went, saving Bear may have saved JPMorgan Chase a lot more than most.

One senior executive calls the issue a matter of splitting hairs, and says the focus was on the good of everyone, even if everyone, by definition, included JPMorgan Chase. "Our issue wasn't our exposure to Bear Stearns, which showed up in numerous press reports," he says. "It was what we thought could happen to the markets. If Bear went out on Monday, we were pretty sure Lehman would be out on Tuesday and then the only question was which firm would be next."

Executives from Dimon on down also lashed out at those who thought that the $29 billion conduit made the deal at all risk-free or easy for JPMorgan Chase. "We took on a shitload of risk," says one senior executive. "The Fed took $29 billion. We took $371 billion. And people-wise, the cultures did not mix. We have risk meetings for days with Jamie, in which we go over everything: our positions, our exposure, and our response to potential crises. Their culture was all about hoarding information, hiding shit, and being dishonest. It's kind of like some mid career Goldman Sachs banker getting hired somewhere else—there's invariably some turbo culture shock, because the Goldman 'Moonie' culture makes them unable to work at other places. And I'll tell you where we screwed up the most. We were way too eager to treat it as a merger of equals. Goldman Sachs would have hired the top 500 to 1,000 people and fired the rest. We offered to hire half of them and pay them double until the deal closed, which was a waste of money in the end."

A rumor also circulated that JPMorgan Chase had made a margin call on Bear—asking it to beef up collateral on various trades and exposures with the larger firm—at the exact moment the investment bank was unable to meet such a demand, thereby forcing it into submission. Dimon found the suggestion absurd. "Some people just don't know what they're talking about," he says. "There may be some truth that we were tightening our lending standards, but so was everybody. And there's no question it reduced certain people's cash. But in this business, you *have to* tightly control counterparty exposure. There are standards you have to follow, for God's sake."

His response didn't exactly put an end to the question whether a collateral call by JPMorgan Chase pushed Bear over the edge. But it suggested that if it had been the case, well, that was a part of doing business on Wall Street. Jamie Dimon would not accept criticism for running his own company conservatively. (Highbridge Capital, the $27.8 billion hedge fund controlled by JPMorgan Chase, also pulled its assets out of Bear's prime brokerage during that first chaotic week. But such a move can also be defended as a prudent one that put investors' interests first.)

The most persistent question, however, was whether Bear's demise was brought on by a cabal of short-sellers ganging up on the company and spreading false rumors in order to profit from a falling stock. *Vanity Fair* fingered the likes of Goldman Sachs, Citadel Investment Group (based in Chicago), and the secretive hedge fund SAC Capital Partners (based in Stamford, Connecticut) as coconspirators in such a scheme. (They all denied it.) Jimmy Cayne later threw the New York hedge fund Paulson & Co. and Hayman Capital (based in Dallas) into the mix. Even disinterested observers couldn't help speculating on the possibility of a conspiracy. One old hand, the value investor Marty Whitman, wrote in a letter to shareholders that Bear was the victim of a "bear raid."

Dimon later said that he didn't know the truth of the matter, but that it was incumbent on the Securities and Exchange Commission to thoroughly investigate and make some determination, even if the determination was "We can't tell." "It's wrong if people trafficked in rumor with malicious intent," he says. "And for the SEC to say it's hard to track a rumor isn't sufficient." In an interview with Charlie Rose, he added to the suspicion with the remark, "I would say where there's smoke there's fire." He also offered a crowd-pleaser when asked about the original $2-a-share offer. "Buying a house and buying a house on fire are two different things."

The deal aside, JPMorgan Chase wasn't exactly a fount of good news in April 2008. With the economy suffering its biggest loss of jobs in five years, the bank suffered along with the competition. The company announced a 20 percent sequential drop in first-quarter net income, to $2.4 billion. It marked down $2.6 billion in leveraged loans and mortgages, and quadrupled its credit loss provision to $4.42 billion from $1.01 billion. Return on equity nosedived to 8 percent, down from 17 percent in 2007.

The company's closely watched tier 1 capital ratio stood at 8.3 percent, however, well above that of its rivals. "We are prepared to manage through this down part of the economic cycle, given the strength of our liquidity, credit reserves, capital and operating margins, and to successfully position our company well for the future," said Dimon. Unlike most of his competitors, Dimon had not needed to go hat in hand to foreign sovereign wealth funds for a capital infusion, and the message was that he wouldn't have to. He had, however, taken advantage of a relative respite in the market's turmoil to issue $6 billion in preferred stock in an opportunity timed sale. JPMorgan Chase also knocked out Citigroup as Wall Street's top underwriter in the first quarter of 2008.

Cayne had regained some of his bearings by the time of the final shareholder vote on the deal on May 29. After the meeting, in which 84 percent of shares voted for the deal (no huge achievement, given JPMorgan Chase's nearly 50 percent ownership), he made a brief speech. "The company that is taking us over, or is merging with us, is a first-class company," he said, to the audience. After the meeting, Dimon called Cayne from Positano, Italy, to make sure the vote had gone through. They talked for just one minute.

In contrast to the wakelike atmosphere of the meeting at Bear, JPMorgan Chase's annual meeting a few weeks previously had a jubilant feel. Wall Street, for all its pretense to sophistication and complexity, is largely a zero-sum game—someone loses, someone wins.

In a comic moment at the meeting, Evelyn Davis, an eccentric gadfly shareholder who has exasperated CEOs for decades, stood up and said, "Jamie, you look strikingly handsome." The crowd laughed and Dimon cracked a smile. "We are fortunate to have Mr. Dimon," Davis continued, "who is the Dudamel"—she was referring to the conductor Gustavo Dudamel—"of bankers in this country." Looking flummoxed, Dimon replied, "I hope that was a compliment."

• • •

Despite the fact that he was playing the highest-stakes game in the world, Dimon had never seemed more at ease. When his old college buddy James Long called him on the afternoon of Sunday, March 16, to catch up, Dimon called Long back a few hours later. "We're just yak-king for a few minutes, and then he says, 'I have to go. We're in this negotiation.' I asked him what negotiation, and he wouldn't tell me. I even brought up Bear Stearns' predicament and he gave me thoughtful answers without telling me anything. A few hours later, I see the news of the deal. It was pretty comical." Likewise, Dimon's longtime friend Laurie Maglathlin called him on the night of March 13 to wish him a happy birthday. After a few minutes, he said, "Laur, I have to go. I'm really busy right now." The next day, the Bear conduit was announced.

The company had said it planned to try to keep about half of Bear's people. It didn't come close to that. By February 2009, 10,000 of the 14,000 people employed by Bear before the deal had either left the firm or been laid off. Dimon extended offers to many executives to stay, but in some areas he made almost none at all. Of Bear's leveraged lending group, for example, only three of 100 people received offers. In asset management, when Bear Stearns brokers demanded the same kind of revenue split they had negotiated with the previous management, they were told in no uncertain terms what they could do with their demands. "They had $28 billion in assets under management when we bought them," recalls a senior JPMorgan Chase executive. "And we had $1.2 trillion. Theirs was such an 'I'm for me' culture that they all thought they would keep their revenue share. We told them, 'We just bought you. The answer is no. So you either come into our compensation struc-ture or we'll shut you down.' And we ended up shutting about 90 per-cent of it down."

Despite reports in mid-April that Dimon had extended an offer to Alan Schwartz to come over to JPMorgan Chase as a nonexecutive vice chairman, Dimon had done nothing of the sort. Dimon took only six people from senior management at Bear Stearns—the former CEO Ace Greenberg, as well as Peter Cherasia, Jeff Mayer, Mike Nierenberg, Craig Overlander, and Jeff Urwin. And three of those six have since left the firm. (Some top earners refused jobs. Shelley Bergman, Bear's star stockbroker, took $1 billion of client assets with him to Morgan Stanley.)

There was internal grumbling at JPMorgan Chase when its invest-ment bank laid off thousands of its own staffers shortly after the deal, while hiring new ones from Bear. "They laid off their own people," says an executive who left the company in 2002. "Why would you fire a single person on your own team? The morale hit was not insignificant."

Despite job-saving offers, many Bear employees chafed at the notion of working for JPMorgan Chase. Those with other options walked right out the door. Bear Stearns was an entrepreneurial place, and that fact ultimately caused its downfall. JPMorgan Chase was viewed as a widget factory, where everything fit into its own little box. That's the smart way to run an organization with $2 trillion in assets, but it's not a recipe for fun, if fun is what you're looking for in a job. There are a number of longtime JPMorgan Chase employees who say that since Dimon arrived in 2004, he has made the place even less fun. His response? "So what?"

Dimon told Charlie Rose that it was unlikely JPMorgan Chase would be in the market for another 48-hour deal any time soon. "If I took a phone call like that again and called up the team and said, 'We have to go do this again,' I think they'd shoot me."

Steve Black, who shouldered the largest part of the negotiations along with Bill Winters, probably would. Prior to this deal, he had always answered the question as to whether JPMorgan Chase would do a deal with an investment bank simply, "Over my dead body." Continuing, he would argue, "There is so much overlap that combining the revenue streams would be like adding '1 + 1' to come up with 1.2. You also have to effectively pay for the company twice because of the amount you have to shell out to convince the people you want to come on board." In retrospect, he says, "There are four reasons Bear worked. First, it wasn't a real full-scale wholesale investment bank. It had bits and pieces, but it wasn't like trying to merge with Goldman Sachs or Morgan Stanley. Second, they had some things we didn't have, like prime brokerage and the commodities businesses. Third, given the price we paid, we could pay people to stick around without it costing double in the end. And fourth, those payments weren't too onerous, as the market for people was itself under pressure at the time. That's why we have an opportunity to create some value here."

Perhaps. But it will take longer than JPMorgan Chase had hoped. It had estimated that the cost of the deal would be about half of Bear's book equity, but the cost turned out to be all of that and more. Instead of a cost of $6 billion to "de-risk" the balance sheet, by November 2008 the total was closer to $15 billion. (Remarkably, one source of significant loss was a "macro" hedge Bear Stearns had against most of the deteriorating positions on its books. When the deal was announced, most markets rallied—equities, fixed income, mortgages—sending the value of the hedge plummeting.) The margin of error Cavanagh had spoken so confidently about was too small. Although Dimon still projected getting $1 billion to $1.5 billion in annual earnings out of legacy Bear Stearns businesses by the end of 2009, the deal's economics didn't look so good anymore.

To say that the deal was not costly would be a mild understatement. "We were selling into the worst market environment *ever*, and it cost us a lot more than we would have wanted," says Black. A sore spot among JPMorgan Chase executives is just how much of that pain should have been taken by Bear Stearns *before* the deal and not by JPMorgan Chase afterward.

On the other hand, some parts of the deal have worked out exactly as planned. There was the building, for one. And even though the prime services unit continued to hemorrhage clients in the wake of the deal, getting a foothold in the business positioned JPMorgan Chase to vacuum up business when Lehman Brothers failed in September 2008 and both Goldman Sachs and Morgan Staneley were on the ropes. By the end of the year, customer balances were back to peak premerger levels. In the first quarter of 2009, JPMorgan Chase snagged the second spot in prime brokerage market share with nearly 20 percent, up from precisely zero the previous year.

Winters would do it again, but differently. "Had we had a crystal ball about the market, we would have been much more aggressive in terms of moving the risk out earlier. We would have sought a greater backstop from the U.S. government. And we would have been more aggressive when it came to cutting costs. We tried to approach it as a merger, and we were too gentle."

On March 17, 2008, Dimon spoke optimistically about what he saw as the coming end of the market's crisis. His logic was straightforward.

Massive de-leveraging was going on at financial institutions, alongside massive capital raising. With no new production of securitized mortgage product, supply and demand had to come into balance at some point—hopefully in 2009. As a result, he suggested that the "financial side" of the market turmoil was probably already half over at that point. He couldn't have been more wrong. The turmoil was just getting started.

In subsequent months, the deal with Bear was eclipsed by even bigger events—the failure of Lehman Brothers, the near-failure of AIG, and the takeover of Merrill Lynch by Bank of America. And that's as it should have been. Bear Stearns, for all its bluster, was too small to matter in the grand scheme of things. Just over a year later, there was absolutely nothing left of the Bear Stearns name save for a small group of high-end brokers kept on at JPMorgan Chase. (By February 2009, Dimon hadn't even found a spot for Bear in a warren of private dining rooms on the fiftieth floor of the company's headquarters paying homage to predecessor companies such as Manufacturers Trust and the Bank of Manhattan. Bear Stearns executives didn't seem to care much about history in any event. When JPMorgan Chase's archivist Jean Elliott went to seek out Bear-related historical materials to add to the company's extensive archives after the acquisition, she found nothing but a pile of annual reports.)

· · ·

Reputations were made, destroyed, and burnished during that tumultuous week in March. Paulson, Bernanke, and Geithner received largely positive press, even if some observers questioned the long-term implications of the government's role in the deal. They had managed to calm the market, had taken out a weak player, and had opened up the discount window at what seemed a critical moment. It all looked fairly smart at the time. All three were later roundly condemned for seemingly haphazard responses to the more dramatic events that came later.

Bear Stearns was neither the greatest deal of all time nor even Dimon's greatest deal. Merging Bank One and JPMorgan Chase was a far more important event with greater ramifications for Dimon's career. Was Bear even a good deal for JPMorgan Chase's shareholders? Dimon said at the time that it would be unfair to judge the deal until a year after the fact. "You cannot judge us on this deal today," he said in May. "We are bearing an awful lot of risk. We are pushing as fast as we can to get it done." Still, by the summer of 2009, it wasn't looking as if it had been worth the effort, at least in terms of dollars and cents. An often over-looked fact is that in doing the deal, JPMorgan Chase paid two costs: the cost of the deal itself and the opportunity cost of deals it might otherwise have done. The latter is a theoretical issue, but it's quite possible that the opportunity cost was large.

Here's what the deal accomplished. It established Dimon as Wall Street's banker of choice, and buffed JPMorgan Chase's reputation to such a high shine that the firm was still benefiting a year later, even as its business continued to deteriorate along with the economy. "In the end, it was a tough deal," recalls the head of asset management, Jes Staley. "With one exception. What it did for our reputation was worth every penny. It was unbelievable. Absolutely."

The result of this enhanced reputation was tangible. The company had $400 billion in money market funds under management at the end of 2007. It took in *another* $200 billion in 2008 alone. Other divisions experienced similar gains. JPMorgan Chase's commercial banking divi-sion, for example, saw 2008 net income surge 27 percent to $1.4 billion even as recession gripped the country.

As Bear had proved, reputation is everything on Wall Street. As Bear's own standing was diminished, Jamie Dimon's rose to towering heights. Bank of America's CEO Ken Lewis hadn't even merited a call when the governors of the Federal Reserve went looking for a rescuer. By calling Dimon, they signaled that they were looking for strong hands at a crucial time for the markets. But they were also making official what a growing number of people already knew. Almost a century after its heyday, JPMorgan Chase—and by extension Dimon himself—was once again the country's bank of last resort.

13. THE NEW POWER BROKER

In the immediate aftermath of the Bear deal, optimism surged about how federal authorities and the private sector had come together to protect the financial system. From its low on March 7, 2008, through May 2, the stock market rallied nearly 10 percent. So what if there was a little moral hazard here, a little government intervention there, the popular thinking went. Better a flawed system than a completely busted one.

On March 18, Lehman Brothers, widely considered the next weakest firm on the Street, announced first-quarter results that were better than expected, boosting its shares 32 percent that morning. Lehman had posted strong results in a few businesses, such as mergers and acquisitions advice and equities, but it also wrote down $1.8 billion of mortgage-related assets. Analyst Mike Mayo (now at Deutsche Bank), a man not known for his sunny forecasts, declared, "Lehman is not Bear." In a piece in late April, *The Economist* magazine said, "That Lehman did not implode is thanks, in part, to the Federal Reserve's decision to lend directly to securities firms for the first time."

Bank executives tried to see past the crisis. Morgan Stanley's CEO, John Mack, told shareholders that the subprime crisis was in the eighth or ninth inning. Goldman Sachs's CEO, Lloyd Blankfein, ventured the opinion that the markets were in the third quarter of the game. Dimon himself was optimistic that the credit crunch might be easing, but he was still disturbed by the weakening economy: "I told my investment banking friends, 'Lucky for you, you're probably through a big part of your pain. It's continuing for some of us with real credit exposures to consumers.' "

Although Dimon was right on that last point, all three were wrong about the credit crunch. By the summer, Lehman and Merrill were fighting for their lives. Lehman Brothers got in a pitched public battle with the hedge fund manager David Einhorn, who aggressively shorted the company's shares, convinced that its accounting couldn't be trusted. He was also convinced that the bank was cooking its books. A $2.8 billion second-quarter loss at Lehman—the company's first quarterly deficit in 14 years—thoroughly spooked the market, and by the end of the month the Dow Jones was in bear market territory. The rest of the summer was just one piece of bad news after another. In July, the government seized IndyMac Bank; this was the second-largest bank failure in U.S. history. Regulators also had to reissue a warning to Citigroup that pursuing any major acquisitions would be unwise in its current state.

The price of oil had gone sky-high—it reached $147 a barrel in July—and short sellers were chasing Merrill and Lehman like bloodhounds after a fugitive. John Thain, Merrill's CEO, had turned into the second coming of Citigroup's Chuck Prince, a man who could be counted on to say one thing and then do precisely the opposite. On April 10, Thain said that the company's cash reserve was "sufficient for the foreseeable future." Twelve days later, Merrill Lynch raised $9.5 billion through an issuance of debt and preferred stock. In May, he said, "We have no present intention of raising any more capital." On July 29, Merrill Lynch tapped the capital markets once again, to the tune of $8.5 billion. On July 18, he said, "I don't think we want to do dumb things. We have been pretty balanced in terms of what we sold, and at what prices we sold them. We have not liquidated stuff at any prices we could get." Ten days later it emerged that Merrill had unloaded $30.6 billion of super-senior ABS CDO product into the market at 22 cents on the dollar. (In retrospect, it is amazing that Merrill made so many moves to shore up its finances yet still found itself insolvent come the fall.)

August, normally a slow month for financial companies, took a toll on JPMorgan Chase. On August 14, the company announced that it was buying back $3 billion in auction-rate securities from investors in a settlement with regulators over whether the company's salespeople had misled their customers about attendant risks. For Dimon, who had a reputation for integrity, this was a bitter pill. (As his predecessor John Pierpont Morgan had said about a banker's reputation at the Pujo hearings in front of the House Banking and Currency Committee in 1912, "[It] is his most valuable possession; it is the result of years of faith and honorable dealing and, while it may be quickly lost, once lost cannot be restored for a long time, if ever.") At the end of the month, the company announced that holdings of preferred stock in the mortgage giants Fannie Mae and Freddie Mac had lost about half their value, resulting in a $600 million write-down. On September 3, Dimon shut down a division that sold derivative securities to municipalities amid a government investigation into questionable sales practices there as well.

JPMorgan Chase stock fell 15 percent in August as investors pondered whether its—or any bank's—business model was the one to bet on in a market gone bonkers. The equity analyst Dick Bove put the concern succinctly: "Bill Harrison, J.P. Morgan's CEO, repeatedly argued that the combination of a consumer finance bank with a capital markets company would be placing two contra-cyclical businesses together, defeating the cycle. Unfortunately, the first time this concept was tested, it did not work. Both cycles seem to be declining in tandem with each other. Moreover, by buying the failing Bear Stearns, J.P. Morgan may have accentuated the negative impact of the capital market downturn."

(In the midst of all those challenges, however, Dimon's softer side once again made an appearance. When JPMorgan Chase's vice chairman Jimmy Lee took his youngest daughter, Izzy, to Bermuda for a weekend of golf before she went off to college, the two arrived at their suite in the Mid Ocean Club to find a bottle of champagne and two glasses waiting for them. Alongside was a note that read, "There are two glasses here for a reason. She's not too young to have a glass of champagne anymore. Have a great time with Izzy, Jamie." Lee, who has spent a lifetime on Wall Street, was blown away. "I mean, what other Wall Street CEO does stuff like that?" he asks.)

Dimon could not argue with the fact that the summer of 2008 was taking a toll. By that point, the company had eaten through all the equity of Bear Stearns and then some in its efforts to scale back the risk on its balance sheet. But he took issue with the suggestion that JPMorgan Chase was the wrong model for a large financial institution, especially when competing investment banks were scrambling to find steady sources of funding in a market that was woefully short on credit.

What's more, in a business centered on people and relationships, Dimon was sure he'd assembled the right team to navigate through the crisis. *Fortune* magazine agreed with that conclusion, and on September 2 ran a cover story titled "The Survivors." The article was another in a lengthening list of stories that trumpeted JPMorgan Chase's relative strengths amid weakening competition.

In terms of the scale and complexity of their businesses, Black and Winters run an investment bank that's bigger than Goldman Sachs, the credit card chief Gordon Smith runs a business that's larger than American Express, and Jes Staley runs one of the largest asset management businesses on the planet. Other executives can make similar claims.

The photo shoot for the story took place at The Cloister at Sea Island in Georgia during a management off-site. In 2004, a G8 summit meeting had been held at the resort, and The Cloister had kept the chair that President Bush had sat in during it. For one photo at the off-site—a photo that ultimately wasn't used—the photographer asked Dimon to sit in this chair and the rest of the team to gather around him. Knowing the irritation that all the glowing, Dimon-centric media coverage caused his colleagues, he cracked wise. "OK, everyone," he said when he sat down. "Look lovingly at me."

Such bonhomie masked a growing concern inside JPMorgan Chase that Dimon's legend had, in fact, obscured the contributions of others. In the public eye, he *was* the firm, to a degree that was unusual even among the giant egos of Wall Street chieftains. What would happen to JPMorgan Chase when Dimon decided to leave? "The stock would drop 20 percent," Bill Winters said in a Harvard Business School case study. "The myth of Jamie is the biggest misconception outside of JPMorgan Chase," Steve Black added. "He's as worried about it as anyone." A number of executives have acknowledged that it could be frustrating to watch their boss get credit in the press for decisions *they* made and results *they* helped deliver.

(Dimon does do his best to make sure his senior executives get the recognition they deserve. He pushes for stories in the media focused on them—not on him—and any time one of his team appears on the cover of a publication, he has the cover framed and sends the person two copies as gifts, one for the office and one for home. And at Sea Island, he refused to pose for any photos that were not group shots.)

Lingering in the background of the summer's turmoil were questions about the ability of Lehman Brothers to remain a going concern. Like Bear, Lehman had plunged headlong into the mortgage business over the previous decade, and also like Bear, the company was facing steep losses in its mortgage portfolio. After the Federal Reserve opened the discount window to investment banks in March, Lehman's CEO, Dick Fuld, had told colleagues, "We have access to Fed funds. We can't fail now." Others, including an increasingly wary group of executives at JPMorgan Chase, weren't so sure about that.

As it had been with Bear, JPMorgan Chase was intertwined financially with Lehman Brothers, more than almost any other firm on Wall Street. Not only did it have counterparty risk on a number of trading positions; it was also Lehman's clearing bank and Lehman's so-called tri-party repo agent, meaning that JPMorgan Chase served as an intermediary between Lehman and a number of overnight lenders to the firm. The company was legally obligated to make sure those lenders were covered in terms of the collateral Lehman provided in exchange for its loans.

Executives in J.P. Morgan's investment bank first became antsy about Lehman's collateral in June. The investment bank's chief risk officer, John Hogan, called Lehman's head of risk management, Chris O'Meara, and asked for $5 billion in additional collateral. Lehman dragged its feet, and not until August did it hand over a package of loans that it said was worth $5 billion. JPMorgan Chase's executives disputed that valuation, and the debate was never actually resolved.

By the time September rolled around, the JPMorgan Chase executives were even more nervous about Lehman's collateral, and the company's chief risk officer, Barry Zubrow, demanded another $5 billion. It was late in the day on Thursday, September 4, Zubrow recalled, and he was dressed and ready to head to the U.S. Open to watch a quarterfinal match between Andy Roddick and the Serbian Novak Djokovic. That $5 billion never made it to JPMorgan Chase.

On Sunday, September 7, the government seized Fannie Mae and Freddie Mac, placing these giants—which held or guaranteed $5.4 trillion in mortgages—in conservatorship. Dimon was meeting with his operating committee in Washington when the news broke, and different groups of JPMorgan Chase's executives had made calls on Secretary of the Treasury Hank Paulson and various leaders of the House and Senate. Dimon and Dick Fuld—Lehman's CEO—had a brief conversation in which Dimon told Fuld that if the terms were cheap enough, his firm *might* be interested in providing funding by buying some preferred shares of Lehman. But he made no promises.

On Tuesday, September 9, the investment bank's co-CEO Steve Black—who was in Washington with Dimon—decided he needed to speak to Fuld as well. "Our intraday exposure was massive and we didn't have enough collateral to support it," Black recalls. "With what was going on in the markets, any rational human being would say, 'Holy shit, that's not right.' So I called Dick and told him we needed more collateral to continue to be comfortable with Lehman. We even worked with them to create a mechanism so it didn't have to come right out of their liquidity by agreeing to a three-day recall." Black ultimately asked for *another* $5 billion, and after some haggling by Fuld, agreed to take $3 billion.

Fuld was still largely in denial at this point, perhaps because the government had stepped in to help Bear, so why wouldn't it do the same for Lehman if the situation came to that point? When Fuld spoke to Black on Tuesday, Black told him that one of his few remaining options looked to be to get a consortium of investors together to rescue the firm, as had been done for Long-Term Capital Management. But the Federal Reserve would need to get involved in herding those cats, and Black suggested that Fuld should be getting those conversations going as soon as possible. Fuld replied that such a move would be terrible for Lehman's shareholders, and he didn't see how he could go ahead with it. "Dick, no one is going to help you keep Lehman Brothers in business just to be good guys," Black said. "They're going to help you because it's in their own self-interest. For that to happen, your shareholders are going to have to pay the ultimate price."

"So then why should I do it?" asked Fuld. "I didn't say you should do it," Black replied. "But I'm telling you if you're getting close to the brink, that's what you should be thinking about." Fuld told Black that he had been talking to Citigroup's CEO, Vikram Pandit, about a possible investment from Citi, and that Citi had a team coming over to comb through Lehman's books that night. Did Black want to send his own team? "I'll send some people over," Black replied, "but I don't think there's going to be anything we can do for you." That evening the head of investment banking, Doug Braunstein, and the risk chief, John Hogan, went to Lehman and came back confirming Black's inclination. There was nothing JPMorgan Chase would—or could—do.

Fuld told Black that he had decided to "preannounce" the company's third-quarter results the next day, including the fact that the investment bank forecast a $4 billion loss in the quarter. Black was flabbergasted. "They had nothing to say," he recalls. "They had no plan. They got on the call and said that they didn't need any new capital, but it was obvious that they did. And they had some plan to spin off their real estate holdings, but that wasn't until February, and people needed to hear some good news right then and there. That was the beginning of the end." The next day, credit default swaps on the company's debt went for $800,000, higher than those of Bear Stearns right before its demise.

On Friday, September 12, Jane Buyers-Russo, head of JPMorgan Chase's investment banking team that covered financial institutions, called Lehman's treasurer Paolo Tonucci and told him that JPMorgan Chase no longer felt comfortable lending to Lehman Brothers on an unsecured basis and that the company wanted the $5 billion Zubrow had requested, and wanted it now. Other customers, lenders, and trading partners were doing exactly the same thing, and by the end of the day, Lehman was facing exactly the same problem Bear had run into six months before. If it didn't find an investor willing to give it a substantial infusion of cash over the weekend, it was likely to fail.

That night, Lehman's bankers huddled with their advisers at Lazard. The next morning, Wall Street's chieftains were once again summoned to the Federal Reserve Bank of New York, and Dimon, Steve Black, and Barry Zubrow all participated in all-day meetings on both Saturday and Sunday with Goldman's Lloyd Blankfein, Morgan Stanley's John Mack, and Merrill's John Thain. The goal was to either find a buyer for Lehman or concoct a solution that would soften the blow of a bankruptcy. "There will be no bailout for Lehman," Paulson told the CEOs. "The only possible way out is a private-sector solution."

A logical buyer of Lehman was someone who wanted a major investment bank and didn't have one. With Bear Stearns, JPMorgan Chase had *two* investment banks, and so there was no interest whatsoever coming out of 270 Park Avenue. "For us, the close-down would have been astronomical," said Dimon, referring to the mass layoffs and shuttering of duplicate facilities such a deal would have necessitated. Although no one officially acknowledged that both Britain's Barclays PLC and Bank of America were taking a very serious look at buying Lehman, Dimon, like everyone in the room, knew the scuttlebutt. What Paulson and Geithner asked the assembled group to consider was another solution in case no deal came to pass. Could the banks put together a financing facility, for example, or a loss-bearing facility of some sort that would allow Lehman to continue functioning?

The meeting was nearly a reprise of the meetings about Long-Term Capital Management a decade previously. Three people were at both meetings—Dimon, John Thain (then representing Goldman Sachs), and Morgan Stanley's chief, John Mack. The difference for Dimon was that in 1998, he was there as Sandy Weill's emissary. In 2008, he was his own man.

At one point, there was talk of a $70 billion financing package. At another, every CEO in the room was asked how much pain his company could bear if forced to eat a portion of Lehman's losses. "Any one of us would have put in $500 million or some number like that, just to stop the event from happening," recalls Dimon. "We knew it was going to be painful for the Street and for the world. The problem was, even if we'd gotten to some number, it wouldn't have been big enough to stop it from happening. Because it was unwinding. People were pulling their money out." *Fortune* later reported that Dimon chastised two reluctant participants, Bank of New York and BNP-Paribas: "You're either in the club or you're not. And if you're not you'd better be prepared to tell the secretary why not." *Fortune* reported that when John Mack later suggested letting Merrill fail as well, Dimon is said to have replied, "John, if we do that, how many hours do you think it would be before Fidelity would call you up and tell you it was no longer willing to roll your paper?"

Bank of America eventually pulled out of the running for Lehman when it snapped up Merrill Lynch in a $50 billion deal that ended a 94-year run for the investment bank. The sole remaining buyer, Barclays, ran into regulatory headwinds and was forced to end its pursuit of Lehman on Sunday, September 14.

Dimon called a board meeting that evening, and told the members that Lehman's end was near. "We think we are going to be fine, in terms of our bank," he told his directors, according to the author of *Fool's Gold*, Gillan Tett. "But it's going to be very, very ugly for others. Worse than anything that any of us have seen in our lives." Shortly after midnight, the 158-year-old Lehman—which had been founded as a dry goods store and cotton trader in Montgomery, Alabama—filed for bankruptcy. "As long as I am alive this firm will never be sold," Fuld had said in 2007. "And if it is sold after I die, I will reach back from the grave and prevent it." He was right. It was not sold—it went bust. The world's stock markets crashed as a result. The Dow Jones fell by 504 points on Monday, September 15. (Barclays later bought a number of Lehman's assets, but not the entire firm.)

Lehman's failure set off a chain reaction. Reserve Primary Fund, a $64 billion money market fund that had been heavily invested in Lehman's debt, broke the buck—its net asset value fell below the crucial level of $1 per share—and nearly collapsed, sparking mass withdrawals. About $500 billion was withdrawn from money market funds in the two weeks that followed Lehman's collapse. On Tuesday, September 16, the government chose to rescue the insurance giant AIG with an $85 billion loan, just one day after Lehman had been deprived of such largesse. (By April 2009, the total amount thrown at AIG was $162.5 billion and climbing.) The firm was later mocked on *Saturday Night Live* for sending executives on a swank retreat just days after receiving the bailout funds. The next day, the Dow fell another 499 points. Investors, it seemed, were losing their last vestiges of faith in the system.

On Friday, September 19, Hank Paulson and the Fed's chief, Ben Bernanke, floated a bailout proposal to Congress that was not rejected out of hand. But the next day, Paulson sent a *three-page* document to the House of Representatives asking for hundreds of billions of dollars, with little or no detail as to how those funds might be spent. On Monday, Congress rejected the flimsy plan, sending the Dow Jones down another 778 points. That same day, Goldman Sachs and Morgan Stanley—the last two investment banks—found themselves the object of some very unwanted attention, and decided the time was ripe to convert to bank holding companies in order to secure permanent access to Fed funding in times of stress.

With Goldman and Morgan Stanley choosing, in effect, to become banks, the era of investment banking had come to an end. Of the five major investment banks, three were now gone (Bear, Lehman, and Merrill) and two had thrown in the towel (Goldman and Morgan Stanley). An era of unregulated excess appeared to have come to a close.

Despite all its collateral calls, JPMorgan Chase ended up undercollateralized after Lehman's failure. (Lehman turned over $8 billion worth of securities in the final analysis.) Still, Wall Street churned with chatter about how Jamie Dimon had sent Lehman over the edge. Steve Fishman of *New York* magazine later reported that Fuld told an associate, "They drained us of cash. They fucked us." Another of Lehman's executives laid the blame squarely on Dimon himself. "Jamie Dimon was doing whatever was in his own personal interest. He knew the consequence [of the collateral calls] was a huge blow to us, and he didn't give a shit."

"That's not true," says Dimon. "I spoke to Dick periodically over those last couple of weeks, and not once did he complain. You have to keep in mind that everyone and their mother was raising collateral on other people. And some of our collateral calls weren't even for us—they were for investors that we represented. If Dick had ever called Steve Black or me and said, 'Hey, this is unfair,' or 'Give us a little more time,' we absolutely would have considered it."

Other executives at JPMorgan Chase are less circumspect. "They didn't go bankrupt because of us," said one. "They went bankrupt because they did nothing for six months, and then did a fucked-up conference call. And then they try to blame David Einhorn, the Fed, and us. It's pathetic."

Neither Dimon nor Black thinks Fuld actually said what *New York* had reported. "We didn't force everything that we could have," says Steve Black. "We could have stopped financing them, but we worked with them. The idea that we put Lehman out of business is just absolute horseshit."

With the perspective of time, former Lehman executives acknowledge this. One investment banker who was subsequently hired by Nomura Holdings in London expressed the tangled emotions surrounding the demise of the firm. "On the one hand, you could say J.P. Morgan was protecting their interests," he said. "But on the other hand, they were fully aware of the implications of what they were doing and you might say they bit off their nose to spite their face. By doing what they did, they knew they were forcing us into a bankruptcy or someone else's hands. One way or another, they were taking out a competitor. But I bet they never thought we'd go bankrupt. I don't think anybody had any indication that Paulson would let us go. My sense is that there's not a lot of animosity toward Dimon, though. Maybe he was a dick for doing it. Maybe he made a mistake. But would anybody else have made a different decision? I don't think they would have. They had fiduciary duties *and* they had the opportunity to step on the throat of a competitor. This isn't Little League, so you do it if you can."

In another, less widely noted, example of JPMorgan Chase flexing its muscles, in September the company briefly stopped doing business with Chicago's Citadel Investment Group because of excessive poaching of JPMorgan Chase's employees by Citadel. After it hired a sixth person, the cohead of the investment bank, Steve Black, called Citadel's head, Ken Griffin, and told him that JPMorgan Chase no longer wanted anything to do with Citadel. One day later, when it appeared that the market didn't buy the argument about poaching—concluding instead that Citadel might be in deep trouble and JPMorgan Chase was just the first to know—Black rescinded the no-business order, but said that it would be reinstated if Griffin made one more hire. "Steve and I thought, 'Oh, God, this is not the right time for this,' " recalls Dimon. "It was intramural politics, but people were reading it the wrong way. It just wasn't the right time to make a stink on our part."

Actions taken by Dimon and his investment bank coheads while both Goldman and Morgan Stanley were under pressure in September and October also suggest that the criticism from Lehman was unfair. After Morgan Stanley's CEO John Mack called Dimon to complain that some of JPMorgan Chase's new hires from Bear Stearns were telling his clients that Morgan Stanley was on the verge of collapse, Black and Winters sent a memo to employees instructing them that they were not to go after clients or employees of either Morgan Stanley or Goldman Sachs using a "predatory" sales pitch.

"What is happening to the broker-deal model is not rational," they wrote, "and not good for J.P. Morgan, the global financial system, or the country." A memo is just a memo, but Dimon was in full agreement. "That's not how you want to beat the competition," he said. "We're going to succeed because over an extended period of time, we built a good company, and not because one of our many competitors runs into a lamppost and is critically injured. That's not fun. No one would wish that upon them. If they get a flat tire, that's a different story. But there's a difference between the two. Everybody's got their own value system. In mine, I want to be buried with a little self-respect one day."

As with Lehman's failure, the word on the Street was that Dimon had pushed Merrill into Bank of America's arms with collateral calls. JPMorgan Chase's chief risk officer, Barry Zubrow, had called Merrill's Peter Kraus on September 12 to ask for an additional $5 billion in collateral from the bank. Again, executives defended the move as protecting their shareholders. "The money never arrived. Merrill complained, but they never even gave us anything," recalls Dimon. "Our lines were open, and the CEOs of those firms knew they could complain if they wanted to."

Paulson called Dimon in early September and urged him to consider adding Morgan Stanley to his list of conquests for 2008—at a cost of literally zero—in the hope of averting a possible collapse of the highly respected investment bank. Hedge funds were pulling their money out of Morgan Stanley's prime brokerage unit, and regulators were worried that another bank run might be in the offing. This time, Dimon balked. Taking over a company with so much overlap, he explained, would result in two or more years of internal bloodbaths, and would be likely to turn the company into a decidedly unpleasant place to work. Although he coveted the investment bank's brokerage subsidiary, Dean Witter, it just wasn't worth all this. "That's too much pain and distraction to get a brokerage firm," he told colleagues.

Paulson was roundly criticized in the fall of 2008 for what seemed at best a finger-in-the-dyke strategy and at worst a policy that clearly favored the interests of his old firm, Goldman Sachs. The rescue of AIG, critics argued, was really a rescue of Goldman Sachs, which had large counterparty exposures with AIG. Goldman maintained at the time that its exposure was "immaterial," but the controversy intensified in March 2009, when it was revealed that the firm was actually AIG's *largest* counterparty, and had received $12.9 billion in payments on underwater credit default swaps from AIG that had essentially come from U.S. taxpayers. JPMorgan Chase, on the other hand, had kept its dealings with AIG at a much lower level, because of Dimon's pervasive risk-management ethos.

Others saw favoritism when Paulson allowed Lehman to fail and then seemed to bend over backward to keep both Goldman and Morgan Stanley from the same fate. "It seems a little more than coincidental that we were the only ones they let go," says a former Lehman executive. "Paulson turned the decision to let us fail into this weak-kneed 'My hands were tied' excuse. That's bullshit. They were changing the rules every day, and they could have done it again. Also, Dick Fuld did suggest to him that we change Lehman into a bank holding company. And

Paulson said no. I guess there are slightly different rules for Goldman Sachs and Morgan Stanley than for Lehman Brothers." The *New York Times* echoed this sentiment when it suggested in September that regulatory decisions regarding Bear and AIG were motivated by a desire to help JPMorgan Chase and Goldman Sachs avoid big losses on their respective exposures. Dick Fuld, it seemed, had too few friends.

Despite the scorn heaped on Paulson after Lehman's failure, Dimon thinks that Paulson had no choice. "There was no way that anyone in the Federal government was going to go in front of the United States Congress to ask for an investment bank to be bailed out," he recalls. "It just wasn't politically feasible, so I don't know why anyone questions him at all on the matter. It would have been far better to have them take it over and have an orderly unwind, but they didn't have the right to do that."

Dimon compared Paulson's task in the fall of 2008 to a game of Whack-a-Mole, with crises popping up left and right. "It's hard to make policy on the run," he said. "I think there have been plenty of mistakes. But I think that in general, and really I'm thinking of Bernanke, Geithner, and Paulson, here . . . in general they acted quickly, boldly, and bravely. They changed their course of action when one wasn't working. Could you and I sit down and say, 'Well, *A* would've been better than *B* and better than *C*?' Absolutely. But you're not up there in the ring. It's pretty easy to say to the guy, 'Hey, don't let him hit you like that!' "

Ever a student of history, Dimon sent Paulson a note including a citation from a speech Theodore Roosevelt made in Paris in 1910: "It is not the critic who counts: not the man who points out how the strong man stumbles or where the doer of deeds could have done better. The credit belongs to the man who is actually in the arena, whose face is marred by dust and sweat and blood, who strives valiantly, who errs and comes up short again and again, because there is no effort without error or shortcoming, but who knows the great enthusiasms, the great devotions, who spends himself for a worthy cause; who, at the best, knows, in the end, the triumph of high achievement, and who, at the worst, if he fails, at least he fails while daring greatly, so that his place shall never be with those cold and timid souls who knew neither victory nor defeat."

On October 9, the Dow Jones closed below 8,600 for the first time since May 2003. The market was increasingly short of patience. The bailout of Bear Stearns caused a rally that had lasted five months. But the nationalization of Fannie Mae and Freddie Mac resulted in just one day of gains. And the relief following the $700 billion bailout endured for just one day as well. "The policy response cannot contain the contagion," the analyst Brad Hintz wrote.

Five years of stock market gains had been wiped out in less than a year. And the tallies for the third quarter were ugly. Through the end of September, Citigroup had taken $55 billion in write-downs on troubled assets, UBS had taken $44 billion, and Bank of America $21.2 billion. JPMorgan Chase's total: $18.8 billion. Not a small number by any means, but a good sight better than the competition's.

• • •

The purchase of the assets and deposits of Seattle-based Washington Mutual—WaMu—in September 2008 was about as perfect a "Jamie Dimon acquisition" as one could imagine. WaMu, which called itself "the bank of everyday people" and had the tagline "Whoo-Hoo!" had seen three straight quarters of losses totaling $6.1 billion and in mid-September fell victim to a good old-fashioned run on the bank. In swooping in to pick up its assets, Dimon showed all the traits investors had come to expect from him: patience (the swooping came after more than a year of stalking the firm), speed, ruthlessness, and a bon mot or two.

In July, Deustche Bank's analyst Mike Mayo had asked Dimon a question during a conference call: "You've been waiting your whole life for this environment . . . so what is the impediment to you pursuing a merger right now in the retail banking side?" Dimon's reply: "Nothing is impeding us. But it's just not up to us." JPMorgan Chase was a buyer, but a buyer still needs a seller for a deal to get done.

Well before Bear Stearns came along, Dimon and his team had been eyeing WaMu and coveting its footprint in both California and Florida, two states where Chase's presence was negligible. (On Dimon's one-pager of potential acquisitions, WaMu sat in the upper left-hand quadrant—a desirable target that had a strong strategic fit, if it could be picked off at the right price.) The retail chief, Charlie Scharf, had put together a report ("Project West") on a possible combination for a management retreat in the spring of 2007. "We always looked at it and we always came up with the same conclusion," Scharf told the *New York Times*. "At the right price, this is No. 1. At the wrong price, this could be terrible."

At the end of 2007, WaMu was the six-largest depositary institution in the country. But along with that ranking came a problem it shared with a number of its peers: major exposure to the subprime market. In early 2008, WaMu was setting up to report a disastrous quarter, and realized it needed to raise some capital. "We had done lots of work on WaMu and we thought, given all the stuff that we were hearing, that we'd get a phone call from them," recalls Scharf. That call came in early March, while a group of JPMorgan Chase executives were in Deer Valley, Utah, at the banker Jimmy Lee's annual private bigwig retreat.

The auction rate securities market had been faltering at the time, and a number of executives were preparing to sit down and talk about the bank's exposures when Dimon's phone rang. It was Kerry Killinger, the CEO of WaMu. Killinger told Dimon that his bank was evaluating capital-raising options and had decided it might also scope out possible merger partners. Was Dimon interested? "Yes, we are," he told Killinger. He then handed the reins to Charlie Scharf and Mike Cavanagh.

The next week, JPMorgan Chase executives sat down at the offices of law firm Simpson Thacher & Bartlett to view a brief presentation by WaMu's management. Talks continued thereafter, and soon plans were made for Scharf, the chief financial officer Mike Cavanagh, the chief administrative officer Frank Bisignano, and the head of strategy Jay Mandelbaum to head out to Seattle for further discussions on Sunday, March 16. When the Bear Stearns deal came out of nowhere, that team shrank to just Scharf and Mandelbaum, as Cavanagh and Bisignano were tied up.

Scharf eventually decided he was ready to start negotiating a transaction that would be part cash, part stock, and he informed the Office of Thrift Supervision (OTS), which oversaw WaMu, about the possibility of a deal. It soon became obvious, however, that the WaMu executives were not negotiating in good faith. In addition to denying Scharf's team access to important financial data, they also forced a ridiculous daisy chain of calls between the two banks and the OTS in which Killinger's team played nice with the regulators and then did the opposite with JPMorgan Chase. "It's always like that, though," says the commercial bank chief, Todd Maclin. "Whoever you're trying to buy, anybody on the other side is going to withhold as much information and try to hide the ball, and you can either decide to play or not."

Part of the problem, it seemed, was Steve Rotella, the president of WaMu, who had run the mortgage business at Chase Home Finance before the Bank One deal. Neither Dimon nor Scharf had ever thought much of Rotella's talents, and when he decamped for WaMu in December 2004, they hadn't been sorry to see him go. Moreover, Rotella was not interested in working for Scharf—or Dimon—again, and he told Scharf so over dinner in March. "No one here wants to do this with you guys," he said. "If we can get some private equity money and get through this turmoil, that's what we want to do. We think we deserve another bat at the plate." Another stumbling block was that Kerry Killinger, the firm's CEO, would be out of a job if he sold to JPMorgan Chase. And he clearly didn't want to be out of a job.

Although Dimon had left the investment bank quite alone when he arrived at JPMorgan Chase, he and Scharf had thoroughly revamped the primary mortgage business. Nearly the entire management team left the firm—some voluntarily and some not. Rotella had been shoved out when Dimon was trying to create an end-to-end mortgage assembly line, from origination to securitization. He and several of his colleagues went to Washington Mutual. And here were Dimon and Scharf, knocking on their door. It was no wonder they were received poorly.

WaMu ultimately spurned a $7 billion offer—roughly $8 per share—from JPMorgan Chase in early April in favor of a capital infusion from a consortium of private equity firms, most notably Texas Pacific Group, which put in $2 billion. There's also the issue of regulators' own self-interest. The weakest portion of a patchwork quilt of regulation, OTS had seen two of the biggest thrifts crater in the past year—

Countrywide and IndyMac—and if WaMu went away as well, there might be no more need at all for the government branch. What regulator would regulate itself out of existence?

The JPMorgan Chase team took defeat in stride. "There is a 50-50 chance that this bank is going to come back to us," Dimon told his executive committee. Dimon and his team saw the quality of JPMorgan Chase's own loan portfolio beginning to deteriorate, and they figured WaMu might eventually face up to $30 billion in losses. Little did they know that the firm would fail just five months later. This time, the phone call to Dimon came from Sheila Bair, chair of the Federal Deposit Insurance Corporation, on Friday, September 19. She was calling a number of banks, including Dimon's, letting them know to keep their pencils sharp and their models up-to-date, because the opportunity to buy WaMu out of receivership might happen sooner than they thought.

"The fact that it came back around in that amount of time was kind of shocking," recalls the chief financial officer, Mike Cavanagh. He is right in the sense that five months is not a long time. But those five months—from April to September 2008—were far from normal. The financial markets had been buffeted by crisis after crisis, from the near-insolvency of the government-backed lenders Fannie Mae and Freddie Mac to Lehman's collapse. By September, WaMu was at the top of every regulator's list of disasters waiting to happen. If the company had gone into receivership with no buyer, it would have swallowed up about half of the FDIC's funds for insured deposits.

On September 8, rating agencies downgraded WaMu's debt rating and sent its stock plummeting. Killinger—who had been at the company since 1983—was fired by his board. But it was too late to try such a cosmetic fix. Depositors began withdrawing their savings en masse. In 10 days, they withdrew $16.7 billion.

Regulators sent WaMu's board an unambiguous message: sell the company or raise some capital, or we're going to have to take you over. When WaMu, which retained Goldman Sachs and Morgan Stanley to pursue "strategic options," came back to JPMorgan Chase hat in hand, it was met with a stiff arm reminiscent of the one it had given Scharf in April. "We got the call that said, 'OK, now we're ready,' " recalls Scharf.

"We told them we would go through the process, but we were also very clear with them. We said, 'Don't count on us to buy the company. We've been through this before.'"

Executives once again sat down with their WaMu counterparts, and found to their surprise that the WaMu team thought there was still some equity value in the company. "They believed their rosy numbers," recalls Mike Cavanagh. "So at a point, we said, 'This is not productive. We'll do the data room stuff and all that, but we have no interest in buying the whole company.' "

On Monday, September 22—just a week after the failure of Lehman Brothers—executives met with regulators at JPMorgan Chase's headquarters to talk about the process. Even though it seemed increasingly unlikely that WaMu could sell the entire firm, the regulators decided to run a dual-track process, and told JPMorgan Chase they were advising potential bidders to consider different options, from buying everything to buying just the deposits and mortgage portfolio.

Neither Sheila Bair nor Tim Geithner was at the meeting—and this meant, by implication, that Dimon didn't need to be there, either. But he was, and he stayed almost the entire time. Rodgin Cohen of Simpson Thacher, there on behalf of WaMu, recalls the significance of Dimon's presence. "This was not a meeting he needed to attend," Cohen says. "And at the end of the day, money talks, but the fact that he was there clearly made an impression on the regulators. But what made even more of an impression was how conversant he was in the details. He was all over it."

The JPMorgan Chase team decided to bid only for the assets of Washington Mutual, leaving behind $18 billion in liabilities. The team members' calculations left them with a range of $1.7 billion to $2 billion, and all that was left was to put a final number on the contract. Someone noted that the number 8 was lucky in both Chinese and Japanese culture and suggested a bid of $1.888 billion. (A suggestion of $1.666 billion was rejected for obvious reasons.) Possibly a little slaphappy from their three-day work blitz, the team members agreed that $1.888 billion was an auspicious bid. At 6:30 P.M. on September 24, Scharf submitted the contract and went home.

He was sitting with his daughters at the kitchen table while they ate their bedtime snack when his phone rang at 8:30 P.M. It was Dimon. "Sheila called me," he told Scharf. "We got the bid; we're the winner." The plan, he explained, was for the FDIC to seize WaMu after the close of business on Thursday, and immediately sell the deposit and loan portfolios to JPMorgan Chase.

To careful observers of the ways and whims of the stock market, there was an unusual wrinkle to the plan. Usually—as was the case with Bear Stearns and on countless other occasions—regulators unveil their dramatic actions after the close on *Friday* so that the representative players will have the weekend to straighten out whatever they can before the opening bell Monday morning. In this case, however, Dimon had more urgent needs.

Because of the uncertainty surrounding Secretary of the Treasury Hank Paulson's three-page, $700 billion bank bailout plan—the market had plunged 778 points on Monday after the House had voted it down—Dimon told Bair he preferred doing the deal on Thursday, so that he could turn around and raise a substantial amount of capital in the equity market on Friday. He wanted to keep his company's tier 1 capital ratio above 8 percent. To do that, he needed about $8 billion in fresh equity, and he didn't want to risk seeing what the weekend—or the following Monday—might bring before obtaining it.

"Jamie learned that from Sandy," recalls Scharf. "When you decide you want to raise money, you don't wait, you get it done. Jamie will think and think and think and make sure he's doing the right thing, but once he wants to do it, he wants it done yesterday. Rumors of what TARP was going to be were all over the place. And he knows that markets can open and they can shut." (The Troubled Asset Relief Program, TARP, was a plan in the works through which the government would buy assets and equity from banks to strengthen the financial sector. It would reach full flower just a few weeks later.) For her part, Bair was worried enough about the run on WaMu that she agreed to do the deal on Thursday, September 25.

Dimon, Cavanagh, and Scharf spent Thursday on the phone rustling up money. They called 10 potential investors, and asked them—

without revealing details—whether, if JPMorgan Chase was interested in raising a substantial amount of capital the next day, they would be buying. Nine investors pledged $7 billion, despite not knowing exactly what the news was.

After the market closed on Thursday, the OTS and FDIC announced that WaMu was being seized in the largest bank failure in U.S. history, and its assets were being sold to JPMorgan Chase. (WaMu had $307 billion in assets. The runner-up, Continental Illinois, which failed in 1984, had just $40 billion.) At 9:00 P.M., Dimon, Cavanagh, and Scharf held a conference call and took analysts through a 21-page summary of the deal. Fifteen minutes later, Dimon sent an e-mail to the entire staff of WaMu, welcoming them into the JPMorgan Chase fold. Around midnight, Scharf boarded a jet for a flight to Seattle and a 7:00 A.M. meeting with WaMu's CEO, Alan Fishman. (One of his messages: You're out of a job.)

(Remarkably, the staff of WaMu found out about the deal before Fishman, who'd been on a plane at the exact moment of the seizure and sale. Because of the importance of keeping the deal under wraps until it was announced, JPMorgan Chase staffers had worked with WaMu's auditors to get access to WaMu's internal network before the news broke. In the process, they secured a list of employee's e-mail addresses without having to get them through WaMu's top management. Within minutes of the deal, too, visitors to www.WaMu.com were greeted by a message from Chase welcoming customers to JPMorgan Chase. This too had been prepared on the sly.)

The deal boosted JPMorgan Chase into first place in nationwide deposits, with $911 billion to Citigroup's $804 billion and Bank of America's $785 billion, and made it the second-largest bank in terms of assets, with $2.04 trillion to Citigroup's $2.1 trillion. (At the end of the first quarter of 2009, JPMorgan Chase was still the second-largest bank, with $2.1 trillion in assets to Bank of America's $2.3 trillion, with Citi slipping into third place.) The purchase also gave the company a foothold in both California (691 branches versus just three pre-deal) and Florida (274 and 13, respectively), and a total of more than 5,000 branches nationwide. What's more, there were cross-selling opportunities, as WaMu had never been big in either wealth management or commercial banking, and JPMorgan Chase could integrate those offerings into its new branches. (History showed any optimism to be well placed. After acquiring the branches of Bank of New York, Chase retail bankers boosted in-branch credit card sales 20-fold and investment sales by 40 percent.)

The cost was a mere $1.9 billion plus $31 billion in write-downs against estimated future losses in WaMu's loan portfolio. (The April prediction of $30 billion in losses, in other words, had been dead-on.) JPMorgan Chase's employee roster jumped from 195,000 to 238,000.

Friday's stock offering eventually reached $11.5 billion. Even though he had obtained an extremely cheap source of funding—WaMu's $188 billion in deposits—Dimon tapped the equity market to bolster its equity ledger, calling it an "offensive" capital raise. "We are raising capital to do a deal, to buy something, to grow," he said in an interview. "We are not raising capital to fill a hole." (A finger in the eye to the likes of Merrill Lynch and Citigroup, no doubt.)

The *New York Daily News* encapsulated the reaction to the deal with the headline "JPMorgan CEO Jamie Dimon Eats Banks for Breakfast." The *New York Times* went with "1-800-CALL-DIMON."

The *Times*'s headline confirmed the success of a savvy public relations strategy Dimon has pursued for much of his career. Not only had he gone out of his way to make himself accessible to reporters; he spent an inordinate amount of time focused on his regulators and their concerns. Some people had wondered what the point of all the outreach was—What did it have to do with generating sustainable earnings growth? Was it just ego gratification?—but the deals with Bear Stearns and WaMu showed the value of a high profile and a carefully cultivated image as a man (and a company) of caution.

"I once heard someone respond to the question of how one can be successful by saying, 'You have to be in the right place at the right time,' " says analyst Mike Mayo, who moved to Calyon Securities in March 2009. "When asked how to do *that*, the response was 'You have to be in a lot of places a lot of the time.' Those two deals are where Jamie's image—and that of JPMorgan Chase—translated into actual transactions. This is now the go-to bank when regulators pick up the phone. It would not surprise me in this environment if Jamie Dimon gets the first call in the next unusual situation we might find ourselves in."

By refusing to step up and buy the whole company, Dimon essentially wiped out WaMu's common shareholders, including the private equity firm Texas Pacific Group (TPG), which got smoked for $1.35 billion on its April investment; TPG had somehow managed to unload $650 million of its exposure in the interim. Dimon also let the bondholders get wiped out. And he ended up buying something estimated to be worth $12 billion or so for just $1.9 billion. JPMorgan Chase's stock rose 11 percent the next day, even though the capital raise diluted shareholders' ownership.

WaMu's president, Steve Rotella, who had indicated in April that he did not want to work for Scharf or Dimon again, was granted his wish and was told he would be terminated. JPMorgan Chase made all the decisions about senior management within five days of the deal, a decisive move that helped stop deposit outflows in their tracks.

There were no niceties tossed into the deal. Executive stock compensation lost in the bankruptcy was not replaced, and no executive was paid a change-in-control provision—a marked departure from the generous retention payments made to Bear Stearns executives in April. On December 1, JPMorgan Chase announced it was laying off 9,200 WaMu employees, about 21 percent of the total. (In February 2009, it laid off 2,800 more, as a result of continued declines in the value of WaMu's mortgage portfolio.)

Despite calling WaMu "a perfect fit," Dimon nevertheless acknowledged that he was doubling down on the American consumer at a volatile time. The company's bank branches, mortgage, and credit card businesses would thereafter account for nearly half of JPMorgan Chase's overall profits. "That's the big risk," he said. But he added that Scharf and the rest of the team had done their homework. They knew WaMu's assets cold by state and by product and had run the numbers on worst-case scenarios for housing prices. "I'm making a bet that we won't have a depression in this country," he said. "If we do have one, the deal will have been a mistake. But that's our job: to make those determinations and figure out what we think is right. It's just like buying a new house.

You may be wrong with your timing, and the price may go down. But what are you going to do? Spend your whole life worrying about being wrong? The price had a huge margin for error in it, but that doesn't mean we won't be wrong. I don't know what's going to happen to this economy."

At a more granular level, Dimon's logic was as follows. Even if the company were to be faced in 2010 with a $10 billion charge due to WaMu's mortgage portfolio, the acquired assets would still be earning $2 billion a year. Seen in that light, the company might end up getting nothing out of the deal in the first four or five years, but in the fifth year it would start pulling down about $3 billion in earnings. "In that case, it will still have been a good deal," he said. "But there's no doubt it's very scary in the meantime. People underestimate how scary that one decision is."

It was such a scary decision, in fact, that JPMorgan Chase was the *only* bank that ended up bidding on WaMu. Wells Fargo didn't show up. Citigroup didn't show up. Neither did Wachovia. It that light, the $1.888 billion bid was arguably a little high. Dimon had no regrets. "Sure, it might have been nice to spend only a million dollars on the thing, but we didn't spend a lot of time wondering what the cover bid needed to be. We just figured out the most we'd be willing to spend, and that turned out to be about $2 billion," he said. "It would have been lucky to have lowballed, yes. But I'd rather have the company." When Sandler O'Neill's analyst Jeff Harte asked Dimon whether he knew how much better JPMorgan Chase's bid had been than that of the runner-up, Dimon had replied, "We don't know, and we don't care." Cavanagh was a little more forthright on the issue. "The FDIC did a good job of running an auction," he laughed.

Dimon later received a letter containing white powder and a note that read, "Steal tens of thousands of people's money and not expect reprercussions [*sic*]. It's payback time. What you just breathed in will kill you within 10 days. Thank xxx and the FDIC for your demise." More than 50 copies of the letter had been sent to multiple Chase bank branches, the FDIC, and the OTS. Dimon's letter also contained a reference to the "McVeighing of your corporate headquarters within six months." All were postmarked Amarillo, Texas.

When federal authorities told JPMorgan Chase they had looked into the matter but had not found many leads, the chief administrative officer, Frank Bisignano, took matters into his own hands. "We're going to nail this guy," he told Dimon. JPMorgan Chase has a significant security apparatus, including former Secret Service professionals, CIA veterans, and all manner of hacker types, to help protect its $2 trillion in assets. The bank's crack security and investigations team first looked for Internet addresses that had searched its website for a list of Chase branches. They found one in Albuquerque, New Mexico, about 300 miles from Amarillo.

The problem was that the address belonged to the free Wi-Fi network at a local community college, so just about anybody could have used it. Given the clear reference to WaMu in the letter, the investigators looked into former WaMu shareholders living in Albuquerque. That is how they discovered 47-year-old Richard Leon Goyette (aka Michael Jurek), who also happened to have taken a class at the community college. Bisignano handed Goyette's data over to the Feds, and Goyette was arrested and charged with several crimes in February 2009. In June of that year, he was convicted and sentenced to nearly four years in prison.

After WaMu, the Street was aflutter with acquisition envy. Citigroup tried to get in on the action, cutting a deal just four days later to buy the banking operations of Wachovia for $2.2 billion. As with Merrill and Lehman, Wall Street's chattering class found cause to blame Dimon for Wachovia's predicament as well. In buying WaMu, Dimon's team had assumed that about 25 percent of WaMu's so-called option ARM mortgages would default. Wachovia had projected that only 12 percent would do so, and so was suddenly faced with a massive write-down.

The Citigroup deal also came with government assistance. Citi's CEO, Vikram Pandit, earned plaudits for stopping a run on Wachovia, but was subsequently embarrassed when Wells Fargo swooped in with a $15.4 billion offer to buy the whole company. That deal, in addition to

Bank of America's $50 billion purchase of Merrill Lynch on September 15, secured Dimon's reputation as a master negotiator. Whereas he paid pennies on the dollar for WaMu, Wells Fargo paid real money for Wachovia. And Dimon bought Bear Stearns for a song—with a government backstop—compared with Bank of America's ill-considered and unsupported grab of Merrill.

The notion of Dimon as the government's banker of choice also won more credence when it emerged that Sheila Bair, the chairwoman of the FDIC, was possibly double-dealing in the Wachovia contretemps. She had publicly supported Citigroup in its squabble with Wells Fargo, but Wachovia's chief, Bob Steel, later said that in private she had been urging him to cut a deal with Wells Fargo. Dimon had received far more solicitous treatment when she teed up the WaMu deal for JPMorgan Chase.

On October 13, 2008, Secretary of the Treasury Paulson summoned the CEOs of leading firms—Dimon, Lloyd Blankfein, Ken Lewis, John Mack, Vikram Pandit, John Thain, and Dick Kovacevich from Wells Fargo—to a meeting. The chief of the Fed, Ben Bernanke; the president of the New York Fed, Timothy Geithner; and Sheila Bair were also in attendance.

It didn't take long. Paulson explained to the assembled group that the public had lost faith in the country's banking system, and that he was using his authorization under TARP to buy $250 billion worth of preferred shares in the nation's largest banks. The hope was that such a large injection of capital would calm fears that the banking edifice itself was on the verge of collapse. Geithner then proceeded to delineate the various allocations, the largest of which went to JPMorgan Chase, Bank of America, Citigroup, and Wells Fargo, each of which received $25 billion. The banks would have to pay a dividend of 5 percent annually for five years and then 9 percent thereafter.

A number of banks, particularly Citigroup, desperately needed the money, but Dimon was in a bind. He didn't need the money but was being asked to take it "for the good of the system," and also put up with the many strings attached to it, including restrictions on executive compensation. Dimon decided he wouldn't stand in the way of the greater good, agreeing to take the money without complaint. (Before he did that, however, he stood up, grabbed the term sheet, and began to walk to the door. "Where are you going?" he was asked. "To send this to my partners," Dimon replied. The majority of the other executives then decided they should do the same.) Wells Fargo's CEO, Kovacevich, was more recalcitrant than Dimon, protesting briefly before accepting the inevitable. Like the deal with Bear Stearns, this was not the kind of thing even the proudest of CEOs wanted to try to refuse.

The meeting was over by 4:00 P.M., and by 6:30 P.M. each of the CEOs had signed a term sheet. Among other things, they had signed away their ability to offer so-called golden parachutes in any new contracts, as well as the tax deductibility of executives' compensation above $500,000. Dimon rarely criticized either the Bush administration's or the Obama administration's bailout efforts, but he repeated, on several occasions, that as far as TARP money went, "We didn't ask for it, didn't want it, and we didn't need it." The market took the news of the bailout badly, falling nearly 8 percent on October 15.

. . .

Despite the growing consensus that Dimon was the banker of the moment and JPMorgan Chase the bank, 2008 ultimately proved another tough year for the company in absolute terms. It was still suffering for past mistakes—overextending in leveraged loans and allowing loan underwriting standards to deteriorate significantly—and was also paying the price for being a bank at a time when banking was not a good business to be in. "You can't outrun the economy," Dimon's former colleague Bob Willumstad observed. "It's the nature of the business."

And the economy was running pretty fast. The negative feedback loop of global de-leveraging continued unabated, with a savage interplay between the financial markets and the real economy. Loan defaults spiked across the board, from large companies to individual credit card holders. Despite JPMorgan Chase's relative balance sheet strength, investors couldn't help being a little concerned about skeletons lurking in its closet. Things were so touchy by late November that when Dimon was reported to be in the Middle East, rumors spread that he was soliciting capital from oil-rich Arabs. He was not; rather, he was celebrating the official opening of the company's Riyadh office.

Full-year results were nothing to brag about. Dimon did not brag. When he received an award at Yale on December 10, he told the audience, "I feel like I'm riding a bronco and holding on for dear life most of the time." The same day, he told CNBC that the company "could very well post a sizable loss for the fourth quarter." The stock fell 11 percent in response, dragging the entire market down 2 percent along with it.

(Judy Dimon found an iron-and-marble sculpture of tiny men literally jumping through hoops and sent copies of it to some senior executives as a holiday present. In one accompanying handwritten note, she christened 2008 "The Year of Jumping through Hoops" and hoped that 2009 would be "The Year of Landing on One's Feet.")

Despite leading the league tables, the company's investment bank saw revenue drop 33 percent in 2008 while nonperforming loans jumped 233 percent to $1.8 billion. The investment bank marked down its mortgage and leveraged loans $10 billion during the year. Similar pressures hit the retail financial services franchise; credit costs climbed 274 percent to $9.5 billion during the year. The company's home lending portfolio, including home equity and both prime and subprime mortgages, was a $328 billion leaning tower of Pisa by the end of the year; of that amount, 36 percent, or $117 billion, had already been deemed "credit-impaired."

The bank had instituted several rounds of credit changes that tightened underwriting standards in 2007 and 2008, but it was too late. At the end of 2008, JPMorgan Chase estimated that about $25.6 billion of its home equity portfolio was extended to households where borrowing exceeded household value, the so-called state of "negative equity." The percentage of the portfolio where households were sitting on negative equity nearly doubled during the year, from 15 percent in January to 27 percent at the end of the year. Much of that negative equity came from California, Florida, Arizona, and Michigan.

Along with its competitors, JPMorgan Chase got smashed by the housing collapse. Citigroup had written down about $101.8 billion in assets from the beginning of the crisis through May 2009, Bank of America about $56.6 billion, and JPMorgan Chase $41.1 billion. Wells

Fargo, by comparison, had seen fit to write down only about $27.9 billion in assets at that point. Although he may have left a few competitors like Citigroup far behind, Dimon still had serious competition.

Both Wall Street and the media fawned over the company's risk management vis-à-vis that of its competitors, but little good can be said about its home equity business. As Bob Willumstad pointed out, on Wall Street, it can be very difficult not to do what everyone else is doing, even if it's stupid, because the profits can be big before the reckoning. In this case, JPMorgan Chase was just as stupid as the rest of them. In discussing changes that had been made in 2008 to underwriting standards, the company announced that borrowers henceforth needed to prove their income—the so-called "stated income" clause had made borrowing during the boom a mere matter of walking into a bank and saying that, sure, you were doing just fine on $75,000 a year, but you needed that extra $25,000 home equity line "just in case."

The sheer size of some of the mistakes made by the JPMorgan Chase team just before the credit bubble burst bring to mind a lingering criticism of Jamie Dimon. A number of people close to him wonder whether he overcompensates for Sandy Weill's penchant for eventually trashing his closest aides. Weill threw important people in his organization overboard all the time, or, more precisely, had someone else do it for him. "But Jamie," says a longtime colleague, "just can't do it. It's a flat spot for him. I don't think it's because he doesn't know. It's because he doesn't ever want it said of him that he's just like Sandy, that he'll just get rid of people." (After having been at the ready to act as Weill's enforcer in the early days, in other words, Dimon was in need of an enforcer of his own by 2009.)

Jamie Dimon learned from Sandy Weill that although playing people off against each other might actually work to your own advantage, what it also does is create a dysfunctional environment that can destroy a company. He often talks of "mature" companies—the likes of Wal-Mart and Johnson & Johnson—and how it is no surprise that a lack of corporate intrigue tends to go hand in hand with long-term success. (It could be said that while many of his competitors were losing their focus, Dimon was running his business just like Wal-Mart itself. Given the

giant retailer's razor-thin margins, its obsessive focus on cost—on counting everything that can be counted—has helped it outrun competitors
for years. Dimon's philosophy is similar.)

Still, instead of holding his most senior executives responsible for
poor decisions, some say, Dimon often goes to the other extreme, taking
personal responsibility for mistakes. On some level, that's a noble and
mature approach; on another, it avoids addressing specific mistakes
made by specific people. The hardest-working man in banking needs to
admit that it's not always about him, that sometimes other people's mistakes are just that—their mistakes and not his own. "There are a lot of
people around here that feel that if he's close to somebody they get more
license than they should on both performance and behavior," says one
member of the firm's operating committee.

Granted, there is an alternative argument: that J.P. Morgan has
managed to outperform most of its rivals precisely because of the stability in its management ranks. And when Dimon speaks fondly of his
team, he means it. He relies extensively on the input and insight of top
management, and rarely does things that he thinks will be a good idea
all by himself. He actually trusts the people working for him, and trusts,
too, that they can learn from their mistakes, as he has learned from
his own.

Wall Street is a pressure cooker, and when the pressure started to get
intense in 2007, the more insecure of its chief executives started firing
everybody around them to make sure outsiders knew where they should
place the blame. Such a strategy does enhance one's short-term job security, but the problem with it is that when turnover gets too high, no one
really knows what's going on anymore. As proof of the point, before
they themselves were dismissed, Bear's Jimmy Cayne, Citigroup's
Chuck Prince, Merrill Lynch's Stan O'Neal, and Lehman's Dick Fuld
had all participated in their own little orgies of firing. Dimon has resisted doing the same thing, and his firm is surely the better for it.

. . .

By December 2008, the Fed had taken 51 measures to address the market's problems, including printing money as if there were no tomorrow.

An astute market seer, Jim Grant, describes the Fed's near-abandon at the printing press: "Frostbite victims tend not to dwell on the summertime perils of heatstroke."

With the rest of Wall Street still busy with cleaning out their Augean stables, Dimon and his team were busy picking up market share in almost every one of the bank's businesses. JPMorgan Chase achieved an unprecedented milestone in 2008. Its investment bank sat atop every single one of the four most important league tables that rank banks by the amount of capital they help customers raise—debt; equity; loans; and debt, equity, and equity-related. The company also earned the most fees of any investment bank, with an 8.8 percent market share. For the full year, the investment bank also set revenue records in foreign exchange, commodities, credit, and emerging markets. But Dimon was anything but complacent. "I don't think it's a given we're going to stay there," he said.

The company led a $60 billion global refinancing of the car finance company GMAC in June, the largest refinancing ever. It participated in two of the biggest deals of the year, the $23 billion purchase of Wrigley by privately held Mars and the $52 billion acquisition of Anheuser-Busch by the Belgian brewer InBev. (With the closing of the InBev deal in November, JPMorgan Chase was an almost inconceivable $100 billion ahead of its longtime rival Goldman Sachs in the mergers and acquisitions advisory rankings for the year.) Money poured into the company's asset management and treasury services divisions, as clients and investors engaged in an unprecedented "flight to safety."

JPMorgan Chase held top three positions in most of its other businesses. In addition to strong positions in commercial banking, treasury services, and asset management, Chase was the nation's largest credit card issuer in terms of outstanding loans and the top issuer of Visa cards in terms of total cards. (Critics who still insisted that Dimon only cuts costs needed only watch *American Idol* in 2009 to see Chase's "Secret Agent Man" ads. In the midst of the what was surely the worst credit card downturn in history, the company was stepping up and buying some of the most expensive airtime on television to bolster the franchise.) The retail bank was third largest in terms of deposits, second in home equity originations, third in mortgage originations, and first in auto loans. All the retail banking market shares had been fought for tooth and nail, but they also left the bank exposed to the roiling recession, and such large exposures took a huge bite out of the company's earnings and continued to do so in 2009.

"What became clear to anybody in finance in 2008 was that JPMorgan Chase was now the dominant financial institution," says Marc Lasry of Avenue Capital, a hedge fund. "We're trying to do more business with them, because when you have more power, they can get more things done. They're in a position now where they can choose who they want to do business with."

By the end of the year, almost any firm lucky enough to still be in business found that its employees would rather be working for JPMorgan Chase. "We feel like we've become an employer of choice," said the cohead of the investment bank, Bill Winters. "We are not doubling or tripling people's compensation in order to attract them, nor moving them two or three rungs up the responsibility ladder." (In May 2009, JPMorgan Chase also supplanted Goldman Sachs as college students' top choice among banks they'd like to work for, a position Goldman had held for more than a decade.)

The company's shares were also fast becoming the stock of choice for investors. In September, the mutual fund giant Fidelity boosted its holdings of JPMorgan Chase to $523 million while at the same time paring its stakes in Merrill Lynch, Wachovia, and Goldman Sachs. A tier 1 capital ratio of 10.9 percent at the end of the year reinforced Dimon's commitment to the fortress balance sheet. In more carefree times, investors sought banks willing to take huge risks. Now, they were looking for banks that actually knew how to manage risks appropriately. And there were few of those. In mid-July 2009, investors valued JPMorgan Chase at $126 billion, versus just $81 billion for Bank of America and a paltry $15 billion for Citigroup.

By the summer, Dimon finally had a minute to catch his breath after the events of the past 15 months. Looking back over the deals for Bear Stearns and WaMu, he thought it premature that people were already calling WaMu a "home run." "We're not ready to call WaMu anything yet," he said. "But I think we're pretty sure about Bear being at least a single by now. It should have been a double or a triple, but it was a single. Of course, the market environment got much worse after that deal."

The cold-blooded competitor in Dimon then made an appearance. "Bear was never a home run, but WaMu will prove to be a great thing for the company over the long run. Will we be able to say that three years from now? At that point, you might very well be asking me, 'How could you have done that in the midst of all those things that were going on?' And I'm going to look at you and say, 'Take your bets, friend. Take your bets.' "

14. WILL GIANTS STILL WALK THE EARTH?

The personal capital Dimon earned by deftly navigating through one of the biggest economic crises in history gave him an opportunity to express views on issues beyond banking. When interviewed by Charlie Rose in June 2008, Dimon identified himself as a deficit hawk, but also made clear his support for short-term fiscal stimulus and directed tax cuts. He called the United States hypocritical for embarking on a heedless spree: borrowing from foreigners and then, when it was cash-strapped, insisting that those same foreigners continue to finance it through purchases of Treasury bonds. He later ripped into the administration for requiring TARP recipients to dramatically reduce their hiring of foreign workers via H1-B visas, calling the move a "disgrace."

He also suggested that in his role as CEO of JPMorgan Chase, he had a greater responsibility than just to his shareholders. "Anyone that I meet that doesn't feel they have some obligation, my level of respect drops for them significantly," he said.

When giving a speech at the Yale CEO Summit in December 2008—at which he was the recipient of a Legend in Leadership award— he took a strong position on the energy crisis and the United States' lack of preparedness. "Shame on us," he said. "This is our third energy crisis. And we still don't have the fortitude as a nation to do anything about it. We are going to earn a fourth. This is not just a financial issue. This is a geopolitical issue. We are arming people who want to kill us. That's what we're doing. What the hell is wrong with us? I find that offensive, because our kids are going to pay for that."

This type of remark does not come without cost. JPMorgan Chase has valuable customers all over the Middle East—the company had just opened its Riyadh, Saudi Arabia, office in late 2008. But Dimon has always been clear about where his priorities lie. When talking of the most important things in his life, he once said, "My family, humanity, my country, and the world. And way down here is J.P. Morgan."

Despite growing criticism of derivative securities and the financial, if not societal, devastation they can allegedly cause, Dimon and his team—particularly Bill Winters, who helped create modern credit derivatives—refused to back away from their involvement in the market, a market one analyst estimated as $1 *quadrillion* in size. "People say derivatives caused our recent problems, but that's just not true," Dimon says. "A lot of those derivatives guaranteed mortgage product. But it was the *mortgages* themselves that were the problem, and those filtered through into SIVs, CDOs, and then into the insurance companies who guaranteed them. Derivatives didn't cause the problem, mortgages did." (Still, it should be pointed out that derivatives can magnify the problem, in much the same way as leverage. Regulators do keep an eye on banks' leverage, but derivatives exposures have reached colossal proportions. Witness JPMorgan Chase's $81 *trillion* as of March 2009 in notional outstandings.)

In large part, he's right. The problems at companies like AIG have been described so many times as a result of "highly complex derivatives," which their users "did not understand," that it has become received wisdom to perceive derivatives themselves as the issue. But this reasoning is almost entirely wrong. The users understood *precisely* what the risks were, but they made the wrong bet—that housing prices wouldn't plunge across the board, everywhere. There were a lot of people who took the bet; they just didn't match AIG's level of recklessness.

There have been some suggestions that the interplay between a company's bonds and its credit default swaps actually exacerbated problems—George Soros wrote convincingly about this phenomenon in the *New York Times*—but that phenomenon was arguably on the margin of a much larger problem: abandonment of risk management controls in pursuit of higher profits. When it came time for the first big test of credit default swaps—in the aftermath of Lehman Brothers' bankruptcy—the settlement of those contracts took place without incident on October 21, 2008.

Dimon has endorsed the creation of a central clearinghouse so derivatives exposures can be more closely monitored. But he considers the bank's CDS business a valuable franchise and doesn't consider it JPMorgan Chase's problem if other investors hurt themselves by mishandling them. (Pointing to a healthy lobbying budget on this score, critics argue that even though he's said the right thing publicly, Dimon and his team are actually stonewalling derivatives reform in order to protect the outsize margins the business generates.) He has also called for a systematic regulator that can anticipate problems in the system rather than merely respond to them. Even though Dimon, as a college student, wrote that admiring letter to Milton Friedman, the king of the laissez-faire economists, he also values the lessons of John Maynard Keynes and Keynes's argument in favor of adult supervision in the markets.

In October 2008, Blackstone's chief, Steve Schwarzman, embarked on a campaign to have so-called "mark to market" accounting rules changed. The rules, he (and others) complained, meant that companies with deteriorating asset values were constantly forced to mark down their balance sheet values; this entailed having to raise capital by selling more assets, which put further downward pressure on those asset values, which . . . a vicious circle. (When prices were rising, no one had a problem constantly marking up asset values, but that's another story.)

Nearly alone among the major banks' CEOs, Dimon did not try to blame the industry's problems on accounting standards. "A lot of those mark-to-market losses will end up being real losses," he said. "They are real losses that are simply being recognized in the market before they're being recognized in expected cash flows." In April 2009, however, regulators buckled under industry pressure, relaxing mark-to-market rules that affected banks. Shortly thereafter, JPMorgan Chase, Citigroup, Bank of America, and Goldman Sachs all announced surprisingly strong quarters. But whereas Dimon made clear during the company's conference call that the accounting change had no effect whatsoever on earnings, Bank of America and Citigroup did no such thing.

At a panel discussion at the New York Stock Exchange hosted by the *Wall Street Journal*, Dimon took aim at the Securities and Exchange Commission, charging that it had no idea that Bear Stearns was on the verge of failure in March 2008. (The chairman of SEC, Christopher Cox, had asserted as recently as the week before Bear failed that he and his colleagues were comfortable with Bear's capital cushion.) "We have a Byzantine, balkanized system where our laws are closer to the Civil War than today," Dimon complained. In response to a question about whether the crisis was abating, he responded, "No one really knows. Clearly we're in the panic stage of unreasonable behavior. [But] the governments of the world will eventually win."

Dimon tried to dampen public anger at JPMorgan Chase with a series of full-page ads in major newspapers including the *New York Times*, the *Wall Street Journal*, the *Washington Post*, and *USA Today* that highlighted JPMorgan Chase's efforts to keep credit flowing to consumers and businesses that needed it. "Your House Is Your Home," the first one, which ran on November 11, 2008, said. "We Want to Keep It That Way."

He also got out ahead of the debate over foreclosures by announcing a moratorium on foreclosures of owner-occupied homes that applies not only to the $350 billion of mortgages the company actually owns but also the $1.5 *trillion* worth that it services on behalf of others. (In a 2009 speech at the Chamber of Commerce, Dimon addressed the question whether JPMorgan Chase even had the right to adjust mortgages it only serviced. Holders of mortgage-backed securities who were inclined to complain about the decision, he said, would just have to "get over it.")

On February 12, 2009, Dimon sent a letter to Representative Barney Frank, chairman of the House Services Committee, in which he pledged that JPMorgan Chase was extending the moratorium through March 2009 while the administration worked on its own $50 billion plan for the housing market. At that point, the company claimed to have already prevented 250,000 foreclosures through a borrower-outreach program that had been in effect since late 2007, and said it was seeking to do the same for 400,000 more home owners.

At a time when nearly everyone in Washington was calling for Wall

Streeters' scalps, Dimon was out ahead of the Beltway crowd, dwarfing its efforts in this area at least. In doing so, he was demonstrating a combination of business skills and public relations savvy that are the required complement of someone looking to run a giant global company.

• • •

Whenever the subject of a possible second career for Dimon in politics comes up—the media were practically demanding it in the fall of 2008—those who know him best cite a number of automatic disqualifiers. The first is his mouth (while he no longer uses the f-word quite as much as he did when he was younger, it's still prominent in his vocabulary). The second is his congenital inability to suffer fools gladly. Those close to him have noticed a mellowing with age, but his temper still flares up. All you have to do is offend his sense of fairness. When the *New York Times*'s columnist Joe Nocera obtained a pass code, called into an employees-only JPMorgan Chase conference call, and asserted in a subsequent article that the company planned to use the federal government's $25 billion capital injection to buy weakened competitors, Dimon was irate.

"First, I don't think it's right to sneak onto an internal phone call like that," he said. "Second, we hadn't even received the TARP money yet. Third, the person he quoted wasn't even in a position to know what we were going to do with the money. And fourth, that employee even said something that essentially contradicted Nocera's point. He said we were going to try to grow our business. Wouldn't that be lending? Because that's what business we're in, the lending business." JPMorgan Chase complained to the *Times* about Nocera's sneakiness.

Dimon also insisted that the bank *was* increasing lending, at least certain kinds of lending. The second advertisement in the company's series "The Way Forward"—which ran on November 20—said, "Our Business Is Lending. And That's Exactly What We're Doing." By late fall, JPMorgan Chase had $60 billion in the interbank loan market, increased its commercial loan balances by 18 percent through the year's end, and also increased both student loans and credit card loans. He also repeated, whenever given the chance, that in the era after World War II, banks had accounted for 60 percent of lending in the economy, but by the turn of the twenty-first century that portion had fallen to just 20 percent. The rest was provided by Wall Street and the so-called "shadow banking" industry, which includes hedge funds, money market funds, and creators of securitized debt.

The seizing up of credit that crippled the global economy in 2007 and 2008, in other words, could not be explained simply by saying that a bunch of banks decided to stop lending. According to a study by the consultancy Oliver Wyman, bank lending decreased by $400 billion from 2007 to 2008, while capital markets lending fell by $950 billion. Given that total net bank lending in 2007 was just $850 billion, the study observes, "it is obvious that banks would never be able to make up for the shortfall from capital markets." In order to understand and learn from the crisis, Dimon argued, it was important to examine all facets of what is now a gigantic and complex organism of credit. What's more, he continued, if it was lax lending standards that caused the crisis, how could he now be criticized for tightening them? "It's a total misconception that banks aren't lending," he says. "They are—and in huge numbers. Where the bottom fell out was in the shadow lending system, where lending almost disappeared. That said, credit standards at banks have tightened. And for good reason—it was loose lending standards that caused a lot of these problems to begin with."

In spring 2009, Dimon met with President Obama and other banking chiefs and referred to TARP funds as "a scarlet letter." Then, during a conference call in April, he referred to it as "TARP Baby." The pseudo-inflammatory nature of the remark aside, the public relations considerations surrounding TARP had indeed become complex. Dimon wanted to pay the money back, but he was sensitive to the administration's concern that in doing so, he might open up a divide between the haves and the have-nots, possibly resulting in a run on banks less healthy than JPMorgan Chase (which was to say most of them). By June, though, Dimon got what he wanted—authorization to pay the money back, along with eight other banks.

On this point, some critics in the media saw Dimon as being selective with the facts. The government supported JPMorgan Chase in ways other than TARP. Dimon's bank was the second-largest user of a debt guarantee program sponsored by the FDIC; the company had borrowed $37.1 billion through the program through April 2009, benefiting handsomely from reduced borrowing costs provided by the guarantee. Dimon insisted that this is not as big a deal as it seems. "Look, it barely saves us money," he says. "And it saves a lot for some other people. We maybe saved a half a percentage point in borrowing costs using the program, while some other people saved *two* percentage points. So it's actually asymmetrically not so good for us. In any event, when we went to Washington, they told us they wanted us to take the TARP money *and* they wanted us to use the guarantee. So that's what we did."

When Secretary of the Treasury Tim Geithner introduced his PPIP initiative—the public-private investment program intended to help investors take bad mortgages off banks' books with government backing—he inadvertently created a whole new set of problems for Wall Street CEOs. Banks like JPMorgan Chase, critics argued, would now be using TARP money to buy one another's bad bets at a discount, with government backing. In April 2009, Dimon and his team had decided PPIP was too hot to handle. "I think we will probably want to stay as far away from that as possible," Dimon said. "We don't need it. It might give a little upside, but so what? To have our motives called into question wouldn't be worth it. We don't need the money."

On his quarterly earnings call, he repeated the sentiment. "We're certainly not going to borrow from the federal government," he said, "because we've learned our lesson about that." (He has since said he went too far with that statement. Still, while eminently capable of cooperating with government, Dimon is without question a businessman. In a conference call in May 2009, he questioned regulators' tendency to pinpoint certain issues without an understanding of the occasional futility of it all. "Say the regulators realize that restaurants are selling soda at a 90 percent margin," he says. "They'll get all excited and make a push to reduce that margin to 10 or 20 percent. I'll tell you what the result will be. The restaurant will raise the price of the burger.")

If he defies the expectations of his friends and colleagues and becomes a statesman in the next incarnation of his career, Dimon will probably need to work further on his filters. Through April 2009, he had done an effective job of balancing endorsing government officials' responses to the crises while waiting for the day he could shake them off his back. But his patience was obviously wearing thin, and his provocative remarks—such as the one about the "TARP baby"—have had a "two steps forward, one and a half steps back" effect on his relationship with the administration.

Despite its general facelessness today, Wall Street was at one point a place where statesmen were forged. But the last "master of the universe" to merit such a description is probably Lazard's Felix Rohatyn, who earned his own comparisons to John Pierpont Morgan when he helped New York City avoid bankruptcy in 1970. (He was also ambassador to France from 1997 to 2000.) Since then, the results have been more mixed; the Goldman Sachs graduates Bob Rubin and Hank Paulson failed to rise beyond the level of technocrat.

Could Dimon revive the tradition? Perhaps, but as a lifelong banker, he does hold certain viewpoints that could easily undermine a political career. Testifying in front of the House Financial Services Committee in February, he insisted that the compensation paid to senior executives at JPMorgan Chase was appropriate. That was just a few weeks after he had awarded $112 million in stock grants to the company's top 15 executives, including more than $11 million apiece to Steve Black, Bill Winters, and Jes Staley. (Dimon took none, although the Associated Press calculated his 2008 compensation as $35.7 million, based on a $1 million salary, stock awards from previous years, and perks.)

"There's a lot of political and social pressure to change compensation, just like there was a lot of economic competitive pressure that drove it up," Dimon says. "So I think there will be change. There are legitimate complaints about compensation that was not properly paid to people who did terrible jobs in hindsight. And sometimes it wasn't even in hindsight. But I also think talent will always be well paid, and I don't think it's fair to lump us all together. We don't have supplemental executive retirement plans. We don't have 401(k) matches for high-paid executives. We've gotten rid of all the change of control contracts and golden parachutes here. I do think that if you're captain of the ship you should pay the price first. But I'm also philosophically opposed to the government being involved in compensation. I think it's ridiculous. Why don't they regulate actors and sports stars and small businesses and doctors and entrepreneurs? Why don't they just tell everyone what we can pay people?"

By the end of 2008, calls to nationalize the country's largest banks were in vogue, especially among influential commentators like Paul Krugman of the *New York Times*. Although it seemed obvious that some banks were insolvent—the stock market knocked Citigroup shares down to $1 a share at one point—Dimon made sure to put space between his bank and the others. "JPMorgan Chase will be fine if everyone stops talking about damn nationalization of banks," he said. "We've got plenty of capital. We're properly marked."

He also kept his focus, refusing to be drawn into venturing opinions on whatever he was asked. When CNBC's anchor Erin Burnett asked him whether former Federal Reserve chairman Paul Volcker might make a good "car czar," he replied, "I have no idea."

Dimon is no neophyte in Washington. In 1997, he and Judy held a fund-raiser for Senator Chuck Schumer of New York, and in Chicago they held one for Hillary Clinton. (This was before they changed their allegiance to Barack Obama.) During the 1990s, the couple gave $167,000 to the Democratic National Committee and the Democratic Senatorial Campaign Committee, and made more than $45,000 in donations to individual candidates.

Nor is Dimon naive about how the game is played in Washington, particularly when it comes to campaign contributions and lobbying fees. In 2007 and 2008, in addition to donating to the campaigns of nine Democrats, he also gave to seven Republicans. And JPMorgan Chase's political action committee's top three donations went to Republicans. The company paid $5.4 million in lobbying fees in 2008 and $5.5 million in 2007. That was more than Bank of America paid but less than Citigroup did—a fact that is not surprising, given Citigroup's much greater need for government support.

He also made no secret of his support for Obama during the presidential race. He was an informal adviser to the candidate in the lead-up to the election, and his wife is close to Secretary of Education Arne Duncan through her work in the Chicago school system. (At one point, Dimon referred to the acquisition of Bear Stearns as a "mission not accomplished," an unsubtle dig at then-president George Bush and his premature declaration of victory in Iraq.)

After Obama's victory, the media and the blogosphere were awash in conjecture as to whether Dimon was on Obama's short list of candidates for secretary of the treasury. Although the rumor took on a life of its own (and resurfaced in early 2009 when Secretary of the Treasury Tim Geithner came under ceaseless fire), nothing came of it. Dimon didn't expect a call and wouldn't have taken the job if he'd gotten one. "There's no way a Wall Street CEO would have been named secretary of the treasury," he said in December 2008, after Obama tapped Geithner for the job. "With all the anger at Wall Street, people understandably want someone that they feel is independent of specific influence." When asked why he didn't quash the rumors, Dimon looked perplexed. "It's kind of presumptuous to announce you're not interested in something that you haven't been offered, isn't it?"

When Obama became president, he singled out Dimon for praise. "There are a lot of banks that are actually pretty well managed— J.P. Morgan being a good example—I don't think Jamie should be punished for doing a pretty good job managing an enormous portfolio." At the company's "investor day" in February 2009, Dimon responded. "President Obama gave J.P. Morgan a shout-out recently," he said. "So I want to give him one, too. I think he's doing a pretty good job!" (Obama did it again at the end of April, when he commended JPMorgan Chase for making sacrifices on the terms of its debt in the Chrysler bailout.)

"It's clear to me that Obama is quite bright," says Dimon. "And quite knowledgeable. When you see him privately and publicly, it's the same thing. It's not like there are two Obamas. He's very knowledgeable about the stuff he talks about. He's clearly ethical, hardworking, and strong. There are many different kinds of strength. He was strong to go through the election. He was strong to state his opinions even though a lot of people hate them. He was strong to shoot drone missiles in Pakistan. He doesn't have a tremendous amount of real-world experience, but I think he gets stuff. He seems to understand things. And he's pretty much doing what he said he was going to do whether you like it or not."

Dimon and his wife were guests at the inaugural celebrations in November. Judy Dimon, ever the spitfire, cornered one of Representative Barney Frank's staffers and implored Frank's staff to stop vilifying banks to score political points. (To go out with the Dimons together is to watch "two balls of hyperenergy colliding," says their friend Peter Maglathlin. "Whenever we get together with them, the decibel level seems to rise. It's pretty funny. You know you're going to have an interesting evening of back-and-forth.")

The esteem in which Obama holds Dimon was revealed by the *Wall Street Journal*'s Monica Langley in a story about a meeting at the White House in mid-March 2009 between Dimon and White House and Treasury officials. "The following day," she wrote, ". . . business executives implored Mr. Obama to get credit flowing again. 'All right,' the president said, according to a transcript of the meeting. He'd have his people 'talk to Jamie.' " On another occasion, Dimon presented Secretary of the Treasury Tim Geithner with a fake check for $25 billion—the amount of JPMorgan Chase's TARP loan. This was an antic you wouldn't be likely to see from, say, Bank of America's Ken Lewis, who was stripped of his chairman's title in April. While humorous, the move also had a cutthroat undertone: the basic challenge of being a bank during a recession aside, Jamie Dimon had far less to worry about than most of his competitors. That was made even clearer during a conference call on May 4, 2009. During a discussion of the impending results of the banks' stress test, Dimon predicted that the government might "still look" to JPMorgan Chase to "do something" in case another firm teetered on the edge.

But even Obama isn't safe from the occasional shot across the bow from Dimon. In March 2008, Dimon lambasted the presidential candidates for their anticorporate populism. "I'm a Democrat," he said. "The Democrats are the worst." In his speech at the Chamber of Commerce a year later, Dimon returned to the issue of demonizing companies, saying that the country was acting like a dysfunctional family. Although it was surely appreciated by the audience, the comment elicited scorn from commentators, who mocked Dimon for seemingly feeling sorry for himself and other CEOs. Dimon's retort: painting everyone with the same brush is counterproductive, especially if you're accusing someone of breaking the law. "I don't believe the corporate world is any more corrupt than anywhere else," he said. "There are bums everywhere."

• • •

It has been said of the great credit bubble and crash that the trouble started when a number of Wall Street firms sold shares to the public. When that happened, the argument goes, Wall Street chieftains, their bankers, and their traders were effectively gambling with other people's money. With skewed incentive systems that favored near-term results, who wouldn't put up the farm on even the riskiest of bets? Few people, it turns out.

Jamie Dimon has never subscribed to that way of thinking. While he's not averse to paying himself an extraordinary amount of money, he has also done well by his shareholders. "Jamie has been a very responsible steward of shareholder capital," says the banking analyst Meredith Whitney. "That's the best thing anyone can say about a CEO. That's all that matters." (This, by the way, is one of the only nice things Whitney said about the entire banking industry between 2006 and 2009.) He certainly has been a responsible steward of his own capital. Dimon's stake in JPMorgan Chase—shares, options, and restricted stock—is worth about $175 million. And that's only about half his net worth, so the family is worth a hefty $350 million or so.

Still, his stewardship would be tested in 2009, as significant exposure to cash-strapped American consumers and businesses meant that the company was due for several more quarters of multibillion-dollar losses and write-downs. "We're as beaten down as anyone else in this environment," said the chief financial officer, Mike Cavanagh, in late 2008. "The culture around here is not one of congratulation and puffing ourselves up. It's 'tear it apart' at all times. And there's certainly plenty to tear apart now."

Jamie Dimon cannot understand how anyone could approach a business differently. "For any of our businesses you can get a reporting packet and it will tell you everything that's going on, including what's good and what's bad," he says. "What we aim for is continuous improvement. It's not like we think we get to a perfect place."

Dimon showed the courage of his convictions once again by cutting the company's dividend on February 23, 2009, a move he explained was vital to preserve JPMorgan Chase's capital. "I'm a large investor in J.P. Morgan," said Brian Rogers, who is the CEO of T. Rowe Price and was a classmate of Dimon's at Harvard. "I was meeting with one of our clients that same day and talking about risks in the financial sector. I told them that one of the few things you could be confident in was the integrity of J.P. Morgan's dividend. When I returned to my office at 4:00 and found out the news, I thought I was going to kill him. When I listened to his explanation, though, I thought, you know, Jamie is probably right. I went from a near apoplectic fit to saying that he was probably doing the right thing for the company. Everyone obviously agreed, as his stock was up in the aftermarket."

In May, when the results of the government's "stress tests" on the country's 19 largest banks were released, Dimon and JPMorgan Chase were right where everyone expected them to be—head and shoulders above the majority of their peers. Bank of America was said to need a staggering $34 billion in new capital, but Dimon's fortress balance sheet was considered adequate as it was. At that point, there was no more debate that any further consolidation in the industry was likely to be led by JPMorgan Chase. The predator was again on the prowl.

Still, although Dimon was receiving the best press—and commanding the most respect—of his entire career, the cheering was somewhat muted by the country's anger with the entire financial system and its recklessness. The billions in bailout funds being paid by taxpayers were one thing. To also owe the bank a mounting credit card bill and a mortgage worth more than one's house quite another.

At one point, the only thing hindering Jamie Dimon's progress was Sandy Weill. By 2009, he was swimming against the tide of an entire industry of overreaching CEOs.

EPILOGUE

For the first half of his career, Jamie Dimon was a character in someone else's story—Sandy Weill's. But by 2009, it was clear that Dimon's star had eclipsed Weill's. And it was also clear that Weill had made a terrible mistake 10 years before when he fired Dimon. When asked about it in his office in December 2008, Weill confessed as much. "I think I made a very bad decision on succession," he said. Today, he has only the highest compliments for his onetime protégé. "Jamie obviously has far fewer blind spots than most people in this business. He's outperformed most of them."

The two deals Dimon pulled off in 2008 showed that he could follow in Sandy Weill's footsteps as an acquisitions specialist. But there was one main difference. Unlike Weill, Jamie Dimon wasn't pursuing opportunities. He was *taking advantage* of them. The U.S. government had practically insisted that Dimon take over Bear Stearns. The last time the government had talked to Weill about acquisitions, in 2005, it was to say that his company, Citigroup, should lay off for a while, as his serial deal making had left Citi dazed and confused. "Jamie has outgrown the comparisons with Sandy Weill," says the analyst Mike Mayo. "As we look back, Sandy Weill apparently cut more corners than people appreciated. But Jamie goes out of his way to ensure that the foundation and plumbing are strong."

What Weill is likely to find quite difficult to believe is a shared opinion of many who worked with both men over the years—that Dimon contributed more to their success together than Weill. "By this point, he would probably consider Jamie his peer, but Sandy's not in the same league as Jamie," says one. "Not anymore."

• • •

There are a number of people who rose to the top ranks of Wall Street unnoticed by most of us. The hedge fund kingpin James Simons comes to mind, at least until he started pulling down more than $1 billion a year. Even Governor Jon Corzine of New Jersey usually stayed under the radar during his climb to the top of Goldman Sachs. Jamie Dimon was not one of those people; we saw him coming a mile away.

Yet it wasn't until 2008 that a complete picture of Dimon emerged. After years of being considered a glorified number-cruncher who only knew how to cut costs, he was finally acknowledged as a leader who knew how to make a company grow. What's more, he was recognized as both a creative thinker and a man with the ability to shape the culture not just of his company but also of his industry and even the country itself. It says something about Wall Street today that only a few people command both the respect of their peers and the genuine curiosity of the outside world. Jamie Dimon is certainly one of them. Although from an early age he preferred wealth to the intellectual pursuits of his brothers, Dimon evolved into a financial philosopher in the spirit of Warren Buffett.

Dimon's 2008 letter to his shareholders was a tour de force, a clarion call for change from the CEO of one of the largest banks in the country. He started work on the letter several months in advance, and spent many weekends refining his message. "I don't write a lot," he says. "So it's very hard for me." In addition to explaining JPMorgan Chase's results, the letter also tackled a bigger question: what had just happened? "That was as much for me as for the shareholders," he recalls. "It was cathartic. I'd given some talks about what had happened and what should be done about it, but I'd never really organized those thoughts. That's what I set out to do." The letter is especially forceful on the effects of excessive leverage, the industry's tendency toward using short-term financing to support long-term assets, and regulatory failures, in particular that of the housing finance concerns Freddie Mac and Fannie Mac. Most impressive of all may have been the understated eloquence of his prose—simple and direct, just like Buffett's.

The letter actually prompted Buffett to send Dimon yet another admiring note. "Jamie," it read, "you have outdone yourself; your letter is a masterpiece." Buffett went on to ask Dimon's permission to distribute the letter at his own annual meeting. He also sent copies of the letter to his friend Bill Gates as well as his colleague Charlie Munger. "It's the best I've seen anywhere," he says. (Both Gates and Munger agreed.) Nearly 25 years after the young Harvard graduate sat in the Seagram Building and marveled at the legendary Buffett's own letters, the legend was marveling right back at him.

Jamie Dimon has always been a winner. By 2009 he was something else entirely. He was a *hero*. In April 2009, at a reunion of his high school at which he was given the alumnus achievement award, he commented on what he considered the "surrealness" of it all. Referring to the school's late headmaster, Charles Cook, Dimon said, "I bet he'd be pretty surprised to see me up here right now."

One of the reasons Jamie Dimon came out of 2008 looking so good is that just as JPMorgan Chase was outperforming its competitors, Dimon was outperforming his CEO peers in his public response to the crisis and the orgy of recrimination it had engendered. Guilt is normally in short supply on Wall Street, but it is shocking just how few mea culpas were heard from bankers who had amassed great personal wealth over nearly a decade of illusory growth. Instead, Wall Street kingpins came across as complainers of the highest order, blaming their problems on everything but themselves—a 100-year storm, short sellers, panicky investors, bad accounting rules. While Jimmy Cayne and Dick Fuld raged about the unfairness of it all, Dimon made no excuses and blamed nobody but himself.

Although he has technically worked for only four companies in his career—American Express, Citigroup, Bank One, and JPMorgan Chase—Dimon has long had a reputation as a Mr. Fix-It who knows how to instill discipline and clean up a troubled balance sheet. In 2008, though, his job effectively became to clean up the entire financial system. And in so doing, he proved a point he's been focused on his entire life: that you can still win while doing the right thing.

· · ·

The question whether the mega-bank model pioneered by Weill and Dimon is viable has never been put to rest. That's in part because the two prime examples—Citigroup and JPMorgan Chase—have seen such starkly differing results. At the same time as it became too big to manage, Citigroup became too big to fail, critics say, putting the entire financial system at risk. Defenders of the mega-bank concept, Dimon included, make an argument similar to the refrain of some people who defend the Second Amendment: "Guns don't kill people; people kill people." The model itself isn't flawed, the proponents of the mega-bank say, though some of the people trying to implement it are.

Through mid-2009, Citigroup had taken $45 billion in new bailout monies, as well as obtaining federal backing on a staggering $300 billion of assets. By that time, the company was practically a ward of the government. "You couldn't design a better footprint or get a better set of assets if you had to build a bank from scratch," Citigroup's CEO, Vikram Pandit, had told *Business Week* in April 2008. Yet in January 2009, Pandit had begun to break the company apart. The house that Sandy Weill built was now a teardown.

Meanwhile, Dimon echoed Pandit's earlier sentiments at his own company's "analyst day" in February 2009. "You can't duplicate this franchise," he said. "If I gave you $200 billion, you couldn't do it."

In early 2009, too, the intellectual underpinnings of the concept appeared to be validated. In the fourth quarter of 2008, JPMorgan Chase's investment bank division had faltered, but relatively strong results in the other five business units had balanced out the loss. Then, in the first quarter of 2009, the investment bank had a terrific quarter while the other five units saw their results deteriorate. This was the rationale of the model. Individual units may have volatile results, but the combination is more stable.

In the end, however, JPMorgan Chase—or, more precisely, Jamie

Dimon—might be the exception that proves the rule. When something gets as big and as complicated as JPMorgan Chase or Citigroup, the issue is not just whether someone has the intellectual capacity to manage it. Someone must also have the desire. At Citi, Chuck Prince didn't have the capacity and Sandy Weill didn't really have the desire. It seems pretty clear that Dimon has both, but this may be because he is a once-in-a-generation kind of person. If mega-banking requires a dozen Jamie Dimons in order to survive, then it is surely doomed.

"He has an amazing sense of risk," says his former colleague at Smith Barney, Bob Lessin, currently vice chairman of investment bank Jeffries & Company. "He understands it intuitively better than anyone alive, so he doesn't do stupid things. The industry has a recent history of dramatically mis-pricing risk relative to return. Jamie never fell for that. If you want one phrase to describe him, that's it."

· · ·

"I think he's one of a kind," says Dimon's college pal Laurie Maglathlin. "There are very few people who can remain true to themselves, know when to turn their job on and off, can run a business like the one he does, yet still prioritize with their family." His high school friend Jeremy Paul says almost exactly the same thing. "There are few people I know who have changed less throughout their lives," he says. "With Jamie, that's really interesting because who has more pressure on them than he does? But he just handles it."

The most successful people on Wall Street have tended to come from one of two camps. The first consists of people who do well because everybody is scared of them. That list includes Jimmy Cayne of Bear Stearns and Ken Lewis of Bank of America. The second group consists of those whom most people like but are *also* scared of. Dimon is in that category.

Is he irreplaceable? Is he the Steve Jobs of JPMorgan Chase? At one point, he will leave the company, and that might come sooner than many people think. Once the current crisis is past, it's hard to see him staying on for too long. At that point, he'll have done it all: building, merging, saving. What else could interest him? You can only wake up on Sundays and read 100-page executive management reports for so long. One thing he is not going to do is go to another big company. "But I'm not going to play golf either," he says.

The list of what Dimon might do next has both obvious and not-so-obvious possibilities. He could teach, most likely in the Socratic confines of Harvard Business School. He could spend the rest of his life investing his own substantial fortune in industries—music or sports, for example—that excite him. One fantasy, according to his wife: opening his own restaurant and turning himself into Sam Malone of *Cheers*. (That, or maybe he might finally go and climb Mount Kilimanjaro.)

He does say that he puts aside an hour so every weekend to think about succession. Although he considers the talent development process inside JPMorgan Chase in need of improvement—he gives the company a C grade on that front—he's pretty sure he's got some strong executives who could step into the CEO position without much difficulty. In case he gets hit by a truck, he says, he's already identified to the board three candidates who could take over. Internal oddsmakers give the best chances to Mike Cavanagh and Jes Staley.

"I'm not one of those people who believes that no one can do the job like I can," he says. "In fact, I think there are several people who could. You might try to tell me that some of them haven't been tested. But if the requirement to be a CEO is to have been a CEO, then you'll never have succession anywhere. At some point, you have to take a chance."

One thing Jamie Dimon learned from Sandy Weill—by watching him do just the opposite—is that you also have to let go, if gradually. Remarkably, Dimon was less hands-on with Bear Stearns than he'd ever been with any of the many deals he's worked on over the years—because he trusted his team to do the job as he would have done it himself. "I think he's realized that it's OK to let people do stuff themselves, because that's how you build a great organization," observes Jay Mandelbaum. Dimon now goes where he's needed, and gives his executives freedom to operate in the meantime. In the process he has turned into what the commercial banking chief Todd Maclin refers to as "the best free-safety I've ever met."

If that truck doesn't hit him, however, Dimon planned in mid-2009 to stick around for the time being. That political career—the one he says he's not sure he even wants—will always be waiting for him when he decides it's time to move on. "I now bleed Morgan blood," he says. "This is what I am going to do until they don't want me here anymore."

It's not as if there isn't still work to do. JPMorgan Chase is hardly out of the woods, and in the next few years it will bear as much of the brunt of the economic crisis as any bank. What's more, a new Wall Street is being built today, and there is surely another Jamie Dimon-in-training ready to take the mantle from the man who took not one but two companies to the top rungs of the industry.

How would he respond to a call to service if the president of the United States asked him to be secretary of the treasury? Even after watching Hank Paulson and Tim Geithner be criticized for almost every decision they made in very challenging circumstances, he would probably accept. One of his regrets in life is never having served his country in an official capacity. (He does believe that being CEO of JPMorgan Chase is a form of public service, but he also acknowledges that others might not see it that way, especially considering the paycheck that comes with it.) Patriotism is one of the stronger currents that run through him.

Wall Street has always been a venue for fly-by-night conquerors. But Jamie Dimon has proved that he is not one of them. As a result, his legend will endure better than most, and it will be that of someone with the unique skills, experience, and temperament to stand above his peers at a crucial moment in history. Some effective Wall Street CEOs have come with all the analytical skills that allow them to understand the business. Some have come with all the magnetism needed to be true leaders. Few in history have come with both. But Jamie Dimon did. "He comes in Technicolor and stereophonic sound," says Warren Buffett. "He has a broad outlook, and he's young, so there's going to be action for him for a long time to come."

The Jamie Dimon of 2009 is the same Jamie Dimon of 1982 who charmed his future wife with his unvarnished character. He hasn't retreated behind the usual veil of legalistic corporatespeak, and this just might be the most refreshing fact about a man who has so much at stake.

And it's impossible to deny that most people who wander into his orbit come away feeling as if they've just encountered a force of nature. At a time when true Wall Street leaders seem in desperately short supply, Jamie Dimon has emerged as a moral and managerial compass for both his industry and the country itself.

BIBLIOGRAPHY

Bookstaber, Richard M. *A Demon of Our Own Design*. Hoboken: John Wiley & Sons, 2007.

Brooks, John. *The Go-Go Years: The Drama and Crashing Finale of Wall Street's Bullish 60s*. New York: John Wiley & Sons, 1973.

Burrough, Bryan, and Helyar, John. *Barbarians at the Gate: The Fall of RJR Nabisco*. New York: HarperCollins, 1990.

Chernow, Ron. *The House of Morgan: An American Banking Dynasty and the Rise of Modern Finance*. New York: Grove Press, 1990.

Cohan, William D. *House of Cards: A Tale of Hubris and Wretched Excess on Wall Street*. New York: Doubleday, 2009.

Friedman, Jon, and Meehan, John. *House of Cards: Inside the Troubled Empire of American Express*. New York: G.P. Putnam's Sons, 1992.

Geisst, Charles R. *Wall Street: A History: From Its Beginnings to the Fall of Enron*. Oxford: Oxford University Press, 1997.

Khurana, Rakesh. *Searching for a Corporate Savior: The Irrational Quest for Charismatic CEOs*. Princeton: Princeton University Press, 2002.

Langley, Monica. *Tearing Down the Walls: How Sandy Weill Fought His Way to the Top of the Financial World . . . and Then Nearly Lost It All*. New York: Free Press, 2003.

Lewis, Michael. *Liar's Poker: Rising Through the Wreckage on Wall Street*. New York: W.W. Norton & Company, 1989.

Lowenstein, Roger. *When Genius Failed: The Rise and Fall of Long-Term Capital Management*. New York: Random House, 2000.

Morris, Charles R. *The Two Trillion Dollar Meltdown: Easy Money, High Rollers, and the Great Credit Crash*. New York: PublicAffairs, 2009.

Stewart, James B. *Den of Thieves*. New York: Touchstone, 1991.

Stone, Amey, and Brewster, Mike. *King of Capital: Sandy Weill and the Making of Citigroup*. New York: John Wiley & Sons, 2002.

Tett, Gillian. *Fool's Gold: How the Bold Dream of a Small Tribe at J.P. Morgan Was Corrupted by Wall Street Greed and Unleashed a Catastrophe*. New York: Free Press, 2009.

Weill, Sandy, and Kraushaar, Judah. *The Real Deal: My Life in Business and Philanthropy*. New York: Warner Business Books, 2006

ACKNOWLEDGMENTS

There are so many people to thank for helping with this book that it baffles the mind wondering just where I should start. So I'll do the obvious: Thank you Jamie Dimon, for your openness and your time.

I am deeply indebted to David Rosenthal of Simon & Schuster for taking on this project. My editor at Simon & Schuster, Colin Fox, was a superb partner, as was the rest of the S&S team, including Priscilla Painton, Victoria Meyer, Tracey Guest, Jackie Seow, and Michele Bové. My agent David Kuhn also deserves my gratitude for putting the idea for this project in my head.

A few people outside Simon & Schuster helped on the front line of *Last Man Standing*. Hugo Lindgren of *New York* magazine performed his usual magic on my raw copy, and for that I am extremely grateful. My two researchers, Brian Burnsed and Miriam Datskovsky, performed yeoman's work with no complaint. Chris Wahl, you also take a pretty fine snapshot.

In recent years, a number of magazine editors have combined to give me work on the journey that ultimately led to this book. When *Red Herring* went bust in 2003, Graydon Carter generously asked me to write a few pieces for *Vanity Fair*. A few years later, Joanne Lipman at *Conde Nast Portfolio* gave me a job. Others warranting mention are Jason Pontin of *Red Herring*, Tony Keller of Canada's *National Post* magazine, and Michael Hogan of *Vanity Fair*. Former *Portfolio* deputy editor Blaise Zerega also knows that I will forever owe him one or two.

But it was *New York* editor Adam Moss who truly kickstarted this project. In a meeting in his office in January 2008 he asked me which prominent Wall Street people we should write about that year. I had just one idea for him: Jamie Dimon. A March cover story in *New York* followed, and the rest is history. Thank you, Adam.

I want to thank all the people who took time out of busy schedules to speak to me during my reporting. To the Dimon family—Judy, Ted, and Themis—thanks for your inti red memories, including Steve Burke, James Long, Laurie and Peter Maglathlin, Jeremy Paul, and Brian Rogers. To Dimon's high school English teacher, Mike Ingrisani, thanks for having a memory that stretched back that far.

Also, thanks to much of the senior management of JPMorgan Chase—Frank Bisignano, Steve Black, Bill Campbell, Mike Cavanagh, Jimmy Lee, Kristin Lemkau, Todd Maclin, Jay Mandelbaum, Charlie Scharf, Gordon Smith, Jes Staley, and Bill Winters. Deserving particular gratitude: Joe Evangelisti, head of communications for JPMorgan Chase. I'm sure that you and your assistant, Loretta Russo, are glad you're done with my phone calls. I will miss harassing you two.

A number of others offered valuable insight, including Ken Bialkin, Dick Bove, Joe Califano, James Calvano, Rodgin Cohen, Marty Haase, John Hsu, Judah Kraushaar, Marc Lasry, Bob Lessin, Bob Lipp, Marge Magner, Mike Mayo, Mary McDermott, Alison Falls McElvery, Joseph Plumeri, Theresa Sweeney, Bob Volland, Sandy Weill, Meredith Whitney, Bob Willumstad, Joe Wright, and Frank Zarb.

Thank you, too, Warren Buffett, for finally taking a call from me after nearly fifteen years of trying.

A number of journalists and authors are owed gratitude for informing parts of this book, starting with Monica Langley, who wrote *Tearing Down the Walls*, a singular feat of reportage. More than a few conversations in *Last Man Standing* are drawn from Langley, who had the good sense to ask people to recollect them before they were lost in history's winds. While there is much discussion of Sandy Weill in this book, it is almost exclusively focused on Weill's influence on the life and career of Jamie Dimon. If you want to read the Sandy Weill story, go buy Langley's book.

To be informed on the subject like this is also to know the work of remarkable writers and reporters like Suzanna Andrews, Bryan Burrough, Richard Bookstaber, John Brooks, William Cohan, Ron Chernow, Suzanne Craig, Eric Dash, Steve Fishman, Charles Geisst, John Helyar, Kate Kelly, Michael Lewis, Heidi Moore, Charles Morris, Floyd Norris, Andrew Ross Sorkin, James Stewart, Gillian Tett, and Shawn Tully. And thank you both, Ken Auletta and Roger Lowenstein, for taking the time to explain to me just how one writes a book such as this.

I need to thank my sounding boards—Joe Burke, David Foster, Carney Hawks, Mike Humphries, Peter Keating, Chris Kerr, Dick Nearing, Bill Stromsem, and my siblings, Scott and Steve McDonald and Julie Carter. Also providing valuable counsel and support: Will Arnett, Shaun Assael, Ira Boudway, Michael Cader, Malcolm Fitch, Karen Keating, Rob Meder, Oliver Prichard, Liam Scott, and Hilary Stout. To the rest of my family and friends, thanks for the overwhelming support.

The encouragement of my parents in this somewhat randomly chosen career gave me the courage to continue it even as my decision to leave Wall Street seemed pretty ridiculous around 1995. So thanks for that, Mom. I love you. I know Dad is reading this book while drinking a beer on the dock of the great cottage of heaven.

Finally, to my wife Caroline: Thank you for your glorious patience during this project, especially as we grappled with the arrival of baby Marguerite. You two are the lights of my life.

To all who helped, I hope the results prove worth the time spent.

New York, July 2009

INDEX